# Parenting

# Parenting

## Larry Cyril Jensen & Merrill Kingston

Brigham Young University

HOLT, RINEHART AND WINSTON

New York  □  Chicago  □  San Francisco  □  Philadelphia
Montreal  □  Toronto  □  London  □  Sydney
Tokyo  □  Mexico City  □  Rio de Janeiro  □  Madrid

*Photo credits:* see page 488

Library of Congress Cataloging-in-Publication Data

Jensen, Larry C.
  Parenting.

  Bibliography: p. 449
  Includes index.
  1. Parenting.  2. Child development.  I. Kingston,
Merrill.  II. Title.
HQ755.8.J46  1985  649'.1  85-21927

ISBN 0-03-069878-2

CBS COLLEGE PUBLISHING
Holt, Rinehart and Winston
The Dryden Press
Saunders College Publishing

# PREFACE

"My parents always treated me with a great deal of respect, as I did them. I was never rebellious. I always felt close to them and knew they loved me very much. Very little harsh discipline was administered, mainly because it was not necessary. I never really had a desire to see how far I could push my parents and don't remember ever being spanked. A disappointed tone in my parents' voice was all I needed to make me feel remorse."

This statement was made by a student in one of our parenting classes. Many family members — parents and children — seek this type of relationship, but it is elusive. Even when captured, it slips away. However, one psychologist found eight couples living in the Berkeley, California, area who were able to sustain this type of family atmosphere; she called it "harmonious parenting." About these families she wrote:

> [Harmonious parents] focused upon achieving a quality of harmony in the home, and upon developing principles for resolving differences and for right living. . . . Harmonious parents were equalitarian in that they recognized differences based upon knowledge and personality, and tried to create an environment in which all family members could operate from the same vantage point, one in which the recognized differences in power did not put the child at a disadvantage. They lived parallel to the mainstream rather than in opposition to it. In their hierarchy of values, honesty, harmony, justice, and rationality in human relations took precedence over power, achievement, control, and order, although they also saw the practical importance of the latter values (Baumrind, 1971).

The above study, based on a very small sample, may be criticized for not being representative of families in general. However, another exceptional study with a larger sample size reached similar conclusions. This second study began 25 years ago when three Harvard psychologists extensively interviewed 379 mothers of kindergartners in the Boston area during the 1950s (Sears, Maccoby, & Levin, 1957). The mothers were evaluated on over 100 child-rearing practices, and personal records and background information on each mother and child were meticulously recorded. Twenty-five years later, when the children were 31 years old, another team of researchers located and evaluated 78 of the children, judging maturation on the basis of independence, self-reliance, and genuine concern for others. They were careful to obtain information on friendships, work experiences, illnesses, organizations the individuals belonged to, and whether they had been in trouble with the law.

What did these researchers find? Surprisingly, specific child-rearing practices were not good predictors of personal growth and maturation. Instead, they concluded:

> How a mother feels about her child is the key to her success. How can parents do right by their children? If they are interested in promoting moral and social maturity in later life, the answer is simple — they should love them, enjoy them, want them around. They should not use their power to maintain a home that is designed for the self-expression and pleasure of adults. They should not regard their children as disturbances to be controlled at all costs. . . . It was the easygoing, loving parents whose children turned out to be most mature. Is that a remarkable finding? Isn't it just common sense? The trouble with common sense is that it is so uncommon (McClelland et al., 1978).

We present these two studies because they set the theme for this parenting book: "Parenting can be harmonious and should be joyful." Our positive regard for parenting will be apparent throughout this text. To illustrate this philosophy, firsthand reports of family life given to us by our students will be amply presented throughout the text. They are important not only as illustrations of concepts, but as insights into unique family situations. We are concerned that we avoid the ivory-tower syndrome sometimes manifested by professors and therapists. By staying close to firsthand accounts of the parenting process, we hope to keep in touch with this day-to-day common sense. Statements and opinions taken from parents participating in parenting workshops will also be included.

In general, these common-sense sources of information agree very much with the research we read. One author using this same approach reports a similar conclusion:

> I remember a pair of young parents who told me they made their first priority one of enjoying their child. They were already obviously enjoying each other. That was fifteen years ago. The enjoyment still goes on today. I feel good every time I am around the family. There are now two other children. Growth is obvious, and there is pride in accomplishment and good feelings about everything. These are not indulgent parents, incidentally, nor is the family without secure and clearly set down limits.
>
> Part of the art of enjoyment is being able to be flexible, curious, and to have a sense of humor. An episode of a five-year-old spilling milk all over the table can be quite a different experience dependent upon what family he lives in and how matters are approached (Satir, 1972).

We have found some beliefs to be commonly associated with successful parenting. They are briefly listed below and will be discussed throughout the text. Though not exhaustive, they provide a good introduction.

1. Work *with* children rather than struggling against them.
2. Mistakes in parenting are to be expected rather than eliminated.

3. Happiness comes through giving rather than receiving.
4. Spousal cooperation is preferable to excess disagreement.
5. Children are opportunities rather than responsibilities.
6. Parents can't make their children happy, but they can provide an environment to engender happiness.
7. Associate with child-oriented environments rather than cultures in which children are not valued (e.g., some singles' cultures).
8. Children are basically good.
9. Have a sense of humor; don't be too serious.
10. Plan to give time to children rather than work them into your schedule.
11. Be in control rather than manipulated by children; however, authoritarian rule is also not desirable.
12. Be an educated parent who learns from others' experiences and knowledge as well as your own mistakes. However, extrapolate from popular concepts and principles, being flexible enough to allow a child's own uniqueness to unfold.

The above discussion should sufficiently introduce our approach to parenting. In Part I we begin by reviewing some of the major historical and contemporary views of children, and follow with a review of some of the most frequently cited parenting research. We feel that research results support our basic parenting philosophies described above.

Part II introduces four of the major theoretical orientations present in child development texts today. It is hoped that familiarity with a variety of explanations for children's development and behavioral functioning will improve understanding of why children progress the way they do, what obstacles impede progression, what parents can and cannot expect, and how varying ideas can be applied in the family setting.

Part III condenses historical, theoretical, research, and our own experimental ideas into a somewhat atheoretical but practical approach to successful and enjoyable parenting. A type of arm-chair factor analysis has produced what we feel are some of the most important components of a progressive family atmosphere.

In keeping with both the research review in Chapter 2 and our own philosophies, successful parenting is most effectively achieved when parental influence and control is neither too authoritarian nor too permissive. However, the parental control necessary for child growth varies with the age, cognitive abilities, and moral and social development of each child. In Part IV we introduce some of the major approaches to child discipline, behavior change, and problem solving by grouping these approaches along the continuum of control from high power to low power. Those working with children must realize that each approach includes techniques that are more appropriate at various periods in a child's life. We also introduce in Part IV one additional source of parental influence — modeling and identification.

Throughout the text, we have attempted to introduce principles and general concepts — often through very specific examples — while encouraging those who work with children to improvise and not to lose sight of each child's uniqueness. Some special situations require additional insight, however. Part V includes such situations in which applying general parenting skills may seem insufficient: infancy and early development; handicapped, hyperactive, and mentally and emotionally hindered children; and emotional crises.

Finally, we would be remiss without pointing out that the "traditional" nuclear family is becoming less of a majority among contemporary family configurations. Rather, single-parent, teenage-parent, step-parent, and foster-parent households are increasing in number and slowly taking over the traditional family idea. Part VI looks at these "less traditional" family units.

We wish to acknowledge numerous students who have provided us with anecdotal stories and ideas, thereby helping us to translate our thoughts into communicable form. Our interaction with students has reaffirmed to us the family's important influence on child development, as well as our belief that, although a growing and trying experience, successful and rewarding parenting is not as elusive as it would seem. We also express our heartfelt love and gratitude to our wives for their help in bringing our dreams for this book into reality.

L.C.J.
M.K.

# CONTENTS

# Parenting

# PART
○ I ◻

# Introduction to Parenting and Research

The task of writing about parenting is not a simple one, largely because numerous beliefs about children and approaches to child rearing exist. This diversity is evident across time, as parenting trends change due to technological advancement, religious influences, media effects, ongoing research in the medical and behavioral sciences, and sociocultural change.

Even among nations of present times, however, diversity in parenting practices may be found, as well as observed among different cultures within the same nation. In Chapter 1, we will consider some samples of this diversity, both historical and current. Following this topic, Chapter 2 presents a summary of current trends in research, whose findings provide a concise summary of the general philosophy appearing throughout this book.

C H A P T E R                                          1

# HISTORICAL AND CONTEMPORARY VIEWS OF CHILDREN

Reasons for having children, and subsequent valuation and treatment of children, vary across time. Additionally, within the same time frame, attitudes toward child rearing vary across culture, socioeconomic group, and other population descriptors (e.g., religion). This chapter will illustrate how these variables affect childhood. Varieties among child-rearing practices are introduced that span time, culture, religion, and socioeconomic status. Finally, the importance of parent education is emphasized. Education programs, including college courses, are sources of valuable information for parents.

## Reasons for Valuing Children

A listing of why couples have children might be as long as the list of couples asked. However, Hoffman and Hoffman (1973) reviewed a number of studies and developed nine basic reasons: (1) adult social status and identity; (2) expansion of the self, tie to a larger entity, immortality; (3) morality, religion, altruism, good of the group, norms regarding sexuality; (4) primary group ties, affiliation; (5) stimulation, novelty, fun; (6) creativity, accomplishment, competence; (7) power, influence, effectiveness; (8) social comparison, competition; and (9) economic utility.

The first reason for having children, the desire for adult social status and identity, is largely a product of social expectations. Society often defines a mature and growing marriage as one including children. This push to parenthood is encountered from different sources: statements by in-laws—"When are you going to make us grandparents?"; neighbors—"Do you have any children?"; pressure from peers; and a pervasive sense of keeping up with society. Consider the following account given by a student in a parenting class:

*One of the reasons my parents had children is because it was expected of them . . . because of social pressure. They were expected to have children within a year after their marriage or else other people (family and friends) would think something was wrong with their marriage or that they had some physical problems.*

Pressure to have children might be particularly true for many women who have been taught to consider it their destiny to bear and raise children. For women with such an orientation, having children may be a fulfillment of their gender identity. However, the changing status and role of women, expansion in educational and employment opportunities for women, advancement of birth-control methods, and a growing awareness of social issues such as population control would presumably soften this push to parenthood. Interestingly, however, some researchers have shown either a steady decline in the incidence of voluntary childlessness (Veevers, 1972) or a small increase between 1960 and 1975, followed by a slight decrease or leveling off (Houseknecht, 1982). Houseknecht (1982) explains this surprising trend by suggesting that: (1) although college-educated and career-committed women are more likely than their differently oriented counterparts to be voluntarily childless, the percentage of college-educated women is still quite small; and (2) a recent revival of the familism theme—in reaction to past emphases on alternative lifestyles and individualism—is creating less tolerance, as well as preference, for childlessness.

It is common to hear parents say, "I sure have had to grow a lot while raising my children." Such a process, exemplifying the second reason for having children, is actually anticipated by many preparent adults as they prepare themselves for what they feel is a necessary step in mature development. Rearing children stimulates the development of responsibility, selflessness, and teaching and listening skills. Having children also ties parents to the community by increasing contact and involvement with schools and other institutions. For some adults, having children assures a sense of immortality, a means of passing oneself on for untold numbers of generations. One student provided an example of how children might be seen as an expansion of the self, an opportunity to pass oneself on.

One of the things I have seen parents enjoy about their children is experiencing missing parts of their own lives in their children's. I have noticed this in my husband's family, which is quite wealthy. His father and mother both started as small-town farm children; they worked themselves up to where they are today. Because they couldn't have many of the things they wanted when they were young, they give these things to their children. One of the youngest has a horse collection that was his mother's idea. . . . My husband . . . was also given a new car and put through college. . . . In some ways I feel the parents enjoy it all more than the kids do.

The third reason cited by Hoffman and Hoffman (1973) that many adults choose to become parents involves religious and moral beliefs. Bringing children into the world is a divine part of the overall plan of life. To have children signifies faith, obedience, virtue, respect, and authority. This view is seen in our Judeo-Christian tradition, "Lo, children are a heritage of the Lord: and the fruit of the womb is his reward" (Pss. 127:3). Consider the views of one student who said, "I think one reason people have children . . . is because it is a commandment of God. We are told to multiply and replenish the earth. . . . [They] feel guilty if they don't have kids." Similarly, individuals not

Some parents choose to have children, in part, because of religious and moral beliefs emphasizing parenthood.

condoning any particular formal church may nevertheless consider child rearing as altruistic and unselfish, and as a means of sustaining their culture.

Children are esteemed as sources of satisfaction and affiliation—reason four. The family is seen as a refuge against loneliness and isolation; having children helps to create that refuge. For women, children might provide desired warmth and affection. This warmth and affection is sometimes sought as compensation for marriage difficulties or other interpersonal hardships. In the event of a divorce, children may become important sources of love and security. Or, single people may desire someone to serve, to love, and to reciprocate that love. Some teenage and unwed female parents, for example, try filling voids in their life by creating a child to provide the love and attachment they have lost during past years of trouble and emptiness. Two students provided the following examples.

◑

*I have a friend who says she has kids so she can do things with them when they get older. She's always saying that she can hardly wait until her children get old enough to go shopping, go on camping trips, etc.*

*This is a big part of why my husband and I want a family also. We love being with people; having a family will give us a ready-made group to do things with.*

*One reason for having children involves affiliation and group ties. My mother was an only child. She always wished she had brothers and sisters to play and go to school with. She had twelve children.*

Among the fifth group of reasons for having children is the desire for increased stimulation, novelty, and fun. One student stated:

*The reason my friend had children was because she was bored. Her husband worked long hours, and she didn't have enough things to occupy her time. She wanted children for stimulation and for something to do.*

Many men and women feel that children are fun and a source of happiness. The joys of child rearing seem to outweigh trials and difficulties, and parents sometimes find it easier to establish a family routine, forgetting outside trou-

One reason parents have children is because of the added stimulation, novelty, and fun children bring into a home.

bles when children are in the family. Fond recollections of their own experiences as children, such as family vacations and outings, create a desire to replicate some of those same memories with children of their own.

Having children is a biological and psychological expression of creativity, the sixth reason for having children. Through this creative process of parenting, many adults experience pleasure and a sense of achievement. Their efforts have helped others to grow and develop; rewards for their efforts are quite often immediate and long lasting. The role of parent can contribute meaningfully to feelings of competence and accomplishment. Consider the following examples.

*My uncle and his family are good examples of having children as a source of competence. The more children they had, the more important they felt. They had four children before my parents even had one, and it was always mentioned in their conversation—"all his wonderful kids." He ended up with ten, and they are very proud of it.*

*My father came from a small town where the entire population was employed by one factory. His father and grandfather were also employed there. It seemed to him that working at the factory was all that was waiting for him also. So, he moved to a town where there were a lot of opportunities for different jobs. He started to expect his children to really make something out of their lives. Whenever we went back to visit my relatives in that small town, my father would always show off my brothers and me. My father shows off his accomplishments and reminds his brothers and sisters that they and their children are still working in the factory.*

In some cultures the seventh reason for having children is evident—having children grants the parent power, especially the mother. The mother, who in some cultures is subservient to her husband, is now in the position to make demands of her children. Mothers and fathers may derive a sense of power from being responsible for them. However, this sense of power may be carried to a pathological extreme if parents, in compensating for a lack of power in their own past, autocratically direct their children without considering individual needs and desires. One young parent had some unique power motives for having children:

*One of my high school friends became pregnant during her junior year. She finally sensed some power and influence over her parents. She struck back at her overcontrolling parents by proving to them she had power to create life.*

The eighth reason for having children is perhaps the most obvious to many people: the boastful father beaming from ear to ear because his son pitched a no-hitter; the proud mother of a daughter who is valedictorian of her graduating class; the parents of children noted for their outstanding service to the community. Children can definitely serve as sources of prestige and competitive advantage. A child's achievements are sources of parental pride and may even be used by the parents as bases of comparison against other children in evaluating their parenting success.

Parents see in their children an extension of themselves. Sometimes prestige is even achieved by having more children than neighbors or relatives. Yet, if carried too far, this orientation may cause the parent-child relationship to suffer. Children start seeing themselves as valuable only in relation to objective achievements; they may feel unimportant as individuals. In addition, a fear of failure may develop in which the child refuses to undertake or participate in challenging and difficult tasks. The child might fear a loss of parental warmth and love if he or she could not perform up to parental expectations.

The last value of children cited by Hoffman and Hoffman (1973) is less relevant in most subcultures in the United States today than in the past. In agrarian societies children were valued for their contribution to the family's productivity. Larger families had more hands to work in the field cultivating

Historically, in the United States, and even in some agrarian cultures today, children proved to be econmomic assets.

resources. In addition, as parents became older, their children provided care and security. Different cultures sometimes have children for unique reasons, some economic and others opportunity oriented. Consider the following three examples. The first is by a religious missionary returning from Korea, the second by a social worker helping juveniles, and the third by a student who had lived in Argentina.

◑

*In the oriental society, parents generally provide a good education for their eldest son because he will eventually take care of them. As soon as the oldest son gets a job, his father usually quits his job and moves in with his son.*

*About a week ago I had the opportunity to work with an illegal alien from Mexico. She was young and pregnant. She was emotionally upset that she was going to be sent back to Mexico. Upon inquiry, I learned that there is a law in the U.S. (or at least there is believed to be a law) which allows illegal alliens to gain a foothold in the United States and eventually achieve citizenship if they have two children born in the States. This woman wanted children to provide her with a certain lifestyle.*

*Living in Argentina for two years . . . I was surprised to see the government encouraging people to have large families. I had previously believed that most developing countries would encourage birth control. Argentina, however, believed that the true patriots were those who raised large families to colonize the remote regions of the country that border Brazil, and to provide soldiers to protect the country from an impending struggle with Chile.*

◑

Today children have become an economic liability rather than an asset, however. Bird (1979) estimates the cost of raising a child through age 18 to be about $100,000. To some individuals this is a factor encouraging voluntary childlessness rather than having children.

Many of the above reasons for having children, and perhaps others not included, are present in varying degrees and different combinations in most families. Regardless of these reasons, however, children are looked upon and treated in some fairly specific ways, depending on the age or time in which they were born.

## Historical Overview
### PARENTING IN EARLIER TIMES

Concern about the relationship between childhood experience and adult character has consistently been a characteristic of American society. However, ideas concerning normal growth and development, and how to cultivate children properly, have changed over the past few centuries. Before considering these changes, it might be interesting to see how childhood was viewed in the year 300 B.C.

Students studying history, psychology, mathematics, physics, astronomy, politics, art, and, of course, philosophy usually learn something about the ideas of Plato and Aristotle. These two ancient Greek philosophers also had opinions concerning child rearing and education. They both perceived political corruption as leading to Athens' destruction. To save their city, it would be necessary not only to use a more successful approach to choosing their leaders, but also to determine a way of preventing the corruption of children who might someday be those leaders.

Plato distrusted the average citizen, believing most adults to have fallen into corrupt patterns that pervaded society. Even parents who were not "unfit" to raise their children would surely use diverse techniques, many of which are "not in keeping with a legislator's recommendations, and tend to bring incongruities into the characters of our citizens" (*Laws* 7, 788, cited in Biehler, 1981, p. 18).

Faced with such a dilemma, Plato concluded that all children must be separated from their parents at an early age. Education and rearing of children would be left up to the State, and each child would be evaluated at various stages in his or her life. From these evaluations, those children considered least capable would become workers. Other children would be chosen and trained as managers and military leaders. Those picked as most capable would receive considerable training and experience before becoming the rulers of Athens. Boys and girls alike, Plato concluded, were to be given equal opportunity to become legislators. Such a process could only be achieved by organized and strict instruction.

> [Self-control] is the aim of our control of children, our not leaving them free before we have established, so to speak, a constitutional government within them and, by fostering the best element in them with the aid of the like in ourselves, have set up in its place a similar guardian and ruler in the child, and then, and then only, we leave it free (*Republic* 9, 591, cited in Biehler, 1981, p. 19).

Although this approach to child rearing might appear to be unduly controlling, Plato felt that overly restrictive, as well as overly permissive, child-rearing styles, would produce children unfit for special contributions to society.

Aristotle, a pupil of Plato, also had ideas concerning the betterment of society. He, too, felt that the most capable individuals should be future leaders, for these were the individuals who would possess the most wisdom. However, Aristotle felt that *only* these individuals should be reared by the state. Family life, he felt, meant personal and social stability and should be taken advantage of. Contrary to Plato, Aristotle saw individual differences in parents' child-rearing techniques as necessary to effectively meet the needs of children, who themselves were quite different from each other. For such a process to be successful, women must devote their energies to child rearing.

Though emerging approximately 2300 years ago, Plato's and Aristotle's viewpoints are in some ways surprisingly similar to contemporary ideas. Plato, for instance, felt that overly restrictive and overly permissive parenting styles were actually detrimental—a finding borne out by present-day research (see Chapter 2). Aristotle felt that children's uniqueness should not be overlooked when implementing child-rearing strategies, and that the family is a source of social stability. Both ideas are stressed in this text as well as many other popular articles and writings.

From the time of Plato and Aristotle up until the eighteenth century, most historians report that children were treated somewhat cruelly (Pollock, 1983). However, opinions range from stating that physical abuse and neglect of children's unique abilities and needs were typical, to suggesting that children, though placed in an adult role, were nevertheless accorded special attention and consideration.

DeMause (1974) took a critical look at treatment of children throughout the centuries. Although perhaps overstating the cruelties, he attempted to document a generally dismal history in which children have been killed, abandoned, beaten, and sexually abused. In ancient Greece, for example, children born with abnormalities were often killed. DeMause claims that from the fourth to the thirteenth centuries, many of the responsibilities we would consider parents to have were neglected. From the fourteenth to the seventeenth centuries, religious doctrines viewed children as innately wicked beings to be broken and molded through strict supervision.

However, Pollock (1983), after reviewing seventeenth-century British and American texts, failed to find supporting evidence that abusive, strict discipline was the rule. In addition, McLaughlin (1974) suggests that as early as the twelfth century, parents showed some tenderness toward children, awareness of their needs, and interest in their development.

In spite of these discrepancies, it is generally agreed that treatment of children in past centuries was less humane than at present. Closely related was the past practice of not allowing children to be children. Rather, they were viewed as little adults and were expected to act and dress as such. Indeed, Ariès (1962) determined that no concept of childhood existed during the Middle Ages. Children were dressed as adults and involved in adult activities such as music and education. Childhood games and toys as we know them were virtually nonexistent.

By the sixteenth century, children's status began to change. They were more readily regarded as sources of parental amusement and relaxation (Ariès, 1983). Parents became ambivalent, not knowing when to consider children adults, or whether to consider them innately good or bad (Tucker, 1974). Yet a recognition that they were different was beginning to emerge. The seventeenth century saw a increased emphasis on childhood and the child's place in the family, and by the the eighteenth century, children were gaining a unique status that was accorded its own manner and dress.

## TWO MAJOR INFLUENCES ON PARENTING

John Locke (1632–1704) and Jean Jacques Rousseau (1712–1778), philosophers from England and France, respectively, were influential in changing many people's attitudes toward child rearing (Maccoby, 1980). Both were opposed to physical punishment, although their recommendations for socializing children differed. Their views will be briefly discussed here, as a similar dichotomy toward child rearing exists even today.

John Locke felt that children are born void of thoughts and ideas; in addition, he felt, they are not innately sinful. This view implies, therefore, that the end product of child rearing (the child's total personality) is a product of his own effort, his caretaker's efforts, and the immediate environment. A lot of power was attributed to the parenting role during a child's early years (a similar emphasis appears in psychoanalytic theory, to be discussed later). It is during childhood that the child's lifelong habits and personality are formed.

Borrowing from previous philosophical ideas, Locke felt that human beings' rationality distinguishes them most importantly from lower animals. This rationality is the ability to reason—to make judgments and choices. Because the child is born without ideas and thoughts, it is the parents' duty to help their children become rational, so as to make proper choices and control their appetites. Contrary to popular opinion, Locke encouraged parents to be patient, thoughtful, and truthful in dealing with a child's curiosity; yet, in order to teach effective control of impulses and appetites, parents must command the child's attention, respect, and affection. Physical punishment would not be needed if this were done successfully.

Rousseau, in contrast with Locke, felt that a parent's all-important teaching must wait until the child is ready. Children should be allowed to grow as nature dictates. Young children are not ready to reason or to form judgments; strict guidance and control at this stage would only be seen as hostility. Rather, children will discover for themselves certain laws through a natural process. Rousseau did not advocate total permissiveness, however: "If there is something he should not do, do not forbid him, but prevent him without explanation or reasoning" (Rousseau, 1974, p. 55). Children were not simply incomplete adults but were to be treated and understood for what they were. This necessitates postponing attempts to teach adult concepts and skills until the child's intellectual capacities are sufficiently mature.

Locke, Rousseau, and others seemed to begin a trend toward more understanding and gentle care, thereby retreating from stringent disciplinary practices. Robert Sunley (1955) identified two other major influences that emerged when Rousseau's and Locke's ideas were becoming prevalent; these two orientations were identified as Calvinism and Early Developmentalism, and will be highlighted when discussing child rearing in America.

## CHILD REARING IN EARLY AMERICA

In early America the typical child was frequently beaten; parents, schoolmasters, and other caretakers felt justified in beating children on the hands, mouth, and buttocks for large or small errors and infractions. Children were expected to show due respect to their elders; they stood when adults entered the room, and sometimes had to kneel before their parents once a day to ask their blessing. In both dress and manner children were expected to emulate their elders. Some children wore special garments reinforced with iron and whalebone, forcing them into adult postures. It is not uncommon to observe straight-faced, rigid children in paintings of that day, fashionably dressed in "proper" and expensive, adult-looking attire, not at all like what we today consider the nature of children. Demos (1970) stated that there was often no clear demarcation of responsibilities and behaviors expected of adults and children. Once infancy had passed, children were expected to act appropriately and to work diligently. A general preoccupation with breaking the child's will existed, which Maccoby (1980) says is attributable to three factors: "widespread acceptance of Puritan religious values, limited medical knowledge, and lack of real understanding of children and childhood."

Some parents self-righteously believed it was their duty to stamp out sin in their children; the Calvinistic idea that children were innately sinful prevailed. John Calvin even decreed the death penalty for children who were chronically disobedient, and such laws were actually passed in Massachusetts and Connecticut (Maccoby, 1980).

An incident quoted in deMause relates how an American Puritan father was teaching his four-year-old son to read. The child was having problems at one point and the father interpreted these difficulties as defiance in the child. The child was taken to the cellar, stripped, tied, and beaten. The father describes the self-pity and suffering he felt as he performed his duty.

> . . . During this most unpleasant, self-denying and disagreeable work, I made frequent stops, commanding and trying to persuade, silencing excuses, answering objections. . . . I felt all the force of divine authority and express command that I ever felt in all my life. . . . But under the all controlling influence of such a degree of angry passion and obstinacy, as my son had manifested, no wonder he thought he "should beat me out," feeble and tremulous as I was; and knowing as he did that it made me almost sick to whip him. At that time he could neither pity me nor himself (deMause, 1974, pp. 8–9).

The second reason cited by Maccoby for this apparently cold parent–child interaction was a very high infant mortality rate, both in the New England colonies and in continental Europe. Disease epidemics often ran uncontrollably, taking the lives of many infants. In addition, a profound lack of knowledge concerning feeding and infant care added to the dilemma. Many mothers considered breast-feeding vulgar and degrading, preferring to send their children to wet nurses, as safe substitutes for breast milk were not available. These wet nurses frequently attempted to nurse too many infants, providing insufficiently for the child's needs. The survival rate of infants put through this process was about 33 percent (Maccoby, 1980, p. 6).

In colonial America, many mothers considered breast-feeding vulgar and degrading, preferring to send their children to wet nurses.

This high mortality rate might very well have been a major contributor to the lack of attachment and warmth occurring in early infant–parent relationships. Parents necessarily learned to protect themselves by remaining distant until their children had escaped an almost inevitable fate.

In addition to neglect of necessities for healthy physical development, parents knew very little about what was emotionally, socially, and developmentally normal. People believed that affection was counterproductive to breaking the child's will, yet children were expected to show affection and reverence to their parents in return. Crawling was looked upon as animal-like, and misunderstandings often occurred due to an ignorance of sensori-motor and intellectual development.

## EARLY DEVELOPMENTALISM

From the previous discussion on parenting in colonial America, it is evident that the father's central role was as disciplinarian and moral and religious instructor. During the nineteenth century (1800–1860), however, a shift of these responsibilities toward the mother occurred. Fathers were increasingly taken away from home by their jobs, a trend partly attributable to developments leading to the Industrial Revolution. The mother was now the central figure, the one to implement the idea of breaking the child's will.

Yet, during this period, the abandonment of physical punishment was encouraged. Independence was desirable; weaning, self-feeding, and toilet training were to be accomplished as soon as possible. And parents were now viewed more as facilitators of a child's growth, not as creators. This developmental approach opposed the belief that children were innately sinful. Rather, children were just ignorant of what was right. Obedience was valued, but adherence could be obtained by gentle firmness and persuasion rather than by physical punishment (Sunley, 1955). This viewpoint is considered a developmental approach "as it emphasized (1) the presence of children's developmental needs; (2) the emerging personalities of children, which parents helped to shape into full development; and (3) the effects that resulted from neglect and harsh punishment as well as from gentle care and nurturance" (Bigner, 1979). Parents were encouraged to be less restrictive and a little more indulgent in their parenting efforts.

## TWENTIETH-CENTURY DEVELOPMENTS

This century has seen somewhat of a seesaw pattern in child-rearing emphases, a pattern uncovered by content analyses performed on advice-giving literature. Celia Stendler (1950) analyzed articles appearing in *Good Housekeeping, Ladies' Home Journal,* and *Women's Home Companion* from 1890 to 1950. Bigner (1972) extended this analysis through 1970.

Stendler (1950) noticed that writers began reversing their advice between 1890 and 1920. Instead of encouraging indulgence of children, a more restrictive pattern of child rearing was advised. The fact that so many of these articles appeared in women's magazines indicates that women continued to be considered the primary child-rearers.

Stendler (1950) then noticed that a highly restrictive era in child rearing began in the 1920s. Strict and consistently regular scheduling of infant care routines was encouraged. J. B. Watson, a psychologist, was partially responsible for this emphasis. He warned parents that showing their children too much love and affection would "condition" children to expect it. In addition, strict control of rewards and punishments would be necessary for proper training, as children are born with very few innate behaviors. However, in the period from 1935 to 1945, Sigmund Freud's ideas swung that shift from restrictive parenting to more permissive caretaking practices. Parents were cautioned that being overly controlling would only repress infantile desires, later increasing the chances of adult neurotic tendencies.

Bigner's (1972) extension of the content analysis of advice-giving literature, from 1950 to 1970, noticed a very slight shift back in the direction of more restrictive but loving attitudes, encouraging parents to be firm and discover their parenting abilities without fear of harming their children. One proponent of this shift was Benjamin Spock, whose articles appeared quite consistently in *Ladies' Home Journal* and *Redbook*. Although Spock's views are claimed to be permissive by some individuals, Spock himself stated, "Goodhearted parents who aren't afraid to be firm when it is necessary can get good results with either moderate strictness or moderate permissiveness" (Spock, 1968, p. 7).

This shift back toward "loving control" is also reflected in the more current writings of authors (e.g., Dreikurs, Ilg and Ames, White, Ginott, Brazelton) who, if their messages are combined, seemed to be saying, "Although parents need not be overly controlling, they must nevertheless provide loving structure and firmness, as a child's upbringing—especially during the early years—has an important impact on his or her life." Indeed, a child's behavior is not solely the product of family upbringing, yet parents' roles are very important and have dramatic influences. As a result, parent education is a valuable part of child rearing.

For example, Ilg and Ames (1955) published the first edition of their book *Child Behavior* in 1955, in which they incorporated and adapted material from a syndicated newspaper column the two had done for quite some time. At the time of publication, many psychologists were blaming parental ineptitude for child behavior problems. Over the years, while this idea changed somewhat, parents continued, nevertheless, to wield a lot of power. In writing the revised edition, Ilg, Ames, and Baker (1981) determined that although specialists had begun considering ". . . [f]aulty behavior [as possibly] merely characteristic of a certain age or a certain personality" (p. 50), they were suggesting that something could be done to prevent it. Although not necessarily the cause of inappropriate behaviors, parents nevertheless had enough power to prevent some of these. Additionally, they could augment their child's positive experiences and learning.

Burton White and his colleagues (White, Kaban, Attanucci, & Shapiro,

1978) published the results of a Harvard preschool project begun in 1965 that focused on child education from birth to six years of age. Conclusions were:

1. Education during infancy is of utmost importance.
2. The family is the major source of this educational development.
3. Inadequate educational influences in the home during a child's first three years may not be overcome in later schooling years.

Brazelton (1974) similarly considered the first years of life as very important. As children struggle for independence and self-mastery, parents must provide support in the form of understanding and tolerance, not permissiveness. Finally, Dodson (1970) and Ginott (1965) both had similar ideas concerning the necessity of loving control, and felt that parents are benefited by increasing their knowledge and understanding of their parenting roles.

In summary, then, parenting trends in America have seesawed back and forth, the most recent of which seems to take the stance that effective parenting involves loving warmth and an attitude toward discipline that is neither too controlling nor too permissive. Children must be provided with adequate control, yet must also be allowed to self-actualize their own strengths and tendencies. These ideas seem to be supported by the researth presented in Chapter 2.

## INCREASED EMPHASIS ON FATHERING

During the period from 1950 to 1970, fathers were also encouraged to take a more active role in the parenting process. An increased participation in child-rearing responsibilities, it was thought, "would result in better personality development of children" (Bigner, 1972). For example, studies began pointing out a father's importance in children's gender identity development—how they identified themselves and their roles as male or female (Bronfenbrenner, 1961; Brown, 1956, 1958; and Sears, Maccoby, & Levin, 1957).

Since the 1950s, research focusing on fathering has increased dramatically and is even becoming a major contemporary research topic. Growing research literature indicates that infants recognize, become attached to, and are distressed by separation from mother *and* father, and that mother and father are responded to differently by their infant children (Belsky, 1979; Kotelchuck, 1976; Lamb, 1976, 1977, 1978; Lester, Kotelchuck, Spelke, Sellers, & Klein, 1974; Ross, Kagan, Zelazo, & Kotelchuck, 1975). In fact, because fathers tend to spend more time than mothers in stimulating, active play, fathers are often preferred as play partners (Clarke-Stewart, 1978). Fathers also have important influences on their children's intellectual development (Clarke-Stewart, 1978; Radin, 1981a).

These findings typify a movement that is considering more closely a father's influence on his children's development. During the past 20 years, dramatic gender-identity changes have occurred. Traditional views that women should remain at home and raise children have been challenged and altered by the women's liberation movement and by economic pressures (Lamb & Sagi, 1983).

Yet, despite these changes, social reformers have ignored the need to consider necessary changes in the male role of traditional breadwinner. As a result, the male role has changed little. In addition, past researchers have neglected to consider ways in which fathers, not just mothers, affected children and the family. What this all boils down to is a dearth in the literature dealing specifically with fatherhood. Most modern societies do not provide clear behavioral guidelines for intensely involved fathers. Yet, in spite of this scarcity of data and guidelines on paternal influences, researchers are looking at this familial aspect with increasing frequency, and some general observations may be made.

Although a mother's role may be growing to include a sharing of the breadwinner role, major studies of paternal participation in the United States, Australia, United Kingdom, and Europe all show that fathers generally show minor participation in the day-to-day child-care responsibilities. Playing with their children is the only child-rearing activity in which fathers tend to expend more than minimal energy and time (Russell & Radin, 1983). Yet, families do exist in which fathers share as much as 40 to 50 percent of child-care responsibilities (DeFrain, 1979; Radin, 1981b, 1982). It is in families with this type of mother–father division of responsibilities that research is beginning to focus its efforts. Consider the following conclusion.

> Increased paternal participation has been reported to have both positive and negative effects on fathers. Reports of positive effects included: fathers feeling closer to and more sensitive towards their children; greater satisfaction and equality in husband–wife relationships; fathers expressing more satisfaction with their parental role and feeling more effective as parents; changes in fathers' attitudes and beliefs about child care and parental roles; and finally, a very small number of fathers reported that their associated reduction in commitment to paid work had a positive effect. On the negative side, increased conflict and tensions were reported particularly with: parent–child and marital relationships; relationships with male peers; father's identities as males (a minor response); and relative commitments to family and paid work. There were also indications of costs in terms of job advancement and success for fathers with a major role in child rearing (Russell & Radin, 1983, p. 155).

Also of interest is the suggestion that fathers could become competently involved as primary caretakers and still maintain a traditionally paternal style of interaction (Thompson, 1983), which may help to explain Radin's (1978) conclusion that children's gender orientation did not differ among families with less- and more-involved fathers. In other words, in spite of the increased participation in child rearing, fathers tended to resemble traditional fathers and mothers—physically stimulating and gentler, verbally oriented interaction styles. This combination of approaches does not seem to change children's gender identities.

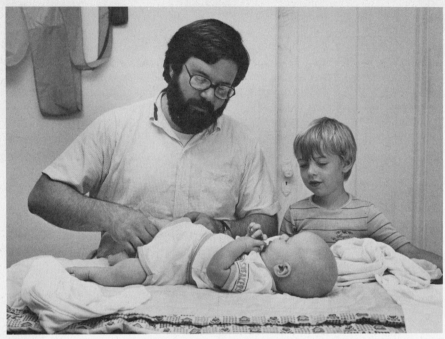
Increased paternal involvement in child rearing generally has positive consequences.

Other findings of families with highly involved fathers include: (1) adjustment and social competence in boys increases (Santrock & Warshak, 1979); (2) children are more likely to assume responsibility for their actions, an attribute central to most definitions of mental health (Sagi, 1982); and (3) daughters are provided increased cognitive stimulation (Radin, 1982).

It appears, then, that increased paternal involvement generally has positive child-rearing consequences. Yet, increased paternal participation in child rearing has not yet caught on in our society. Reasons for this delay are many and include: traditional roles and beliefs, fathers' own socialization experiences, employment restrictions and inflexibility found in some occupations, and economic difficulties requiring increased time spent in earning money.

## Parenting Today
### POPULAR CONCEPTS OF CHILDREN

In a recent parenting text (Wood, Bishop, & Cohen, 1978), different views about children that are held by today's parents were identified. Wood classified parents into four patterns of child rearing: the potter, the gardener, the maestro, and the consultant.

The parent who is a "potter," according to Wood et al. (1978), exhibits the following beliefs:

1. *Parents should take full responsibility and authority for their children.* They feel that enriching experiences are necessary for proper development, and that they must provide these experiences by carefully structuring and guiding their children's growth. These parents feel they must answer all the child's questions, because they are the household authority.
2. *Parents determine what a child becomes.* A child's behavior reflects upon the parents. Therefore, teaching a child correct principles is a very important responsibility.
3. *These parents regard mistakes by their children as failures.* Mistakes are considered the result of poor teaching and are therefore avoidable by proper training.
4. *These parents explain their children's feelings to them.*
5. *These parents stress constructive activities.* Becoming a successful, productive member of society is highly encouraged.
6. *These parents have a strong sense of duty.* A sense of duty is felt toward family, occupation, religion, and society. This sense of duty is instilled into their children.
7. *Desirable behavior should be rewarded.*

The parent who is a "gardener" can be typified by the following:

1. *Gardeners believe in the innate goodness of man.* Children must only be given the opportunity for growth; it is a parent's responsibility to provide these opportunities. Given the opportunity, children will develop into mature, competent adults.
2. *These parents have learned what to expect at different stages of development.* This knowledge is acquired through observation, study, and dialogue with other parents.
3. *Each individual's uniqueness should be accepted.* The speed of growth and abilities developed in this process are different for each child; patience and understanding are necessary.
4. *These parents rely on example and modeling rather than the imposition of lots of rules.*
5. *Children should be free to explore their own interests.*
6. *These parents set limits that are necessary for their children's safety and health.*
7. *Childish behavior is accepted as appropriate and right.*

The "maestro" parent believes:

1. *Democracy should be a tradition.* Everyone's opinion is listened to and respected.
2. *Pride is taken in group achievement.*
3. *Each family member's personal life needs to be protected.*
4. *The home environment needs to be carefully designed and structured to meet goals.* Parenting is highly regarded and taken very seriously, as children benefit most if their lives are carefully organized.
5. *Children should be assigned responsibility as soon as they are ready.*

The parent functioning as "consultant" can be identified by several beliefs:

1. *These parents work hard at understanding themselves.* This is a prerequisite to relating effectively to others.
2. *Children and parents are constantly learning and growing.*
3. *These parents know and accept themselves.* They have confidence in their abilities, while also accepting their limitations. This acceptance is passed on to their children.
4. *Children are related to as peers.* Children's moods and feelings are accepted as unique.

5. *These parents don't worry too much about what other people think* (p. 267) (Wood et al., 1978).

Evident in Wood's classifications are the same themes recurring in past attitudes on parenting (e.g., Aristotle, Plato, Locke, Rousseau): permissiveness vs. restrictiveness or control vs. autonomy; parental warmth and acceptance vs. detachment and strict expectations; the child as innately good vs. innately "evil" and problematic; and the child as born without personality or predisposition vs. the child as born with definite personality traits. The ideas of researchers and prominent figures past and present (see Chapter 2) can be situated along these continua. Approaches to discipline and parental control can also be "fitted" somewhere along these dimensions, as will become more apparent in Part IV of this text.

## OUR VIEWS ABOUT CHILDREN

In our discussions with parents, students, and other professionals, we have found not only that modern parents do have very identifiable views about the nature of children but that these views are similar in many respects to classifications previously discussed. Views that parents hold influence how they treat and react to children. We choose to classify these viewpoints under five orientations:

1. The child as a seed.
2. The child as a "miniature adult."
3. The child as a "bundle of sin."
4. The innocent child as a noble savage.
5. The child as a "blank slate" or *tabula rasa.*

With these concepts in mind, we asked mothers how they viewed their children, and what effects those views had on daily interactions with their children. From these discussions, the following characterizations about parenting styles were developed.

Parent 1 believes that the child begins as a *seed,* a small spirit in an embryo stage. Such parents are constantly aware of the example they are setting for their children, and are always careful to fill their minds with good things. They feel that as parents they should do their best to enhance their children's ability to become whatever they are to become. One such Parent 1 commented: "My son was born with his own personality. He has always been jovial, but as parents we have also been able to insure that his good qualities continue to grow." If they are expecting other children, they know that more, distinct personalities will appear, and they hope to be able to encourage individuality by allowing their potential to develop.

With a different view, Parent 2 sees the child as a *miniature adult,* and feels that the child is highly intelligent and able to express his or her feelings, wants, and desires in an acceptable (i.e., adultlike) manner. In the home, children are expected to treat visitors with respect. Clothes are always worn and proper etiquette observed. Since these parents see their children as little adults, they treat them as little adults, and they, in return, are expected to act accordingly.

One student reported about a principal who viewed children as a *bundle of sin* (Parent 3). Perhaps her views were distorted by her own subjective observations, but her ideas are descriptive.

*My principal in high school believed children, as well as older people, were simply "bundles of sin." All people needed to be controlled and patrolled. As soon as he came to our school, there seemed to be an immediate tension—for both faculty and student body. Before a big school event, he always anticipated the worst. He gave us lengthy lectures over the PA system, warning against our evils and what our punishment would be. He immediately began to control all he could. He made rigid rules about leaving the classroom—and to enforce it, we had "hall monitors." He insisted that teachers be objective-oriented; they were required daily to write our objectives on the board, and he conveniently stopped by on occasion to make sure they were. The poor man thought he had to have us all under control. Because of his rigidness, no one seemed to like him—student and teacher alike.*

One woman (Parent 4) appeared to believe her children were *noble savages*, although basically good. An observer reports:

*This lady has five children, the middle one having Down's syndrome. In the last couple of years, she has tried to avoid spanking, expecting them to get out of line on occasion. She talks to them about her feelings. For example, if one of the children starts to yell, she says, "Oh, I feel so bad when you scream." She feels that kids generally want to please their parents, so they are free to choose everyday encounters, although their inexperience may produce inappropriate behavior.*

*The older ones have to help with the dishes. If they don't help, they have the option of not eating or getting dirty utensils from the dishwasher. She believes in following logical consequences, and she finds it is hard to stay consistent in disciplinary areas. When her children fight, she tries to steer them away from conflict while trying not to act as referee. They have to learn how to handle it themselves; if she were to step in, the main issue would not be resolved. She views children as having their own distinct personalities, to be treated with respect and courteousness, at the same time realizing that they don't have the ability to choose as we do because they haven't had the same experiences.*

The *tabula rasa,* or blank slate, theory is common to many parents. Below is a positive example of a father who holds this point of view.

*Bill Brown is the principal of an elementary school and a father of 12 children. He is a very busy individual, but always has time to speak to any parent or child no matter how trivial the subject. His appearance is calm and gentle, but he can be firm and unrelenting when administering consequences of misbehavior; he feels that misbehavior has at some point been reinforced, so he must reverse the faulty learning.*

*The notes that come home to parents typically state, "We are here to help your child grow and develop. What can we do to help make time in school a learning experience for him or her?"*

*Mr. Brown is predictable in nature, and the atmosphere at school is positive. He is concerned, helpful, and relays the feeling that he regards children in his charge as stones to be carved into capable and responsible citizens. To do so, these children are disciplined and not allowed to hurt one another, and are consistently reinforced for behaving in socially and academically positive ways.*

These five views are certainly broad generalizations and are not exact. For most of us, a mixture of views is more common. A parent may fit many of these views simultaneously or on occasion consider one more correct or accurate than others.

We encourage you, as you read this book, to develop what you consider to be the most accurate and comprehensive view of the nature of children.

## CULTURAL DIFFERENCES IN PARENTING

Even though the experience of raising children is universal, intra- and intersocietal differences shape different and unique environments. Such environmental differences influence child rearing by adapting families to different hazards, resources, and goals. Before discussing examples of parenting diversity, however, we must, first consider common goals that parents everywhere seem to share.

Levine (1974) proposed three goals that all parents have for their children:

1. The physical survival and health of the child, including (implicitly) the normal development of his reproductive capacity during puberty.
2. The development of the child's behavioral capacity for economic self-maintenance in maturity.
3. The development of the child's behavioral capacities for maximizing other cultural values—for example, morality, prestige, wealth, religious piety, intellectual achievement, personal satisfaction, self-realization—as formulated and symbolically elaborated in culturally distinctive beliefs, norms, and ideologies (Levine, 1974).

Levine (Fantini & Cardenas, 1980) mentions that a natural hierarchy exists among these categories. Physical survival is normally of greater concern during the first few years of a child's life, while developing economic self-maintenance and behavioral capacities for maximizing cultural values becomes more important only later. In addition, each of these goals is a prerequisite for the ones following. For example, physical survival is a prerequisite to developing economic self-maintenance.

Concerning this hierarchy of goals, it is important to understand that environmental hazards and constraints determine which goals are most emphasized. Levine (Fantini & Cardenas, 1980) compares and contrasts tropical African (primitive) and American societies to illustrate this point.

Populations of tropical Africa are primarily agricultural; infant mortality is high and subsistence is precarious. Parental goals, therefore, focus on the child's physical survival and the family's economic future. Having many children helps compensate for increased infant mortality rates while at the same time contributing to the labor force.

Frequent childbirth also influences feeding schedules and affection given to the infant during infancy and later in childhood. The tropical African woman usually bears a child every two or three years. The infant is breast-fed for 18 to 24 months, a precaution against dehydration from diarrhea—the most frequent cause of infant death. The child is fed upon demand whenever it cries, necessitating that the mother sleep with the child and carry the child with her most of the time. This process continues until weaning, at which time the mother is ready to give birth again and to devote the same amount of attention to a new baby.

Economic restrictions require African children to share sleeping space, food, clothing, and possessions, thereby engendering interdependence among family members. Obedience is heavily emphasized to secure compliance with subsequent demands of contributing to the family labor force. Even the small child is taught to carry items at parental command and to perform useful tasks in the fields and at home.

It becomes obvious that American society lends itself to different parenting strategies. The concerns for infant survival and economic utility are generally not major. Instead, a major theme is independence. Children are often provided with separate rooms and innumerable personal possessions. They are not given the intense physical attention evidenced in the African culture; rather, the child learns a primitive capacity for self-comfort. American children receive frequent praise for their performance in acts considered commonplace and necessary in the African culture.

Observing other cultural parenting strategies reveals further differences. Whiting and Child (1953) studied the behavior of individuals in 75 primitive cultural settings. Examples of weaning and toilet-training philosophies are given below.

Kwoma infants up to the time they are weaned are never far from their mothers. . . . Crying constitutes an injunction to the mother to discover the source of trouble. Her first response is to present the breast. If this fails to quiet him, she tries something else. . . . Thus during infancy the response to discomfort which is most strikingly established is that of seeking help by crying or asking for it (Whiting, as cited by Whiting & Child, 1953, pp. 91–92).

In contrast, Ainu children are . . . put into the hanging cradle . . . the poor little creatures could not get out, and for the rest they were free to do whatever they were able. This usually meant a good deal of kicking and screaming until tired of it, followed by exhaustion, repose, and resignation (Howard, as cited by Whiting & Child, 1975, p. 93).

The Dohomean . . . child is trained by the mother who, as she carries it about, senses when it is restless, so that every time it must perform its excretory functions, the mother puts it on the ground. Thus, in time, usually two years, the training process is completed. If a child does not respond to this training, and manifests enuresis at the age of four or five, soiling the mat on which it sleeps, then, at first, it is beaten. If this does not correct the habit, ashes are put in water and the mixture is poured over the head of the offending boy or girl, who is driven into the street, where all of the other children clap their hands and run after the child singing, "Urine everywhere" (Herskovitz, as cited by Whiting & Child, 1953, p. 75).

In the practices of the Siriono, however, almost no effort is made by the mother to train an infant in the habits of cleanliness until he can walk, and then they are instilled very gradually. Children who are able to walk, however, soon learn by imitation, and with the assistance of their parents, not to defecate near the hammocks. When they are old enough to indicate their needs, the mother gradually leads them further and further away from the hammock to urinate and defecate, so that by the time they have reached the age of 3, they have learned not to pollute the house. . . . Not until a child has reached the age of 6 does he take care of his defecation needs alone (Holmberg, as cited by Whiting & Child, 1953, pp. 75–76).

Turnbull (1972) relates how the Ik people of Uganda turn their children out of the house at age three. The children are left to fight the elements of nature on their own. They band together to find food and shelter, and to protect themselves against older children. Darwin's "survival of the fittest" principle is the rule in this society, and is quite adaptive for the Ik people, because survival is a primary goal.

Societies often rear children in accordance with certain societal goals. With the Ik people, as indicated above, survival is a primary goal, so leaving children alone to "brave" nature is the chosen child-rearing strategy. In the American culture independence and knowledge are goals; tasks tending to these goals are emphasized and praised (e.g., tying one's own shoes, dressing oneself, preschool performance). Even within American society, however, differences abound. The Hopi Indian society is primarily agricultural. Children are taught obedience and diligence so as to be productive in the fields (males), or to help out at home (females) while everyone else is out working in the fields or caring for sheep (Dennis, 1972).

## SOCIOECONOMIC DIFFERENCES IN THE UNITED STATES

One needn't study cultures of other countries, or even different racial groups within the United States, to observe different parenting techniques. Bronfenbrenner (1958), for example, conducted a survey spanning 25 years and found consistent trends in feeding, weaning, and toilet-training practices among different social classes. From 1930 until the end of World War II, working-class mothers were generally more permissive than middle-class mothers. However, this trend reversed itself after the war, when middle-class mothers were seen as more permissive.

Some researchers, though still finding differences, conclude that social classes differ very little (Erlanger, 1974; Gecas & Nye, 1974). Nevertheless, differences are still being reported, regardless of how minimal they are. According to sociologist Melvin Kohn (1977), working-class and middle-class parents differ as to what is punishable and why. White-collar parents stress the development of internal standards of control. Self-control is reacted to more frequently than consequences of the behavior. The child is more likely to be disciplined according to an interpretation of the child's intent or motive, not the consequences of his or her behavior. For example, a child's loss of temper indicates a lack of self-control; this loss of self-restraint is punishable. If, however, similar consquences due to "wild play" were observed, these consequences would not be punishable. Working-class mothers, howevr, place greater emphasis on conformity; consequences of behavior are generally reacted to. In the above example, punishment would likely be employed following "wild play" *and* loss of temper, since the consequences of both are similar.

Maccoby (1980) condensed a large body of research on the relationship between parenting and social class, relying a great deal on the work of another researcher, Hess (1970). Comparisons between high- and low-socio-economic status families revealed the following differences (socioeconomic status will be abbreviated as SES):

1. Lower-SES parents tend to stress obedience, respect, neatness, cleanliness, and staying out of trouble. Higher-SES parents are more likely to stress happiness, creativity, ambition, independence, curiosity, and self-control.
2. Lower-SES parents are more controlling, power-assertive, authoritarian, and arbitrary in their discipline, and they are more likely to use physical punishment. Higher-SES parents are more democratic and tend to be either permissive or authoritative. They are more likely to use induction (that is, point out the effects of a child's actions on others, or ask the child how she or he would feel in the other's place) and to be aware of and responsive to their children's perspectives.

3. Higher-SES parents talk to their children more, reason with them more, and use more complex language.
4. Higher-SES parents tend to show more warmth and affection toward their children (Maccoby, 1980).

These social-class differences seem to hold across race and culture in the United States. However, Maccoby (1980) emphasizes that these differences are based on averages. In other words, both higher- and lower- SES families may have variable parenting styles; some lower- SES families obviously exist that reflect higher- SES parenting styles and vice versa.

Vander Zanden (1981), in contrast to Maccoby, reviewed a number of research studies and concluded that although some social- class differences in parenting do exist, "the differences between the classes are not very large. Indeed, this seems the safest conclusion at the present time" (Ellis, Lee, & Petersen, 1978; Wright & Wright, 1976).

## PARENT EDUCATION IN MODERN AMERICA BEGINS

Parent education in the United States has been of special interest to behavioral and social scientists in the last two decades. Research findings show the unequivocal need for the training of parents (Fantini & Cardenas, 1980; Harman & Brim, 1980; Harmon & Zigler, 1980; Waggoner, 1970). In particular, results show that what parents know about child development is positively related to their ability to provide a stimulating and supportive environment conducive to positive development (Stevens, 1984).

While schoolteachers are required to complete a rigid four-year training program prior to taking full responsibility for children in their classrooms, prerequisites for parents are nonexistent. This is a somewhat ironic phenomenon when one considers that parents are indeed the primary influence, and in the best position to promote healthy adjustment of their children (O'Dell, 1974). It is claimed that while millions of men and women become parents each year, few have the knowledge, skills, and confidence to pursue this overwhelming task (Pickarts & Fargo, 1971; Powell, 1978).

The need for parent education has become increasingly accepted in recent years and many books have been written to help parents (e.g., Dobson, 1970; Dreikurs & Soltz, 1964; Ginott, 1965; Gordon, 1970; Spock, 1957). In addition, lectures, seminars, and workshops have also been developed to help meet this need (e.g., Dinkmeyer & McKay, 1976; Soltz, 1967). Parents who have become involved with materials aimed at improving parenting strategies report them to be highly successful.

Well-designed educational programs for parents were sporadic prior to the last two decades of the nineteenth century. In 1888, the Child Study Association of America was founded by a small group of mothers meeting together in New York City for the purpose of determining how they might become better parents (Auerbach, 1968). The first White House Conference on Child Welfare was held in 1909, and the Children's Bureau was founded in 1912 (Croake & Glover, 1977). Issues concerning the improvement of child rearing continued to attract interest from this time forward. Only in the last 20 years, however, has the parent education movement begun to unfold and develop into a "legitimate" area of academic concern.

Parent education programs are being offered through colleges and universities, community education centers, school districts, and churches. Why the sudden interest? Is it a result of the ever-increasing divorce rate, a possible moral decline in this country, apathy with regard to families, or just plain ignorance among the current generation? Karpowitz (1980) feels the American family is alive and doing well but is dealing with so many rapid changes that the functioning of the family unit has been altered. Because families are constantly changing, they would be benefited by means or programs that help them deal with problems that beset them (e.g., parent education programs). This text is one means to that end.

## Summary

It should now be obvious that environments, children, and parents differ. It is anticipated that parenting techniques will also differ—across time, culture, socioeconomic status, and religion, to name just a few. Also different are theories concerning child development and psychological attitudes toward discipline, moral and emotional development, the handling of special problems, and many other aspects of family life. (Topics such as these will be the focus of subsequent chapters.) Again, this text will attempt to provide a wide range of views on topics, attitudes, and techniques concerning child rearing.

Differences in parenting techniques, as pointed out in this chapter, are a function of all of those influences cited above—time, culture, SES, religion, and contemporary thought. Also not to be forgotten are pure and simple fads. One author points out the continual ebb and flow of parenting advice, calling this the child-rearing "pendulum."

> In the absence of a validated system of child rearing, American practices seem to operate in terms of fads and cycles. For example, in 1914 the government published the first edition of *Infant Care,* a book that has gone through umpteen editions and sold tens of millions of copies. As the various editions have been published, however, there have been some remarkable changes in the advice given to mothers.
>
> In the 1920s, thumb-sucking and masturbation were looked upon as dangerous impulses that must be curbed. As late as 1938 the book showed a stiff cuff that would stop the baby from bending its arm, thus preventing thumb-sucking. Yet in 1942, readers were told that masturbation and thumb-sucking were harmless. In 1951 the caution was voiced that too much pampering might result in the child becoming a "tyrant." In the present decade, *Infant Care* takes a markedly permissive attitude toward such things as weaning, masturbation, thumb-sucking, and toilet training. . . . And so it goes (Kephart, 1981, p. 423–424).

In spite of the many variations in child rearing across time, culture, SES, religion, and contemporary thought, several parenting themes or concerns constantly recur. How much control should parents take in their children's lives? How do parental expectations, presence or absence of warmth, and acceptance of children affect their development? Are children's personalities inborn or are they a product of the environment? These and similar questions will be addressed in the following chapters.

# SELF-CHECK

1. Hoffman and Hoffman (1973) identified reasons that parents value children. Which of the following is not as applicable in the United States today as it was in the past?
   a. Morality, altruism, religion, norms regarding sexuality
   b. Creativity, accomplishment, competence
   c. Economic utility
   d. Stimulation, novelty, fun
2. Plato distrusted the average citizen and felt that children
   a. were more of a liability than an asset.
   b. should be educated and reared by the state.
   c. should be beaten on the mouth, hands, and buttocks.
   d. All of the above are true.
3. Which of the following child-rearing practices was much more common from 1600 to 1700 than it is today?
   a. Physical punishment
   b. Dressing and treating children as adults
   c. Preoccupation with breaking the child's will
   d. All of the above are true.
4. John Locke of England and Jean Jacques Rousseau of France were influential in changing many people's attitudes toward child rearing. Both of them
   a. condoned physical punishment.
   b. opposed physical punishment.
   c. felt physical punishment was appropriate only when children were young.
   d. None of the above are true of both men.
5. Which of the following is true concerning child-rearing emphases in the twentieth century?
   a. Permissive parenting philosophy
   b. Restrictive parenting philosophy
   c. Parenting techniques influenced by scientific theory
   d. Child-rearing emphasis in somewhat of a see-saw pattern.
   e. Both c and d are true.
6. In our discussion with parents, students, and professionals, we have found modern parents to have very identifiable views about the nature of children. Which view is not included in the generalized views identified in your reading?
   a. The child as a "miniature adult"
   b. The child as a "gardener"
   c. The child as a "bundle of sin"
   d. The child as a "noble savage"

7. Which of the following is *not* a common goal that parents everywhere seem to share as identified by Levine (1974)?
   a. Raising children so that they will take care of their parents when they become old
   b. Development of the child's capacity for economic self-maintenance
   c. Development of the child's capacity for maximizing cultural values
   d. Physical survival and health of the child
8. Concerning the hierarchy of parents' goals for child rearing (Levine, 1974), which of the following is important to understand in determining the goals?
   a. The sex of the child
   b. The age of the child
   c. Religious values and beliefs
   d. Environmental hazards and constraints
9. When studying the relationship between parenting and social class, Maccoby (1980) found that
   a. lower-SES parents tend to stress happiness, creativity, and ambition.
   b. lower-SES parents are more controlling, power-assertive, and authoritarian.
   c. higher-SES parents talk to their children less, yet seem to communicate better nonverbally.
   d. higher-SES parents tend to be cold to their children and to each other.
10. Which of the following is true of parent education in the United States?
    a. Well-designed parent education programs have been sporadic until about 20 years ago.
    b. Parents are not required to complete training programs.
    c. The need for parent education is great.
    d. All of the above are true.

KEY:1–c; 2–b; 3–d; 4–b; 5–e; 6–b; 7–a; 8–d; 9–b; 10–d

# C H A P T E R

# 2

# SOME RESEARCH CONTRIBUTIONS

In Chapter 1 the influence of time, culture, socioeconomic status, and religion on parenting was introduced. Great fluctuations in child-rearing techniques have occured due to these and other variables. As we mentioned, at one point in history it was believed by theologians that the child was born in sin and, therefore, full of the devil. Parents were instructed that if they wanted "righteous" children they should "beat the devil out of them"—and beat them they did. One can still observe the influence of some early philosophies espousing a belief in the evil nature of humanity. Translated into the family, parents were to teach children to overcome, or at least control, their (evil) desires.

Later, John B. Watson, the leader in American Behaviorism, offered a more "scientific" approach to raising children. The following is his prescription offered to parents:

> There is a sensible way of treating children. Treat them as though they were young adults. Dress them, bathe them with care and circumspection. Let your behavior always be objective and kindly firm. Never hug and kiss them, never let them sit in your lap. If you must, kiss them once on the forehead when they say good night. Shake hands with them in the morning. Give them a pat on the head if they have made an extraordinarily good job of a difficult task. Try it out. In a week's time you will find how easy it is to be perfectly objective with your child and at the same time kindly. You will be utterly ashamed of the mawkish, sentimental way you have been handling it (Watson, 1928, p. 113).

Watson's influence on child-rearing techniques can best be described by this excerpt from an old text, *Guidance of Childhood and Youth:*

> From this point of view the child is considered as primarily neither moral nor immoral, but capable of acquiring both a form of behavior that is socially acceptable, and a set of attitudes that [is] essentially social and moral or the opposite (Gruenberg, 1926).

Thus, all children could be properly socialized with appropriate manipulation. Being born without predisposition, this approach considered children and their behavior (whether socially appropriate or not) to be a product of parental techniques. Psychologists had abondoned the basic "evil nature concept" in favor of the *tabula rasa* or blank slate theory, teaching that human beings were born neither bad nor good, but were molded for better or worse by outside influences.

However, this viewpoint was later coupled with the popular Freudian emphasis on a child's early years, and the effects of a strained parent–child relationship on subsequent personality development. As a result, a more permissive or needs-oriented form of child-rearing replaced the rigid, methods-oriented styles condoned by Watson. Of course, all of these practices were

According to John Watson, the leader in American Behaviorism, proper child rearing involved an emotionless, objective approach—producing, if all went well, totally behaved children.

built on the premise of maximizing parental influence in producing a psychologically secure, well-adjusted, intelligent individual.

Today parents are often similarly divided into camps ranging from rigidly controlling and authoritarian to indulgent and permissive. Others can be classified somewhere along that continuum, as they try to find the best approach for their particular family.

While we still have much to learn about a parent's influence on child personality and social behavior, a tremendous increase in parent–child research has served to clarify some effects of parent behavior on children. From research findings investigators have conceptualized meaningful dimensions of parental behavior. These theoretical models are at present still in development and, therefore, not absolute, but information can be gained to assist in formulating a child-rearing philosophy. Although it would be impossible to include *all* significant research, a sample will nevertheless be presented in this chapter.

## Schaefer's Work

### CLASSIFYING PARENTS

Schaefer (1959) organized several studies of maternal behavior and determined that in all cases, two major dimensions can be isolated: control

Figure 2.1    Schaeffer's Model of Parental Behavior

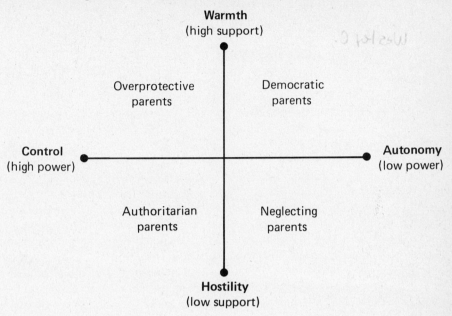

**Warmth**
(high support)

Overprotective
parents

Democratic
parents

**Control**
(high power)

**Autonomy**
(low power)

Authoritarian
parents

Neglecting
parents

**Hostility**
(low support)

vs. autonomy and love (warmth) vs. hostility. Each of these two dimensions contains opposite ends of a continuum, and each dimension is independent of the other. In other words, a parent may be placed somewhere on the control–autonomy continuum regardless of his or her position on the love–hostility dimension. For example, a parent may be controlling and warm or controlling and hostile; or, a parent may exercise little parental power and be warm or hostile (see Figure 2.1).

If these dimensions were considered separately, limited generalizations could be made about parental behavior. However, by coupling these two dimensions, as shown in Figure 2.1, Schaefer was able to classify parental behaviors into more meaningful generalizations. Parents exhibiting low power (permissive, allowing autonomy) and low support or love (rejecting, hostile) could be classified as neglecting, while parents who demonstrated low support coupled with high power (dominating, controlling) were considered authoritarian. Low-power parents who were highly supportive (accepting, loving) of their children were classified as democratic, and parents coupling high power with high support were termed overprotective.

Although easy to understand, the simplicity of this two-dimensional model is problematic. In particular, identifying only four parent descriptives (overprotective, democratic, neglecting, authoritarian) limits the dimensions' applicability. Schaefer (1959), realizing this problem, developed another model based on the same two dimensions of autonomy–control and love–hostility, but now incorporated different degrees of parental *involvement* on the two continua. Not only do the original four behavior descriptions remain, but more specific parental descriptions could be added. Whereas only four general parenting types had been available, there are now eight. A similar model is used by Becker (1964) and will be described below.

Wesley C.
## Becker's Contributions

Becker (1964) tied a number of parental behavior studies together through a statistical procedure called *factor analysis* (Baldwin, Kalhorn, & Breese, 1945; Becker, Peterson, Hellmer, Shoemaker, & Quay, 1959; Becker, Peterson, Luria, Shoemaker, & Hellmer, 1962; Roff, 1949; Sears, Maccoby, & Levin, 1957; Takala, Nummenmaa, & Kauranne, 1960). From his work, Becker also concluded that a third dimension of parental behavior is important to consider. Retaining Schaefer's original love–hostility and restrictiveness–permissiveness dimensions, Becker's model added an anxious/emotional vs. calm/detached involvement (high-anxiety vs. low-anxiety) dimension (see Figure 2.2). He notes, for example, that two different parents may both be warm and permissive (or restrictive), yet differ in their emotional involvement. For example, both the democratic and the over-indulgent parent, by definition, are considered warm and permissive, but the indulgent parent is high on emotional involvement, while the democratic parent tends to be low on this dimension (calm/detached). Both the organized, effective parent and the overprotective parent are high on warmth and restrictiveness, while the overprotective parent again shows more anxious/emotional involvement than the organized, effective parent (Becker, 1964).

Becker provides a description of parental attitudes on these three dimensions. The warmth-vs.-hostility dimension is defined at the warm end by parents who (1) are accepting, affectionate, approving, understanding, and child-centered; (2) use explanations and praise when disciplining; (3) respond positively to dependency behavior; (4) use little physical punishment; and (5) (for mothers) are rarely critical of their husbands. The hostility end of the dimension would define parents with the opposite characteristics: (1) rejecting, nonaffectionate, disapproving, and critical; (2) using physical punishment; and (3) meting out little praise or explanation when disciplining. The restrictiveness-vs.-permissiveness dimension is defined at the restrictive end by parents who use many restrictions and strictly enforce expectations in the areas of sex play, modesty, table manners. toilet training, neatness, orderliness, care of household furniture, obedience, and aggression toward siblings, peers, and parents. Permissive parents, on the other hand, might provide little restrictions or clearly defined guidelines, letting their children roam unmonitored. Anxious/emotional involvement vs. calm/detached is defined at the anxious end by parents who exhibit high levels of concern and anxiety to the point of being babying, protective, and solicitous of their children. Calm/detached parents are not easily overexcited by their children's troubles and difficulties, at times appearing almost aloof, although they may be very much aware and involved (Becker, 1964). By using these three dimensions, Becker produced a model that is neither too general nor too specific.

## Figure 2.2 Becker's Model of Parental Behavior

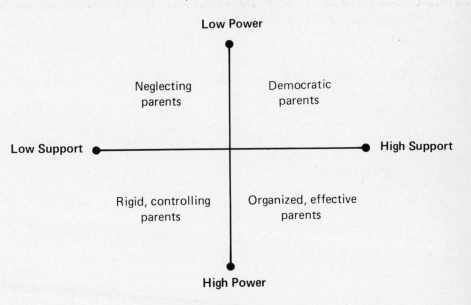

Low–Anxiety Parents
(calm/detached)

**Low Power**

Neglecting parents | Democratic parents

**Low Support** ———————————— **High Support**

Rigid, controlling parents | Organized, effective parents

**High Power**

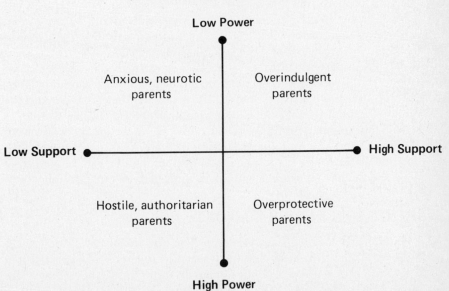

High–Anxiety parents
(anxious/emotional involvement)

**Low Power**

Anxious, neurotic parents | Overindulgent parents

**Low Support** ———————————— **High Support**

Hostile, authoritarian parents | Overprotective parents

**High Power**

By examining Figure 2.2 it is evident, as Becker pointed out, that the only difference between democratic and overindulgent parents is the amount of emotional involvement (anxiety). The same difference is found between organized, effectives and overprotectives, between rigid controllings and hostile authoritarians, and between neglecting and anxious neurotics. Now, by employing Becker's three dimensions, eight parent types can be described as follows:

|  | Affection | Authority | Worry |
|---|---|---|---|
| Democratic | High support | Low power | Low anxiety |
| Overindulgent | High support | Low power | High anxiety |
| Organized, effective | High support | High power | Low anxiety |
| Overprotective | High support | High power | High anxiety |
| Rigid, controlling | Low support | High power | Low anxiety |
| Hostile, authoritarian | Low support | High power | High anxiety |
| Neglecting | Low support | Low power | Low anxiety |
| Anxious, neurotic | Low support | Low power | High anxiety |

Since Becker and the writers of this text feel that anxiety level affects parental behavior, we will briefly define and discuss anxiety. While it may seem similar to fear, a significant difference between fear and anxiety exists. Fear is related to some objective danger wherein emotions are appropriate to the magnitude of risk. Thus, a person who has been bitten by a dog is appropriately afraid when confronted by a vicious dog. She has previously felt a dog's teeth puncturing her flesh and has heard its growl, so it is no surprise that she is fearful when confronted with this cue.

Anxiety, on the other hand, is not so easily understood because it often has no object of focus. If it has, the object is difficult to detect and is frequently inappropriate for the magnitude of emotion felt. For example, if a man has a strong, pervasive feeling of fear when walking into a schoolroom, he is experiencing anxiety. Anxiety is a vague fear, usually without object attachment.

Anxiety in parents can come as a result of many factors either directly related to the parenting role or not. Anxiety could affect a mother's interaction with her children if she is afraid she is not adequately prepared to be a mother. Or, a father may be afraid of what his child will do if he doesn't let the child know (regularly) who the boss is. Anxiety may be indirectly involved, on the other hand, when a father is a tyrant with his children because he feels threatened about losing his job at the factory; a mother may be indulgent because she doesn't want the neighbors to think she is a cruel person.

## PARENTS LOW IN LOVE-SUPPORT

With the three dimensions of love, power, and anxiety briefly described, it is now appropriate to discuss characteristics of the parent types presented in Figure 2.2 (For a more in-depth discussion of the research creating these generalizations, see Shaefer, 1959, Becker, 1964, Maccoby, 1980, and Baumrind, 1971.) Since the majority of literature is related to the four parent types revolving around the high-support axis (overprotective; organized, effective; democratic; and overindulgent), most of our discussion will focus on these four. First, however, we present the four parent types having low support as a common bond (neglecting; rigid, controlling; anxious, neurotic; and hostile, authoritarian).

**Neglecting parents.**    Neglecting parents (low support, low power, low anxiety) are characterized by a lack of concern for their children. Usually hedonistic, they tend to leave children to their own devices. These parents lack warmth and are either neglectful in exercising parental control or highly inconsistent in discipline use. A significant percentage of delinquents come from this type of home. They usually exhibit aggressive and poorly controlled behavior.

**Rigid, controlling parents.**    Rigid, controlling parents (low support, high power, low anxiety) are both restrictive and hostile and tend to promote counterhostility in their children without allowing it to be expressed in their behavior. Under such conditions, children tend to become neurotic. These children are socially withdrawn, shy, anxious, and highly self-punishing. This

Neglecting parents, low in support, love, and emotional involvement, often produce delinquent children.

combination of low support, high power, and low anxiety fosters considerable resentment, with some of it being both turned against the self and more generally experienced as internalized conflict and turmoil.

**Anxious, neurotic parents.** Anxious, neurotic parents (low support, low power, high anxiety) transfer their anxiety to their children. They, too, are probably the product of rigid controlling or hostile, authoritarian parents. Their anxieties are focused inward and often exacerbated by the belief that the world is out to get them. They, therefore, see their children as perpetrators of their own weaknesses. Children are viewed by anxious, neurotic parents as a symbol of punishment and constant reminder of their inability to function as a "normal" parent. Children from these homes reflect the anxiety modeled by their parents and are motivated toward antisocial behavior; they are often socially aggressive and punitive.

**Hostile, authoritarian parents.** Hostile, authoritarian parents (low support, high power, high anxiety), like rigid, controlling parents, are restrictive and punitive. However, their authoritarianism is primarily a result of high anxiety. They may be frustrated people who try to appease their feelings by striking out at their children. Anxiety experienced by hostile, authoritarian parents is generally from sources outside the family. The children of hostile, authoritarian parents tend to be like those from rigid, controlling homes—specifically, socially withdrawn and self-punishing.

## PARENTS HIGH IN LOVE-SUPPORT

Our discussion now turns from the basically non-nurturant parent type to those parents who share the common denominator of love or support for their children. It is often said that it makes no difference what you do to or with a child as long as you love him. However, the literature reveals that *highly supporting, highly anxious* parents at either end of the power dimension are generally socially undesirable. One type, overprotective parents, tend to "smother" their children with love, while the other family type is highly supportive but exerts very little control over the child for fear of crushing the child's development. A closer look at these two parent types is warranted.

**Overprotective parents.** Overprotective parents (high support, high power, high anxiety) are intrusive and focus their whole lives around their children's behavior. They are also quick to respond to threatening child behavior or misbehavior. Qualified power-assertion methods are preferable to physical punishment; they find the threat of withdrawal of love and other emotional tactics more effective in controlling a child's behavior than punitive methods. They try to remove obstacles or prevent situations that might be problematic for their children, and usually set high standards. The children, in an attempt to please their parents, usually set unrealistic goals for themselves. These children are highly compliant and extremely dependent on their parents for guidance and approval. They develop very strong consciences in order to protect themselves from a withdrawal of love.

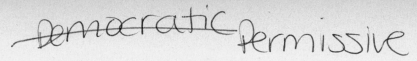
~~Democratic~~ permissive

**Indulgent parents.**   Indulgent parents (high support, low power, high anxiety) seem to live with an extreme fear of frustrating their children; therefore, they set few, if any, limits or restrictions on their children's behavior. Like overprotective parents they are quick to remove obstacles from their children's lives. However, they exert very little control or power over them. They are warm, supportive, and unconditionally accepting of their children.

The children from indulgent homes are extremely independent and are great manipulators, ~~especially of their parents.~~ They are frequently aggressively antisocial, not only toward peers but also toward parents and other adults. With few limits and unconditional acceptance, the child never has the opportunity to develop a conscience and is left, therefore, both noncompliant and mischievous.

Noncompliant and mischievous children have a greater tendency to come from indulgent homes.

The two remaining parent types—democratic and organized, effective—generally rear children who are better adjusted and more socially mature than do the other six parent types. Both democratic and organized, effective parents are low in anxiety and high in support or love, although the organized, effective parent asserts high power, while the democratic parent uses power sparingly.

**Democratic parents.**  Democratic parents (high support, low power, low anxiety) are very warm and supportive of their children and, like indulgent parents, use very little power and assertion. Behavior limits and ground rules are mutually accepted and set by parents and children. Characteristic of the democratic family is the family council, in which every member has equal say and power. If, for example, three children decide to vote against Mom and Dad, they can instigate family change themselves. Democratic and indulgent parents differ largely as a function of anxiety or emotional involvement. Indulgent parents act in fear, while democratic parents express confidence in their children and reflect an attitude of cooperation.

Democratically raised cildren are very creative and highly independent. Their independence is founded on confidence as opposed to the rebellion expressed by children from an indulgent home. These children are socially outgoing and accepting of others. Their sense of achievement is based on a self-rewarding structure. In other words, they would measure their success by their own happiness, not by worldly standards such as wealth and prestige. Their conscience is usually based on a "golden rule" type of philosophy that respects others' rights. Generally, democratically raised children are friendly nonconformists who like to "do their own thing" and allow others the same privilege. On the other hand, these children have also been criticized as being rowdy and lacking in obedience and submissiveness.

**Organized, effective parents.**  The organized, effective parent is similar to the successful, highly motivated businessperson who seems to devote all of his or her time and energy to the success of the business. Such a person is organized and effective at work. Imagine this same motivation and energy directed toward a family's success. This is a picture of the organized effective parent (high support, high power, low anxiety). As would be expected from a controlling parent, parent-set limits would be highly structured. Unlike the home of the overprotective parent, however, there would be fewer limits, and these limits would be rationally selected for the child's benefit. Organized, effective parents are not so quick and intense in response to their child's misbehavior. Very methodical in choosing a course of action, they base their decision on what is best for the child. While setting high standards of excellence for their children, they do not expect perfection unless their children are realistically capable of achieving such a goal. They just push them to operate at the peak of their abilities. Organized, effective parents are confident, warm, supportive, and success-oriented people.

*Authoritarian*

Characteristics of organized, effective children are like those of their parents. They have high achievement striving and are very responsible. They lack, however, the freedom to become as independent or creative as children from more democratic families. Independence and creativeness need the freedom and encouragement of democratic parenting styles to fully develop. Organized, effective children have a strong conscience and are extremely compliant and respectful to persons in power or authority. In short, they are the "model child" as prescribed by our Western civilization.

Table 2.1 summarizes in simple fashion some of the most salient points made in the preceding discussion.

The parenting dimensions of control, warmth, and anxiety-involvement, and the eight subsequent parenting types described above, provide a general guide to how parenting styles affect children's emotional and social devel-

**Table 2.1   Description of and Possible Outcomes of the Eight Parenting Types**

| Types of Parents | Characteristics of Parents | Possible Traits of Children |
|---|---|---|
| Democratic | Warm and supportive; rules set by parents and children | Confident, independent, socially outgoing |
| Indulgent | Lack of definite standards and limits | Independent, manipulative, antisocial, aggressive |
| Organized, effective (authoritative) | Structured limits; high standards; confident, warm, supportive | High achievement; responsible |
| Overprotective | Intrusive focus on their children's behavior; high standards | Dependent; strong conscience |
| Rigid, controlling | Restrictive and hostile | Neurotic, socially withdrawn, shy, anxious, self-punishing |
| Hostile, authoritarian (dictator) | Restrictive, punitive, frustrated | Socially withdrawn, self-punishing |
| Neglecting | Lack of concern and warmth; hedonistic and neglectful; low parental control | Delinquent |
| Anxious, neurotic | World perceived as out to get them | Anxious, antisocial, aggressively punitive |

opment. Although these eight styles are not hard and fast, research does tend to support the basic idea that parental love and warmth are positive, and that both overly controlling and overly permissive parenting styles may be problematic. We now turn to additional research supporting these general ideas.

## The Baldwin Study

Though the contributions of Schaefer (1959) and Becker (1964) provide a summary and basis for many studies of parenting types, their work was actually preceded by other significant studies. Baldwin, Kalhorn, and Breese (1945), in a cooperative research project with the Samuel S. Fels Research Institute, observed 125 families over several months, subsequently identifying three major "syndromes" of parental behavior. In other words, parenting responses to children could be classified along three dimensions, which are remarkably similar to the three later identified by Becker (1964).

The first syndrome, *democracy,* describes parental control from democratic to autocratic, and resembles Becker's (1964) power or control dimension. Democratic parents: (1) talked with their children frequently, (2) were noncoercive in policy-making, allowing children input into family decisions; (3) answered children's questions and offered explanations for family rules; (4) respected children's individuality and freedom of choice; and, (5) encouraged self-reliance. Autocratic parents demonstrated the opposite of these characteristics.

In a subsequent report, Baldwin (1949) identified some differences among the children of families with different levels of democracy. Children of highly democratic parents were above average in planning ability, leadership, emotional security, intellectual development, fearlessness, social involvement, and vigorous physical activity. However, they were also more aggressive and bossy. It seems, then, that democratic child-rearing techniques produce not only positive child attributes, but some nonconforming ones as well. Recall that Becker's (1964) democratic parents seemed to have children who were similarly creative, independent, and self-reliant, but also rowdy and lacking somewhat in obedience.

The second syndrome identified by Baldwin et al. (1945) was termed *acceptance,* ranging from rejecting to accepting parental attitudes, and resembling Becker's (1964) warmth-hostility or support dimension. Accepting parents were more affectionate and less critical of their children. They also enjoyed a better rapport with their children and their homes were more "child-centered." Rejecting parents, on the other hand, were more hostile, unaffectionate, disapproving, and emotionally distant.

This acceptance dimension appeared to be the most important or basic. If parents were accepting, they were classifiable in any number of ways according to their placement on the other two dimensions. On the other hand, rejecting parents were generally skewed to the "less desirable" end of the other dimensions as well. In other words, there seemed to be fewer ways to reject children than to accept them.

The third syndrome was *indulgence,* ranging from the indulgent to the nonchalant parent, and resembling Becker's (1964) parental anxiety dimension. Indulgent parents were seen as protective, babying, and solicitous, but also accepting. Nonchalant parents were less anxiously concerned and involved, evidencing less neurotic behaviors.

## The Baumrind Study

Diana Baumrind, through several research projects (1967, 1971, 1973), identified three parenting patterns: authoritative, authoritarian, and permissive (see Table 2.2). These studies show some similarities with the earlier work by Schaefer (1959) and Becker (1964).

Authoritative parents were somewhat controlling and demanding, but also warm, receptive, and rational. They tended to direct children's activities in a rational manner, encourage discussion, value disciplined conformity along with self-reliance, and recognize children's uniqueness while also setting standards.

Authoritarian parents valued obedience, attempted to shape, control, and evaluate children's behavior and attitudes according to an absolute set of standards, and did not encourage discussion. In comparison to authoritative parents, then, they allowed for little child individuality and input. In addition, they were less warm and more emotionally detached from their children.

Permissive parents were noncontrolling and nondemanding, rarely exercising power to create conformity. Rather, they turned to reasoning when interacting with children, consulted with them when making family decisions, and presented themselves as a resource. These parents were also warm and accepting.

### Table 2.2   Baumrind's Parenting Types

| Type | Parent Behavior | Child Characteristics |
| --- | --- | --- |
| Authoritative | Controlling; demanding; warm; receptive; rational; verbal give-and-take; values discipline, self-reliance, and uniqueness | Independent; socially responsible; self-controlled, explorative; self-reliant |
| Authoritarian | Stricter control and more critical evaluation of child's behavior and attitudes; little verbal give-and-take; less warm and more emotionally detached | Withdrawn; discontented; distrustful of others |
| Permissive | Noncontrolling; nondemanding; little punishment or exercising of power; use of reasoning; warm and accepting | Lacking in self-reliance, self-control, and explorative tendencies |

Children of each parent-type had distinguishable behavior differences. Children of authoritative parents were more independent and socially responsible than children of the other two parenting types. They were also characterized as self-reliant, self-controlled, and explorative. Children of authoritarian parents were somewhat withdrawn, discontented, and distrustful of others. Children of permissive parents were the least self-reliant, explorative, and self-controlled.

Parental warmth alone was not related to social responsibility or independence in children, although parents of the most competent children were *both* warm and somewhat controlling. Again, as in studies reviewed earlier in this chapter, parental control and warmth (acceptance) interact to influence children's development in different ways.

More current research is also supportive of Baumrind's suggestion that parenting styles are correlated with differences in child development. Endsley, Hutchens, Garner, and Martin (1979), for example, found that authoritarian mothers had less curious children. Similarly, McCall (1974) found that children who progressed the most intellectually had warm, controlling, and reasoning parents.

## Major Parent Dimensions

From the studies discussed previously, some general parenting dimensions can be identified. The first, restrictiveness vs. permissiveness, seems to appear in all the studies cited. The second, warmth vs. hostility, is dealt with specifically in Becker's results, but can be extrapolated out of other studies, as the effects of warm and hostile parenting styles appear logically to have different parenting results.

## RESTRICTIVENESS VS. PERMISSIVENESS

A generally consistent conclusion from Shaefer's, Becker's, Baumrind's, and Baldwin's work is that parents who are too rigidly restrictive and authoritarian, or who are too permissive, may create undesirable attitudes and behaviors in their children. Results of these and other studies examining restrictive vs. permissive styles find that restrictive discipline produces inhibition and permissive discipline produces uninhibited behaviors (Becker, 1964). Symonds (1939) found that children of dominating (restrictive) parents were better socialized and more courteous, obedient, neat, generous, and polite. However, they were also more sensitive, self-conscious, and shy. Children of permissive parents were more irresponsible, disobedient, disorderly in a classroom situation, and lacking in sustained attention and regular work habits.

Becker also cited a significant Fels longitudinal study (Kagan & Moss, 1962) that considered the child's age in relation to mother's restrictiveness. For both boys and girls, restrictiveness after the age of three tended to produce higher hostility toward the mother. Restrictiveness before three appeared to produce inhibition; these children were more conforming and dependent on adults, and less dominant and competitive with peers. Becker concluded that "it would appear that restrictiveness at ages three to six is more likely to generate aggression, but the aggression is manifested in socially approved forms (competitiveness, indirect aggression to peers, and justifiable ventilation)" (Becker, 1964, p. 192).

## HOSTILITY VS. WARMTH

During Becker's investigation, a number of studies were found that explored consequences of restrictive vs. permissive parents who were primarily warm or hostile. This dimension seemed to interact with restrictive and permissive discipline styles as indicated in Becker's original set of axes. "In general, the studies show that permissiveness combined with hostility maximizes aggressive, poorly controlled behavior, while restrictiveness combined with hostility maximizes self-aggression, social withdrawal, and signs of internal conflict" (Becker, 1964, p. 193). Studies on delinquents indicate that permissive–hostile conditions tend to produce noncompliant, aggressive, and poorly controlled behavior (Bandura & Walters, 1959; Burt, 1929; Healy & Bronner, 1926). Several other studies indicate that neuroticlike conflicts are more often generated under restrictive–hostile conditions (Lewis, 1954; Rosenthal, Finkelstein, Ni, & Robertson, 1959; R. R. Sears, 1961; and Watson, 1934).

Considering now the effect of parental warmth, "results showed that children reared in a warm, permissive home were more independent . . . , more friendly in interaction with adults (cooperation), moderately persistent in the face of an impossible task . . . , more creative, and less hostile. . . . Children reared in a warm, restrictive home were more likely to be dependent, unfriendly, to be either very high or very low in persistence, less creative, and to show more fantasy hostility" (Becker, 1964, p. 196).

## CONTEMPORARY SUPPORT OF THESE DIMENSIONS

The general findings of this chapter were supported by more current research as well. For example, Quinton and Rutter (1984) determined that families living in an upper London borough who were experiencing serious child-behavior difficulties tended to have mothers who were low in expressed warmth to the child and who were insensitive to their children's worries and distress. Similarly, these families exhibited inconsistent discipline practices; aggressive control was often used and conflicts were often unresolved. These familial characteristics stood out in comparison to families with similar-age children, where major child difficulties were not apparent.

Barron and Earls (1984) also concluded that negative parent–child interaction and high family stress are associated with poor behavior adjustment in children. Negative parent–child interaction included low parental warmth and affection, and increased parental irritability and criticism. High family stress was evaluated by considering, among other variables, parental anxiety and feelings of inadequacy, and marital discord.

The variables emerging out of these two studies are highly reminiscent of the major parenting dimensions discussed earlier. Parental warmth is still an important and positive influence on a child's emotional and social development—warmth vs. hostility dimension; likewise, disciplinary styles still retain their influence—restrictiveness vs. permissiveness dimension (Quinton & Rutter, 1984). Also, a parent's emotional involvement is still considered as a variable affecting child development (anxious/emotional involvement vs. calm/detached).

In our previous discussion, we also considered the effects that various parent characteristics might have on the development of child traits. For example, parents low in support or warmth and high in power or control (e.g., rigid, controlling and hostile, authoritarian) tend to have children who are shy, withdrawn, and self-punishing. Similarly, Turner and Harris (1984) found children of neglecting, restrictive parents to have lower self-esteem. In addition, organized/effective parents (high support, high control, low anxiety) were found in our previous discussion to have higher-achieving children. Similarly, Radin (1971, 1973) determined that parental warmth, acceptance, and nurturance foster achievement motivation and intellectual development. "In summary, the most effective pattern of parenting for facilitating children's success in school as well as their general intellectual development, seems to involve being nurturant without being too restrictive, responsive but not overly controlling, and stimulating but not too directive (Belsky & Spanier, 1984, p. 66).

However, it must be noted that, in spite of the evidence presented in this chapter, influence in the family unit is not so linear and simple. In other words, it is not true (1) that parenting styles are unchanging across time, social situations, and family development, (2) that only parents influence children; and (3) that parents and families are not in turn affected by children themselves. Current thinking is much more inclusive. Belsky and Spanier (1984) exemplify this trend in family research, stating that children, parents, the family unit, and the larger environment are all developing, changing organisms, each influencing the other. Children are influenced by parenting strategies. These strategies are in turn influenced by children's personalities and behaviors. In this fashion, children influence their own development.

In addition, families move to new cities, increase in size, and children get older, all of which serve to change parenting styles and children's behaviors. Neighborhoods and communities each have unique compositions and experience various changes and crises. Human existence is basically social, and child development is therefore influenced by both the family and the environment. To just say that certain parenting styles produce certain child characteristics is too simplistic.

# Summary

A more complete summary of findings relevant to these two dimensions—warmth vs. hostility and permissiveness vs. restrictiveness—can be found in Becker's (1964) article. It becomes apparent upon considering these and other studies that parental warmth is a positive factor in child rearing. In addition, absolute permissiveness or restrictiveness seems to have negative side-effects; however, a "slightly restrictive" permissive atmosphere, according to Becker's model, tends to create a "democratic" environment producing independent, friendly, creative, active, socially outgoing, and minimally self-aggressive children who are facilitated in adult role taking and require minimal rule enforcement (Baldwin, 1949; Levin, 1958; Maccoby, 1961; Sears, 1961; Watson, 1957).

The importance of these two dimensions will be repeatedly emphasized through this text. We will later introduce various family units (e.g., single, teenage, and stepparenting), special children (e.g., mentally retarded, hyperactive), and special parenting situations (e.g., infancy). Although parents require varied and different knowledge and skills in each of these conditions, the basic concepts reviewed in this chapter are nevertheless applicable.

This chapter has focused on "research" findings as they pertain to parenting styles and child characteristics. It must be pointed out, however, that the studies cited as references are *correlational* in nature. In other words, certain parenting styles were found to be correlated with specific child characteristics. Yet, causality cannot be determined. These studies do not demonstrate conclusively that warm, semirestrictive parenting *causes* friendly, creative, active, and socially outgoing children—only that they are correlated.

It could be that other parenting variables not yet identified are involved. Perhaps if controlled experimental studies were conducted in which parents raised their children in certain prescriptive ways (e.g., warm–restrictive, hostile–permissive), these influences on child personality could be more conclusively determined. Unlike controlled experimental designs with animals, however, such studies would be unethical for humans, even if financially, emotionally, and logistically possible in the first place. In spite of the limitations on correlational data, however, the results are nevertheless impressive enough to conclude that parenting styles affect subsequent child behavior in very significant ways—most probably in ways similar to what Becker has suggested.

Part I of this text has focused on a variety of factors influencing what we today call "parenting." Our children's lives are subtly affected by where we live; by our religious beliefs, income, and parenting styles; by scientific research and study; and even by the reasons we have children in the first place. Everyday events become reality, and these factual events have some bearing on our children's destiny. This is not to suggest, however, that we are solely a product—or victim—of our environments. Yet, environmental influence cannot be underestimated.

Part II will introduce some of the less objective influences on the parenting process in its discussion of psychological theory. Theories of human development and behavior are not always amenable to empirical validation; they cannot always be proven by adhering to the scientific method. Yet, based on astute observations of human behavior, psychological theory nevertheless provides additional structure to our understanding of child rearing.

# S E L F - C H E C K

1. Schaefer (1959) organized several empirical studies of maternal behavior and determined that in all cases, two major dimensions can be isolated. They are
   a. control vs. rejection; warmth vs. permissiveness.
   b. control vs. warmth; hostility vs. autonomy.
   c. warmth vs. hostility; control vs. autonomy.
   d. None of the above are true.
2. When contrasting anxiety and fear, which of the following is related to an objective danger wherein emotions are appropriate to the magnitude of the risk?
   a. Fear
   b. Anxiety
   c. Both a and b are correct.
   d. None of the above are correct.
3. Parents who are high in all three of the dimensions identified by Becker (high support, high power, high anxiety) are termed
   a. anxious, neurotic.
   b. neglecting.
   c. democratic.
   d. overprotective.
4. Baumrind (1971, 1973) identified three patterns of parenting (authoritarian, authoritative, permissive). Of these three, children of _____ parents were the most independent and socially responsible.
   a. authoritarian
   b. authoritative
   c. permissive
5. A general conclusion consistent with Baldwin's parental control is that parents who
   a. are too rigidly restrictive and authoritarian may create undesirable attitudes and behavior in their children.
   b. are too permissive may create undesirable attitudes and behavior in their children.
   c. Both of the above are true.
   d. None of the above are true.
6. What are some possible traits of children whose parents are restrictive, hostile, and high in anxiety?
   a. High achievement, responsible
   b. Neurotic, socially withdrawn, shy, anxious
   c. Independent, manipulative, antisocial, aggressive
   d. Confident, independent, outgoing
7. A parent who is warm, confident, and supportive, and who has high standards and structured limits, can be classified as

a. organized effective.
b. overprotective.
c. indulgent.
d. anxious-neurotic.

8. Children from which type of parent may be quite manipulative and have a difficult time developing a conscience?
   a. Anxious, neurotic
   b. Democratic
   c. Indulgent
   d. Rigid, controlling

9. For centuries, what has been a global assumption about parental behavior?
   a. It strongly affects a child's development.
   b. It is the cause of individual differences.
   c. Neither of the above are correct.
   d. Both of the above are true.

10. John Watson, one of the leaders in American Behaviorism, said the following about child raising: "Never hug and kiss them, never let them sit on your lap." Which of the following can be said of Watson?
    a. His was a "scientific approach."
    b. He was very affectionate with his children.
    c. He favored a psychoanalytic approach.
    d. He would be considered high on Becker's support (warmth) dimension.

KEY:1–c; 2–a; 3–d; 4–b; 5–c; 6–b; 7–a; 8–c; 9–a; 10–a

# PART

## ○ II ▫

# Parenting and Psychological Theory

In Chapter 1, changing parenting styles were shown to reflect somewhat the development of various theories. Both Rousseau and Locke influenced child rearing by their assumptions of child development. Similarly, Sigmund Freud and John Watson later influenced parenting techniques by making explicit their observations and theoretical viewpoints on human behavior. As you'll recall, their influence was noticed in trends appearing in advice-giving literature.

Part II of this text presents four of the major theoretical orientations toward child behavior and the different explanations each one offers of child development and child rearing. Granted, volumes have been written on each approach, so the summaries presented are limited at best. Nevertheless, familiarizing oneself with the basics can facilitate more effective and enjoyable child-rearing experiences. Many parents feel more comfortable in their roles when able to use conceptual frameworks to guide their parenting decisions. In this sense, popular theories can serve as guides for parents; yet integrating these theories' ideas and applying them to unique family situations are the parents' responsibility. No theory presented here is intended to be unalterable in its application.

Chapter 3 discusses psychoanalytic and behavioral theories, perhaps the two most visible to the lay public. However, this is not to suggest that they are any more important than the cognitive development and phenomenological theories presented in Chapter 4. In actuality, it is these latter two that usually receive major attention in most child development texts.

C H A P T E R 3

# PSYCHOANALYTIC AND BEHAVIORAL THEORIES

"Do you want facts or theories?" We do not see the conflict expressed in this popular phrase. First, notice that *facts* have changed in almost every discipline. Even basic physics updates and supplants previous *facts* with new information. And, of course, old theories are also supplemented and/or eliminated. Nevertheless, the practical application of physics uses facts and theory hand in hand. It is necessary to apply both simultaneously when uncovering the governing laws of the universe.

In the behavioral sciences, theory is even more necessary and useful for practical advancement, because variables under study are more complex and subjective, and determining cause and effect among these variables is more difficult in the behavioral than in the physical sciences. Variables in the physical sciences can often be easily regulated or specified; weights, concentrations, and temperatures are easily measured, held constant, and varied. In human behavior, however, variables such as motivation, learning, personality traits, and sensitivity to environmental influences cannot be easily defined and controlled.

Accordingly, facts from one era or culture are likely to differ among settings and across time. The effects of punishment on children may not be the same in 1970 as they were in 1930, on females as they are on males, for the Joneses as for the Smiths, nor in the United States as in Samoa. Information about the effects of punishment is much harder to generalize than is information about the weight and strength of steel, or the boiling and freezing temperatures of saline solution. It is impossible to find facts about human reactions that include all possible interactions among individual differences and environmental influences. Therefore, when discussing human behavior, the wisest procedure is to find useful rules or models that facilitate prediction, understanding, or problem solving.

An additional reason for employing models or theories follows from the quotation credited to Charles Darwin: "Any observation to be of value must be for or against some point of view." Factual information is of greatest value after the student has acquired an understanding of various theories and models. Facts can then be seen as meaningful, for they add to or detract from various points of view already being considered. In addition, not only does factual information enhance our understanding of models and theories, but, because theories provide a conceptual framework, we can more easily understand and recall the information, while viewing the facts as meaningful and relevant. Hence, we present in this and the next chapter some basic practical theories of child personality development and propose that thereby can additional information and findings on parenting be most efficiently and appropriately used as a supplement. Both facts and theories are seen as valuable and complementary.

In this chapter we will briefly describe two popular theories about the nature of children—psychoanalytic and behavioral—while trying to simplify them and to point out their present relevance. Try to consider each of them as having some truth and usefulness, and then pick and choose those parts of each that seem most appropriate.

## Psychoanalytic Theory

### SIGMUND FREUD

Sigmund Freud has probably been the most influential, yet also the most controversial, figure in the field of psychology. Basing his theories on observations of adult neurotics during the neo-Victorian era, Freud noticed, through psychoanalysis, that neuroses seemed to stem from frustrated drives and urges occurring during childhood. Unconscious impulses to satisfy these deep sexual and aggressive urges were massively repressed and allowed expression in certain symbolic patterns; thus neurotic processes developed.

The major tenets of Freudian theory challenged existing ideas of human functioning: (1) unconsciousness rather than consciousness is the core of the mind and, therefore, of human functioning; (2) sexual and aggressive drives are the source of all personality problems (in essence, these libidinal energies were hypothesized to be the source of personality in general; society existed to bridle and channel these energies into acceptable behaviors); and (3) problems occurring in adulthood are a product of frustrated or improperly curbed urges during the first five or six years of a child's life.

In order to understand more clearly how Freud's evolving ideas influenced child rearing, a brief overview is given of Freud's theories of the structure and dynamics of personality, and of the psychosexual stages of development.

**Personality dynamics.** Freud postulated the personality to have a three-part structure: id, ego, and superego. The *id* is that mental province composed of inherited instincts. Urges emerging from the id seek immediate satisfaction; the id functions according to the *pleasure principle*. A child, for example, experiencing any sort of internal imbalance such as hunger, becomes tense and uncomfortable and desires immediate satisfaction of the drive state—the child cries.

Freud emphasized that drives are primarily sexual (only later did he designate aggression as a second major internal drive state). The idea of infant sexuality shocked many people at that time and still causes many lay individuals today to consider Freud a mere lunatic. It must, however, be emphasized that these sexual impulses were perceived as energies deriving gratification through erogenous zones. Today we tend to look upon the gratification of such impulses as sexual from adolescence on. Yet Freud thought that children, even infants, seek gratification and pleasure in like fashion. For example, a child's tendency to suck his or her thumb would hardly be considered sexual to a majority of people; yet, Freud considered thumb sucking an effort to gratify sexual impulses that at that developmental period were orally focused; the mouth was the erogenous zone. It is important to understand that these instinctual urges seek immediate gratification in an irrational manner. (Freud's psychosexual stages will be discussed later in this chapter.)

The *ego* is an outgrowth of the id. It necessarily develops to help the id rationally delay the discharge of its tension-producing impulses until the appropriate order and environmental conditions are present. The ego functions according to the *reality principle*. The older child, experiencing hunger, is, therefore, aided in its tension-reducing search by this *reality principle;* he or she may wait for dinner time or perform logical actions to acquire food instead of screaming out in frustration. The ego is in contact with the external world and serves as an executive, considering safety and self-preservation in seeking realistic means of expressing impulses and releasing tension.

The third part of the mental structure is the *superego,* and is a product of parental influence and of the morals and standards of society. The superego has been termed "the conscience"—the judge between good and bad. Again, using the example of the hungry child, the child with a well-developed superego refrains from stealing or acquiring food through other inappropriate means. Whereas the id seeks pleasure (food now), and the ego tests reality (delay of gratification by developing rational means of satisfying hunger), the superego seeks perfection by desiring socially and morally acceptable means of acquiring food and thereby releasing tension resulting from hunger.

It is readily apparent that constant conflict among these three sources is both inevitable and continuous. Biological urges, such as sexual energy, are restricted from immediate expression by societal (environmental) restraints. These restraints become internalized in the older child, and the warfare continues internally. Freud implies that this dynamic interaction between biology and environment during the first few years of life determines the course of personality development. The *libido* (a fixed quantity of sexual energy) is present at birth and is apparently the source of all mental energy. Society and the superego control that energy.

Warfare between the energies of id and superego is the source of anxiety. *Neurotic anxiety* occurs when the person fears that his or her instincts will get out of control and cause behavior that is socially unacceptable and that will produce punishment. *Moral anxiety* occurs when the person feels guilty about unacceptable acts or thoughts. Anxiety produces a state of painful tension; if this anxiety cannot be dealt with effectively through realistic methods, the individual resorts to the use of unrealistic or overly used defense mechanisms.

**Defense mechanisms.** Defense mechanisms hide the internal conflict between id, ego, and superego from oneself and others. Examples of defense mechanisms include:

*Repression:* "The forgetting, or ejection from consciousness, of memories of threat, and especially the ejection from awareness of impulses in oneself that might have objectionable consequences" (White, 1964, p. 214). Aggressive impulses, for example, may be repressed by the ego for fear that expression of these impulses would be dangerous.

An important indicator of repression is a *refusal by the person to examine and consider any motives for a given action other than the one which he or she will consciously admit.* Thus, a father may spank his children quite severely, he may forget their birthdays, he may never spend time with them at enjoyable activity, and he may continually scold them. An observer may gather the impression that such behavior expresses hatred and dislike of the children. He asks the father why he treats his children so. The father says, "Because I love them, and I am trying not to spoil them. I am trying to raise them right." If the observer asks him, "Could it be that you don't like your children?" the father might become quite indignant and refuse to explore this possibility. He is repressing hostility toward his children. To admit that he dislikes his children might threaten his self-structure to a profound and catastrophic degree. However, repression is not so common in children as is the less complicated mechanism of suppression.

*Suppression:* Suppression is the conscious, rather than unconscious, forgetting of something or stopping an action because of fear. This occurs when a child deliberately refuses to face a responsibility or task that has been frustrating. Rather than think about something unpleasant, it is simply put out of mind. In fact, "out of sight out of mind" applies to children very well. Parents repeatedly hear children say, "I forgot."

*Projection:* In projection, "the person's own unacceptable impulses are inhibited and the source of anxiety is attributed to another person" (Mischel, 1976, p. 34). For example, a woman experiencing considerable anxiety over sexual impulses may attribute these impulses to another person or to the environment. By defending herself against "sexually permissive" friends or environments, the person avoids anxiety by not admitting sexual desires in herself.

*Reaction Formation:* In reaction formation, the unacceptable impulse is replaced by its opposite. For example, an individual frightened by his pornographic obsessions might openly denounce pornography and even crusade against adult bookstores.

*Sublimation:* In sublimation, the anxiety-producing sexual or aggressive impulse is displaced or redirected through socially acceptable means. A young woman, fearing the release of sexual impulses, might divert her energies to athletics.

*Regression:* Parents frequently see their children return to a more infantile behavior that they had thought to be outgrown. This frequently occurs under stress when, for example, a parent becomes too preoccupied to give the child the attention he or she is used to, or when a new baby takes away a child's position as center of attention, or when a child begins school. In these situations the child may return to earlier patterns of behavior that have been successful in the past. One two-year-old who recently received a new baby brother began crawling and cooing again so as to regain some of the attention she had recently lost.

Regression means, basically, growth "in reverse." When a person

A young man, according to psychoanalytic theory, may sublimate sexual urges through athletics.

regresses, it may be a highly *selective* regression, where only one trait changes from its present form to one that was typical of the person at a younger age; or, it may be a more *global* regression, where all aspects of the personality become more "primitive."

Clinical and experimental studies have warranted the generalization that regression is a reaction to stress, frustration, and deprivation. If ego strength is relatively low, the person cannot preserve his or her present level of performance under stressful conditions; the person may, therefore, come to manifest more primitive and childish reactions.

*Rationalization:* Among all defense mechanism, rationalization is probably most common among verbal adults. Rationalization is an explanation of one's actions that explains them in motives other than the real or genuine reasons. Usually not a conscious lie, it is rather a self-deception.

Suppose a boy asks an attractive girl for a date, and the boy's friend suggests he is asking this particular girl because she is known to be a "heavy petter." If the boy is threatened by the thought of himself as a sexy young man, this explanation may be anxiety-provoking. He may insist he is dating this girl because, and *only* because, he wants to discuss the class they have together. This is a rationalizing of motives.

If these and other defenses become inadequate, or are pathologically adhered to, neurotic anxiety might be the cause as well as the result. Neuroses

## Table 3.1   Freud's Psychosexual Stages of Personality Development

| Stage | Age | Source of Pleasure | Possible Personality Traits If Needs Are Frustrated or Overindulged |
|---|---|---|---|
| Oral | 0–1 | Sucking, biting, chewing | Dependent, gullible, generous, argumentative, sarcastic |
| Anal | 1–3½ | Elimination and retention of feces | Excessively shy, clean, shameful, impulsive, stingy, stubborn, hostile, aggressive |
| Phallic | 3½–6 | Genital stimulation | Homosexuality, flirtatious behaviour, excessive guilt |
| Latency | 6–12 | Need for pleasure is repressed | A period of learning, no definite effect on personality development |
| Genital | adolescence | Sexual and affectual relationships with the opposite sex | Inability to form lasting, meaningful adult relationships |

have their roots in early childhood, even though symptoms might not emerge until later on in life. The emphasis, then, is on the child's early upbringing, which is quite clear in Freud's theory of personality development through psychosexual stages.

**Psychosexual stages.**   Freud theorized that the child passes through five stages of personality development: oral, anal, phallic, latency, and genital stages (see Table 3.1). The first three stages cover the first five or six years of a child's life; only these three will be clarified here to give the reader an idea of how Freud suggests a parent may instill pathologies into his or her child.

During each of these stages, libidinal energy is focused on erogenous zones characterizing a particular stage. Experiences encountered at each stage, in the form of overindulgence or deprivation, may produce *fixation*. Fixation occurs when the sexual impulses at one of these early stages is fixated (arrested), leading to a character structure that is built around the unresolved conflicts at that stage.

*Oral Stage (0–1):* During the first year of life, the focus of sexual pleasure is the mouth. Gratification is achieved through sucking, biting, and chewing. Anybody around infants has noticed how almost everything picked up is put in the mouth. At the same time, infants are dependent upon others for care and satisfaction of needs. If the child's needs at this stage are frustrated, he or she is said to "fixate" at the oral stage. This child will likely become dependent on others in adulthood, become friendly and generous to others, yet feel that the world "owes him a living." Depending on where in the oral stage the child fixates, and whether this child's fixation is due to frustrated needs or to overindulgence, the child may later become gullible, or sarcastic and argumentative. An unaffectionate mother may produce a child who later in life tries to take in love by acquiring wealth (material objects).

It becomes obvious that such an orientation attributes strong importance to proper feeding schedules and weaning techniques. Yet, Freud offered no practical suggestions for the interested parent, only a concern about one's possibly harmful parenting techniques.

*Anal Stage (1–3):*   At about one to three years of age, pleasure shifts to the anal functions of elimination and retention. As the child faces parental attempts to complete toilet training, and a conflict between societal demands and these pleasures develop, different outcomes are possible. "If children view their feces as a possession, toilet training experiences may be the foundation for a host of attitudes about possessions and valuables (Baldwin, 1967, in Liebert, Poulos, & Marmor, 1977, p. 276). From demands of toilet training the child may develop excessively clean, shy, shameful, or impulsive tendencies. If these demands are met with ease, self-control is established. Difficulties in the process may result in aggression, hostility, stinginess, or stubbornness.

One student, in describing toilet training with his two-year-old daughter, related the struggle suggested above. His daughter was able to hold her bowel movements, she knew when she needed to go, and she had even used the toilet on occasion by herself. Repeated attempts to control or train her bowel habits, however, were met with opposition. She was defiant, would sit on the toilet without defecating, would become constipated, and would even defecate in her diapers immediately after her father gave up and removed her from the toilet.

According to Freudian theory, this struggle is commonplace. Children struggle between wanting to gratify their urges on the one hand, and responding to authoritarian societal rules of proper health habits on the other. Had this father persisted in forcing training at this point, excessively clean, shy, and shameful personality characteristics could have emerged in this child's later adult life.

*Phallic or Oedipal Stage (4–6):*   At about four years of age, the genital region becomes the erogenous zone. Conflict in this stage arises out of what Freud terms the Oedipal and Electra complexes for male and female children, respectively. The young boy, desiring his mother, experiences a competitive fear of his father. He senses that his father is jealous and might hurt him. This fear is sufficiently anxiety-provoking so that the child gives up sexual longings for his mother and identifies with his father. This identification process is instrumental in facilitating superego development; the boy incorporates his father's attitudes and values, and proper gender role and moral development is achieved. Through a reversed though somewhat similar process, the young girl comes to identify with her mother as she forces longings for her father out of consciousness. Again, a complete identification process is necessary for proper gender role and moral development.

One college instructor went with his wife and five-year-old daughter to the grocery store. He decided to wait in the car, and his daughter wanted to stay with him. While the mother was in the store, the professor's daughter jumped in his lap, turned to him, and said "You don't love Mommy, do you? You just love me, huh Daddy?" In Freudian terms, this story exemplifies an Electra complex. Should this complex not be adequately resolved, should the daughter not force sexual longings for her father out of consciousness and identify with her mother, then she may grow up feeling masculine in many ways. Such a process could theoretically occur if father was subtly seductive and mother was essentially nonthreatening (e.g., infrequently present or very passive by nature.).

*Latency and Genital Stages (6–12):* According to psychoanalytic theory, the preceding stages are the most significant stages for childhood determination of adult personality. The two later stages, latency and genital, occur during the years 6 to 12 or 13 and after puberty. During latency the strong id is temporarily suppressed and the child is not as strongly buffeted by sexual and aggressive forces. It is a tranquil period of development, and much cognitive learning takes place. Later, when adolescence occurs, all the energy not expressed during latency explodes and the personality structure experiences increased stress. These are the difficult years of adolescence that Freud did not discuss as thoroughly. The best discussion of these years has been written by Erik Erikson, to be presented below.

**Summary.** With this description of Freud's personality development theory, it should be easier to understand the increasing emphasis on childhood that developed during the early 1900s. Whether we agree with Freud's theory or not, if we know what he said we can understand the massive change in social attitudes as his ideas received widespread public acceptance. In addition to the responsibility placed upon parents to provide proper childhood experiences and training, it was recognized that psychopathologies developing during adulthood might be traced to unresolved childhood conflicts. These conflicts probably resulted from improperly strict or permissive parenting styles. By the mid-twentieth century, a well-balanced, flexible personality became an ideal in parenting. "Implicit in his theories, at least from the American viewpoint, was the promise that, if a child's early experiences were pleasurable and if he suffered a minimum of frustration and was given a maximum of encouragement and understanding, he developed into a well-adjusted person" (Lomax, Kagan, & Rosenkrantz, 1978, p. 64).

## ERIK ERIKSON

Erik Erikson is regarded as a "neo-Freudian," taking Freud's basic framework of personality development and fashioning it according to his own ideas. Instead of basing his theory of development on a series of psychosexual stages (as does Freud), he designates a set of "psychosocial" stages, which advantageously include developmental crises occurring in a person's life even after childhood and adolescence.

Some of Erikson's chief concerns as a psychoanalyst and an interpreter of Freud's work are summarized in his book *Childhood and Society* (1963). Taking the Freudian idea of five psychosexual development stages, Erikson therein reformulates and expands them into a sequence of eight psychosocial stages through which the personality is perceived to be constantly developing. At each stage a specific developmental task must be accomplished for normal development. With each developmental task, an individual's success is measured on a continuum between two extremes, successful task completion or

**Table 3.2  Erikson's First Five Stages of Psychosocial Development**

| Stage | Age | Developmental Task |
|---|---|---|
| Trust vs. mistrust | 0–1½ | Believing in the security of one's environment and a basic confidence in oneself |
| Autonomy vs. shame and doubt | 1½–3½ | Asserting one's own abilities and individuality |
| Initiative vs. guilt | 3½–5 | Bringing one's autonomy under conscious control |
| Industry vs. inferiority | 5–12 | Carrying out real tasks to completion |
| Identity vs. role diffusion | Adolescence | Integrating personal needs, talents, roles, and identifications with other individuals |

lack of completion. If the individual is found along the positive end of the continuum with each task, he or she has a greater probability of healthy personality development. The resolution of crises existing at each task becomes critical, and the nonresolution of developmental crises results in pathological aspects of personality that continue throughout life.

The eight developmental, bipolar dimensions that Erikson describes are: (1) sense of trust vs. mistrust, (2) sense of autonomy vs. shame and doubt, (3) sense of initiative vs. guilt, (4) sense of industry vs. inferiority, (5) sense of identity vs. identity diffusion, (6) sense of intimacy vs. isolation, (7) sense of generativity vs. stagnation, and (8) sense of integrity vs. despair (see Table 3.2). Erikson purposely uses the term *sense of*, "because the affective feeling of having achieved or failed to accomplish a stage of trust, autonomy or initiative, industry, identity, etc., is the most important determining factor for development in succeeding phases" (Maier, 1969, p. 30).

**Sense of trust vs. mistrust (0–1½).**  Erikson describes the developmental task of the first phase as a sense of trust vs. mistrust, the cornerstone for all future personality development. The critical time for developing a sense of trust is during a child's first year or year and a half. A sense of trust is actually twofold: a basic belief in the security of one's environment, and a basic confidence in oneself and the capacity of one's own organs and systems to cope with urges. Maier (1965, p. 31) describes a feeling of trust as arising from " . . . a feeling of physical comfort and a minimum experience of fear or uncertainty. . . . In contrast, a sense of mistrust arises from unsatisfactory physical and psychological experiences. . . ." A person who achieves this sense of trust is one who will willingly face new experiences in life. An example of this trusting personality might be a four-year-old who, on the first day of nursery school, enters the classroom without excessive fear and apprehension.

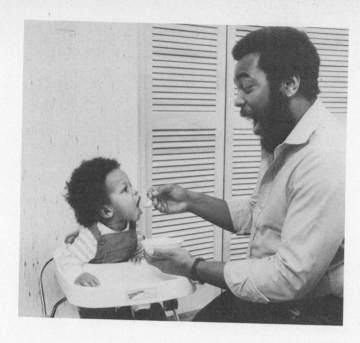

If a child's needs are regularly met early in life, a sense of trust develops.

The task of helping a child achieve this sense of trust is largely the responsibility of parents. An infant is dependent upon others for the satisfaction of physiological needs such as food, water, and warmth. If these needs are regularly satisfied, "the child comes to associate his inner sense of well-being with the consistent behavior of the persons who care for him" (Sawrey & Telford, 1968, p. 315). From this statement it seems evident that familiar, consistent, regular, and predictable infant care provided by a parent or parent substitute constitutes the basis of trust in a child's personality.

However, Erikson warns that it is not just the skill, amount, or quantity of care that is important in helping a child develop trust in the world, but the quality or underlying attitude of parent care, plus a personal quality of trustworthiness that parents must possess. It is this type of sensitive and dependable care that helps a child identify with parents and assimilate their characteristics of trust. A quotation from Maier (1969) gives further insight into this type of parent–child relationship:

> Erikson says that child training efforts fail when they become parent training rather than child training. How many mothers have said, "I was so nervous with my first child," or "My first child came along and taught me, then with my second child I was more confident." Erikson would say that under these circumstances the child with the confident mother would probably develop more trust or confidence within himself (p. 36).

Two other aspects influence this type of parental child care. One is the support and confidence that a parent receives from other people in the environment, the most important person being the spouse. If he or she is supported and given confidence, then the child will experience a more trusting, stable atmosphere. The second is a parent's preoccupation with other interests, such as occupational pursuits. This type of preoccupation can, for example, lead to a developmental crisis if "the mother turns from the baby as the primary focus of her attention to other pursuits given up during pregnancy and early postnatal life of the child" (Sawrey & Telford, 1968, p. 316). From this idea it appears that sudden or long separation of the parent and child can also lead to development of mistrust.

**Sense of autonomy vs. shame and doubt (1½–3½).** When children reach the age of about 18 months and have learned to trust their environment and themselves, then they begin to realize they have minds and wills of their own. A quote from Spock (1945) illustrates this point:

> One year old is an exciting age. Your baby is changing in lots of ways—in his eating, in how he gets around, in what he wants to do, and in how he feels about himself and other people. When he was little and helpless, you could put him where you wanted him, give him the playthings you thought suitable, feed him the foods you knew were best. Most of the time he was willing to let you be the boss, and took it all in good spirit. It's more complicated now that he is around a year old. He seems to realize that he's not meant to be a baby doll the rest of his life, that he's a human being with ideas and a will of his own (p. 260).

For the next two years the development of this sense of autonomy in contrast to a sense of doubt and shame will be the developmental crisis in focus. Up to this point the child has been very dependent upon others for the satisfaction of his or her needs. At this stage, however, a physiological maturation takes place in the body and the child is able to coordinate muscular movements such as walking, talking, and holding onto and letting go of objects. With these new abilities the child adopts a "me do," "I can do" outlook. This new attitude expresses individuality and helps children gain self-esteem. For example, when they first learn to walk, they practice it over and over for the enjoyment of walking, but they also realize that they now have status—they are people who can walk like others—and they can travel considerable distances in their environment.

To achieve the fullest sense of autonomy, Erikson believes that:

1. Children must first have developed a strong sense of trust because trust and autonomy go hand in hand. If children have not achieved a sense of trust in their environment and in themselves, they will be fearful of moving out on their own in exploration of the surrounding environment. A child who has not achieved a sense of trust will still feel a need to be dependent.
2. Children must have choices. Some of the choices that Erikson mentions are given in *A Healthy Personality for Every Child: The Fact-Finding Report of the Midcentury White House Conference on Children and Youth* (1951). These include:

a. Whether to sit or whether to stand.
b. Whether to approach a visitor or to lean against one's mother.
c. Whether to accept or reject offered food.
d. Whether to use the toilet or wet one's pants.

(Many psychologists and people in the field of child development focus their concerns primarily on children's toilet training. In actuality, however, control of the bladder and bowel movements—whether to let go or hold back—is only representative of the many decisions that must be made at this age.)

Parents must be prepared to grant freedom to the child in certain areas and to maintain control in others lest the child experience shame and doubt. Shame is a feeling of self-consciousness. At this age, children can easily experience shame if parents do not safeguard them from venturing into areas where they cannot physically control themselves. This shame and doubt is often felt as frustration in two-year-olds, and is seen in their temper tantrums. On the other hand, if parents do not provide any freedom while the child is adopting the philosophy of "me do"—if parents are always saying "No, you're too slow to walk," or, "No, you're too little"—then shame and doubt develop.

Spock (1945) gives several suggestions on this subject. For instance, if a child happens to pick up an object that could be easily broken and/or is something you do not wish the child to play with, remember that chidren are easily distracted at this age. Give the child another toy to play with. If you've gone to the park and the child persists in eating the dirt in the sandpile, give him or her a cracker to keep the mouth busy. Dr. Spock (1945) also gives ideas for parents on how to keep babies from hurting themselves around the house.

> First of all, you can arrange the rooms where he'll be so that he is allowed to play with three quarters of the things he can reach. Then only a quarter have to be forbidden. Whereas, if you try to forbid him to touch three quarters of the things, you will drive him and yourself mad. . . . Practically speaking, this means taking breakable ashtrays and vases and ornaments off low tables and shelves and putting them out of reach. It means taking the valuable books off the lower shelves of the bookcase and putting old magazines there instead. Jam the good books in tight so that he can't pull them down. In the kitchen, put the pots and pans on the shelves near the floor and put the china and packages of food out of reach. One mother filled a lower bureau drawer with old clothes, toys, and other interesting objects and let the baby explore it, empty it, fill it to his heart's content (p. 268).

3. Children must be allowed to practice newly acquired skills such as feeding and dressing themselves. To assist the child in mastering these tasks, buy those things that help make this possible. For example, purchase smaller clothes with big necks and elastic at the waists.

4. Children must be allowed to simply play. Play "provides the child with a safe island where he can develop his autonomy within his own set of boundaries or laws" (Maier, 1969, p. 40). When children are given experience wtih small toys that they

can manipulate and play with according to their own rules, shame and doubt are less likely to develop.

**Sense of initiative vs. guilt (3½–5).**   At the ages of about three and a half to five, the child engages in another task, that of achieving a sense of initiative vs. a sense of guilt. Whereas in the previous stage children were concerned with finding that they are persons in their own right, with their own self-wills, at this stage they become concerned with bringing their autonomy under conscious control. Instead of merely asserting self-will, often defiantly, initiative enables children to plan and undertake tasks. Achieving this sense of initiative is a necessary motivational basis for all acts an individual later undertakes.

This stage in a child's life is a time of vigorous learning and great imaginings. A child at this age has sufficiently mastered language and is continually questioning. He or she is also often interested in all kinds of adults—doctor, postal worker, truck driver, or police officer. Since children are trying to discover what kind of people they are, they need the example of these adults, and an opportunity to try out such roles through play.

Erikson gives suggestions for parents or adults to use with children at this age. One is very similar to that given during the stage of autonomy—that parents maintain control in some areas, but grant freedom in others so that the child will not get the idea that he or she is faced with a universal "No." In the White House Conference Report (*A Healthy Personality*, 1951, p. 15) this is summarized: "It is very important, therefore, for healthy personality development that much leeway and encouragement be given to the child's show of enterprise and imagination and that punishment be kept at a minimum."

An example of this would be a preschooler who draws a picture and the parent doesn't know what it is. The parent should find something good on which to base a compliment. The *danger* of this stage according to Erikson (1950, p. 224) " . . . is a sense of guilt over the goals contemplated and the acts initiated in one's exuberant enjoyment of new locomotor and mental power[s]. . . . " Hence guilt occurs when children contemplate or attempt tasks that their bodies actually cannot do or that they are not allowed to do by their parents.

This sense of initiative entails two major aspects: the development of conscience and appropriate gender roles. Up to this point in a child's life, parents have played a major role in whatever was attempted; they have been designating "right" and "wrong." At this stage, however, the conscience begins to develop. Parents' own values become incorporated into their children and this inner voice now directs them in what is right or wrong. When they do not obey parents or heed this inner voice they experience guilt. Development of conscience occurs at a time when people outside the child's immediate family are for the first time having a significant relationship with him or her. This development is very appropriate, for, at a time when parents are no longer continually with the child, this inner voice becomes capable of taking control.

At this time children also notice and become interested in and curious about differences in the opposite sex. Freud, as mentioned earlier, goes into great detail on how a child learns appropriate gender roles through the resolution of what he calls the Oedipal complex. Although Erikson does not go into as much detail about gender-role development, he still believes that a young child does have great affection for its opposite-sex parent, while at the same time identifying and competing with the same-sex parent. Only if a child has achieved a strong sense of trust and autonomy will he or she be able to relinquish some affection for the opposite-sex parent and turn it to others. If the child cannot do this guilt will be experienced.

**Sense of industry vs. inferiority (5–12).**   At about the age of five and continuing until age 12, the critical conflict is a sense of industry or accomplishment vs. a sense of inferiority. Whereas up to this point, a child has been involved with only initiating and starting projects, at this stage the White House Conference Report (*A Healthy Personality,* 1951, p. 7) says that a child "wants to be engaged in real tasks that he can carry through to completion . . . he wants to settle down to learning exactly how to do things and how to do them well." Hence this major theme gradually supersedes the whims and wishes of play.

This sense of industry vs. inferiority is closely tied to the major tasks that children of most cultures are involved with at this age in school. Erikson, in the White House Conference Report (*A Healthy Personality,* 1951, p. 17–18), says that inferiority will be experienced:

1. If the child has not yet achieved a sense of initiative.
2. If the child's experiences at home have not prepared him or her for school.
3. If the child finds school a place where previous accomplishments are disregarded or talents and abilities are not challenged.
4. If the individual child's needs are overlooked—if too much is expected, or if the child is made to feel that achievement is beyond his or her ability.

With this in mind it seems that the position of teacher in today's schools is an enormous one. The teacher is responsible for making sure that each student has at least one task that he or she can do well, and from which to feel a sense of accomplishment. A sense of inferiority or low self-esteem will develop in children if not helped to know that they are doing well. Conversely, succeeding in school develops industry.

School is not the only place where a sense of inferiority or industry can be gained, however. The home is also very important, since brothers and sisters are very competitive. It is important that parents not only find tasks that each child can do well but give them genuine encouragement and recognition for them. Parents at this stage could buy raw materials for children so that they will be able to try out their skills and become competent in them. For

When children aged 6 to 12 acquire skills and carry them to completion, a sense of industry develops.

example, simple tools and building supplies or cooking tasks are enthusiastically received by children of this age. Many youth organizations, such as Boy Scouts, Camp Fire Girls, and Girl Scouts, are also geared toward helping youth achieve "a feeling of mastery and worthwhile endeavor."

It is noteworthy, however, that at this period of life, family members seem to have a declining importance in children's lives. Peers become the measuring rod for success, and children at this age are often heard to say, "I can do something better than Jane," "I'm in the best reading group," or "I've got more stamps in my collection than any of the kids."

**Sense of identity vs. role diffusion.** As children reach the age of adolescence, they enter into a new stage of development. At this stage, the individual will seek to achieve a sense of identity vs. a sense of role diffusion. Sawrey and Telford (1968) define identity in three parts:

1. The development and maintenance of a feeling of "inner sameness and continuity," which is matched by the sameness and continuity of one's meaning for others.
2. A conviction that the individual's ways of achieving in the personal and vocational areas are successful variants of the ways other significant people in his or her culture achieve these goals and acquire recognition for such achievements.
3. The feeling that one is learning effective social skills and developing a unique personality with reference to a tangible future within a social context that is understood.

At the onset of adolescence, a youth's body undergoes many physiological changes, including rapid body growth and genital maturity. With these physiological changes comes the desire for sexual fulfillment with the opposite sex. It is no wonder with all these changes occurring that the adolescent continually asks, "Who am I to be?" "What is my role in society to be?" "Am I a child or am I an adult?"

There are various processes by which an individual can achieve a sense of identity, but all imply exploration and a temporary "trying on" or commitment to various philosophies or religions. Before individuals can make a final commitment to a role in society, they must first integrate personal needs, inherited gifts, identification with significant people in their lives, and previous roles. If these contributing influences are integrated, the individual will achieve a sense of identity—will "find himself." The danger of this stage is achieving a sense of role confusion or diffusion, or a nonintegration of all aspects of one's personality. A character in Arthur Miller's *Death of a Salesman* is experiencing this condition when he says, "I just can't take hold, Mom. I just can't take hold of some kind of life."

Our society, which has no definite rite of passage to define a youth's admittance into the adult world, provides for a psychological moratorium; Maier (1965, p. 57) describes it as "an authorized delay of adulthood." At this point the adolescent is granted time when he or she can work through the problems of identity. This delay often allows young men and women to prolong identity issues (e.g., Who am I? What are my strengths and weaknesses? What will I become?). In fact, research suggests that the most extensive advances in identity formation occur during the college years, not during high school (Waterman, 1982).

In the adolescents' search for answers to questions of identity they often "overidentify" or cluster together in stereotyped groups, "and fasten on petty similarities of dress and gesture to assure themselves that they are really somebody" (*A Healthy Personality,* 1951, p. 13). Oftentimes, members of these groups are very intolerant and even cruel to people not in their group, that is, to those who are "different." Erikson warns, however, that such behavior in youth should not be severely condemned by adults or others, for it helps adolescents find their identity. An intolerance toward others who are different at least gives them an idea of something they are not. Also supporting Erikson's belief that overidentifying with a peer culture should not be condemned by parents is the assertion that although youth achieve a form of independence through overidentification, the process does not necessarily indicate concurrent rejection of parental values (Fasick, 1984).

A second way youths overidentify is through "falling in love." This young love is often based a great deal on conversation. At this stage, Erikson (1950, p. 228) describes adolescent love as "an attempt to arrive at a definition of one's identity by projecting one's diffused ego image on another and by seeing it thus reflected and gradually clarified." This is why so much conversation is needed.

Youths also select certain adults to become meaningful to them (e.g., teachers, social workers, or parents). The adolescents' selection of such adults is based not so much on "social function," but on what they are doing for

Youths overiden-
tify by falling in
love.

them during this time of confusion. It becomes apparent, therefore, that
adults, especially parents, who want to be influential in helping their adolescent children need to allow youths the freedom to try out different roles,
mentally or behaviorally. Failure to allow this freedom may create adolescent
resistance and rebellion.

Parents must be able to talk to their teenagers, for talking seems to have
a special significance at this stage. Adults and parents must refrain from labeling youths as "delinquent" or "lazy good-for-nothing," even though they
might be temporarily exhibiting such behavior. Labeling only forces youth to
accept a negative identity (even if negative performance is only temporary)
rather than a nonidentity.

As mentioned earlier, Erikson's psychosocial stages include developmental crises that occur throughout a person's life. However, due to the subject matter of this text, the last three stages (sense of intimacy vs. isolation,
sense of generativity vs. stagnation, sense of integrity vs. despair) will not be
discussed.

## Behaviorism

While Freud's ideas were gaining acceptance in America, a more dis-
tinctly American view, known as Behaviorism, was broadening under the

intellect of John Watson. The behavioral emphasis can be summarized as emphasizing rewards and punishments: Reward desirable behavior and punish undesirable actions. Behaviorism can be seen as a revolt against the emphasis on subjective criteria, such as internal energy states, personality dynamics, and psychosexual stages of development. In explaining and predicting human behavior, such subjective criteria seemed inapproprate. Watson stated that observable phenomena must replace consciousness as the subject of research.

## JOHN WATSON

Watson's ideas were influenced by Edward L. Thorndike and Ivan Pavlov. Thorndike suggested that learning occurred because an act causing pleasurable consequences tended to be repeated. A typical experiment illustrating Thorndike's ideas was performed by placing a cat in a cage while locating food outside the cage. The cat had to perform a response, such as pressing a lever, to open the door and get the food. Sooner or later the cat "accidentally" pressed the bar and succeeded in getting at the food. Thorndike observed that on additional trials, "All the other nonsuccessful impulses will be stamped out and the particular impulse leading to the successful act will be stamped in by the resulting pleasure . . ." (Thorndike, 1898, p. 11). In addition, he stated that the process of rewarding and punishing to increase or decrease behavior did not require a *conscious* interpretation by the individual being rewarded or punished. Watson added to this principle by saying that this was a reflexive process—the individual reacted passively.

**Classical conditioning.** Watson expanded his ideas on reflex by discovering the work of Ivan Pavlov. Pavlov found that dogs began salivating (unconditioned response–UCR) as food (unconditioned stimulus–UCS) was presented. They even began to salivate *before* they saw the food if they were able to anticipate its arrival. Pavlov presented a second stimulus, the ringing of a bell, with the food. When the food was presented, the bell was run. The dogs came to pair the bell with the food and the bell (conditioned stimulus–CS) was subsequently able to produce salivation (conditioned response–CR) by itself (see Figure 3.1).

Theoretically, almost any stimulus to which we as humans are sensitive (auditory, visual, gustatory, tactile, or olfactory) can become a CS (Schwartz, 1978). If home, for example, has a positive stimulus value, then returning home after several weeks (UCS) would be quite an emotionally positive experience (UCR) for most individuals. If, when arriving home, a certain color (parent's clothing), taste (homecoming meal), or sound (music on the radio) was particularly prominent, that stimulus (CS) could later elicit positive feelings (CR) even under conditions other than a homecoming.

It is important to note, however, that the most effective conditioning situations involve presentation of the CS immediately prior to the UCS (Beecroft, 1966). If, in Pavlov's experiment, the bell was heard *after* the food was

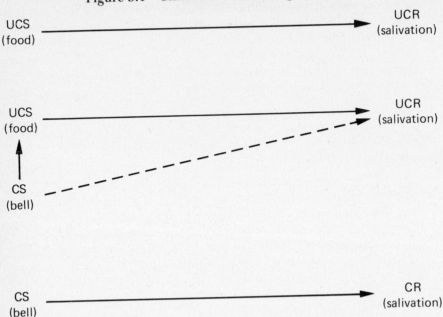

Figure 3.1   Classical Conditioning Paradigm

UCS (food) ——————————————→ UCR (salivation)

UCS (food) ——————————————→ UCR (salivation)

CS (bell)

CS (bell) ——————————————→ CR (salivation)

presented, or even at exactly the same time, conditioning would have been less likely to occur. Ringing the bell a few seconds *before* presenting the food is optimal. In addition, if presentation of the food only occasionally followed the bell, conditioning would not occur (Rescorla, 1967). It is as if the animal or human unknowingly computes probabilities. If the food (UCS) is more likely than not to follow the bell (CS), conditioning is facilitated.

Watson adopted this idea of *conditioned reflex* to explain types of learning. This conditioning, he said, began early in life. The infant is born into this life with few innate responses; even the majority of inborn instincts become conditioned. Behavior is predominantly learned; not only physical movements but personality traits, such emotions, can be a result of conditioning.

This rationale was supported in the now-famous experiment with little Albert, a healthy 11-month-old baby. Albert was conditioned to a fear of furry objects through *classical conditioning*, a process similar to Pavlov's. Each time Albert touched a rat that was presented to him, a steel bar was struck behind his head, frightening him and causing him to cry. Soon Albert developed a fear of rats; this fear later generalized to all furry objects such as a rabbit or a fur coat.

Watson's ideas became radical as he further concluded that all learning occurred through the modification of existing stimulus–response mechanisms by conditioning. Training required strict and logical control of rewards and punishments. Improper conditioning is evidenced in behaviors such as little Albert's fear of furry objects.

Give me a dozen healthy infants, well-formed, and my own specified world to bring them up in and I'll guarantee to take any one at random and train him to become any type of specialist I might select—doctor, lawyer, merchant, chief and, yes, even beggar-man and thief, regardless of his talents, penchants, tendencies, abilities, vocations, and race of his ancestors (Watson, 1914/1958, p. 104).

These basic tenets of Behaviorism—reinforcements, punishments, and conditioning—are easily evident in many simple behaviors. However, more complex behaviors don't appear to be as easily controlled through behavioral techniques. Yet, behavioral theory attempts to explain these as well, through processes such as those presented next.

## B. F. SKINNER

Around 1930, B. F. Skinner began formulating a description of behavior. This was based on his observations of animals through the use of the now well-known "Skinner box," a caged enclosure in which a rat could learn that by pressing a bar or lever, food would be presented. Recall that Thorndike used a similar paradigm, except that the food was visible outside the cage. The animal could see the food and learned to elicit a response to obtain the stimulus (food). However, in Skinner's box, the food was not visible. The stimulus (food), in this case also the reinforcer, was contingent upon the response, or operant.

In a Skinner box, a rat learns to press a bar to receive food.

**Operant conditioning.** Skinner called this behavior *operant* (sometimes called *instrumental*). No particular stimulus is needed to induce the behavior; a crawling baby is an example of operant behavior. No particular stimulus may have been elicited to make the baby respond by crawling; he or she just crawled. However, the occurrence of operant behavior is influenced by environmental events—in particular, rewards and punishments. Based upon past funtioning, the baby has learned that crawling is rewarding (e.g., parents' oohs and aahs, obtaining a goal).

Behaviors immediately preceding reinforcement are more likely to be repeated in the future. If, for example, a child were to perform all sorts of attention-getting behaviors before the parent finally notices and smiles, the particular act immediately preceding the desired attention would most likely be tried first in the future. Skinner proved this tendency by identifying what he called *superstitious behavior* (Skinner, 1948). If a bird in a cage was strutting around, preening itself, and pecking, and food was suddenly presented, the bird was likely to "superstitiously" repeat the behavior that had immediately preceded the food's presentation, in hopes that the food would again appear.

It is also important to understand the effects of various reinforcement schedules. If a reinforcer always follows a desired behavior, then a *continuous reinforcement* schedule is in operation. However, various types of reinforcement schedules can be used, each resulting in differing response strengths (Ferster & Skinner, 1957).

Reinforcement schedules may differ according to the passage of time between reinforcements *(interval schedule)* or the number of responses required before reinforcement occurs *(ratio schedule)*. In addition, these two schedules can vary in consistency *(fixed* vs. *variable)*. As a result, four additional reinforcement schedules are possible (see Table 3.3).

For example, a bird may be required to peck a colored disc before receiving food. Initially, all pecks are reinforced by food to ensure learning of the response (continuous reinforcement). However, the bird may later be reinforced only when pecking the disc after a certain time period following the previous reinforcement—say, one minute. Pecks before the minute has elapsed are not reinforced. After the minute has elapsed, the next peck is reinforced. This is a fixed-interval reinforcement schedule. However, the

### Table 3.3   Reinforcement Schedules

| Schedule | Reinforcement Follows |
|---|---|
| Continuous | Every desired response |
| Fixed-interval | A set time period or interval after the preceding reinforcement |
| Variable-interval | A variable, or changing, time period after the preceding reinforcement |
| Fixed-ratio | A set number of responses |
| Variable-ratio | A variable, or changing, number of responses |

interval of time required between reinforcements may be varied. For example, when pecking, the bird may be reinforced one minute after the previous reinforcement, 30 seconds after the next, 90 seconds after the next, and so on. After each reinforcement, a certain time period is still required before another peck can be reinforced, but this time period is a variable interval.

Ratio schedules require that a set number of pecks occur before reinforcement is given (e.g., two, four, or six pecks). A fixed-ratio schedule may reinforce the bird with food after every fourth peck. A variable-ratio schedule, on the other hand, varies the number of pecks required between reinforcements; initially, four pecks may be required, then two, then seven.

Interestingly, variable schedules are the most resistant to *extinction,* a process whereby the bird will stop responding if reinforcement is permanently discontinued. The next most resistant to extinction are fixed schedules, followed by continuous schedules. If a parent, then, wanted to extinguish a child's crying for attention by ignoring it, how much and how long the child cries would depend on the parent's previous reactions to the crying. If the parent responded to the crying regularly and then quit, extinction would occur more quickly than if the parent had previously responded to the crying intermittently or variably.

Reinforcement schedules also influence the child's tendency to behave as parents would like. If parents reward children for every correct behvior, the children will quickly stop behaving in the same fashion if reinforcement does not follow for some reason. However, intermittent reinforcement ensures that correct behavior continues though not always rewarded.

*Operant conditioning,* then, explains the occurrence of complex, voluntary behaviors intended to reach some goal or gain some reward. The behavior occurs before the desired stimulus is obtained. We as humans do not always respond reflexively according to a *classical conditioning* paradigm, where a presented stimulus automatically elicits a certain response, the behavior occuring after the presented stimulus. All behaviors are not just the result of stimuli paired together as demonstrated by Pavlov's dogs. Skinner used both types of conditioning, classical and operant, to explain complex forms of behavior; this is Skinner's major contribution. Based on the knowledge of principles to be explained below and in Chapter 7, practically all human behaviors, no matter how complex, could be explained by stimulus–response and reinforcement–punishment laws.

Complex animal behaviors can also be conditioned, learned, or taught using these same principles. Pigeons have been taught to play a game of ping-pong on a small table by pecking at a ping-pong ball; they were taught to guide military missiles with greater accuracy than the electronic equipment available during World War II. These accomplishments are only a few of the more dramatic examples of behavioral control obtained by B. F. Skinner of Harvard University.

Skinner, probably one of the world's most renowned research psychologists, has in this regard developed a model of human behavior based on only a few fundamental principles (Skinner, 1953, 1972). Using his approach, many adherents claim to have transformed entire units in mental health institutions from a chaotic state into well-organized wards. Other adherents have improved juvenile systems for delinquents and the prevention of crime. Teachers are said to have acquired control over unmanageable classrooms. Even autistic (severely withdrawn) children have shown increases in speech and other socially accceptable behaviors when skillfully coached according to some of these fundamental principles.

According to this theory, human behavior can be best understood or predicted by analyzing the surrounding environment. Accordingly, strict Behaviorists disregard internal behavioral causes, considering only the surrounding environment when explaining human behavior. They document their point of view by giving numerous examples in which the behavior of old and young, healthy and unhealthy, poor and rich, and male and female has been predicted and controlled using only information about stimuli outside the person. Inner causes such as the following are ignored: self-concepts, drives, needs, mind, will, abilities, desires, motives, ids, egos, superegos—in fact just about everything written about human psychological functioning is eliminated. It is proposed that when these internal dynamics are ignored, and focus is placed on external events, *the manipulation, prediction, and control of human beings is much more effective.*

## BEHAVIORAL THEORY APPLIED

Essentially, events that strengthen behaviors are called *reinforcements* or *rewards.* A person behaves in a manner that brings about pleasing consequences or rewards. Responses not part of a person's behavioral repertoire are those that either have not been reinforced or that have been weakened through certain negative consequences occurring after the response; the latter is called *punishment.*

If behavior is followed by reward or reinforcement, the probability that that behavior will occur on subsequent occasions is increased. A person might be courteous with one group of friends but not with another—why? Possibly because the one group rewards courtesy, and the other may not . . . or may even punish it.

Environmental consequences can do more than just strengthen or weaken existing behavior. Consequences in the environment can also help create new responses. For example, when an athlete practices a skill such as tennis, he occasionally will make responses that depart from his usual performance. If these departures are followed by positive consequences, these responses will be strengthened.

At this point the question probably arises, How do events that follow a behavior affect it? Or, in other words, if a person performs a certain behavior, how can a reward that *follows* affect that behavior—don't causes usually precede the event being affected? In explanation, the reward does not affect the particular response that has already taken place; it affects the probability that the person will again make that *type* of response in the future. So, when a person making a particular movement on a tennis court scores, her move is rewarded. That class of responses is then more likely to occur in the future than if it had not been followed by a reward.

The words *reward* and *reinforcement* have been used interchangeably, but behavior theorists distinguish between the two. Although a given event or stimulus is reinforced, the reinforcement may be rewarding *to one person but not rewarding to another.* Or, it may be rewarding at one time and not at another time or place. In addition, what to some is considered a punishment, may to other people be regarded as a reward. For example, Alfred, age eight, is told by his mother, "I'm going to leave for a while. When I come back, I don't want you to have played in the kitchen or else you'll get a spanking." The moment mother closes the door, Alfred goes straight to the kitchen and gets everything out. When mother returns, the kitchen is a mess, so Alfred receives a spanking. The same thing happens on the second day and third day. If behavioral theory is true, the boy ought to stop going to the kitchen because he's not getting any reward; in fact, he's getting punished. But, what is not understood, as often happens, is that the purported punishment of this child is actually a reward. It may be that this is the only time Alfred receives any attention from his mother. Commonly, show-off misbehavior among young children occurs for attention's sake. Even mild punishment is attention and, therefore, rewarding.

There is some controversy as to whether it is better to ignore conflicting or competing responses, or to punish the competing behavior. A reasonable number of psychological experiments indicate that teaching is as efficient when correct responses are rewarded and incorrect responses ignored, as when correct responses are rewarded and the incorrect punished. It follows, then, that training becomes easier if there is no need to punish incorrect responses. In addition, when punishment is introduced, a new set of problems such as frustration or resentment must be faced. Therefore, it is best to eliminate those concerns by simply reinforcing the correct and ignoring the incorrect. The relative effect of a positive approach as opposed to a more punitive method can be seen in the following excerpt from the writing of Benjamin Franklin (1969, p. 247).

> We had for our chaplain a zealous Presbyterian minister, Mr. Beatty, who complained to me that the men did not generally attend his prayers and exhortations. When they enlisted, they were promised, besides pay and provisions, a gill of rum a day, which was punctually serv'd out to them, half in the morning, and the other half in the evening; and I observ'd they were as punctual in attending to receive it; upon which I said to Mr. Beatty: "It is, perhaps, below the dignity of your profession to act as steward of the rum, but if you were to deal it out and only just after prayers, you would have them all about you." He liked the tho't, undertook the office, and, with the help of a few hands to measure out the liquor, executed it to satisfaction, and never were prayers more generally and more

punctually attended; so that I thought this method preferable to the punishment inflicted by some military laws for non-attendance on divine service.

A specialist in behavior modification made an observation to one of the authors when attending a conference. He said, "The success of a therapist using behavior modification is not dependent on how much he knows about either the technique or the trainee. Primarily, it's a matter of creatively using a few simple rules. With only a small amount of guidance or training most lay people could effectively use these principles." Over the years this has proven to be a correct statement. Many undergraduate students, after attending developmental psychology courses, have been able to successfully utilize these principles to *modify human behavior*. A subsequent chapter (Chapter 7) will be directed toward showing how this theory can be applied with children.

## Summary

Psychoanalytic and behavioral theories have been very influential in shaping parenting trends. With psychoanalytic ideas came the belief that rigid, strict parenting neurotically inhibited personality growth and subsequent adult functioning. A child's needs would fixate somewhere during early development if parents were too demanding and premature in their controlling efforts. Developmental growth was proposed to be greatly influenced by biological drives, and these could not be manipulated at will without creating difficulties. The result: many parents chose to be more permissive in their techniques.

A frequently studied theory in child development today is that provided by Erik Erikson. Taking Freud's concept of stages of personality development, Erikson expanded the idea to include developmental tasks during adulthood as well. During each stage developmental crises are reached, the resolution of which allows for adaptive growth and advancement to the next developmental stage.

Behaviorism, on the other hand, focused on environmental stimuli and organismic responses. A child's behavior is a product of adult manipulation or control of reinforcements and punishments. Deviant behavior, according to this paradigm, results from overly permissive or otherwise improper usage of these principles. The result: many parents have chosen to be more structured and controlling in their techniques.

# S E L F - C H E C K

1. The major tenets of Freudian theory that challenged existing ideas include all but which of the following?
   a. Sexual and aggressive drives are the source of all personality problems.
   b. Problems occurring in adulthood are a product of frustrated or improperly curbed urges during the first five or six years of life.

c. Personality has a two-part structure.

d. Unconsciousness rather than consciousness is the core of the mind and, therefore, of human functioning.

2. Which mental province did Freud consider to be governed most by the "pleasure principle"?
   a. Superego
   b. Id
   c. Ego
   d. None of the above

3. Freud emphasized that the basic drives are
   a. sexual.
   b. aggressive.
   c. both of the above
   d. neither of the above

4. If you were to become angry at your father, but rather than admit or express that anger you were to go out and split logs, which defense mechanism would you be using?
   a. Sublimation
   b. Reaction formation
   c. Projection
   d. Repression

5. If a child becomes excessively clean, shy, shameful, or impulsive, what might Freud postulate was the probable cause?
   a. Fixation at the oral stage
   b. An unresolved Oedipus complex
   c. Genital anxiety
   d. Excessive demands during toilet training

6. Erik Erikson's psychosocial stages include which of the following concepts?
   a. Developmental crises occur throughout a person's life, not just during childhood.
   b. At each stage, a developmental crisis must be overcome for normal development.
   c. Nonresolution of developmental crises results in personality aspects that continue throughout life.
   d. All of the above

7. The bias of Behaviorism can be summarized by which of the following statements?
   a. Internal energy states and personality dynamics are important to understand.
   b. Reward desirable behavior.
   c. Rewarding and punishing to increase or decrease behavior requires a conscious interpretation by the person being rewarded or punished.
   d. If you don't want your dog to salivate on the carpet, don't ring a bell.

8. If a rat learns to press a bar to obtain food, it has learned through the process of
   a. operant conditioning.
   b. classical conditioning.
   c. punishment.
   d. chance.

9. Little Albert, an 11-month-old baby, developed a fear of furry objects through the process of
   a. operant conditioning.
   b. extinction.

c. successive approximations.

d. classical conditioning.

10. Which one of the following persons did not contribute significantly to Behaviorism?

a. John Watson

b. Edward Thorndike

c. Benjamin Spock

d. Ivan Pavlov

e. B. F. Skinner

KEY: 1–c; 2–b; 3–c; 4–a; 5–d; 6–d; 7–b; 8–a; 9–d; 10–c

# C H A P T E R 4

# COGNITIVE DEVELOPMENT AND PHENOMENOLOGICAL THEORIES

During the 1960s the dominance of Behaviorism over other psychological viewpoints decreased; keen interest in understanding the mind developed, as did interest in each person's subjective experience. Researchers wanted to know how people perceive and use information—in "general" developmental as well as unique, subjective ways. A foremost authority in the area of cognitive development was Jean Piaget. Topics such as "age-related changes in information processing and intellectual development" were the focus of his work. An attempt will be made to outline Piaget's theory simply and accurately, while pointing out some parental applications. While it is a complex theory, many parents will want to have a basic concept of this way of viewing children.

Carl Rogers (1951, 1961, 1969) is one of the most significant contributors to phenomenological theory. We will attempt to describe how his and others' contributions facilitate an understanding of children by learning to view the world as they themselves experience it.

## Cognitive Development and Piaget

*Cognitions* are those mental processes through which knowledge is acquired, the process by which sensory perceptions are translated into systematized, understandable information for our intelligent use. *Cognitive development* theories attempt to explain how children build these internal models of the world and how they use these models to explain, interpret, and predict the world around them. Jean Piaget, a Swiss psychologist, is father of perhaps the most widely known theory of cognitive development.

Maccoby (1980), after reviewing work by Piaget and other researchers, listed four major themes from Piaget's ideas:

1. As children mature, their conceptual abilities develop in certain fairly predictable sequences. At any given time an individual child may make use of several levels of thought and may not make use of the highest levels of which he or she is capable. Nevertheless, within this variability is a consistent thread of forward movement.
2. Most children go through sequences without skipping steps and without going backward. That is, progress is relatively irreversible.
3. The developmental changes in thinking are structural changes. That is, they represent changes in the way information is organized and in the mental activities, or operations, that the child performs with the information at hand. Structural change is not just a matter of accumulating more and more items of information.
4. The impact of any environmental event on a child will depend on what the child takes from the event—how the child interprets what has happened and how the new information is integrated with what the child already knows. Children are active participants in their own learning. Indeed, they set the pace (p. 20–21).

Unlike psychoanalytic theory, which stresses internal states and drives, and unlike Behaviorism, which stresses environmental reinforcements, Piaget emphasized that developmental change stems from experience with the environment *and* from genetically guided maturation. The rate of developmental change is variable; although children progress through a developmental timetable, they may proceed at different rates, which is basically dependent upon biological change. Children at later ages are capable of grasping concepts they could not grasp in earlier stages due to biologically determined maturation. Experience might provide added knowledge to a child's abilities, but only to a limited extent.

Piaget's theory of cognitive and moral development is invariant and irreversible—every child proceeds through each stage in a specified order. However, a child's social experience can influence somewhat the ease with which he or she progresses through the stages. So, although progression through the stages is invariant and irreversible, significant others in a child's life can make a difference as to whether progress will be retarded, accelerated, or normal.

## INFORMATION PROCESSING

To better understand Piaget's ideas, picture the brain as an information-processing machine. Various units *(schemata)* within the brain are capable of storing information. When an infant is born, he or she inherits a certain number of storage units, but only through environmental experience and information processing do the various schemata come into use. These schemata form a framework into which incoming information fits, although the framework is continually changing its organization to assimilate new information.

The schemata adapt to new information through the invariant functions of assimilation and accommodation, two functions found in all biological organisms. In *assimilation,* information is taken into the brain and put into its proper category or schema. If the information does not fit into a pre-existing category, then the brain changes, or *accommodates,* its schema to fit the new information. To illustrate: A small child knows how to grasp certain objects in one hand. If a new object is sighted that deviates only slightly in size from previous objects, she will *assimilate* the object to her "grasping" schema and grasp it. If, however, she has difficulty grasping the new object because it is quite a bit larger than what she is used to, she will modify the schema so she can grasp it with both hands. In this instance, she is accommodating her behavior and building a new schema. This second adaptive process is *accommodation*—incoming information forces a change in the existing schema.

The critical distinction between assimilation and accommodation lies in the degree of difference between new information and old schemata. If new information does not radically depart from information in an existing schema, then this new information can be assimilated into storage. However,

Young babies assimilate their environment by putting things in their mouths.

if the new information is quite different or unique, the existing schema must change to accommodate it. When these two processes are in balance, a state of equilibrium exists, and adaptation is at its maximum. All structures move toward a state of equilibrium.

One can easily observe examples of assimilation and accommodation by observing infant behavior. Give a young baby something and he will undoubtedly put it into his mouth. This is how external stimuli are experienced or assimilated. Occasionally, however, the environment introduces something new to the child that cannot be assimilated in the usual manner. The infant may find that a pillow or a large, colorful object cannot be easily placed in the mouth. Therefore, new action qualities are introduced—accommodation. For example, the child may begin to explore the new object with her hands. An infant familiar with balls of all sizes and shapes will find her assimilatory expectations frustrated when first introduced to soap bubbles; as she reaches for the bubbles they pop, and she must change her schema to accommodate this new kind of ball. Her expectations are not met, and she encounters an exception that, along with other exceptions, leads to differentiation between physical properties of different objects.

When experiences do not fit into existing schema, a state of cognitive *disequilibrium* is said to exist. When this occurs, the organism, in this case the child, attempts to accommodate the information into a new schema. As she does so, *equilibrium* is again reached. However, it often happens that children face experiences they are not cognitively able to understand. At that point in their ideological development, their mental capabilities are not sufficient to accommodate the new information. It is either discarded, ignored, or distorted to fit existing schema; it is improperly assimilated if distorted. For example, a child of five will maintain that a large styrofoam ball is heavier than a smaller one of lead. Cognitive functioning at this age is insufficient to think in terms of size *and* density. As a result, the experience is distorted rather than accommodated.

As children mature through developmental stages, they become better able to accommodate new experiences into developing schema. "Each phase of development has its pseudoequilibration, the achievement of a level of more realistic thinking, until towards the end of the final phase a near perfect equilibration is achievable" (Maier, 1978, p. 23).

A parent or teacher could take advantage of these processes by introducing new objects that are somewhat familiar to the child, yet have varying action qualities. If the bounds of familiarity are exceeded, the new object is either ignored by the child, or the child explores the object by assimilatory means he found successful in the past—the cat's tail gets bitten, or the magazine gets pulled apart, or the bowl of cereal gets pushed off the table.

It should be obvious to most observers that a child's assimilatory expectations or schemata expand to handle increasingly sophisticated stimuli. However, to prevent a child from ignoring presented stimuli and to reduce frustration and discouragement when children are faced with cognitive tasks exceeding their abilities, it would be wise to view the developmental sequence as defined by Piaget.

## DEVELOPMENTAL PERIODS

Piaget views cognitive development as a continuous changing of cognitive structure. Within this continuous process, however, he defines four distinct phases or periods of development. Maier (1969), in describing the phases, says:

> Each phase reflects a range of organizational patterns which occur in a definite sequence within an approximate age span in the continuum of development. The completion of one phase provides a passing equilibrium as well as the beginning of an imbalance for a new phase (p. 92).

Maier emphasizes here what to Piaget is crucial to understand. Although a child's age at each period is somewhat fixed, the invariant sequence of the different developmental phases and stages is of greater importance.

**Period of sensorimotor development (0–2).** The first period of Piaget's developmental sequence is that of sensorimotor development. During this period, a child's inherited reflexes will develop into flexible and planned movements through a series of six stages. Sensory and motor experiences are integrated so that by the end of the first two years of life, a child is flexible and self-directed in much of his or her physical behavior.

During *stage one,* up to about one month of age, the infant is involved mostly in "reflex exercise." Reflexes present at birth are being exercised (e.g., sucking and rooting reflexes). During the *second stage,* approximately one to four months old, the infant begins to repeat sequences of events—*primary circular reactions.* More specifically, primary circular reactions are sequences of events focusing upon the infant's body, not on the environment. The first event in the sequence is stumbled upon, after which the event is reenacted to recapture the experience. For example, the infant may accidentally place its thumb in its mouth and suck on it. The action is repeated and thumb sucking is established.

Between the fourth and eighth months of life *(stage three)* infant behaviors begin to aim at sustaining environmental events originally due to chance—*secondary circular reactions.* For example, the child may pick up a rattle and shake it. After the noise is heard, the action may be repeated to hear the noise again. Colorful mobiles hanging on the child's crib will dance and move, if not also make noise, when the child hits or shakes the crib by kicking. The child perceives this and repeats the action. During this stage the child begins to look for objects removed from view—*object permanence.* Prior to this time, "out of sight, out of mind" was the rule. Experiencing the removal of objects did not fit an existing schema and was unable to be accommodated, so the experience was discarded—the child went on to something else instead of looking for the object.

*Stage four* (between months 8 and 12) sees the acquisition of instrumental behavior. The infant performs an act to reach a goal. For example, the child may pull the blanket from her crib rails to see through the slats.

During *stage five* (12 to 18 months) the infant begins exploring the relationship between action and object—*tertiary circular reactions.* Through trial and error, the child may search for the connection between her actions and environmental events. For example, one student related how her child, wanting to get to a drawer out of his reach, after many attempts at reaching finally pulled the highchair close enough to climb up on.

During *stage six* (18 months to two years of age), the child no longer requires trial-and-error experimentation to find solutions to problems. Rather, the child is able to come to solutions through "internal" as opposed to external manipulation of objects in problem solving—*insight*; it can be thought out without trial and error. At this point, the attainment of goals and desires has come a long way from the simple, reflexive movements present in stage one.

**Preoperational stage (2–7).** Leaving the sensorimotor stage and entering the stage of preoperational thought is identified by the above-mentioned ability to internally manipulate symbols that represent the environment. Before this stage, the child is only capable of interacting directly with the environment. Vander Zanden (1981) states:

> Symbols are things that stand for something else. They free children from the rigid boundaries of the here and now. Using symbols, they can represent not only present events but past and future ones. Symbols become increasingly effective as children gain skill in language (p. 290).

Although children gain the ability to manipulate symbols, thinking remains concrete, as they are yet unable to evaluate or synthesize actual events. For example, the child has the ability to imitate the actions and speech of people in the environment but does not have the capacity to comprehend another person's point of view because a point of view is not tangible. The child's ability to accommodate new experiences increases, but he or she does not understand that others view the world *differently*. This perspective is often referred to as *egocentricity*. To illustrate this concept, Piaget and Inhelder (1956) seated children in front of a display containing three toy mountains of unequal heights. A doll was placed elsewhere in relation to the display, so that the mountains would appear in a different configurational pattern from the doll's point of view. When asked to describe how the display would look to the doll, children under the age of seven or eight generally described what they themselves saw.

When a child gets angry at her mother for not playing with her "because she is sick," or is outraged at Father's exit for work instead of staying home to read her a story, or is certain that Mother "loves the baby most of all" because she spends more time with the infant, she is demonstrating an inability to comprehend another person's point of view. She believes everybody sees and feels things as she does. The young child who can't understand why the grocery clerk can't find her "Mommy" (in a store full of "mommies") is frustrated by egocentrism.

As a child proceeds through this stage, imitations become increasingly representational rather than overt. In other words, the child may remember certain actions that he or she saw and imitate them at a later time. These internal representations refer to or "signify" external objects or events. Also, the child begins to form *significants*—"that which the signifiers refer to." In watching a child at this age one can observe him, for example, blowing out a stick (pretending it is a candle) or moving blocks of wood around as if they were cars. According to Roe (1971), "this ability to treat objects as symbolic of other things is an essential characteristic of this stage" (p. 207).

A child's thinking during the first part of this stage (2 to 5 years) is only preconceptual; that is, he or she does not understand the relationship between an object and the class to which it belongs. For example, the child may, when walking through the woods, see several snails and not be sure if he or she is seeing the same snail repeatedly, or if they are different snails (Berlyne, 1964).

A child at this stage also does not reason in the same fashion as adults. Adults generally reason from the general to the specific (deductive reasoning) or from the specific to the general (inductive reasoning). Children at this age, however, reason transductively—from the specific to the specific. This means that, according to Berlyne (1964, p. 317), a child will think that "if A causes B, then B causes A." Sometimes valid conclusions are reached transductively. In Piaget's observations of his daughter Jacqueline, she once said, "Daddy is getting hot water, he must be going to shave since he shaved after getting hot water yesterday" (Berlyne, 1964, p. 317). At other times, however, transduction leads the child to false suppositions. An example of this would be the four-year-old boy who, through his own experience, has concluded that big things are heavy. When this boy is confronted with a large chunk of styrofoam, he will undoubtedly judge it as too heavy to lift.

Another characteristic of a child's thinking at this stage is *irreversibility*. Reversibility, according to Phillips (1969, p. 60), is the ability to return to a point of origin. For example, $3 + 5 = 8$, $8 - 5 = 3$; add something to a quantity, take away the same amount, and you will end up with the original amount. Children in this stage cannot mentally perform these operations, producing mistakes in reasoning. A simpler example can be illustrated by pouring water into a tall, narrow container from a shorter, wider one. To help the child remember what the water in the first container looked like, a third container, identical to the first and with the same amount of water, will also be used. Because of the child's inability to "reverse" the operation in his or her mind, the child will maintain that the third container contains more water than the second, because the water level is higher. Other variations of

A preoperational child cannot "reverse" operations in his or her mind, and will, therefore, falsely suppose that of two containers containing the same amount of liquid, the thinner, taller one contains more.

this experiment consistently show the child's inability to attend to more than one dimension at a time.

Irreversibility, inability to put things in categories, and transductive reasoning are all closely related to a phenomenon called *centering* (or *centration*), which is the inability to focus on more than one detail of a question or problem at a time. Adults have the ability to discern more than one detail at a time (e.g., in the water experiment adults can see that even though the water level is shorter or lower, the beaker is wider and so the water content is the same as in the narrower beaker). Adults can also focus on more than one aspect of a person; when a person changes clothes, he or she does not need a new name. A child's thinking at this stage, however, is still based on perceptions, not adult logic. If the child perceives a water level to go higher, then, indeed, to him or her there *is* more water in a beaker, based on perception; if a stranger changes clothes, then certainly a different person has appeared.

*Some applications.* Piaget's ideas suggest some important characteristics of learning that can be applied by parents. First, there is an emphasis placed on the child's physical world during the sensorimotor and preoperational stages. The child learns best when having physical objects to manipulate. In our modern world of gadgetry and expensive toys, parents and teachers are constantly bombarded with propaganda on the importance of stimulating young children as much as possible in order to maximize intellectual growth. There is some evidence to support the assumption that early environmental-stimulation is advantageous, but it is also important not to overstimulate young children. Infants surrounded by many enticing objects become "stimulus bound" and show difficulty in selecting things to play with, spending less time enjoying one toy or object. Many children, regardless of background, are probably overstimulated rather than understimulated. To a young child, the whole world is new and stimulating, so a few simple objects will probably provide a wide variety of action possibilities. One particular child spent a fascinating half-hour sorting paper clips into a small, plastic container.

Children are not passive learners soaking up knowledge as they sit. To expect them while young to learn sufficiently from a book, or a lecture, or from watching television is a fanciful wish. Children are busy, active participants in the game of life. The processes of touching, tasting, manipulating, and experimenting with real objects in the immediate environment teach children much more and have greater impact on them than passive experiences do.

Parents should not be discouraged if a preschool child seems to spend all his or her time doing the same thing over and over. Repetition is important for helping a child assimilate the environment. A preschool child may elect to build with blocks for several days in a row. Each day she may appear to follow the same sequence, but if the child's activity were carefully scrutinized, slight variations in routine would become evident. Not only does the child gain confidence in her ability to duplicate activity, but she learns that although she varies the process, she can still produce predictable results. We would, therefore, emphasize that variations in process, experience, and results lead to a greater understanding of the environment. Whereas repetition is assimilatory in nature, variation enhances the process of accommodation. Since young children do not process information as quickly and cannot tolerate change as readily as adults, they must move at a slower pace and experience change in small increments. Many changes come by accident rather than conscious intent, and much of a young child's learning in this stage is by accidental discovery—the "ah-ha phenomenon."

Parents would also do well to not become too frustrated and/or eager to discipline their preoperational children for not being able to perceive events as they themselves do. Because the child's perceptions are egocentric, it would be harsh, for example, to scold a child for not being able to perform a task as the parent has done, or to become angry when a young child who wants to play with something selfishly takes it away from an equally interested sibling. In this latter case, the parent of a child early in the preoperational stage may just have to intervene and help both children find something to play with; another's viewpoint is not able to be accommodated. However, an older preoperational child may be coached into seeing others' viewpoints by explaining how the selfish act has hurt another—the child may be able to accommodate the new information.

**Period of concrete operations (7–11).** "Since the concrete-operational child also operates on the same plane [as the preoperational child], the question arises: what are the differences between the two? . . . It is simply that the older child seems to have at his command a coherent and integrated cognitive system with which he organizes and manipulates the world around him" (Flavell, 1963, p. 165).

The concrete-operational child has learned that certain processes, or transformations, are reversible. He has learned to "decenter," focusing on more than one detail of a problem or question at a time. Seeing water from a tall, thin beaker poured into a shorter, wider one, the child is able to determine that the amount of water has remained the same.

The child in this period also begins to master the concept of *classification*. He or she learns, for example, that the class of "dogs" is made up of poodles, terriers and all other types of dogs; that is, the child understands that the larger class of "dogs" is composed of several smaller classes of dog types. Prior to this time, if presented with five terriers and two poodles and asked the question, "Are there more dogs or terriers?" the child responds with more terriers.

In addition, the child has lost some egocentricity and is now sensitive to contradictory views. Not only can he entertain different viewpoints of other people, but he can also consider contradictions within his own thinking. Yet, this increased cognitive sophistication is still limited by an inability to develop abstract hypotheses about conceptual relationships. "Although concrete-operational children understand relationships among specific events in the environment, they are unable to produce formal, abstract hypotheses. They cannot imagine possible events that are not also real events, and thus they cannot solve problems that involve formal operations" (Liebert, Poulos, & Marmor, 1977, p. 179). The next period, that of formal operations, will now be discussed. Although ages 11 to 15 may be an interval for the beginning of this next stage, for many individuals cognitive development continues well into adulthood.

**Period of formal operations (11–15).** Unlike children in the concrete operations stage, adolescents in the period of formal operations have the ability to entertain "possibilities"—to imagine hypothetical events, to infer hypotheses from observable events, and to deduce or induce principles about their surrounding environment. This ability to transcend present objects and events enables logical and abstract thought, which can be illustrated by some experiments done with children by Inhelder and Piaget (1958).

In the first experiment, adolescents were presented with an object hanging from a string—a pendulum—and permitted to vary the string's length, the suspended object's weight, the height from which the pendulum was dropped, and the force with which they pushed the object. These factors were all allowed to be changed in an effort to see which one, or which combination, influences how quickly the pendulum swings. The concrete operations child would soon give up after randomly approaching the problem. However, formal operations children would systematically deal with the problem. In one case, a girl would imagine all possible factors influencing the pendulum's speed and would begin to test each one empirically, realizing that to alter

The formal operations child is able to entertain and test hypotheses to reach conclusions.

## Table 4.1    Piaget's Periods of Cognitive Development

| Period | Age | Cognitive Abilities |
| --- | --- | --- |
| Sensorimotor | 0–2 | Inherited reflexes develop into flexible and planned movements; child is increasingly able to explore relationships between action and object, to learn through trial and error, and to become goal-oriented |
| Preoperational | 2–7 | Thinking and reasoning are concrete, preconceptual, transductive; able to internally manipulate symbols; limited by egocentricity, irreversibility, and centering |
| Concrete operations | 7–11 | Child is now able to decenter and reverse operations, and to classify; is less egocentric; still unable to develop abstract hypotheses about conceptual relationships |
| Formal operations | 11+ | Can entertain possibilities, hypothetical events, and reason deductively and inductively |

more than one dimension at a time would not allow her to determine which one was responsible for a change if a change did occur. "After having selected 100 grams with a long string and a medium string, then 20 grams with a long and short string, and finally 200 grams with a long and short, [she] concludes: It's the length of the string that makes it go faster or slower; the weight doesn't play any role. She discounts likewise the height of the drop and the force of her push" (Inhelder & Piaget, 1958, p. 75).

Another experiment was used by Inhelder and Piaget (1958, p. 109) to investigate the same reasoning abilities. They provided the child with five flasks containing colorless, odorless liquids, of which the combination of a certain three produced a yellow color. The experimenter had previously combined some of the liquids in separate flasks to demonstrate the reaction, then asked the child to reproduce the color, using any combination of the flasks he or she wished. As in the previous pendulum experiment, the child younger than 11 would unsystematically approach the problem after maybe trying all second-order combinations first. This approach would often lead to the child giving up. The formal operations child, however, is able to systematize and to test all 15 combinations of the flasks, even fourth-order combinations, until the desired color is attained (see Table 4.1 for a summary of these developmental periods).

*More applications.* Although Piaget did not write his theory of cognitive development specifically for the parent, many of his ideas do have considerable significance for child rearing. Piaget's theory conceptualizes how a child progresses from one stage of intellectual development to another. According to many, one of the purposes of psychology is to help a child reach higher levels of intelligence. Piaget introduces various strategies to help children through this series of continuous, yet invariant, stages.

One teaching strategy suggested by Sigel (1969, p. 473) is called "confront[ing] the child with the illogical nature of his point of view." Seeing an illogical point of view creates disequilibrium in the child. The child then "strives to reconcile the discrepancies between what he believes and what he perceives and thus evolves new processes by which to adapt to the new situation." Several methods are suggested by Sigel to accomplish this confrontation:

1. Verbal techniques such as asking probing questions
2. Demonstrations such as pouring the same quantities of water into jars of different shapes
3. Environmental manipulations such as allowing children to view events from other perspectives

Verbal experiences with other teachers, children, and parents foster cognitive development. Parents must be aware that just because children can use certain words, this does not mean they really understand the meaning. Children only comprehend the definition of words according to their degree of cognitive development. Teachers and parents should evaluate and develop methods to clarify what children really understand.

## AT THE RIGHT TIME

It was established by Piaget that certain stages of an academic curriculum must be presented at the right time in the child's learning sequence; yet, how does one know what time is right in the child's life? Or, how does a teacher know what stage a child is in? Some (Hooper, 1968) say that Piagetian tasks should be used to assess a child's level of thinking. Although Piagetian tasks or tests have not been standardized into formal IQ tests, studies show positive correlations between Piagetian tasks and psychometric scales of intelligence in infant, preschool, and school-age populations (Sattler, 1982, p. 45). Cognitive development is related to intelligence.

The ultimate goal of these Piagetian tests, according to Hooper (1968), is that they will "be valuable adjuncts to those measures designed to determine grade or level placements, and subject matter readiness" (p. 424). They could also be used in "corrective or remedial instruction programs." A basic concept of Piaget's theory is that cognitive abilities develop through distinct stages, each requiring mastery before the next stage is attainable. Thus, before children can function effectively on the preoperational level, they must first be adequately prepared through sensorimotor experience. As a result, an infant who is introduced to an enriched environment (rich in sensorimotor stimuli) during the sensorimotor stage will progress to the preoperational stage faster and more efficiently.

Historically, babies were placed in surroundings void of sensory stimuli; the nursery was painted in pastels with blankets and toys to match. Using Piaget's cognitive theory as a model, we should shun the placid environment of the traditional nursery and introduce surroundings that would stimulate the infant's sensory perceptions. An array of brightly colored butterflies, for example, dangling over the infant's crib would engender cognitive activity. This notion of visual stimulation could be applied to clothing, blankets, toys, and other stimuli, all in an effort to stimulate several senses (e.g., touch, hearing, smell, and taste).

Similarly, the preoperational child could be worked with to facilitate the development of reversibility and classification. Majares and Fox (1984), for example, administered to children a modified concept-learning task and found a marked increment in performance between the ages of five and six. However, it must be re-emphasized that cognitive development is limited by biological maturation. It would be inefficient and perhaps futile to work excessively with children in an effort to advance their cognitive skills if their maturation level precluded grasping of the concepts being taught.

This idea has been stated in the title of the book *The Hurried Child: Growing Up Too Fast Too Soon* (Elkind, 1981). Elkind advocates Piaget's theory but finds excessive pressure to achieve and move ahead too much for most children. He especially objects to pressures for children to read, get into sports, or become socially and sexually mature at an early age. He concludes his book by saying:

> No matter what philosophy of life we espouse, it is important to see childhood as a stage of life, not just as the anteroom to life. Hurrying children into adulthood violates the sanctity of life by giving one period priority over another. But if we really value human life, we will value each period equally and give unto each stage of life what is appropriate to that stage.
>
> A philosophy of life, an art of living, is essentially a way of decentering, a way of looking at our lives in perspective and of recognizing the needs and rights of others. If we can overcome some of the stresses of our adult lives and decenter, we can begin to appreciate the value of childhood with its own special joys, sorrows, worries, and rewards. Valuing childhood does not mean seeing it as a happy and innocent period but, rather, as an important period of life to which children are entitled. It is children's right to be children, to enjoy the pleasures, and to suffer the pains of a childhood that is not infringed by hurrying. In the end, a childhood is the most basic human right of children (pp. 199–200).

It would behoove parents, therefore, to be flexible and patient in their attempts to facilitate children's cognitive and intellectual growth. A knowledge of cognitive development can enable parents to provide additional stimulation and training when children are approaching new "stage" skills. However, overanticipating cognitive changes and creating excessive expectations can be problematic. Reconsider the effects of authoritarian, demanding parenting styles presented in Chapter 2.

# Phenomenological Theory

Piaget's cognitive theory draws attention to the mind and how that mind generates meaning. The same event experienced by different-aged children is perceived and interpreted differently. It follows, then, that a child's behavior will vary in response to these individual perceptions. Such thinking typifies the phenomenological approach to understanding human beings.

*Phenomenological psychology* assumes that since behavior is determined by the individual's own perceptual field, the only way to truly understand and influence another person is to understand his or her reality; what to one person is reality may not be for someone else. Understanding another person's subjective experience, then, is the beginning of interpersonal influence. Indeed, the application of principles outlined in this section will, according to this viewpoint, enable the reader to begin influencing children in positive, therapeutic directions. Such an expectation could only spring from a belief or trust in the positive nature of human beings.

Specifically, three beliefs or assumptions distinguish this position from other theories of human nature. The first is that reality is based on an individual's perceptions, and this perceptual reality determines behavior. Second, growth forces residing in all individuals move them toward healthy maturity. Third, an individual's self-concept is the most important perception to be considered in understanding someone else. So, while we all possess growth forces pushing us toward physical health and intellectual maturity, development of the self-concept is most important because it heavily influences behavior. In the following sections, we will describe each of these assumptions in detail.

While phenomenological theorists once represented a small minority within psychology, its adherents have been very vocal and convincing, and their number has been multiplying. This viewpoint finds ready adoption among those in helping professions such as teaching, counseling, psychology, and nursery schools. In addition, this approach is appealing to many parents. Its usefulness and appeal are enhanced because it is based on therapeutic methods used to help people change.

## PERCEPTIONS OF REALITY

The story is told of a traveler who asked an elderly resident what the people were like in his city. The resident, in turn, asked the traveler what the people were like in the town from which he had come. The traveler then described their selfish, negative, and hostile nature. The wise resident advised him to move on, for the people were the same in this city. When a second traveler stopped to ask the same question, he was also asked what the people were like in the town from which he had come. This second traveler pointed out that the people he had known were friendly, positive, and commendable. The resident then advised the second traveler to stay, for the people in this city were the same.

It appears that certain constant, fixed, physical events exist in the universe. Nonetheless, it is still striking how diverse the effects of these same events are on different individuals. Teachers notice, to their chagrin, that while some students find their lectures most inspiring, others are lulled to sleep. Obviously, the words, content, gestures, temperature, and other physical factors are relatively constant for all students. Nevertheless, some have positive experiences while others have negative. It could be predicted that a child whose older siblings describe tales of terror in the schoolroom will likely find the first day of class to be traumatic and fearful. On the other hand, a second child who has been led to believe that school is a friendly, exciting, and loving place will likely react differently. A teacher's humor, requests, and detailing of classroom rules will evoke different reactions because children have contrasting perceptions of both the teacher and the general classroom climate. Or, the same person on different days may perceive a similar event differently. A father having experienced extreme distress at work will, upon returning home, find the attention demands of his young child overbearing, when ordinarily he finds it a delight to have his child pulling at his leg.

An individual's perceptions originate from sensory input, but need not be restricted to immediate sensory stimulation. In other words, a person's perceptions can also originate from within, in dreams, for example. Or, past experiences and learning may influence immediate perceptions. Lewin (1935) remarked that knowledge of a desired goal—e.g., food in the kitchen—will lead to pursuing that goal, even if the food is not seen or smelled. Past experience of finding food in the kitchen is sufficient.

Objectively, a person's perceptions may be highly inaccurate. Nevertheless, for that person or child they are reality and govern his or her behavior. A young child who perceives a stuffed animal as vicious is certainly mistaken. Nevertheless, the experienced fear is real, although based upon erroneous perceptions. To an adult, children's perceptions often contain error and illusion, and we regard them as faulty or immature, but they are reality for the child. In fact, even a sampling of adults shows there is no consensus as to how things in life should be interpreted or perceived.

On the other hand, certain perceptual commonalities are the rule. People separated as geographically and culturally as the Eskimos and Australian aborigines, for example, have common perceptions regarding objects controlled by gravity, weather, and other natural phenomena. Their environments have common elements. Anthropologists have noted similar patterns in language, gesture, and communication in peoples throughout the world. Thus, perceptions are different yet still very similar in some instances.

**Perceptions are the key to understanding children.** The perceptual worlds of children have common elements as well as differences, and these commonalities and differences vary from individual to individual and from time to time. Nevertheless, according to phenomenological theory, optimal understanding of children can occur if adults acquire the ability to construct and understand a child's perceptions. If an observer is interested in predicting how a child will behave, even the child's future perceptions must be estimated; this step will make the observer more knowledgeable about probabilities of the child's subsequent behavior.

The following general principles apply to children's perceptions:

1. Perceptions change rapidly.
2. Perceptions are generally organized and serially related—earlier perceptions influence later perceptions. The child who has had experience with balls and circles is more likely to perceive the letter O than one who has not been taught to separate circles and balls from blocks and squares. Children's TV programs, such as "Sesame Street," spend a great deal of time repeatedly presenting the configurational elements of the letters in the alphabet. Children exposed to this soon perceive the symbols' identifying elements more easily.
3. Perceptions generally have meaning, often emotional meaning. Place before a child a scribble on a piece of paper or a shape of almost any kind, and soon the child will be seeing a car, an animal, or something else in his or her experience. Generally, the child will react positively or negatively to even ambiguous stimuli. (Incidentally, the same is true for adults, which forms the basis of many popular projective tests in the field of psychology.)
4. A person's mind will impose organization upon perceptions. Experiments have shown that perceptions of distorted objects, for example, when recalled from memory tend to be more organized and regular.
5. When any complex stimulus is presented, only certain aspects will be attended to at any given moment. (This is generally referred to as the *figure–ground relation-*

Optimal understanding of children requires that adults construct and understand children's perceptions—from their point of view.

*ship*). When a child observes a novel, complex stimulus, only the most dominant or familiar elements will be initially noticed; the child focuses on only part of the presentation. A parent who angrily scolds a child may be surprised that the child does not hear and remember the verbal reprimands. Rather, the child is probably being so attentive to the adult's strong emotional expression and physical gestures—the figure—that the words become background and are not perceived. At other times, the child may be so intent upon understanding instructions that he or she fails to recognize the communicating adult's feelings.

Sociologists George J. McCall and J. R. Simmons (1966) have said, "We interact, not with individuals, and objects, but with our images of them." Images must go beyond physical perceptions of others—how they look or act—and focus on underlying personality traits. From these inferences we build subjective frameworks or schemata for relating to people and predicting their behavior.

When developing schemata of another's phenomenal field, however, we must not become easily swayed by the *primacy effect*. Primacy is the psychological effect we know as "first impressions." It is a common belief that first impressions are strong and lasting, yet first impressions are not always correct. Psychologists explain that the primacy effect is caused by being committed to first perceptions and rejecting subsequent discrepant information (Freedman, Carlsmith, & Sears, 1970). Solomon Asch (1944) researched the primacy effect by using a procedure in which adjectives describing a hypothetical person were read one at a time to listeners who were then asked to describe the subject. A person described as "intelligent, industrious, impulsive, critical, stubborn, and envious" was evaluated much more positively than one described with the same adjectives in a different order; "envious, stubborn, critical, impulsive, industrious, and intelligent." In their subsequent descriptions, subjects used the initial adjectives to interpret the later ones. The stubbornness of someone first known as intelligent and industrious was explained as integrity. The person whose description began with "envious" was perceived as having his good qualities restricted by the bad.

**Focus on the present.** Within the phenomenological framework, behavior is caused by perceptions *at the moment of action*. Behavior is not seen as the result of a long reinforcement history or early childhood experiences. This is not to say that reinforcement histories, childhood trauma, or Oedipal complexes do not influence present perceptions; it is acknowledged that they do. However, to change behavior one need not delve into the past. The cause of present behavior is *present* perceptions.

In traditional psychotherapy, treatment involves assisting the patient to return to the past, face old dilemmas, handle previous feelings, recognize complexes, and work out old problems. The patient may be taken into the past to relive segments of life. However, dealing with the past is considered unnecessary by those who stress phenomenology. Neither the traditional analytic nor the behavioral conditioning approaches are necessary to the phenomenological viewpoint. One can change either present or future behavior by directly altering current perceptions. While perceptions are influenced by past conditioning and experiences, they are not totally determined.

**Individuality and uniqueness.** Because each person's behavior—attitudes, values, dispositions—is determined by perceptions, and because perceptions are unique, it follows that each person is unique. Because perceptions are in constant flux, it also follows that each person is continually changing. Each person must be regarded as an individual.

Knowledge and research of external environmental factors as causative agents is considered insufficient to fully explain human behavior. An individual's interpretation of these elements, however, directly influences human action. Perceptions determine behavior, and one cannot anticipate what children will do unless they are studied individually and unless insight regarding their own unique views of the world is gained. Maslow (1962) points out this emphasis on individuality: "We have, each one of us, an essential nature which is intrinsic, given, 'natural' and, usually, very resistant to change. . . . Every person is, in part, 'his own project' and makes himself" (p. 213).

**Perceptual bias.** Still another phenomenon affecting our perceptions is the tendency to "see what we're looking for." This effect is based on the perceiver's own needs and values. Rubin (1968), for example, hypothesized that preferred persons are seen as taller and more imposing. He found that two-thirds of a sample of Californians planning to vote for John F. Kennedy in the 1960 election perceived him as being taller than Richard Nixon. More than half of those planning to vote for Nixon perceived him as being at least as tall as Kennedy.

One tends to accentuate characteristics of things or people as they relate to one's personal needs and desires. Cold water tastes best when thirsty, and food always tastes and smells best when hungry. Similarly, never has there been a more beautiful, kinder, understanding, affectionate, and totally wonderful person than the one with whom you're in love. Or, is there any cuter baby than the one born to a woman who has tried for 15 years to become pregnant? Loving another person sometimes creates a tendency to focus attention upon the loved person, forget other people, and become oblivious to things that would otherwise command our attention. A spouse often overlooks ordinarily bothersome attributes of the beloved's personality and accepts them.

Hardy (1975) describes an experience Maslow had during the Depression. He had purchased a cup of strawberries, a rare delicacy for his family at the time, and his wife served them in separate bowls for each family member. The children ravenously gulped theirs down before the parents had time to finish, and then proceeded to beg their parents for more. Maslow then gave his strawberries to the children. Later, a visitor in the home acknowledged the unselfishness of this act. Said Maslow, "Not so. I received more enjoyment from giving them to my children than I would have received had I eaten them myself" (Hardy, 1975).

# CHANGE AND BECOMING

While the existence of an identity or concept of self is stressed within phenomenological theory, it is also recognized that through repeated interactions with the environment this self-concept changes. Change is considered unavoidable and desirable. At no one point in life is there an established standard toward which each individual is to develop and then cease to change. Rather, change is inevitable and must be remembered when trying to understand children. For the humanist or phenomenologist this change is welcomed and is compatible with an optimistic view of humanity. Change will generally be toward positive self-development and fulfillment.

**Growth: the basis of positive change.** Traditional psychoanalysis growing out of the Judeo-Christian heritage of Western societies has assumed that human beings are basically bad or evil, or at least antisocial. Social institutions such as governments, families, and churches are necessary to control the human being's antisocial, irrational, and compulsive tendencies. These institutions teach, control, and direct a person's development or growth. More recently, the scientific or behavioral point of view assumes that human beings have no basic or innate nature, but that they are extremely pliable, being influenced and shaped by environmental circumstances referred to as *stimuli*. Having this plasticlike quality, the individual can be directed in almost any direction by environmental stimuli, because no particular inner force influences the person's growth.

The position represented in this section assumes that in all human beings exists a growth force taking them toward mental health and desired social behavior. This growth tendency directs each child toward self-fulfillment or, in Abraham Maslow's words, "self-actualization." Maslow, in his book *Motivation and Personality* (1954), describes the characteristics of self-actualizing persons:

1. They are realistically oriented or have a concrete and accurate view of reality.
2. They accept themselves, other people, and the natural world for what they are, emotionally and behaviorally. Typically, both emotions and behavior are spontaneous.
3. They devote their attention to tasks or duties that cut out time for themselves; that is, they are problem-centered rather than self-centered.
4. These people seek privacy and, while enjoying other people, concentrate their energy on developing rich and deep relationships with a limited number of people.
5. They are self-directing and independent, able to remain autonomous in the face of rejection or unpopularity.
6. They appreciate and have the capacity to see the basic beauties and purposes of life; for example, enjoying an early morning sunrise, the smile on the face of a child who does well in school, beautiful music, etc.
7. They frequently have mystical, spiritual, or some kind of rich, emotional experiences. These may or may not be religious in character.

Phenomenological theory assumes that human beings are innately innocent and good. Only when not allowed to express natural and potential tendencies does the person become disordered and destructive.

8. They identify with all of humanity rather than with just a small family, state, or country; they feel a belongingness with people in general.
9. The interpersonal relationships they develop with a few immediate people who surround them are extremely profound, deep, and warm, rather than superficial.
10. They evaluate people as individuals and not by race, social status, or other more artificial types of distinction.
11. They have a basic set of ethics and values upon which they can draw to govern and guide their behavior. Their sense of humor and enjoyment of life is not hostile but is more philosophical in nature. The human dilemmas or predicaments of life are the main focus as opposed to reactions against control of authority.
12. They have a great deal of creativeness in their actions and interest.
13. They are quite individualistic and not conforming.

Indeed, these characteristics are positive, and it is Maslow's belief that each person has a growth tendency moving him or her in this direction. Therefore, what is consistent with the maintenance and enhancement of an individual is also consistent with the maintenance and enhancement of society. Freedom is allowed because a child's self-growth is entirely consistent with the welfare and general promotion of the human race. Carl Rogers, a major contributor to this belief, rejects the notion that the human being is innately selfish, negative, and potentially destructive. When allowed to express natural potential and tendencies, the individual will live a reasonably ordered, constructive life without the necessity of being held in check by social institutions and controls. Only when these natural tendencies are frustrated and inhibited do individuals become violent, mentally ill, and chronically unhappy.

## INDIVIDUAL SELF-CONCEPT

Perhaps all theories of personality have included within their assumptions the idea of a self and an awareness of that self at some level. In other words, these theories assume that we are aware of ourselves as an identity, and that we can estimate who we are and what we are doing at any given moment. Phenomenological theory places great importance on this idea of self and on the necessity of coming to know oneself accurately and thoroughly.

**Self-perceptions.** A person's most important perceptions are his or her own. In fact, some authors believe that the individual's motivation is to enhance and protect the self-concept (Snygg & Combs, 1949). Research data show that a person's self-satisfaction is related to his or her performance in a wide range of areas: success in school, marriage, athletics, vocation, personal adjustment, and social relations. When people feel positively about themselves, they are free to learn more about the world and themselves, since they do not have to censor incoming information to see if it would damage their self-images. By not needing to screen all information, a person with a positive self-concept can act more intelligently because of access to a fuller range of experience. Conversely, someone with a negative self-concept is threatened by a wide range of information, and therefore limits negative input through psychological barriers.

**Self-esteem and interpersonal perceptions.** Self-esteem has a great effect on social relationships. Zick Rubin, a prominent social psychologist, describes an experiment investigating the impact of self-esteem on romantic choice (Rubin, 1968). In the first part of a session, men were led to believe they had scored very well or very poorly on an intelligence test they had taken. Each man was then escorted to a canteen where he "by chance" met a college student, a confederate participating in the experiment. In half of the meetings she was extremely attractive, and in the other half she was very plain. In the group scoring high on the intelligence test, men made romantic advances toward the attractive woman, but not the plain one. In the low-scoring group the plain woman, not the attractive one, was most often approached. Results suggest that if self-esteem is lessened by perceived failure, individuals may be less bold, daring, or assertive in their social relations. Lefevre and West (1981) similarly found low self-esteem to be correlated with less assertiveness.

Low-self-esteem individuals have also been found to have a higher demand for approval (Daly & Burton, 1983), to experience more social anxiety (Geist & Borecki, 1982), to perform more poorly when facing extended failure (Brockner, Gardner, Biermann, Mahan, Thomas, Weiss, Winters, & Mitchell, 1983), and to experience more depression (Zemore & Bretell, 1983; Prosen, Clark, Harrow, & Fawcett, 1983).

The self-concept circle.  People learn about themselves by the way they are treated. A prominent psychiatrist, Harry Stack Sullivan, proposed that we define ourselves in light of others' reactions to us. How we are treated and the regard we receive from others tell us what we are like, and if we are successes or failures. If those around us provide positive feedback and act toward us in positive ways, we develop a positive self-concept or esteem. On the other hand, negative reflections from significant adults lead to lowered confidence and a tendency to withdraw.

It was suggested above that individuals with higher self-esteem are less threatened by new experiences and information. As a result, they are more free to learn from the world around them and to accurately perceive themselves; they then are able to set more realistic goals and to achieve their expectations. This result only reinforces the original positive view of self. Yet, this self-concept chain originates out of definitions reflected or mirrored from significant adults, usually parents. If parents convey the idea and feeling that the child is loved, capable, and accepted, this positive self-concept circle is set into motion. Figure 4.1 describes the cycle of how a positive self-concept is developed through positive experience or feedback.

## TOWARD UNDERSTANDING AND HELPING CHILDREN GROW

Having reviewed phenomenological assumptions regarding the reality of perceptions, the nature of positive growth, and the idea of a self-concept, we can now discuss applications in the parenting process. Just how does a parent take phenomenological theory and translate it into parenting techniques and decisions?

How to know a child's perceptions.  If one wishes to influence, predict, or understand children's behavior, one must come to appreciate and understand how children perceive the world—not only how children *in general* perceive the world, but how *particular* children perceive it. Most of us recall how one of our parents was able to predict the preferences, tastes, and reactions of his or her spouse. You might have asked, "Would Father like gloves for Christmas?" to which your mother replied, "Your father would be delighted." This ability to predict accurately the other's perceptions and reactions was probably a constant aid in decision making.

Parents can be equally insightful with their children. They know which

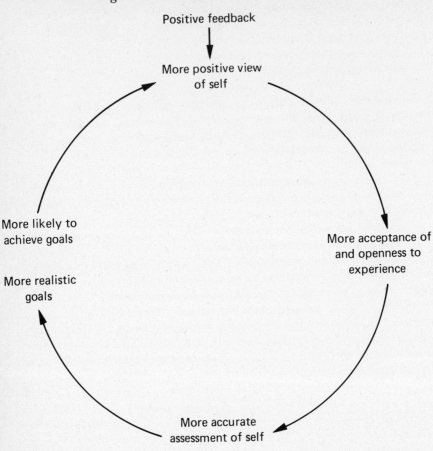

Figure 4.1  The Self-Concept Circle

Positive feedback

More positive view
of self

More acceptance of
and openness to
experience

More accurate
assessment of self

More realistic
goals

More likely to
achieve goals

one is nervous about moving to a different city. They are "tuned in" to the teenage girl who is confused about the dating process. The accuracy with which insightful, sensitive parents can pinpoint problem areas is astonishing.

Each individual interprets incoming stimuli in different ways, creating a different perceptual field. However, people know themselves and are able to do a good job of predicting their own behavior—predicting with about 80-percent accuracy their activities for the following day (Sorokin & Berger, 1939). A starting point in discovering another's perceptual field, therefore, is, ask! The question may be direct—"How do you feel today?" or "What do you think about that?"—or indirect—"What's on your mind?" Generally, it is held that responses to such questions are accurate and can be trusted. Although people do distort and are sometimes unaware of their true feelings, a person's self-report is the best single indicator of his or her perceptions. So, parents can come to know their children's reality by merely asking about thoughts and feelings.

Besides asking questions, inferences can be made about another person's perceptual field by observing behavior, especially in those situations where a specific response is not required. When a child is asked to finish an incomplete story, or is simply watched while interacting with other children, personal information is disclosed.

Observing how a child behaves during certain events in his or her life is also helpful. If a child delays in preparing to go to school, this could mean that school is seen as hostile, threatening, or boring. Further listening and observation will clarify these perceptions and help construct the child's perceptual field. Listening and observing are techniques that can be used by parents and teachers in developing more accurate inferences about a child's perceptions.

In discussing the observation of behavior, questions arise about the accuracy of observer perceptions. Are they biased, prejudiced, or logically related? Is the inference based on an isolated instance of the subject's behavior? To reduce inference errors, a few checks are recommended.

First, check to see if your perceptions are logically consistent with other things known about the child. If the child delays in preparing to go to school, you might find a correlation between this behavior and negative statements about school. Second, find out if other observers come to the same conclusions. Does the child's teacher detect an apprehension about school in the child? The fourth way to check the accuracy of an inference is to see if it helps predict future behavior. With the child who does not want to go to school, you might arrange a situation to see if you could predict that behavior, by offering a choice of going to school or staying home and helping clean the

One way to find out children's perceptions is to ask.

house. If the child decides to help clean house, you can be rather certain that school is unpleasant to the child.

In summary, a person's statements or behaviors provide information and clues about how he or she perceives the world. Individual behaviors could even include artistic productions, stories, documents, letters, preferences in reading materials, dreams, self-reports, and music preferences. All can be used by the sensitive, insightful person to help understand the child's perceptual world.

**Motivating children toward positive growth.**  One important application arising from the phenomenological orientation is that a parent need not feel obligated to motivate or externally force a child to become something. Simply put, the child will naturally progress toward positive growth. Emphasis should instead be on helping children benefit and profit from experiences they will inevitably encounter in the continuous growth process. When combining the notion of continual change in perceptions with the values of positive growth and individuality, it would seem unwise and detrimental to identify or construct a mold for the growing child to fit. Instead of identifying goals, target behaviors, or specific responses, it is advisable to provide critical growth elements such as trust, knowledge, support, and expectancies. Parents should then be concerned about the general direction and rate of growth rather than specific behaviors.

**Developing a child's self-concept.**  A positive self-concept is important within the phenomenological framework. "The most important single cause of a person's success or failure has to do with the question of what [a person] believes of himself" (Maslow, 1954). Yet how is this self-concept developed? We discussed the idea that children's self-esteem develops if parents convey positive, realistic images of their children. Positive, realistic reflections can be transmitted in several ways.

First, parents must show children that they care. Care can be felt through parents' listening, giving, and empathic efforts. Parents who feel and share in their children's joys and sorrows, who give of their time and energy, and who objectively listen to children's problems and concerns are telling their children that they care. "The care which the child receives serves as evidence that he is of worth to those who are doing the caring. The security that he receives from a sense of belonging also signifies to him that someone thinks he is special" (Felker, 1974).

Second, self-esteem can develop through parental encouragement. Rather than just praising or rewarding children when they accomplish something, their efforts need to be encouraged. In this fashion, children develop an intrinsic sense of rewards, rather than learning to rely on what they do as a measure of worth. (This idea will be elaborated in Chapter 9 when we discuss moderate power influences on behavior.)

These first two suggestions provide the initial positive feedback as input to the self-concept circle (refer again to Figure 4.1). It seems fairly obvious that positive feedback from parents is important. In fact, many professionals feel that positive or encouraging statements from parents to children should outweigh negative, disciplinary statements (e.g., "Don't do that," "Don't you listen?") by about six to one. Yet how many parents would approximate this suggestion if they counted their positive and negative statements for a few days? Too often, in our busy, demanding lives, we slip into a tendency only to pay attention to children when they are "out of line"; a negative reflection usually follows.

Parents can also increase positive self-esteem by breaking into the self-concept circle itself. For example, parents who provide a variety of experiences and challenges in a secure environment enable their children to be open to new ideas and experiences. According to the self-concept circle, the child will then begin to more accurately assess self. Or, parents can help children to evaluate realistically and to set goals (Felker, 1974); as these goals are accomplished, a more positive view of self develops, and the cycle begins again.

A fourth suggestion for helping children develop positive self-esteem stems from the previous discussion on "Motivating Children Toward Positive Growth." Children should be allowed to grow at their own rate. Typical progress rates or developmental stages can be used as guides, but quantitative and qualitative deviations from these guides are expected. Children should be allowed individuality and uniqueness—expectations should be reasonable and realistic.

How do these suggestions translate into a parenting style? Recall the parenting styles emerging out of research presented in Chapter 2. It would appear that parents who engender positive self-esteem in their children are high on warmth (as opposed to hostility), and are neither too permissive nor restrictive. They democratically establish identifiable standards and rules. Indeed, this is supported by research findings (Coopersmith, 1967).

## CONCLUSION

If the child is innately good and has a positive growth tendency, what is the need for a caretaker or parent? The answer is provided by an analogy. A small acorn has a growth tendency to develop into a large, beautiful, healthy oak tree. Nevertheless, for maximal growth to occur, the acorn and growing tree require the proper climate, essential nutrients, oxygen and water, and a limited temperature range. As with the tree, a child's maximal growth will more likely occur when an optimal climate is provided. The needed climate for children's growth will be presented in Part III.

## Summary

This chapter presented two additional theoretical orientations for describing child development and behavior. Examples of parenting techniques consonant with these orientations and those in Chapter 3 were given;

additional parenting techniques can be extrapolated after becoming familiar with the theories.

These theories have strongly influenced parent behaviors as they became prominent in the literature. Psychoanalytic theory suggested more permissive styles, whereas Behaviorism caused many parents to increase control and restriction within the home environment. Cognitive development and phenomenological ideas suggest that understanding children better is essential to effective parenting. Through understanding comes increased love, tolerance, and skill. Restrictive parenting is not necessary. Rather, a controlled environment allowing the child latitude and autonomy to develop as he or she may is most desirable. Notice how this shift reflects parenting styles as described in Chapter 1, and contemporary parenting research in Chapter 2.

At this point, introducing our *home climate theory* is appropriate, as it espouses many of the latest developments in this observable parenting trend. Part III is organized to present our theory.

# SELF-CHECK

1. Piaget's cognitive development theory includes all *except* the following:
   a. Most children go through a certain developmental sequence without skipping stages.
   b. Developmental changes are structural or qualitative changes, not quantitative changes.
   c. Although children are active participants in their own learning, environmental influences can accelerate or decelerate the developmental process to a certain degree.
   d. Biological and genetic influences are not important in this process.
2. When new information does not fit a pre-existing category in the child's mind, a category changes to fit the new information. This process is called
   a. schemata.
   b. accommodation.
   c. assimilation.
   d. equilibrium.
3. Which of the following is the first stage of Piaget's developmental sequence?
   a. Formal operations
   b. Informal operations
   c. Preoperational stage
   d. Sensorimotor development
4. Which of the following is characteristic of the preoperational child?
   a. Egocentricity
   b. Irreversibility
   c. Centration
   d. All of the above
5. During what stage is one generally able to entertain hypotheses for the first time?
   a. Sensorimotor development
   b. Preoperational stage

c. Concrete operations

d. Formal operations

6. The following belief or assumption distinguishes phenomenological theory from other theories of human nature:

   a. Reality is based on an individual's perceptions.

   b. Development of a person's cognitive abilities is the most important influence of behavior.

   c. Both a and b are correct.

   d. Neither a nor b is correct.

7. Which one of the following principles does not apply to perception?

   a. Perceptions are often unorganized.

   b. Perceptions change rapidly.

   c. Perceptions generally have emotional meaning.

   d. When any complex stimulus is presented, only certain aspects will be attended to at any given moment.

8. _____ is the psychological effect we know as "first impressions."

   a. "Focus on the present"

   b. Primacy

   c. Becoming

   d. None of the above

9. According to the phenomenological theory, the basic cause of present behavior is

   a. stimuli.

   b. past perception.

   c. present perception.

   d. All of the above.

10. Phenomenological theory views the human being as basically

    a. bad or evil.

    b. neutral.

    c. good.

    d. None of the above

KEY: 1–d; 2–b; 3–d; 4–d; 5–d; 6–a; 7–a; 8–b; 9–c; 10–c

# PART
○ III ▫
# The Home
# Climate
# Theory

As a complement to Chapters 2 through 4, we wish to present a simple and, we hope, practical way of conceptualizing parenting. We feel that child rearing can be most successful when the preceding ideas are broadened to include the entire home climate. The climate produced in a home, whether positive or negative (warm or hostile), has a major influence on parents' efforts to raise their children.

We conceptualize the ideal home climate as consisting of two parts: love and organization. More specifically, if a warm and loving atmosphere along with sufficient order and predictability exists within the home on a day-to-day basis, children will generally respond positively. Parents should therefore begin by trying to establish these climates. The components of each climate are:

*Love*

A climate with feelings
A climate with freedom and choice
A climate attaining uniqueness and individuality
Love and affection
A feeling of belonging

*Organization*
A safe and nourishing physical climate
A climate with meaning: values and beliefs
Knowledge and truth about self and world
Work and play
Structure

In our opinion, if a positive and organized psychological and social climate is provided, children will develop successfully. An adjusted, well-balanced, and responsible individual will emerge. When the ideal climate is provided, the need to do more will be minimized. This concept will be explained in Chapters 5 and 6, which focus on describing the two basic climates of love and organization.

# C H A P T E R  5

# HOW LOVE
# IS EXPRESSED
# IN THE HOME

Love is mysterious and difficult to define. Is it something you feel, possess, or act out? Are there different kinds of love? Is it best understood by the poet, minister, or scientist?

We propose a simple definition when it comes to parenting. *Love* is the total of all caring and positive acts directed toward another person for their benefit. In this chapter we present five elements of love needed most by the child in a family setting. While there are more elements and aspects to love than these, we think these are the most important and basic. We call them the *climates of love*.

The first climate is that of feelings. Having more positive than negative emotions is the key to successful emotional learning. In addition to feelings, freedom of choice is important. In our view, love provides freedom and choice, for humans flourish and grow when they are free to choose. Unfortunately, too many parents fear giving more freedom to children. The third component of a loving environment is respecting each child's uniqueness and individuality. We see individuality as genetically determined and believe it is a mistake to try to mold children according to our own preconceptions. Affection is the fourth element; this need among children for physical comfort and affection is amply documented. Finally, the fifth and last element is belonging. Children need an environment where they feel and know they are accepted. In our culture, the family must provide this acceptance for optimal development.

## A Climate with Feelings

### A WIDE RANGE OF FEELINGS

With feelings, we are alive; without them, we are dead. Ministers tell us to fill our lives with love and charity. Governments ask for loyalty; husbands ask for devotion; wives ask to be cherished. Endlessly, people desire emotion in others and seek feeling for themselves. Feelings make life worth living. For children it is necessary that they live in a world where they can come to know feelings—a full range of feelings. A brief glimpse into a positive environment for healthy emotional growth was given by a student:

*As a child, I was raised in a loving home. That's not to say there were never any displays of negative feelings—there were. I remember Mom and Dad disagreeing about things, but I was also able to see them work things out and be happy again. This helped me in many ways. It showed me that people could have problems and still work them out. It also helped me to know I could go to my folks for help to handle my own feelings if I was upset or didn't understand. I feel that I was better*

*prepared to deal with my own feelings and interactions with others later in life because of this environment.*

This student insightfully noticed that negative as well as positive feelings can exist in a happy home. Negative emotions need not be deleterious, as many individuals seem to believe. Parents and children will experience hurt, sadness, disgust, embarrassment, and jealousy, to name just a few.

## DIFFICULT FEELINGS

Although feelings are a necessary part of our lives, they can be dangerous. Uncontrollable anger, rage, or hate have literally ruined the lives of potentially happy people. While these violent, high-energy emotions are obviously dangerous, less visible emotions of depression, despair, and anguish are equally destructive. It was advantageous for the above student to know that in his family, opportunity was provided to handle feelings so that they did not ruin his life.

While the home climate must present opportunities for children to handle and experience a wide range of emotions, it can also be a safe place to shelter a child from difficult feelings. Rejected and frightened children return home, run to their parents, and find security. Home provides a haven from frightening, disintegrating emotions, not only for the young child, but for the older child and adolescent as well. To illustrate this, consider the importance of a home for this student in one transition period of her life:

*Richard and I had dated all summer. When we came back to college he started dating someone else, and I felt like I had been used for his "summer fling." This breakup was extremely hard on me because I had never fallen in love with someone enough to feel like I could marry him as I did with Richard.*

*The depressed, rejected, low feelings I was having were not just going to leave in a couple of days. I had never felt so depressed in my whole life. Everything I saw, everything I heard, touched, or thought about reminded me of Richard. I spent more hours of the day on my knees and crying than anything else.*

*The best way I could handle the whole situation was to leave it. So, I withdrew from school and went home. . . . Those negative feelings lasted from September to December and luckily my family was considerate enough to let me have my time and not to get on my case about being down. I had to find my own way out. I had to get rid of the feelings, and I could never have done that properly if I had received pressure from my folks.*

Home needs to be a haven where difficult feelings can be expressed.

Providing a nonthreatening climate in which a person can work on emotional problems is needed at all ages. Having a place to turn when emotional problems were present resulted in a growth experience for the above student. She concludes:

*It took time to overcome my feelings of rejection; but once I did, once I had overcome them, I felt like I was ready to tackle the world again.*

*Now that I've been through the experience and it's over, I know I can handle things like that; and I can overcome hurt, rejection, and depression.*

◑

Two aspects of feelings in a healthy climate have been identified thus far. First, the climate should provide a wide range of emotional experiences. Second, help should be provided for the child to handle difficult feelings.

## AVOID EXTREMES

Extremes should often be avoided. In providing a full and wide range of emotional experience, parents must be careful not to overwhelm the child with intense feelings. Children will differ in temperament, and a safe level of emotional responding will vary among children. States of low emotional arousal are often desirable, and the child's daily schedule should have ample opportunity for him or her to rest, dawdle, and experience the contentment of childhood. In our modern society, the stresses of employment, time schedules, and achievement come all too soon. Often, parents who have grown accustomed to this world bring their high level of tension into the lives of their children before they are ready to cope.

A child can also be overwhelmed with emotion caused by family discord and strife. Young children see their powerful parents strike and tear at each other, throw objects, and scream. This must be an upsetting spectacle in the eyes of young children. Some children see these immature emotional displays and physical abuses continuing day after day, producing emotional scarring. Cummings, Zahn-Waxler, and Radke-Yarrow (1981) found that young children were distressed by expressions of anger. Repeated interparent anger increased the likelihood of negative emotional reactions in children.

As a second extreme, some parents deny emotion in themselves and will not allow children to express their feelings. This is often done with the honorable intention of helping children control "unacceptable" emotions. Frequently, these are emotions that are threatening to the parent. Consider the following statement:

◑

*When I was a child, sexual feelings, sadness, and anger were not really acceptable in our home. I had such feelings, of course, but was not helped to deal with them. Since my emotions were not acceptable, I concluded that I was bad. I also repressed those feelings. As an adult, I have experienced severe depression as a result of turning anger inward. I have also suffered a great deal because I feel that I am still a bad person.*

◑

Children will inevitably feel a variety of emotions in their lives; the helpful climate is one in which even negative, embarrassing, or personal feelings can be expressed and openly confronted. Suppressing or hiding them provides no service to children, who must then deal with the feelings inwardly on their own, often keeping them inside and producing anxiety.

When suppression becomes extreme, emotions may move into the subconscious, where they are less accessible, and it becomes more difficult for children to recognize that they even have these feelings. Neurotic symptoms begin at this point. Parents may say, "I don't know why he does these things," or "It's all so irrational; it doesn't make sense." Even the child may be totally unaware (at a conscious level) of why he or she does things that are motivated by suppressed emotions.

A third extreme deals not with the amount of emotion present, but with the type. The first two dangers were either denying and not allowing enough emotion in the child's life, or overwhelming the child with intense emotions. This third danger deals with the balance or ratio of positive to negative emotions. More positive than negative emotions must be present for optimal psychological development. The National Institute of Mental Health and the National Opinion Research Center at the University of Michigan developed tests for measuring mental health, and studied what caused happiness and psychological well-being. While they studied adults, the principles they uncovered apply to children as well. After studying a large sample of people living in four communities, the most significant findings are as follows:

> In analyzing further the relationships betwen happiness and other aspects of well-being, we came to the conclusion that a person's sense of well-being can be understood best as a function of the relative strengths of the positive and negative feelings he has experienced in the recent past. The data show clearly that these are two distinct and independent dimensions associated with different aspects of a person's life. Forces contributing toward increased negative feelings, such as anxiety, marital tension, and job dissatisfaction, do not produce any concomitant decrease in positive feelings, and those forces which contribute toward the development of positive feelings, such as social interaction and active participation in the environment, do not in any way lessen negative feelings. Thus it is possible for a person who has many negative feelings to be happy, if he also has compensatory positive feelings. Only by knowing the relative balance of feelings can one make predictions about people's happiness (Bradburn & Caplovitz, 1965).

A person having many negative feelings in life will still report being happy if negative feelings are outweighed by a larger number of positive feelings. In a later study, Bradburn and Noll (1969) used a test called the Affect Balance Scale, measuring psychological well-being as the difference between scores on positive- and negative-feeling items. Interestingly, they found that people who reported experiencing many feelings were not happier than those who reported fewer. It was the proportion of positive to negative feelings that determined happiness. The presence of positive emotions was correlated with social involvement and new and varied experiences.

While it is inevitable that negative emotions will occur in everyone's world, and that it is the ratio or balance of positive to negative that is important for healthy psychological growth, there is still no evidence that negative emotions or feelings have beneficial effects. Emotions of hate, anger, resentment, rage, and jealousy cannot be shown to be helpful or beneficial. At best, they are inevitable and must be dealt with appropriately. On the other hand, positive emotions enhance a child's development and personal-social adjustment.

One prominent child psychologist writes in her text, "If a child grows up in a home *environment* where happiness prevails and where friction, animosity, jealousy, and other unpleasant emotional experiences are kept to a minimum, the chances are that he will become a happy child" (Hurlock, 1972, pp. 205–206).

## A Climate with Freedom of Choice

*The decision I faced was the choice of going on a mission for my church or continuing school with a baseball scholarship. I approached my father on this matter, knowing that he favored my baseball career over serving a mission. Needless to say, I was impressed by the way he handled the situation. . . . As we sat together, he made a list of the positive consequences of each choice and a list of the negative. After acting as my counselor, my father gave me the lists and left the final decision to me. He had discussed his experiences and shared his knowledge, which gave me greater insight into my own choices. Yet, I never felt pressured by him to respond one way or another. He realized that I needed to be satisfied and happy with my choice in order to succeed in the direction I chose to go. After reviewing the pros and cons we had drawn up, I chose to go on a mission at that time in my life.*

### GROWTH THROUGH CHOICE

Sometimes the element of growth comes from actually making the choice, since making the choice itself is often more important than the specific choice. We learn by facing choices and trying to understand their consequences. The growth this young person realized, being able to freely make a decision, is not limited to just older children. Decision making can benefit even small children. One mother would pick out three outfits and then give her 2½-year-old child freedom to choose one of the outfits. As the child grew older he learned more about clothing and how to dress, but, more impor-

We learn by
making choices
and trying to
understand their
consequences.

tantly, he was learning how to make decisions. The following incident was related:

*My four-year-old nephew is a very independent little boy, and when his mother asks him to make his bed, he gets cranky and isn't willing to do it. But when she gives him freedom to choose between making his bed and picking up his toys, he is more than happy to do it!*

## RESEARCH FINDINGS

How necessary to psychological development is the freedom to act for oneself? Is there evidence supporting or refuting the notion that we must experience freedom in order to effectively progress? Although the question is general, we argue that for healthy psychological development there must be controlled freedom, and that the most critical time for humans to experience controlled freedom of choice is early childhood.

Psychologists have looked specifically into the question of freedom and control as discussed in Chapter 2. Here, we wish to again present some relevant findings as they relate to this issue of freedom. Secord and Backman (1974) concluded that restrictive parents interfere with independence. Restrictiveness can too easily lead to fearful, dependent, and submissive behaviors. However, unrestrained permissiveness decreases persistence and increases aggressiveness, despite the fact that permissively raised children are generally assertive, sociable, and intellectually striving.

Similarly, Diana Baumrind (1974) was interested in the difference between children raised in authoritarian (restrictive), authoritative, and permissive homes. Authoritarian parents attempt to shape, control, and evaluate the child's behavior with strict and absolute values. Unquestioned obedience is stressed, forceful discipline preferred, and verbal give-and-take discouraged. Her findings showed that children raised in this type of home were discontented, withdrawn, and highly distrustful. These children also had high anxiety and fear levels.

Permissive parents were nonpunitive and accepting. However, when children were allowed total autonomy in regulating their own behavior, Baumrind found that these children lacked self-reliance, self-control, and exploratory behaviors. They had high levels of indecision and uncertainty.

Finally, Baumrind studied a third category of parents—the authoritative. Parents in this category provided firm direction but gave children considerable freedom within limits agreed upon by both parent and child. Their control was not rigid, intrusive, or unnecessarily restrictive. Reasons were given for family policies, and there was a high amount of verbal give-and-take. Parents were concerned about children's wishes and needs. The results of this study found that children raised in the authoritative home were self-reliant, self-controlled, explorative, and content. They were also able to develop interpersonal competency (Baumrind, 1974, pp. 1–103).

We will not attempt to present all research demonstrating the advantages of providing freedom and autonomy to the young child (refer to Chapter 2 for a more complete summary). Yet, other research continues to show that in our society children given a large measure of freedom and autonomy develop stronger and more desirable personalities. While the exact mixture of permissiveness and restrictiveness cannot be prescribed, a general rule might be to provide the child with as much freedom as possible, while at the same time monitoring the child's behavior so that it stays within the limits of acceptability.

There will be times when strong obedience pressures may be necessary and even beneficial. Zern and Stern (1983), for example, found that obedience pressures facilitated IQ and self-concept growth when they were operating to resolve difficult dilemmas for the child, such as situations perceived by parents to be dangerous. However, obedience pressures were detrimental to IQ and self-concept growth in more neutral situations.

## BEING GENUINE

Sometimes parents' attempts to provide freedom result in humorous learning experiences. For example, in one family during a meeting between parents and children, the children decided to exercise their voice in family decision making by choosing what foods should be prepared for a week. They insisted on a diet of soda, ice cream, cookies, cake, and other snack foods. They also wanted to eat from paper plates so they would not have to do any dishes. Looking back upon this incident, one of the children recalled:

*After Mom and Dad discussed this proposal, they decided to let us do as we wanted, for they knew we would learn a great deal. Well, by the middle of the week, all of us didn't think very much of our idea and tried to talk Mom into cooking just one meal. She made us stick to our agreement. By the end of the week, we learned a great deal about nutrition and the consequences of wrong choices*

Providing freedom of choice involves genuineness. If honesty and genuineness are absent, the benefits of responsibility may not be realized. One student recalled having to make the decision of whether to go home or stay at a university:

*I had called home almost every night crying and feeling really down. I told my mom and dad I was thinking about coming home, but what I really wanted was for them to just say, "Come on home!" My parents told me they would be supportive if I made my own decision. Well, within the next few days I had sold my contract, withdrawn from school, and booked a flight home for the following week. That night I called home to tell my parents what I had decided to do. When I told my mom I had withdrawn from school and booked a flight home, all she said was, "Karen, you didn't!" in a disappointed tone. I was so upset after she had said that. I felt like I had really disappointed her and let her down. After I had gone home she didn't ever say anything negative about my decision again but her initial reaction spoke louder than anything. The thing I want to stress is that parents, after letting the child make his/her own decisions, should support the child.*

This example reveals the importance of genuine approval of a child's decision. If approval cannot be given, a parent should be open with that hesitancy rather than indicating otherwise.

To summarize, research examples were cited to show that climates or home environments exhibiting freedom and autonomy benefit a child's psychological development. This is not a recommendation for permissiveness—that bounds, limits, or consequences should be removed. Instead, the democratic-type, authoritative approach seems to be optimal in Western culture. Throughout this book, recommendations will be made on how to create and implement this type of climate.

## A Climate Encouraging Uniqueness and Individuality

During childhood, most of us remember wanting to be *best* in something. By adulthood, most find this dream impossible. However, the psychological search continues. We want our team to be number one and we like people who call us special. Most people like to be called by their first name and even find they can laugh at and take pride in their individual differences. Underlying this peculiar human quality is the nature of human beings to search for self, to become his or her true self.

### INDIVIDUAL DIFFERENCES

Psychology has a subdiscipline called *individual differences.* Textbooks written in this area repeatedly point out each human being's uniqueness and individuality. Geneticists show that being alike is only possible in those rare cases of identical twins, and, even here, differences emerge. Those acquainted with identical twins often find that they seek to be different. A student related the following story about two identical twins named Ray and Ron. This account illustrates the strong motivation to be unique.

Even in cases of identical twins differences emerge.

◑

*From the time they were very young, everyone in their family and all their friends grouped them together instead of speaking of them or treating them as separate individuals. They were always referred to as "the twins." They went everywhere together, had the same friends, and dressed alike. No effort was made to enhance each boy's talents, differences in personality, and likes and dislikes.*

*As Ray and Ron grew older, they rebelled in an all-out effort to be totally different from each other. If one twin was getting good grades in school, the other would "take care" to do mediocre work. They never wore matching clothes or even matching colors on the same day. They made sure they played different sports and had different friends. However, the boys still weren't free to be individuals because they really were interested in many of the same things and yet didn't feel able to express it.*

*When Ron and Ray were 19 years of age, they ended up in different parts of the world. During the next two years, neither of them lived under each other's shadow. For the first time in each boy's life, they felt able to be totally themselves.*

*Upon returning home, this new-found measure of expression and self-confidence continued. Ray and Ron found they had much in common. They each chose the same college, majored in the same field, and both did well in school. They attended many of the same social functions and enjoyed the company of mutual friends.*

*It is interesting that these identical twin boys ended up as they had started out—very much the same in many ways. However, the end result was of their own choice, and came about because each person was allowed his individuality and therefore felt free to make that decision.*

◑

The positive climate, respecting individuality and uniqueness, does not endorse being different for difference's sake; rather, it emphasizes that individuality must be respected. If similarities occur, they can be welcomed.

## BIOLOGICAL AND GENETIC CONSIDERATIONS

Again, it is difficult to ascertain why we seek uniqueness and individuality. Perhaps from the beginning biological differences provide a push in this direction. Even at birth, clear differences exist among infants. Thomas, Chess, and Birch (1970) found that 40 percent of the infants they studied could be classified as easy-to-warm-up, 15 percent slow-to-warm-up, 10 percent difficult, and 35 percent inconsistent. Easy-to-warm-up children (1) were regular in sleep and eating cycles; (2) responded positively to new objects or people; (3) adapted easily to environmental changes; (4) exhibited mild emotional reactions, regardless of the emotion; and (5) were generally friendly, pleasant, and joyful. Difficult children exhibited the opposite of these tendencies: irregular sleeping and eating cycles; withdrawal from new people and objects; slow adaptability; intense emotional reactions; and unpleasant moods. Slow-to-warm-up children were generally classified somewhere in the middle on each of these dimensions.

Follow-up studies at five and ten years showed the continued stability of these traits, and it is suggested that they may continue into adulthood (Carey & McDevitt, 1978). Bridger (1965), after observing hundreds of infants, developed similar conclusions. He noticed that newborns react very differently to a variety of stimuli, and that these unique reactions tend to remain constant. Eysenk (1982) analyzed the results of several studies of twins and determined that 40 percent of the variation among children in sociability and impulsiveness is due to genetic factors.

These results suggest a clear biological predisposition toward certain personality characteristics. The implications for parents are clear—children must be allowed to develop without pressure to conform or change in ways significantly different from innate personality dispositions. Segal and Yahraes (1978), for instance, have commented that slow-to-warm-up children "should be allowed to adapt to their surroundings at their own speed. Pressure to move quickly into new situations may only strengthen their tendency to withdraw" (p. 51).

Simple personality traits are not the only characteristics that research has shown to be determined, in part, at birth. Mental disorders and intellectual abilities are also genetically influenced. Schizophrenia (Gottesman & Shields, 1974; Kety, Rosenthal, Wender, & Schulsinger, 1971; McClearn & DeFries, 1973; Rosenthal, 1970, 1971), depression (McKnew & Cytryn, 1973), alcoholism (Goodwin, Schulsinger, Hermanson, Guze, & Winokur, 1973; McClearn & DeFries, 1973), and criminal behavior (Cadoret & Cain, 1980; Crowe, 1974; Schulsinger, 1972; Slater & Cowie, 1971) have all been shown to run in families. Yet, how does that prove that similarities within families are in part genetically determined? Might they not be wholly a result of environmental influence?

Most of the above-mentioned studies were *twin* or *adoption* studies, which help to determine the presence of genetic influences. In twin studies, identical (maternal, monozygotic) twins are compared with nonidentical (fraternal, dizygotic) twins and with other nontwin siblings. These studies show conclusively that if a child has one of the disorders introduced above, his or her identical twin is most likely to exhibit the same disturbance. Nonidentical twins are next most likely and nontwin siblings are least likely to have the disorder, even though raised under the same roof as the afflicted child.

Adoption studies provide even stronger support by looking at children of mentally ill parents who were adopted and raised by somebody else. Invariably, children whose biological parents were emotionally disturbed are more likely to suffer emotional disturbances themselves, whether they were raised by their biological or adoptive parents.

The degree to which genetics is thought to determine intellectual ability depends upon what research one reads and adopts. The classical position suggests that 80 percent of the variance in intelligence test scores is attributable to genetic differences (Jensen, 1973; Herrnstein, 1973). Jencks (1972), however, concluded that genetic differences explain approximately 45 percent of the variance. Kamin (1974), on the opposite pole, claims that no data conclusively supports the idea that IQ test scores are heritable to any degree.

Brody and Brody (1976) feel that these discrepancies are largely due to different research and statistical methodologies and to the different populations used by the researchers. When the large variety of opinions are distilled, we could assume that genetics accounts for 45 to 50 percent of the variance among IQ scores. In other words, although environment can enhance or retard intellectual development (Bloom, 1964), 45 to 50 percent of a child's intellectual abilities are delimited upon birth.

This research on personality and intellectual development does not suggest that genetics is the sole determining factor. Rather, a *genetics (predisposition)* × *environment* interaction model is most appropriate. Environmental influences, specifically the home environment, can enrich or retard growth of certain intellectual abilities and personality characteristics, although authors differ somewhat on the degree to which they emphasize genetics or environment (Lindon & Young, 1981).

With regard to mental illness, a similar model is at work. This model, *diathesis-stress,* suggests that inborn traits or emotional weaknesses (diathesis) may predispose a child toward some form of emotional disturbance (e.g., schizophrenia, depression, alcoholism, criminality). However, emergence of that characteristic depends on environmental influences (the *stress* part of the model). The more negative, hostile, and inconsistent the home environment is, for example, the less of a diathesis or predisposition is needed for the emotional disturbance to occur. Contrariwise, if the home environment is highly warm and supportive, a child with a moderate to high predisposition toward mental disturbance may not exhibit the disorder to its fullest extent.

With regard to sex, there are really very few inherent differences between boys and girls (Maccoby & Jacklin, 1974). However, some researchers suggest that some differences do appear early in life and seem due to biological determinants. Parsons (1980) maintains that, among neonates, girls are more responsive to tactile and oral stimulation, while boys are more irritable. Others suggest that girls have greater verbal abilities (Maccoby & Jacklin, 1974) and that boys have greater visual-spatial and mathematical abilities (McGee, 1979). It has been suggested that these differences are due to hormonal differences between the sexes (Broverman, Klaiber, & Vogel, 1980). Another suggested influence is differences in brain lateralization. For example, girls appear to have a headstart in verbal skills, which are located in the brain's left hemisphere. As such, they may be predisposed to verbal, left-brain approaches to problem solving in general, making them more verbal and less spatially-oriented than boys.

However, such differences are small and the evidence is still inconclusive:

Even without total control of relevant sex-role variables, i.e., even when likely environmental sources of variance are left uncontrolled, the amount of variance attributable to sex is typically *at most* 5 percent. Hence any biological factors contributing to [sex] differences are relegated to a very small role (Sherman, 1978, p. 66).

Also of interest are findings that newborns of different cultures show some differences in basic predisposition (Freedman, 1979). Chinese-American newborns, for example, were found to be less perturbable and changeable, to habituate more readily, and to be calmed more easily than Caucasian newborns.

These findings suggest that individuality is partly determined at birth. Parents would do well to refrain from trying to change innate characteristics of their children, particularly subtle personality attributes, some emotional weaknesses, and intellectual abilities. Indeed, individuality is real.

## INDIVIDUAL IDENTITY

The human being's desire to be treated uniquely and as an individual may stem from a knowledge that he or she is different from others. Although we are often classified and treated as a member of a group, this classification process is not congruent with the genuine knowledge that we are in some way different. To accept anonymity would be like living a lie. The knowledge that we must not behave and respond precisely as predicted, demanded, or expected causes us sometimes to rebel against the grouping. We do not want to be someone else and, therefore, avoid the artificiality of placement in a classification system.

The healthy home environment allows and accepts individuality. An example of such treatment in a family setting was related by a young girl, describing the relationship between her brother and father.

*My brother is not the kind of son my father had hoped to have. Instead of interests centering around athletics, the outdoors, etc., he was interested and talented in the field of art. My father wanted a son he would be able to do things with, but he knew that my brother's interests didn't comply with his, and he didn't push it. He had respect for him and his talents and encouraged him to develop them. He often said that he wanted for us what we wanted for ourselves. My brother, my sister, and I are very different from each other; there is nothing wrong with that. My parents allowed each of us to become separate individuals with our own identities, which in turn gave us confidence in ourselves.*

The healthy home
environment
accepts
individuality.

Erik Erikson pointed out that adolescents universally face a developmental task of searching for an identity. One girl, going through this identity search, deliberately attempted to be an individual during the ninth grade:

*Throughout grade school, and most of junior high, I was always trying to be someone else. Of course, that person was always the most popular girl, because the popular girls seemed to be having all the fun. By the ninth grade, I decided that these girls were all the same. None of them had their own personality. They talked, dressed, ate, sang, and walked the same, at the same time, in the same place. All of a sudden I wanted to be me, Rebecca, my own person. Who was I? What was I like? I was determined to find out.*

*The first thing I did was find a new best friend, someone who wasn't part of the crowd. Then, I did the hardest thing of all—I started acting like me. It was hard at first because I didn't know who I was. But gradually it came easier, and by the end of tenth grade, I was confident enough to do my own thing and not care what anyone thought or said. My friends were very close to me (no artificial surface stuff), and they turned out to be the officers of my senior class and student body. Individuality was worth some of the lonely times that I experienced. I knew who I was and what I wanted long before a lot of my friends did.*

Unfortunately, in family situations the emphasis on meeting expectations and belonging to the group often forces a uniformity that is unhealthy. For example, parents often want their children to have opportunities and advantages that they missed, or to meet potentials that they regret not reaching themselves. If a mother never had the opportunity to take piano lessons, or frittered them away when she was younger, she may force lessons on her daughter because she regrets her past decisions. Perhaps a father who never met his potential sees in his son a way of extending himself. Unfortunately, forcing a personality upon children is rarely successful and results in frustration and rebellion.

When children's true selves are not accepted, and forced into roles they do not fit, low self-esteem is a frequent by-product. This is reflected in positively checked items on self-esteem tests such as, "I often wish I were someone else."

A good example of an emphasis on individuality is given by the following girl:

*As I was growing up, individuality was emphasized more than conformity in my family. Although my parents did not particularly try to be nonconformists, our lifestyle was very different from that of other families we knew. My parents placed considerable emphasis on helping us develop our own unique talents and abilities. I accepted these unstated but implicit values.*

*There were three things that tended to give me an identity apart from my peers. One was membership in my church. A second difference was my ability to perform well in school. The third thing that tended to set me apart was my interest in classical music. I played the flute, and it was very important to me.*

It is recommended that individuality and uniqueness not only be tolerated but actually encouraged in the ideal family climate. While acceptable role behavior and rule following is necessary, a wide range of personality differences can be both accepted and encouraged. In this way, parents are most likely to nurture the biological uniqueness inherent in every child.

# A Climate with Affection

*Years ago when my three daughters were babies, I realized that what-
ever else I achieved as a parent was of little value if my children didn't
know I loved them. It was not enough that I simply loved them, but my
children must know in their hearts that they are loved by me. And so
as the years sweep by it is still my hope that my children can always
feel my love.*

## FROM THE BEGINNING

How important is it that your child is aware of your love? Maternity
wards, after implementing "mother love" programs, have shown decreases in
infant mortality rates. In hospitals where much infant handling and affection
occur, the old, often fatal disease of marasmus has become nonexistent. The
traditional foundling home has largely been replaced by foster homes where
the child can better receive individual and personal care needed so early in
life (Vander Zanden, 1980).

Some professionals feel that the sooner mother and newborn can contact each other after birth, the better off both are. Observations of premature
infants show early contact as an important factor in child–mother attachment
development. Klaus and his colleagues (Klaus, Jerauld, Kreger, McAlpine,
Steffa, & Kennell, 1972), for example, divided 28 mothers and their first-
borns into two matched groups, In one group, mothers were given their
babies to care for in bed for one hour in the first two hours after birth and
for five hours on each of the next three days of life. The other group of
mothers received routine hospital care—a glimpse of the baby at birth, brief
contact six to eight hours later, and 20- to 30-minute visits every four hours
for feeding.

One month later the "early contact" mothers showed closer ties to their
babies. They were more concerned, more soothing, and fondled their infants
more. Even at two years of age noticeable differences still existed. These
mothers spoke to their children with a greater number of words and questions and used fewer commands. At five, these children had superior verbal
performance.

Additional studies suggest similar influences of early, close contact
between mother and infant following birth. Consider the following:

1. More eye-to-eye contact, fondling, and caressing by mother 36 hours later (Hales,
   Lozoff, Sosa, & Kennell, 1977)
2. Babies who cried less and smiled more (DeChateau & Wilberg, 1977)
3. Increased infant weight gain (Rice, 1977; Kramer & Pierpoint, 1976)

However, these results do not suggest that mothers who for some reason cannot have early contact with their infants (e.g., cesarean birth, high-

risk infants requiring incubation and/or other medical care) are not able to develop adequate bonds with their children.

Babies first seek out their mothers at an early age. Schaffer and Emerson (1964) studied the development of attachment in 60 Scottish infants during the first 18 months of life. They identified three stages in the development of infant social responsiveness. During the first two months of life (the first stage) infants are affected by *all* parts of their environment. They seek arousal from human and nonhuman aspects. The second stage, "indiscriminate attachment," occurs about the third month, at which time infants protest the withdrawal of any person's attention, whether that person is familiar or strange. The third stage begins at seven months, in which babies enter into "specific attachment." They begin to prefer a particular person and show greater desire to be with this certain individual, usually the mother. Babies will show "separation distress" when withdrawn from this particular individual, or will cry or become upset when the individual they have grown "specifically" attached to pays attention to another (Schaffer & Emerson, 1964). Other attachment behaviors include close proximity between infant and mother, and contact-seeking when the mother returns after an absence (Ainsworth, Blehar, Waters, & Wall, 1978).

In the past decade, much has been learned about infant attachment; yet, there is still much that is not known (Ainsworth, 1982). Nevertheless, some research results appear somewhat conclusive. First, attachment "leads to the development of affectional bonds" between mother and child (Bowlby, 1980). Second, there appears to be a link between attachment to the mother early in life and later social-emotional development (Ainsworth, 1982; Lieberman, 1977; Waters, Wippman, & Sroufe, 1979). Well-attached children are later less withdrawn and socially resistant, are sought out more by others, and exhibit more leadership tendencies.

Ainsworth (1982) maintains further that the major dimension of maternal behavior leading to adequate attachment is the degree to which the mother is sensitive to and responds to her infant's signals and communications (e.g., responsiveness to crying and infant indications of hunger). Certainly, maternal behaviors contrary to such sensitivity (e.g., child abuse) interfere with attachment (George & Main, 1979).

One possible consequence of early parental affection and sensitivity to a child's needs is the child's subsequent ability to develop similar behaviors. Some studies show that babies can love and feel compassion. According to Piaget, a child under six or seven is too egocentric to understand another person's point of view. Psychologists, however, are finding that many babies are capable of comforting others who are in distress. Twenty-four young mothers with babies 10 to 20 months of age began a study by participating in a training period, becoming more aware of their own babies' cries, startles, and facial expressions. A psychologist gave each woman a tape recorder and instructed her to dictate a brief report every time someone in the baby's immediate environment showed affection, happiness, pain or discomfort, sorrow, anger, or fatigue (Yarrow, Scott, & Waxler, 1973).

For nine months each mother faithfully recorded what her baby did or said on such occasions, as well as her own actions, taping her report as soon as possible after the event. The mothers were amazed to see how sensitive their babies were to persons around them. Some babies as young as one year old actually tried to comfort people who cried in pain. They snuggled up to them, patted them, or hugged them, and sometimes tried to help them. One 13-month-old boy was busy eating his cereal when his tired father sat beside him, resting his head on his hand. The baby pulled the father's hand away and tried to feed him cereal.

In another instance a 15-month-old was watching a doctor swabbing his mother's sore throat. The mother made a strangling noise and was rescued by her small son, who tried to knock the swab out of the doctor's hand. Yarrow collected 1500 such incidents, many of which illustrated how toddlers react to others' miseries as well as how parents shape their reactions.

Five years later these mothers and children were again observed for a period of three months. It was found that about two-thirds of the children clearly had not changed their particular patterns of response to another's distress. Children identified for their high empathy were still exceptionally empathetic. Those who tended to be less responsive or to flee from the situation at 18 months still did so.

Clearly, infants become attached to and search out close contact with significant figures (e.g., parents) at a very early age. In addition, early and close contact with parents can have sustained effects. It would seem that the influences of parental affection begin early and have profound developmental consequences.

## THE INFLUENCE OF AFFECTION

Discussed elsewhere in this text is the study initiated by Robert Sears, Eleanor Maccoby, and Harry Levin (1957). Seeking to identify parenting techniques influencing personality development, they interviewed 379 mothers of kindergarteners and rated each mother on 150 different child-rearing practices. Twenty-five years later, David C. McClelland interviewed and tested many of those children, who were then 31 years old, most with children of their own.

McClelland and others concluded that practices such as breast-feeding, toilet training, and spanking were not all that important. How parents "feel" about their children made the difference. "Mother's warmth" was found to be the key determinant of adult maturity. For example, it mattered whether a mother liked her child and enjoyed playing with the child or whether she considered the child a nuisance with negative characteristics. And children of affectionate fathers were more likely as adults to show tolerance and understanding than were children of other fathers. These researchers concluded:

How can parents do right by their children? If they are interested in promoting moral and social maturity in later life, the answer is simple: they should love them, enjoy them, want them around. They should not use their power to maintain a home designed for the self-expression and pleasure of adults (McClelland, Constantian, & Stone, 1978, p. 46).

The following statement, illustrating this type of parent, was made by a student in a parenting class.

*There were many times I didn't understand my father. And although he never told me, I knew he loved me. How? He spent time with me and seemed to enjoy it. He carried me around a lot, put his arm around me, and kissed me good night. I decided at a young age that he enjoyed being a dad.*

Contrast the above with this less cheerful story:

*My mother was an overworked woman with several children and didn't seem to enjoy any of us. She complained a lot, spanked and slapped us around daily, and made comments such as, "Maybe when you kids are grown, I'll be able to have nice things again."*

It is clear that children from households differing like those described above would be influenced in significantly differing ways. The expression of love is a necessary component of healthy personality development. Even in discipline love can sometimes be expressed:

*Tory was about 2½ years old. Although he was ordinarily quite well-behaved, one day he just had a bad day. Outside in the sandbox, he threw sand at another child and picked on those children smaller than he. In the house, he got into one thing after another. Finally, he did something (I can't remember what) that just seemed to be the last straw. He looked up at his mother with an expression that said, "Uh oh, I'm going to get it now!" And she looked at him with an expression that said, "That was the last straw! You're really going to get it now!" Then she stopped. Finally she said, "Tory, I think what you need is a little loving." She sat down in the rocking chair and held her arms out to him. He quickly scrambled onto her lap and they rocked for a little while. He was very good for the rest of the day.*

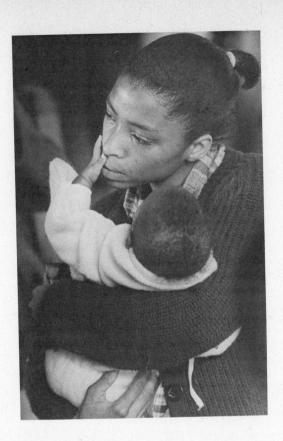

Physical contact often says more than words.

Physical contact often says more than words. Time spent this way is a form of unspoken communication, and discipline often becomes unnecessary when love is felt. For example:

*My fifteen-month-old child is a very loving, intelligent child and was in the habit of going to sleep at a certain time each night. When she was a little over one year old, this willingness to go to bed began to change to unwillingness. I couldn't understand why, because nothing else in her behavior had changed significantly. I was puzzled for quite some time and unable to find a satisfactory resolution for both of us.*

*One night after she had fussed and cried, I went in and lay down with her for a few moments and just told her I loved her and that what I enjoyed about the day were the things she did that made me happy. This seemed to satisfy her and in a few minutes she was ready to go back to bed and sleep.*

It may be surprising, but giving love often cuts down on the time demanded by young children. One mother, after having twins, was experiencing difficulties with her two older children.

*Sibling jealousy in five-year-old Douglas has improved since I decided to spend 20 or 30 minutes every other evening with him alone. He has my complete attention and we talk about anything he wants, read or tell stories, or play games. I make sure to give him a lot of physical affection during these special periods we have together.*

*Erik, eight years old, demands equal time, of course; the evenings I'm not with Douglas, Erik and I have our turn. His requests include long conversations, scripture stories, or working out problems he encounters with work or playmates at school. I have also found this to be an ideal time to introduce books and discussions about "the birds and the bees." Erik has cut down on his constant demands for my attention because he is sure his turn will come.*

## EVEN FATHER'S AFFECTION

Can men be as nurturant and loving as women in caring for their offspring? Perhaps in their own way they can. Men have the potential to be as good caretakers as women. Parke and Sawin (1977) observed the behavior of both middle- and lower-class parents of newborns in hospital maternity wards, finding fathers just as responsive as mothers to their infant's vocalizations and movements. Fathers touch, look at, talk to, rock, and kiss babies in much the same way as mothers. But, while fathers are more likely to "talk" to babies, mothers are likely to "touch" more. Fathers were more likely than mothers to look at their babies, although mothers smiled at their babies more. The researchers concluded that fathers and mothers are not interchangeable; each contributes to the child's needs in a unique way.

Not only are fathers affectionate to their children in some unique ways, but that affection may influence children in ways that are somewhat specific. Nurturant, competent, and available fathers help sons and daughters develop a broad range of adaptive abilities beyond narrow gender-role stereotypes (Biller, 1981). As males and females, these children feel more positive about their roles. Paternal nurturance is also positively related to boys' vocational adjustment and success in peer relationships (Biller, 1974, 1976), cognitive competence (Ziegler, 1979), and girls' personal and marital adjustment as adults (Biller, 1974; Block, 1971; Fish & Biller, 1973).

How deep love can be between a father and child and how vital it is even during later childhood was touchingly expressed by a student in a parenting class:

*When I was 16 years old, I was having a very hard time in school, both with my grades and my social surroundings. I would spend quite a bit of time in my bedroom and no one seemed capable of talking to me. In general, I did not have a good atittude about myself or anyone else.*

*But one evening while I was reading in my room, my father came in and sat on the edge of my bed. My father is not a very affectionate man physically or verbally. It's a difficult thing for him. In any case, on this particular night he started to open up. He said that being a parent to a 16-year-old was a new experience for him, the same as being a 16-year-old was a new experience for me. He said that we were both making a few mistakes and getting a little bit confused, and that he would do all he could to do better.*

*Then my father looked at me and said he loved me. He had never said that to me before and I didn't know quite how to react, but inside it changed me and my attitude toward my father. Somehow I was able to see a part of him that craved for the same love and affection as I. He told me I was valuable to him and that I had many capabilities. I knew then that I was worthwhile. I really believe that experience is what caused me to get better grades in school and to improve my social functioning. It only took that simple phrase, "I love you."*

## A Climate with Belongingness

### A FUNDAMENTAL NEED

Defining and measuring subjective emotional states and needs is diffi-cult. Thus, there is no direct research to show that the need to belong is one of the individual's basic needs. Nevertheless, both psychological and socio-logical theory stress the importance and pervasiveness of a fundamental need for membership in a primary group. Back in 1890, a father of psychology, William James, wrote:

> No more fiendish punishment could be devised . . . than that one should be turned loose in society and remain absolutely unnoticed by all mem-bers thereof. If no one turned around when we entered, answered when we spoke, or minded what we did, but if every person we met "cut us dead" and acted as if we were nonexisting things, a kind of rage and impo-tent despair would ere long well up in us, from which the cruelest bodily tortures would be a relief . . . (James, 1890).

Indeed, separation from one's group has been used throughout centu-ries as a punishment; children were separated from parents, citizens exiled from their countries, prisoners placed in solitary confinement, and persons stripped of membership. Human beings constantly seek friends, conform to expectations, obey rules, and join groups.

## GROUP MEMBERSHIP

Besides the inborn strivings to belong, many social customs sustain group membership. Family names are often used to help a child be aware of his belonging—"I'm an Adams." Formal membership often begins even in children's neighborhood clubs. Perhaps more important than names and formal membership are informal activities such as participating in decisions, sharing resources and time, and assuming group responsibility. These actions cause a person to feel secure and to belong. To show how she became more closely tied with a feeling of family membership, one student related the following:

*In our family we all "belong" to each other very much. I would say that the main reason for this feeling is that we were often given the opportunity to contribute to family functioning. An example, while we were growing up, concerns our many financial difficulties. Of course, it was my father's basic responsibility to provide for our family, but there were many hard times when my father's paycheck just didn't cover everything. My parents called us together and asked us to contribute all of our savings into a family "pot." It made us feel very much a part of a good cause—our survival. We felt that everything we had was "ours," not "mine." We had to get together and work for the welfare of our family and it brought us closer together.*

Conditions making the family important to a child may be seen by others as having little value. The family is, however, the child's first primary group and despite voiced objections still seems to be the most prevailing, enduring primary group. A sense of belonging to this group is important to children. One student recalls:

*Another experience I enjoyed was coming home after school to a pile of ironing or something cooking—I knew Mom was around somewhere. Every day after grade school, junior high, or even high school, I often looked forward to coming home. Mom would give my sister and me a quarter to get an ice cream cone. This made me feel close to my mother and my sisters.*

Some parents give considerable time and effort to activities that cement a group feeling of solidarity. The enduring results of this type of effort were explained in this way:

Family activities can cement a group feeling of solidarity or belongingness.

*They shared time with us in many ways, but, in my case, two things left a great impression on me. First, my mother would read to me. As a result, I am an avid reader today and enjoy a closeness of interests with my mother in the things we read. Second, my father practiced all kinds of sports with me, whatever I happened to be interested in at the time. We went through swimming, basketball, baseball, football, boxing, and trap and skeet. As a result, I am interested in most sports and enjoy a closeness with my father. I fondly recall the times my father and I would go fishing or camping together. Our discussions of life, my future, and his experiences laid a foundation of closeness that now enables us to talk freely when communication is important, but perhaps not so easy.*

Being involved in sharing problems, helping to establish and maintain rules, sharing feelings and ideas, and playing and working together can be quite satisfying. Contrariwise, a feeling of not really belonging to a family group can be especially devastating to children, often resulting in seeking membership outside of the family unit. One such case was described:

◑

*I had a girlfriend in high school who was really close to me. Her parents were divorced, she had step-brothers and -sisters, and home life was essentially unhappy. The tension got to be so bad that she dreaded the thought of returning home after school. She avoided her home as long as she could. This usually meant she would come home with me. She soon "adopted" us as her family and we began to see her as another member of our family. She ate with us, went on family activities with us, and even began doing chores around the house. She and my mother became quite close, and she even called her "Mom." She really did belong. For all intents and purposes she was a member of our family.*

◑

Teachers and other adults working with children can relate countless examples of children who seek out other groups when they do not have strong family ties and a sense of belonging. It was fortunate for the child in the above example that the family she adopted accepted her. Many are not so lucky and often desperately cling to peer groups, which are frequently neither stable nor supportive.

Oftentimes, even professionals underestimate the importance of primary group membership for young children. The family and other primary groups can provide a sense of security in a changing and, what might be for a child, frightening and disorganized world. Families support children and frequently know "what is best" during difficult periods.

The examples given show not only the benefits from a sense of belonging to a group, but its indispensability for optimal psychological development. We hope these examples provide illustrations of how to identify and develop this important part of a healthy psychological climate for children. As additional assistance, the following material lists suggestions for developing the climate of love discussed in this chapter.

## PRACTICAL SUGGESTIONS

Developing Feelings—Preschool Children

1. Help children identify emotions correctly. If they can identify their feelings they are more likely to feel confident in dealing with them. Learning about feelings begins through ordinary conversation when a parent labels feelings, such as "I know you are very angry," or "You seem very happy this morning."

   Emotions are a part of our genetic heritage. Fish swim, birds fly, and people feel. Sometimes we are happy, sometimes we are not; but sometimes in our life we are sure to feel anger and fear, sadness and joy, greed and guilt, lust and scorn, delight and disgust. While we are not free to choose the emotions that arise in us, we are free to choose how and when to express them, provided we know what they are. That is the crux of the problem. Many people have been educated out of knowing what their feelings are. When they hated, they were told it was only dislike. When they were afraid, they were told that there was nothing to be afraid of. When they felt pain, they were advised to be brave and smile. Many of our popular songs tell us "Pretend you are happy when you are not."

What is suggested in place of this pretense? Truth. Emotional education can help children to know what they feel. It is more important for a child to know what he feels than why he feels it. When he knows clearly what his feelings are, he is less likely to feel "all mixed-up" inside.

How can we help a child to know his feelings? We can do so by serving as a mirror to his emotions. A child learns about his physical likeness by seeing his image in a mirror. He learns about his emotional likeness by hearing his feelings reflected by us (Ginott, 1969, pp. 39–40).

Learning to label feelings in nonstressful situations is easier than after strong emotions have overcome a child. One method professional therapists use is to give children pictures of faces with different emotions and ask the child to tell whether the face is happy or sad. For a young child, simply use a semicircle (a mouth) on a round sheet of paper (a face) that can be turned up or down to indicate a smile or a frown.

2. Children can also be helped to know ways to constructively deal with strong feelings. In most families, dealing with anger by hitting others is not allowed. The child needs to learn acceptable means of coping with anger—perhaps shouting or simply getting up and leaving the room.

3. Help children to not feel guilty about having feelings, as having feelings is inevitable. Children are often unable to identify feelings and confuse one emotion with another. They may feel guilty about being emotional because some of the emotions are labeled "bad" or "wrong" by parents. Sexual arousal or overexcitement, for example, are sometimes annoying and repugnant to parents, and they label these as bad. The child then learns to fear these and similar feelings, and may even inhibit communication of other moods and feelings. If a child has too many negative or unacceptable emotions, ignore them, or indicate clearly that *those* types of expressions are unacceptable. At the same time, it is well to specifically endorse positive feelings. The value of positive emotions can be directly communicated.

4. Children will generally respond the way parents do. Let the child see how you react to various situations. For example, when you hit your thumb with a hammer you might want to control your language and refrain from throwing the hammer.

**5.** Parents should not dictate the feelings children should have, but rather give them freedom to feel. Whan parents let children own their own feelings and experiences, it shows them that their parents care for and love them.

Developing Feelings—Older Children

**1.** Discuss emotional episodes with the child, usually after strong emotions have passed.
**2.** Look for signs of emotional suppression, such as enuresis or nail biting.
**3.** Help the child learn that, while it is okay to feel emotions, it may not be okay to act on them. Appropriate reactions can be taught.
**4.** Help the child distinguish between temporary feelings and more permanent ones. Example: "I don't think you hate me, but I know you are very angry with me right now."
**5.** Create a one-to-one relationship with the youngster (father–son or mother–son) by scheduling a weekly activity that stimulates interaction; this should help the child to be more open in expressing feelings. Another idea for children who have difficulty verbally expressing feelings would be a box, placed somewhere in the home, for notes to parents.
**6.** Schedule a special weekly time or parent–child interview as a means of expanding love, communication, and trust between family members. This provides parents a time to focus on frustrations that children may be experiencing and to monitor their feelings toward school, family, church, friends, or other areas.

Freedom and Choice—Preschool Children

**1.** Provide simple choices and let them have the freedom to decide. Total freedom is not advocated, but rather a structured variety of choices. For example, let the child select which gift to give to someone else, what to have for breakfast, what clothes to buy, or when to do homework or study music.
**2.** Provide freedom through discipline. Discipline is necessary for true freedom. When an unskilled child wants to climb trees, he or she may lose "freedom" by having an accident. On the other hand, the child who is forbidden to climb will become rebellious and will climb when no one is watching. A happy medium would be to teach the child how to climb. The child can also be allowed to make choices in disciplinary situations. When children are arguing at the supper table, they may be told, "You either stop arguing or leave the table; you decide."

Freedom and Choice—Older Children

**1.** The child should be given as many choices as possible, including the choosing of responsibilities, friends, clothes, and activities outside the home.
**2.** Make sure children follow through on their decisions, teaching

them that this is a part of decision making. An elementary-school-age child may buy a bike, for example, that will require additional chores to pay for the item. After the child brings the bicycle home, he or she needs to follow through on the contract; responsibility and maturity are fostered.

Uniqueness and Individuality—Preschool Children

1. Children can know that their parents are unique. Let them spend time with neighbors or other family members so that they will not only be exposed to new ideas, but can also see the differences between family and friends. However, if the family climate is radically different, the child may feel embarrassed or strange when in another environment.
2. Parents can show that they value the child's developing personality. Commenting favorably on a child's strengths can encourage the child to continue developing in those areas. At the same time, parents need to express their confidence that the child will perform adequately in other areas. Parents can encourage individuality by treating children as individuals rather than always placing them in a group by saying "the boys," etc. (This is especially important in the case of twins.)

Uniqueness and Individuality—Older Children

1. Most children want to be best at something, have shown some indication of the areas in which they can excel, and can be given special lessons or training in those areas. These years are a good time to start activities such as music lessons, scouting, and organized sports.
2. By the end of childhood, the peer group will have become much more important, making the encouragement of uniqueness difficult. Therefore, it is important to emphasize individual development while the child is still responsive to it.
3. Parents should not make an issue of individuality in unimportant areas. For example, children could be allowed to dress as they choose even though they may be conforming to peer group fashions, as long as they remain modest and clean. Parents can encourage individuality in more critical areas.

Love and Affection—Preschool Children

1. Parents can show love and affection by: expressing love verbally, hugging, kissing, holding, rocking, tousling hair, spending time playing, singing, setting reasonable limits, talking, and maintaining eye contact.
2. Parents can convey a climate of love and affection through psychological safety. Psychological safety includes being relaxed as parents, avoiding sudden surprises, being open and

honest with children, and not giving mixed messages in which words and body language are contradictory.

## Love and Affection—Older Children

1. Parents need to show love and affection regardless of children's achievements; children need to feel valued apart from their accomplishments. This can be implemented by remembering that children need the safety of nonjudgment. Love will be continually felt by children if parents separate the performance from the children themselves. One father told his child, "Whenever personal worth is dependent upon performance, personal value is subject to cancellation with every misstep."
2. When one says "You . . . ," it is followed by a judgment, while "I . . . " is followed by personal feelings. For example, compare "You are such a slowpoke" with "I'm worried you'll be late for school." Judgments are similar to smokescreens in that they prevent love from coming through.
3. Cherish the child's specialness, even though his or her behavior may not always be acceptable. This attitude is essential for expressing unconditional love and affection. Refuse to take your child's uniqueness for granted, and treat him or her with the same respect *you* would want.
4. Young children are usually receptive to direct expressions of love. As they become older, however, they may become embarrassed by open displays of affection. However, they still need to know that they are loved; this can be verbally expressed during moments of private closeness. A quick squeeze in passing, rumpling of the hair, or pat on the shoulder can be effective at this age.

## Providing a Sense of Belonging—Preschool Children

1. As soon as possible, start a system of personal responsibility for chores around the house—no matter how small the chore, responsibility creates a sense of participation, of being needed in the family.
2. Spend a little time with each child at bedtime. Make up bedtime stories that include each child as characters and that portray their importance in the family.

## Providing a Sense of Belonging—Older Children

1. Never use threats of separation from family as punishment, which could be construed as not loving the child.
2. Teach children about the family's name, heritage, and ancestors to develop pride in the family.
3. Involve the whole family in decisions such as purchasing a new car or possible change of residence.

# SELF-CHECK

1. In your reading, five "climates of love" were considered as important and basic when it comes to parenting. Which of the following does *not* belong to this list?
   a. Feelings
   b. Freedom of choice
   c. Consequences
   d. Affection
2. Which of the following is *not* true about feelings in the home?
   a. Feelings can be dangerous.
   b. Proportionately more positive than negative emotions are the key to successful emotional learning.
   c. A child must be able to experience a wide range of feelings or emotions.
   d. All of the above are true.
3. According to Diana Baumrind (1974), _____ parents attempted to shape, control, and evaluate the child's behavior with strict and absolute values.
   a. authoritarian
   b. authoritative
   c. permissive
   d. democratic
4. The study by Thomas, Chess, and Birch (1970) that categorized infants into "easy to warm up," "slow to warm up," and "difficult" categories is famous because of the following results:
   a. Clear differences exist among infants even at birth.
   b. "Easy-to-warm-up" infants talked sooner because of warmer parents.
   c. Differences among infants existing at birth may continue into adulthood.
   d. a and c are both correct.
5. Which of the following is not true concerning contact between a mother and her infant?
   a. Early contact is an important factor in child–mother attachment development.
   b. Babies seek out their mothers at an early age.
   c. Children under 6 or 7 haven't been found to be able to love and feel compassion for others (Piaget's theory).
   d. Babies at 7 months will show "separation distress" when withdrawn from the mother or an equivalent primary caretaker.
6. MacClelland, Constantian, and Stone (1978), when following up a study began in 1957, concluded that
   a. how parents "feel" about their children is the principle factor in child outcome.
   b. breast-feeding and toilet training practices are crucial in determining child outcome.
   c. only the mother's affection (not the father's) was found to be important.
   d. None of the above is true.
7. Parke and Sawin (1977) observed the behavior of both middle- and lower-class parents of newborns in hospital maternity wards. They found that
   a. fathers were usually out chasing nurses.
   b. the father and mother weren't interchangeable; each provided for a child's needs in a unique way.

c. the father and mother were not distinguishable in their behaviors toward infants.

d. mothers, being tired from childbirth, smiled less at their babies.

8. Which of the following is true about the need to belong?
   a. Both psychological and sociological theory stress the importance and pervasiveness of a fundamental need for membership in a primary group.
   b. A feeling of not really belonging to a familly group can be especially devastating to children.
   c. Besides inborn strivings to belong, there are many social customs that sustain group membership.
   d. All of the above are true.

9. Which of the five climates in Lesson 3 advises that parents be neither too restrictive nor permissive?
   a. Feelings
   b. Freedom of choice
   c. Uniqueness and individuality
   d. Affection
   e. Belongingness

KEY: 1–c; 2–d; 3–a; 4–d; 5–c; 6–a; 7–b; 8–d; 9–b

# CHAPTER 6

# HOW ORGANIZATION IS DEVELOPED IN THE HOME

In Chapter 5, an accepting, warm climate was advocated—in which the child is encouraged to experience feelings and develop uniquely through personal choice. The reader may have wondered if such a positive, "unstructured" environment is certain to produce growth, if at all possible in the first place. Certainly, an obedient though autonomous child is ideal—one who feels that he or she belongs, who feels loved, and who is progressing toward becoming a productive member of society. However, such growth is not possible without some planning and organization. Children must be provided with a predictable structure in which they feel safe; they must have expectations and guidelines placed upon them; they must be taught to contribute to the good of the family unit through efforts of their own; they must be able to derive meaning from what is going on around them and to acquire knowledge about themselves and their surroundings. Such organization is the topic of the present chapter. We will discuss the role of five separate elements providing this organization: structure; work and play; knowledge and truth about self and world; a climate with meaning; and a safe, nourishing climate.

We would like to stress here, as we will in subsequent chapters, that each child, family, and culture is different. Personal experiences and insights must be relied on for effective parenting. The suggestions in this text have been researched and found to be important. However, they provide a working base for parents to branch out and individualize their own techniques.

## Structure

Structure in a home has been called different things: rules, expectations, limits, standards, encouragement, guidelines, and laws. None of these terms is inclusive, however. Expectations, encouragement, and guidance help provide structure in a healthy growth climate. They are positive terms, implying freedom for the child. On the other hand, rules, laws, limits, and standards are more restrictive terms, often carrying negative connotations. Yet, both the dos and the don'ts are necessary. As mentioned in the previous chapter, children must have freedom to develop autonomously, being guided by parents' expectations. However, lack of experience and maturity necessitates adequate limits and rule setting for younger, less socially mature children. Some unfortunate children would benefit by a few limitations and restrictions. One child was heard to say, "I wish there was a fence around our yard so I would know where I can go."

### EXPECTATIONS AND DEMANDS

Research has looked at parents who establish definite expectations and define rules to bring about compliance. Summarizing research evidence to support her conclusions, a prominent psychologist, Eleanor Maccoby, states that children with this type of parent are low in aggression, altruistic rather than egotistic, and above average in competence and agency (1980). Low demands, on the other hand, have been associated with high aggression, low impulse control, and immaturity. Furthermore, Maccoby states that when parents consistently enforce rules and prevent their children from taking control, the children are better able to control aggressive impulses. She states:

> A demand is a goal that the child is expected to meet, and goals vary. Some parents expect help with their household tasks or child care, others demand politeness and consideration in interpersonal relationships. When parents make few demands, they may be underestimating the child's capacity and maturity level, or they may be so disinterested and preoccupied that they find it easier to do things themselves than to get the child to do them. . . . The positive outcomes of high demands—especially a sense of competency—can only be expected if the child has the necessary skills to meet the demands. . . . In other words, high parental demands that are appropriate to the child's age and are accompanied by training can provide a stepping stone to self-reliance (pp. 382–383).

Expectations, though similar to demands, are more conducive to the development of freedom and trust. For example, the following account illustrates an expectation and its consequences:

*I remember a time when my mother applied expectations to set limits on my behavior. I had begun to date, and we were discussing the time I should be home. She said, "I'm not going to set a specific time for you to be home. You've always shown good judgment. I'm trusting you." I felt that I would rather break my neck than break her trust. If I were to abuse her trust, she would have to set a specific rule. I felt greater motivation to get home early by her trusting me than I would have with a rule.*

Because immediate, total compliance to expectations is not always experienced, they are often discarded by parents in favor of stricter rules and demands. In this fashion, the power of simple expectations is usually underestimated. And, in doing so, parents communicating many demands to their children can create difficulties. The following story illustrates how restrictive demands may inhibit a child's growth:

*My father always seemed to want me to be like him—I am the only boy in my family. One of the earliest experiences I remember (I was*

*about seven) involved ice-skating. In his youth, my father was a fine figure skater. As far back as I can remember he wanted me to enjoy it as much as he did, and to become as good as or better than he had been. Unfortunately I can't, and never could, tolerate ice-skating. I just don't like it.*

*My father never seemed able to understand or accept my feelings about ice-skating. He would often make me go to the local rink, or arrange parties, thereby forcing me by social pressure to go. He gave me his old figure skates, and even though they didn't fit, I wore them to please him. They would hurt, but one particular night the pain was especially bad. When I got home, my dad saw my broken and bleeding blisters; he finally seemed to understand. After that he never pressured me about skating again.*

Had this father continued with his demands, the child might have pursued a pastime from which he was deriving no pleasure, possibly preventing personal excellence in desired areas and interfering with a positive father–son relationship.

Expectations, however, when accompanied by trust and freedom, will sometimes produce more growth than demands because individuals assume some responsibility for their personal actions. This is expressed in the following:

*As a child growing up, I wanted to meet these "expectations" because I wanted to please my parents, even though I did not feel pressure to act a certain way. I always knew I had the freedom to meet or not meet these expectations. The fact that they were implied and not hard and fast rules helped us kids experience individual responsibility and freedom to perform as we wished. Most of our actions, decisions, and behaviors were condoned and supported by our parents.*

It is important to note that demands may be necessary at times. Some parental control is necessary for adequate development of self-control in the child (Baumrind, 1967; Levy, 1943). We want to point out, however, that heavy and continued reliance on unalterable demands may bring about temporary compliance, though leading to increased antisocial behaviors when parents are not present.

Often, adults do not know how to state expectations or establish rules. Simply stated, it involves letting children know what is expected in advance, giving them a chance to practice it, and helping them understand the consequences. As will be discussed later, allowing the child to participate in establishing rules or expectations will result in greater success.

The total range of behavior can be included in rules, demands, and

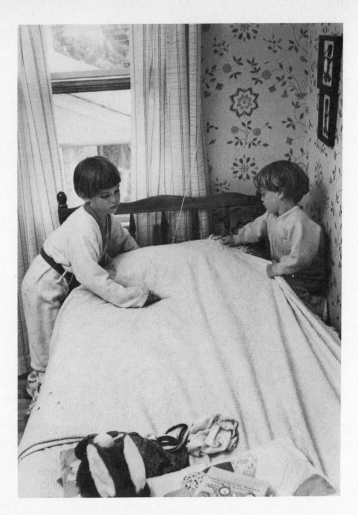

Parental expectations, when accompanied by trust and freedom, are necessary for individual growth.

expectations. Some examples of reasonable expectations were given by a mother of several pre- and elementary-school-age children:

*My children know there is a difference between inside and outside play, and they are expected to act accordingly. Inside, they must play reasonably quiet games; no running or chasing is allowed. Outside, the sky is the limit as long as they play safely and don't disturb the neighbors.*

*They also realize that although good manners are expected at all mealtimes, eating in a restaurant requires extra effort. They know we use quieter voices and observe stricter table etiquette.*

*The kids have been taught that we give the same respect to other people's homes as we do to our own. When they are at a friend's house, they know that they should be just as polite and considerate of inside rules as they are at home. They have found that they are always welcome guests because they behave in an acceptable fashion.*

Expectations will not be effective unless there is follow-through; parents must evaluate a child's treatment of parental expectations. Sometimes parents simply forget; other parents have so many things going on they are unable to notice, neglecting to provide the necessary guidance. In the long run, these parents will have less time for their children, and will soon believe that simple expectations do not work. The children will then believe that expectations are not important to the parent. One mother who realizes this danger states:

*We have a family council whenever it seems necessary. My son has had real difficulty accomplishing his responsibilities at home and at school. We sat down in a council and talked to him about his feelings. He felt the problem was that he was lazy and had too many demands on him at school and home. We negotiated at home and dropped one of his jobs. We talked to the teacher at school. Apparently, he was goofing off at school instead of doing his work. The other children were able to accomplish their work plus do extra, so there wasn't negotiation in this area. Each Friday we checked with his teacher and got a list of his homework. Expectations were made clear that if he caught up on his school work he had privileges to do specific activities he liked to do; if he wasn't caught up, the weekend was spent doing school work.*

## EXPECTATIONS VS. RESTRICTIVENESS

An important distinction should be made between parents who thoughtfully establish expectations and demands, and those who are simply restrictive. As mentioned earlier, expectations and demands imply action whereas restrictions imply the "don'ts." Maccoby (1980, p. 385), in reviewing studies, finds that restrictive parents produce children who lack empathy. They are more timid and not as motivated. When parents use a great deal of power in being restrictive, an even clearer pattern of child behavior emerges. Characteristics of children of these authoritarian parents include: lack of empathy; low self-esteem; low internalization of moral standards; lack of spontaneity, affection, curiosity, independence, and responsibility. While obedience and submissiveness may be obtained, it is at a heavy price.

Rather than being simply restrictive, it is beneficial to impose environmental structure in the form of expectations and demands. These require follow-through and effort, but assist the child in developing social maturity and acceptable behavior. It is felt that these expectations will not be resisted but actually welcomed by the child. In some cases, children seek expectations for help in their lives. Ironically, one teenage daughter called her father late at night from a party. Her father was not expecting her home for some time, but they had the following conversation:

*Daughter:* "Dad, do I have to come home now?"
*Father:* "No, of course you don't."
*Daughter:* "Oh Dad, why do I have to?"
*Father:* "You don't. I said you could stay late tonight."
*Daughter:* "Please Dad, just this one time."
*Father:* "You want me to tell you to come home?"
*Daughter:* "OK, I'll be right home."

## Work and Play
### WORK RESPONSIBILITIES

*In my home we all had our own small chores to do. Through these chores I learned that responsibility was part of having a job. When I found my first job outside the home, I already knew what responsibility was, and by being responsible I managed to get promotions over people who had been there longer than I. This helped my self-esteem very much and made me want to work that much harder. My parents taught me the importance of work, and how to enjoy work no matter what it may be.*

Contrast the previous statement with this description:

*I compare myself to my girlfriend who never had Saturday chores. When we were little, I was so envious. Now I see how differently we've grown up. She never finished high school, had a baby out of wedlock, spent time in jail for drugs, and spent most of her adult life on welfare. She's told me since that she wished she would have had parents who cared enough to teach her to work so she would have learned to make something out of her life. I'm grateful that my parents cared enough to teach me to be productive.*

These two examples illustrate the significance of work and responsibility in even a young child's life. One psychologist (Staub, 1979), when reviewing studies on moral development of children, concluded that one of the most effective ways to engender moral maturity is to assign work and responsibility to children.

I have previously suggested . . . that an important influence on a child learning to behave prosocially is the focusing of responsibility on them by parents and other socializing agents to engage in behavior that enhances others' welfare.

Responsibility assignment may also be more structured; a child may be expected to take care of a younger sibling whenever the mother is not home or when she is otherwise occupied, or may have obligations for the maintenance and welfare of the family or some of its members.

I am proposing that involvement with responsible activities will lead to a sense of personal responsibility toward others, which, as the research showed, is an important influence on prosocial behavior (pp. 189–194).

Work and responsibility seem to transform one's outlook on the world. It is as if people must themselves experience that life does not simply meet their own personal needs, but that they must look beyond themselves to understand the meaning of their existence. The importance of work has been repeatedly stressed by those who have studied it; David Macarou (1970), for example, points out that some believe work to be a human instinct.

**Work ideals.** While it is believed that work develops a sense of responsibility, it is also true that the human being has assigned different meanings to work. In ancient Greece, work was at one time considered menial activity; for early Christians it was God's punishment on the human race. It was the Protestant work ethic that eventually classified work as an end in itself, an ethical duty to be engaged in, not for material necessity, but because of resulting personal development.

The idea of hard work has also been abused, especially during the Industrial Revolution, when young children were brutalized by working long hours in deplorable conditions. Such abuses often affected physical and intellectual development for the worse. This is not to suggest that work is necessarily undesirable for children. Rather, the conditions and goals of work can be neglected and abused.

Contemporary parents sometimes falsely asume that the true value of work cannot be taught if children do not grow up on a farm, or in a family business, where they are heavily involved in providing for the family's subsistence. Consider this "old-fashioned" work experience:

*When I was a child, living on a ranch in eastern Oregon, I had many opportunities to contribute to our family. We didn't have power lines where we lived, so we were without electricity. We used a wood-burning stove to cook and heat our home. The entire family worked together to get the wood we needed. We would go into the forest and Dad would cut a tree and saw it into blocks. Mom split the blocks with a maul and wedge, and my brothers and sister and I loaded it into the truck. At home we unloaded it, stacked it, and later carried it to the house. We all felt our contribution to be meaningful.*

*We also helped with the haying from a very early age. Dad would mow the hay, and he and Mom would rake it. Then he would load it onto a hay wagon and we would tramp it down so the load was bigger. We also helped tramp the hay into good, solid stacks once it was taken out of the field.*

Some parents feel that in our modern, technologically advanced culture it is impossible to provide this type of experience for children, but home management experts point out that there is ample work in the contemporary family. One sucessful way of organizing work in the family was related as follows:

*In our family we were all expected to do chores. We sat down as a family and decided what was to be done, how it would be divided, and what the consequences would be if the work wasn't completed. We all had a voice in the matter, and all of us had to agree on the terms. It helped us in our work and chores to know we all had decided it.*

Another student related that one of the most enjoyable, pleasant childhood memories she had was working with her father each Saturday. Sometimes it was in the yard, sometimes in the basement, and sometimes doing errands around town. She loved to go with him and share his company. It made her feel important. Indeed, children can learn responsibility through work no matter what the family situation or culture.

**Benefits.**　　Two benefits of teaching children to work at an early age are evident: moral maturity and a sense of responsibility. Another benefit of work is the appreciation of life and hard-earned possessions that develops. The following story was related about a brother who came to value something he himself had worked for:

*When my little brother was eight years old he wanted a certain skateboard very badly. The only problem was that the skateboard cost over $100. Mother told him if he really wanted it, to save his money, and that he could also earn extra money by doing odd jobs around the house. She made sure there were plenty of things to be done and opportunities for him to earn that money. After a few months of long, hard work, he finally had enough money. That skateboard was his most prized possession and he guarded it with his life.*

Perhaps the most significant attribute of work is its effect on children. When work that is appropriate to the mental and physical abilities of children

Teaching children to work at an early age engenders moral maturity and a sense of responsibility.

is diligently undertaken, children feel better about themselves and are generally happier. One father noted that in his large family there frequently came times when children would say, "I don't know what to do." They would whine, fight, and become grouchy and negative. At such times he knew some type of activity was needed. Generally, he organized the home so that a short work assignment was given to each child and a small treat arranged at the task's completion. He reports that almost without exception, this procedure resulted in greater happiness despite occasional reluctance by the children to participate.

## PLAY

Children have always played. In ruins in China, Egypt, and other ancient civilizations toys have been found. Although once thought to be frivolous, even sinful and a waste of time, children's play is considered now by psychologists as important, even critical, for social and personality development. In a popular textbook on child psychology, Vander Zanden (1981, p. 346) states the following about play:

1. It is a vehicle for cognitive stimulation.
2. It prepares children for life where they can experience themselves as active agents.
3. It provides opportunities for rehearsing adult roles.
4. It helps children build their own individual sense of identity.
5. It allows for both reality and fantasy; it is a medium that enables children to come to terms with their fears of villains, witches, ghosts, lions, dogs, and so on.

In almost every child psychology book, play is regarded as an important childhood activity. It is advisable to give children the opportunity, time, toys, and encouragement in this activity. In one textbook, a little girl is seated on the stairs with a dog, rabbit, mouse, jack-in-the-box, picture book, Raggedy Ann doll, and baby bottle of milk at her feet. The author states:

> There is little doubt that this young girl enjoys a rich and exciting world of imaginary play. Contrary to popular opinion, she probably has fewer problems and is more intelligent and advanced in language skills than children without imaginary playmates (Gander & Gardner, 1981, p. 271).

How do parents engender or facilitate children's playfulness? Barnett and Kleiber (1984) found that playfulness in male children was positively related to the use of noncommercial games in which the children could make up their own rules and design their own playthings—using a kind of creativity. In particular, boys who possessed specific sports equipment were inflexible in their play. In addition, male children whose parents (mother and father) played with them regularly and for longer periods were more playful.

Although these same factors did not correlate with playfulness in female children, girls with younger and more educated mothers had more playful orientations.

## Knowledge and Truth about Self and World

◖

*A five-year-old child was playing in the water when he hit his head and began to drown. Coughing and spitting, he was pulled out of the pool. As you might expect, he had a hard time getting back in the water. To help him overcome his fear, his parents enrolled him in a swimming class. Still, he resisted instructors, who had a hard time even getting him to put his face in the water or to let go of the side of the pool. He had to repeat the class more than once. While driving home one day, the little boy began asking his father questions about death and dying. The next week he put his head under the water and swam. After this lesson the little boy said, "I swam today and I didn't die."*

◖

One basis of personal confidence is knowledge and truth. When one does not understand one's environment, the results of one's actions, or the logic behind them, confidence gives way to uncertainty. For this reason, we seek to educate ourselves, to be informed, and to acquire knowledge. The human being is curious and desires to know. Repressive governments have learned that they cannot keep people from seeking knowledge and truth, and we propose that a continuous input of knowledge and environmental stimuli is essential to healthy functioning.

The ideal climate for children is one in which both information and truth are amply available. Not only should children's questions be answered, but truth is important. This is not to say that children cannot believe in Santa Claus. However, being eager to learn and know, they will develop more if they can find honest answers to their questions. Depending on age and readiness, children are not able to grasp certain concepts, however. But having knowledge available when the child is ready to learn is important. Many a parent, for one reason or another, will refrain from discussing human sexuality and reproduction with a child although the time may be appropriate. What generally happens is the child finds his or her own answers from peers who may or may not understand and explain things as the parent would have wished. Or, if the parent provides some mythical answer to postpone what seems an uncomfortable discussion, the child may develop false ideas or come to distrust the parents as a source of information. Even a parent who lacks the ability to adequately answer the hundreds of questions such as "Why is the moon only half tonight?" or "What is an earthquake?" may teach the child that the environment is somewhat of a mystery, perhaps unwittingly causing a lack of confidence and control in relation to the surroundings.

An attitude of respect for truth and knowledge is important. For example, the father in the following account helped his son learn the importance of intelligent problem solving:

*I wanted a hamster. I knew that my mother didn't like rodents, but that she would go along with my father if he said it was all right. I also knew that my usual methods of convincing my father in situations like this didn't work very well. So I had to change. A short time ago I had been the unwilling recipient of one of my father's lectures about the virtues of information and knowledge. I thought, why not try it, it can't hurt. So I went to the library and read all kinds of material on hamsters, their habits, characteristics, and care and feeding. Then I sat down and figured out all the reasons why I should have a hamster, all the reasons against it, and counterarguments to what I expected my father to say. It worked so well I was absolutely amazed. Armed with all my information, I went in to talk with him. Fifteen minutes later we were on our way to the pet store to buy a hamster. That one experience made more of an impression on me than all the lectures my father had ever given.*

Allowing children to explore the world through experience increases their fund of truth and knowledge.

Sometimes it is hard for a parent to provide knowledge or to be honest with a child, for fear that the child may be embarrassed or might not understand. While it may seem at the moment that it would be more kind to allow an error to pass unnoticed, the child depends heavily on parents for accurate information. Consider the following episode:

*A child had been working on spelling new words and had finally mastered a difficult word. He went proudly to his mother and spelled the word to her. In the process he had missed one letter. The mother did not correct the child. The child then went to his father to spell the word for him. Several moments later the child returned and quizzically asked the mother why she had not corrected him.*

## EVEN WHEN IT'S DIFFICULT

In our parenting classes, we often debate whether it was fair and wise for the following mother to share the upsetting and personal circumstances behind her separation with her children:

*A year ago, my father left my family, which was a total shock and surprise. My mother, needing support and wanting to do the right thing, felt it better to inform my sister and me about the circumstances involved in the separation and the reasons behind it. She thought we were old enough and mature enough to handle this.*

When discussed in class, most students felt that even though it might produce mental stress and anguish for a young child, it is better for them to understand personal things such as divorce, death, adult mistakes, and family finances. However, parents should not dump all their heavy emotional problems on children. There exists a fine line between informing children of sensitive family decisions and situations and, on the other hand, using children for support and comfort, or providing children with information they are unable to handle because of cognitive and emotional immaturity. This logic underlies the consensus among professionals that parents should talk about sex education with their children. Yet, it is understood that the type and amount of information given should be appropriate to the child's maturational level and ability to comprehend.

## ARRANGING LEARNING EXPERIENCES

While the emphasis has thus far been on placing knowledge and truth at the child's disposal when he or she is ready to receive it, it is sometimes necessary to arrange learning experiences designed to increase understanding. A visit to the zoo, educational films, trips, visiting sick relatives in the hospital, and other planned experiences provide enrichment. For example, instead of preaching about the dangers of playing with matches, a student said his mother did the following:

*Mother had problems with my two oldest brothers, Tony and Mike, when they were kids. They liked to play with matches. Mom told them not to, but they would hide and play with them anyway. She was really worried that they would hurt themselves or someone else. So she sat them down in a safe place and let them play with as many matches as they wanted to. After they burned their fingers a few times while sitting there, they decided playing with matches wasn't as much fun as they thought it was.*

Experience in handling hazardous parts of our environment can often increase competence and decrease personal danger. Like the previous example, this can apply to firearms, knives, animals, and automobiles.

## KNOWLEDGE OF SELF AND ENVIRONMENT

The need for truth and knowledge about the outside physical environment has been emphasized. An understanding of the environment engenders social competence. Also important is that which we learn about ourselves from the knowledge and truth available to us. In many discussions on the self, it is simply pointed out that one should have a positive self-concept, while the need for an *accurate and realistic understanding* of the self is often overlooked. In reviewing research on the self-concept, a distinguished child psychologist, Boyd McCandless (1967), states:

> This study ... suggested honesty about oneself, which may also be thought of as accuracy, as an important aspect in the self-concept, and may be related to good adjustment (p. 268).

> Two studies, then, suggest clearly that accuracy of self-estimate is associated with a number of other indices of good adjustment. Although another study suggests that this relationship is affected by whether the self-concept is *high and accurate* or *low and accurate,* the former condition would be more likely to accompany good adjustment (p. 282).

It is difficult to know whether it is more important to have a positive self-concept or an accurate self-concept. Ideally, the optimal self-concept would be both accurate and positive. Imagine you have two mirrors to look into each morning before you leave to face the world each day. One mirror is in a well-lighted room. It reflects you accurately, showing all blemishes and imperfections. Looking into this mirror is sometimes discouraging as you are likely to note each of your imperfections. The other mirror, on a wall away from adequate light, tends to reflect a more pleasing image. After looking at yourself in this mirror, you generally conclude that you look pretty sharp. It is a question of which mirror best prepares you for the day ahead.

## A Climate with Meaning: Values and Beliefs

### A LIFE PURPOSE

The meaning and purpose of life to various individuals is a topic that, in the past, has not been amenable to scientific study. However, most individuals are greatly influenced by what they see as the purpose of their existence, or the confusion they feel by not being able to come to grips with their purpose in life. Leo Tolstoy, referring to himself, wrote the following:

> I felt that something had broken within me and on which my life had always rested, that I had nothing left to hold on to, and that morally my life had stopped. . . .
> Behold me then, a man happy and in good health, hiding the rope

in order not to hang myself to the rafters of the room where every night I went to sleep alone; behold me no longer going shooting, lest I should yield to the too easy temptation of putting an end to myself with my gun.

I did not know what I wanted. I was afraid of life; I was driven to leave it; and in spite of that, I still hoped for something from it.

All this took place at a time when so far as all my outer circumstances went, I ought to have been completely happy. I had a good wife who loved me and whom I loved; good children and a large property which was increasing with no pains taken on my part. I was more respected by my kinsfolk and acquaintances than I had ever been; I was loaded with praise by strangers; and without exaggeration I could believe my name already famous. Moreover I was neither insane nor ill. On the contrary, I possessed a physical and mental strength which I have rarely met in persons of my age. I could mow as well as the peasants, I could work with my brain eight hours uninterruptedly and feel no bad effects. . . .

What will be the outcome of what I do today? Of what I shall do tomorrow? What will be the outcome of all my life? Why should I live? Why should I do anything? Is there in life any purpose which the inevitable death which awaits me does not undo and destroy?

These questions are the simplest in the world. From the stupid child to the wisest old man, they are in the soul of every human being. Without an answer to them, it is impossible, as I experienced, for life to go on (Tolstoy, 1882, pp. 153–155).

While Leo Tolstoy wrote about himself as an adult, the foundation for understanding life, its purpose and meaning, begins during childhood. The purposes of one's life need to be sought, although indoctrination into a specific religion or ideology is not the object.

One of the most respected and popular textbook writers on personal adjustment speaks of our need to solve human problems,

. . . of our need to solve the uniquely human problems of acquiring both "know-how" and "know-why." For the individual, this means trying to find the answers to three key questions: Who am I? Where am I going? Why? (Coleman, 1974, p. 11)

A survey of personal adjustment books reveals the belief that human beings must find meaning in their lives for optimal functioning. Little research evidence can be mustered to support such claims, but clinical reports of practicing therapists repeatedly stress the importance of meaning in one's life. What does this mean to parents? Essentially, parents can help children consider their existence and present them with a rational value system. Traditionally, this has been done through various belief systems, religions, values, and attitudes. These need not be formal, but they must be salient. That is, parents must speak about right and wrong, and purpose and meaning. It is best to do this in a spirit of freedom and choice rather than through the imposition of absolutes upon the child.

## PARENT EXAMPLE

Example and style of living are perhaps the two most practical ways to bring meaning into existence. One student describes her family as follows:

*While living at home, I never saw my parents lie, steal, or put something over on someone. They were honest with everyone and as I grew older, I realized that their values prevented a lot of day-to-day problems and worries. Also, my parents would punish us worse if we lied than if we just took the blame for a particular wrong-doing. That provided an incentive to tell the truth.*

Consider another illustration:

*The best example of service I have ever witnessed is my mother. People always call her when something needs to be done, because they know that she is helpful and dependable. Also commendable, I feel, is what she does to make others happy. About once a week she makes a special cake, or fresh bread, or something else homemade and has it anonymously delivered to a family. She wants them to know that they are special.*

It would appear obvious that these mothers effectively modeled and probably instilled certain values into the lives of their children. A child's willingness to recognize and accept these values can be compared with those families in which parents exhort, preach, and insist that a set of beliefs be accepted. Oftentimes the child rebels. One student writes:

*After all this teaching and structuring of our values and beliefs, one of my brothers rebelled and escaped to live in another value system, which, of course, had different beliefs. His wasn't a forceful, violent rebellion, but rather an outward demonstration that he had his own beliefs and values and would no longer follow the rest of the family.*

Fortunately, in this particular instance the parents allowed him freedom and he eventually came back and accepted his parents' values.

Parents help their children develop values, beliefs, and meaning through their own example. Life consistently presents occasions when parents can in this manner assist children in understanding issues related to values. The following are examples of issues parents deal with that children will observe and often incorporate into their own value systems.

1. Aggression toward others
2. Physical health
3. Property rights
4. Sexual behavior
5. Responsibility and work
6. Telling the truth, keeping promises
7. Respecting rules and authority

Children frequently face similar issues; how they interpret and understand them depends on the values they have seen their parents model.

## VICTOR FRANKL

A dramatic example of how meaning is demonstrated to be important for psychological functioning is given by Victor Frankl, a psychotherapist. At the age of 37, Frankl began a three-year ordeal of torture and cruelty in the Auschwitz concentration camp. He was one of few to survive this ordeal and attributes his endurance to a belief in the human capacity to find meaning and purpose in life in the face of overwhelming suffering. Gordon Allport wrote in the Preface to Frankl's book *Man's Search for Meaning:*

> How could he—every possession lost, every value destroyed, suffering from hunger, cold, brutality, hourly expecting extermination—how could he find life worth preserving? A psychiatrist who personally has faced such extremity is a psychiatrist worth listening to (Frankl, 1962).

Frankl's theory stresses the importance of possessing a *will to meaning.* His psychological theory, called *logotherapy,* is named for the Greek word *logos* or "meaning." For Frankl, a lack of meaning in life creates neurosis. In one form it is characterized by meaninglessness, purposelessness, aimlessness, and emptiness in life. He had seen this not only in the lives of his fellow prisoners, but also in his patients. To overcome this neurosis, Frankl proposes that a person must obtain a vital sense of meaning and purpose in life. Three factors are necessary to facilitate this process: spirituality, freedom, and responsibility.

While Frankl's logotherapy is treatment oriented, his principles can be applied toward creating a preventive environment. In this case, the parent, by providing meaning for a child, develops a climate for healthy personality development.

# A Safe and Nourishing Physical Climate

*Between the 6th and 7th grades, my family moved to a large city. Two girls at the start of that 7th year decided it would be fun to pick on me. I was harassed by these two girls for two years. They never left me alone—going to school, at school, or coming home from school. They used physical as well as verbal abuse and I was so averse to fighting that I just took it all. I was so fearful that my grades hit rock bottom! I would cry at night because I had made it home safely. In any case, because I was in such fear for my safety I could not function properly—socially or otherwise.*

The removal of security in this young girl's life had a tremendous impact on her daily routine. Imagine the possible devastation had she not had a secure home. Under constant fear, it would have been impossible to function properly in other areas of her life.

Similarly, deprivation of physical needs is also disrupting and can produce lasting effects. One student writes about her father:

*My father's parents died while he was quite young and he was, therefore, raised by his older brothers and sisters (the oldest being 16 at the time of their parents' death). He went without many physical needs. They didn't always have enough to eat and their housing was poor. My father has expressed to me many times the lack of security that he felt because he didn't know from one day to the next if he would get enough to eat or if he would have proper clothes to wear. He worried about these conditions so much that he would become lax in his school work, or get behind because he had to go out and earn money. It would appear that people need to take care of their physical needs before they can become productively involved in other pursuits. He has seen to it that we have all of our physical needs met. Even now after I have been in college for five years, he always asks if I have enough to eat, if I am sleeping right, or if the house is warm enough.*

## HIERARCHY OF NEEDS

The above two examples illustrate a fundamental psychological concept proposed by Abraham Maslow in 1943, a theory of human motivation that even today continues to have appeal. He stated that people begin their lives by satisfying basic needs and then moving to higher needs. Before a person can meet higher needs, lower needs must have been adequately satisfied:

> If all the needs are unsatisfied, and the organism is then dominated by the physiological needs, all other needs may become simply non-existent or be pushed into the background. . . . For the man who is extremely and dangerously hungry, no other interests exist but food. He dreams food, he remembers food, he thinks about food . . . and he wants only food . . . life itself tends to be defined in terms of eating. Anything else will be defined as unimportant. Freedom, love, community feeling, respect, philosophy, may all be waved aside as fripperies which are useless since they fail to fill the stomach. Such a man may fairly be said to live by bread alone (Maslow, 1943, p. 373–374).

Maslow has qualified his theory to explain how some people become independent and rise above physical and safety needs. What is important here, however, is the obvious and supportable belief that a healthy, positive growth climate needs to provide safety, health care, and physical necessities to ensure the proper development of psychological and social needs.

A humorous incident was related by a student, illustrating how higher needs of modesty and social propriety were influenced by lower-order needs:

> *I was raised on a ranch, and my family was not well off financially. Our biological and safety needs were met on a level that was barely adequate. We usually had enough to eat, but seldom had treats of any kind. We had enough clothing to provide adequate protection, and my mother tried to make what we had as attractive as possible. However, we wore only as much as was required by the weather. In the summer my brothers, sister, and I wore only cotton underpants.*
>
> *I can clearly remember a particular incident when I was about five years old. One of my father's friends came out to the ranch. He did not come to the house, but stayed down by the shed. He sent word to us that if we would come down to his pick-up, we could have some soda pop. Since we had few visitors on the ranch, we were very curious about the man, in addition to really wanting the pop. However, we were old enough to be embarrassed by our lack of clothing. Mom tried to find something for us to wear, but couldn't. Finally our curiosity and desire for the pop overcame our embarrassment enough that we went down to the pick-up.*

Maslow's proposed safety needs include more general elements than those of actual physical and emotional threats. Maslow (1943) states:

> Another indication of the child's need for safety is his preference for some kind of undisrupted routine or rhythm period. He seems to want a

predictable, orderly world. For instance, injustice, unfairness, or inconsistency in the parents seems to make a child feel anxious and unsafe. This
attitude may be not so much because of the injustice *per se* or any particular pains involved, but rather because this treatment threatens to make
the world look unreliable, or unsafe, or unpredictable. . . . Perhaps one
could express this more accurately by saying that the child needs an organized world rather than an unorganized, or unstructured one (p. 377).

Most parents would agree that children profit from a safe and nourishing environment. Children who do not feel this security may grow unconfi-
dent in their own abilities to determine their future. One way parents have
an influence on the security of their children's environment is the physical
surroundings they provide.

## THE PHYSICAL ENVIRONMENT

Obviously, a safe, nourishing physical climate is more complicated than
would appear at first glance. We will now look more specifically at aspects of
the physical environment that have been shown to have a powerful impact on
psychological development.

Physical needs include food, water, air, sleep, and shelter. Without
question, deprivation of these would have serious physiological effects, but
would deprivation also (adversely) influence psychological development?

Failure to provide conditions conducive to sleep has negative psychological effects. The classical sleep-deprivation study has individuals go for
long periods without sleeping. When deprived of sleep, individuals exhibit
behavior similar to drunkenness: incoherency, rambling speech, decreased
coordination, and even hallucinations (Oswald, 1962, pp. 178–191). Yet,
although sleep-deprivation studies are interesting, they have little applicability to the average child. More pertinent are the findings of Renshaw, Miller,
and Marquis (1983) that showed children who experienced a continued
shortened sleep schedule to become peevish and irritable, and to develop
acute conduct problems. These children were put on varying six-hour sleep
schedules, some staying up until midnight and rising at 6 A.M., others going
to bed at 9 P.M. and rising at 3 A.M. The effects described above are in addition
to fatigue, concentration difficulties, and physical illnesses that often occur
when children do not get sufficient sleep.

Chronically malnourished children experience growth retardation not
only physically, but also psychologically. Tests show a decline in mental abilities with prolonged food deprivation (Scrimshaw, 1968, pp. 274–277). Malnutrition directly affects psychological development by impairing neurological growth due to a nonavailability of amino acids for protein concentration
in brain tissue. However, indirect effects are seen in altered motivational
states, and decreased energy and strength. These secondary effects were illustrated in an experiment by Shneour (1974). In this study, conscientious
objectors to military service volunteered to be deprived of food for a number

aged, had periods of depression, and were unable to sustain mental and physical effort.

Interesting data has also come from studies on housing conditions. Improper and adverse housing conditions such as overcrowding, poor lighting, and inadequate space have been shown to have adverse psychological effects, especially on children. Mandelker and Montgomery (1973) found four major psychological consequences of crowded living quarters on children.

1. They challenge the sense of individuality. Because he or she is so rarely alone, the child does not learn to search out the real satisfactions in life.
2. They challenge the child's illusions about other people. Brought into contact with adult weaknesses, young children find it difficult to build up images and identification with strong herolike adults, who can display ideals for human conduct.
3. They challenge the development of mature concepts about sex. Crowding makes the physical aspects of sexual life more apparent and primary, while de-emphasizing the personal relationship aspect of sexual behavior.
4. Because children are so much in contact with other children and adults, it is hard for them to objectively observe life because they are so much a part of it (Mandelker & Montgomery, 1973, pp. 25–26).

Other researchers studied the psychological effects on children of a move from poor-quality housing to good-quality housing (Wilner, Walkley,

Crowded and inadequate living conditions may impede psychological and social development.

Pinkerton, & Tayback, 1962). They concluded that poor housing originally contributed to feelings of despondency, depression, impulsiveness, poor anger control, as well as nervousness. However, there seems to be improvement in these aspects of psychological development when a move to more adequate housing is made. These results coincide with Quinton and Rutter's (1984) finding that half of families having children admitted to a mental health facility lived in rather crowded conditions.

Failure to meet physical needs does not simply result in temporary discomfort, but impedes necessary psychological development. That adults should provide for the safety and physical needs of children seems obvious, but so many don't. Physical neglect may manifest itself indirectly through a neglected child's behavior. Children who appear lazy, tired, and indifferent may, in actuality, be suffering from poor eating habits. It may be hard for many low-income families to provide for their children's physical needs as they would like. Nevertheless, parents experiencing financial difficulties can insure that their children have balanced though often simple meals.

Sometimes, while environmental deficiency may be more imagined than real, it may yet have negative influences. If children are insecure and frightened because of feeling they don't have "good" clothes and food like their friends, it does not matter that parents may have concluded there is no threat to their safety or welfare. In such cases, the child's imagined interpretation is as real as if a physical threat actually existed. The child's fears should be acknowledged and attempts made to alleviate these fears. Parents may need to defer at times to what appear to them to be unreasonable requests.

In some instances, it may be wise for the parent to conceal real environmental difficulties, rather than expose children to potentially threatening realities. In one family, the parents did this in an ingenious way:

*This family had an "emergency bank." Whenever the family ran into financial problems, the parents would tell the children that they could use money from the bank, but they would rather make it without bothering the money in their "emergency bank" if they could. So, all the children did whatever they could to earn money and they never did have to use the "emergency bank" funds. Years later, the children found out that there was no "emergency bank," but because they had all along believed otherwise, they never grew up with a fear that often accompanies poverty and hard times.*

## The Climate and Consequences

The best-made plans go awry and things don't always turn out as planned. How do you explain that some parents very sucessfully provide loving and organized home climates, as described in this and the previous chapters, and yet their children are real problems? You have likely been most surprised to meet a very obnoxious child living with the most gentle, kind, and delightful of parents. There are several explanations why desirable behaviors sometimes fail to appear in a positive growth climate.

1. On closer inspection the climate is really not so positive.
2. Prior to experiencing the present positive climate, the child had lived in a predominantly negative climate.
3. The child is simultaneously heavily influenced by other less desirable climates such as those produced in the neighborhood, in the school, or by relatives living in or out of the home.
4. The child may have handicaps or deficiencies, causing negative reactions that overpower home-climate effects. For example, an extended illness with accompanying mental or physical pain is going to have a definite impact, even though the general climate is very positive.
5. Unfortunately, for many children, traumatic events intrude. These include war, death, and divorce.
6. The time of observation may color assessment of the home climate. Positive effects develop slowly and require years. Patience is required; expecting immediate results is not realistic.
7. The child's misbehavior may not be appropriately handled. In other words, misbehavior may be ignored or even reinforced. Similarly, positive behavior may not be attended to.
8. Finally, recall in Chapter 5 that some children are innately more difficult or "slow to warm up." In other words, some children will naturally be less responsive, adaptable, or well behaved. In these cases, parents must learn to work with the child in a patient manner.

In parenting classes, examples of children are discussed who seemingly come from positive growth climates, but who have been negatively influenced. Consider the following example:

*Sue lives in a home with many necessities of a positive growth climate. Her home is filled with love, trust, knowledge, and belongingness. Basically, Sue is a happy child from a happy family, but there is one problem. Sue gets anything she wants. If she leaves her bed unmade, Mother makes it. When Sue leaves clothes and belongings around the house, Mother picks up after her. When she wants a new dress, bike, or whatever, Father rushes down to buy it. Sue is becoming more and more dissatisfied. Her mother and father say, "There's nothing more we can do. We give her everything she wants. Why is she still unhappy?"*

Sue is obviously being rewarded for negative behavior. If she doesn't make her bed, her mother *rewards* her by making it herself. If she becomes overdemanding, her parents reward her by granting her desires. From this example, it is apparent that a positive home climate is a necessary but not sufficient condition for positive growth. In other words, providing a positive climate, while neglecting to attend properly to a child's subsequent positive or negative behavior, might not produce the expected results. All children behave improperly at times, regardless of a home's positive climate. These negative behaviors must be discouraged, and good behaviors must be rewarded.

The reverse is also true. If consequences fit the behavior, but the home climate is negative, positive personality growth will be hindered. A student from Norway described a negative climate in which parents appropriately rewarded good behavior and punished the bad:

*I'd like to write about a friend of mine. His mother was very strict and punitive when he was bad, but rewarded him for doing good. His father had a violent temper. Both parents were very suspicious people and all members of the family fought a lot. My friend now has his own family, and he is a very rigid and authoritarian parent. He only sees his side of an argument, being very closed-minded. He's very suspicious and jumps to conclusions about people and his own children. He had five children, all of whom are now grown. He has lost every one of them because he refuses to accept that they do not always agree with him.*

We have constructed a model (see Table 6.1) as an example of how home climates and consequences *may* interact to influence a child's personality development. This is only a model. In reality, individuals will show

#### Table 6.1  Personality Outcome from Different Environments

| Climates | Consequences | Personality |
| --- | --- | --- |
| Positive Climate | Reward good and punish bad | "Ideal" |
| Positive Climate | Disorganized consequences | Weak and immature |
| Positive Climate | Reward bad and punish good | Socialized criminals and likable deviants |
| Negative Climate | Reward good and punish bad | Rigid-authoritarian |
| Negative Climate | Disorganized consequences | Alienated and neurotic |
| Negative Climate | Reward bad and punish good | Psychopathic and seriously disturbed |

combinations of the six personalities presented. Formal case studies can be used to document some of the less-often-found combinations of climate and consequences such as the last category—a negative climate with bad behavior rewarded and good behavior punished. One such example concerns an eleven-year-old boy named Oswald, who was taken to a clinic for frequent, unprovoked abusive behavior against friends and siblings. That Oswald did receive rewards for aggressive behavior is seen in the following quote from the book *Case Studies in Deviant Behavior* (Leon, 1974):

> Mrs. Williams continued to discipline the children primarily by shouting at them. She stated that she constantly had to yell at the children, and that they tended to ignore her. She felt that the children were in control of her emotions, because they could get her very anxious or very angry in a short moment's time, depending on what they were doing. Mrs. Williams reported that lately she had to resort to physical punishment more often to get the children to mind her. . . .
>
> In Oswald's home, the parents were most ineffectual in their attempts to prevent fighting, so that each child's place in the pecking order was determined by whom he or she could beat up. The only way that Oswald could stop his brothers and sisters from teasing him or taking things that belonged to him was to fight with them. Aggressive behavior was therefore an extremely dominant response in his behavior repertoire, in part because persons in the environment failed to reward alternate behaviors.
>
> In terms of family role models, all of the children observed their father engaging in a great deal of physical punishment (pp. 59, 71).

Climates and consequences have been introduced and shown to be important. By combining the two principles, parents can be maximally effective. This goal is described in Table 6.2, and calls for accepting some undesirable behaviors that inevitably occur in an imperfect world. Parents begin by establishing the climate and then responding appropriately to the child's behavior. If a positive growth climate is established, the parent may not need to deliberately and consciously always reward good behavior or punish bad. Instead, natural contingencies in life, both within and outside the home, will often be sufficient to maintain adequate consequences for strengthening desirable behavior. However, if the ratio of undesirable to desirable is not satisfactory, parents must act. Four basic modes or options are possible.

## WHEN UNDESIRABLE BEHAVIOR CONTINUES

It is not the nature of people to be all good or all bad, and this is especially true of children and their evolving personalities. Four logical options are available to the parent when too much undesirable behavior exists.

1. The parent can accept a different ratio of good and bad behavior. Sometimes it is best to say: "I'll just have to accept my child that way." Some children are going

## Table 6.2 A Realistic Goal for Parents

| Climate | Behavior | Consequences |
| --- | --- | --- |
| Increase the positive growth climate<br>  Love<br>  Organization | | Following desirable behavior, allow:<br>  Material rewards<br>  Social recognition<br>  Positive activities<br>  Attention and approval<br>  Affection* |
| Decrease the negative climate<br><br>  Anger<br>  Hate<br>  Suspicion | Accept mixture of desirable and undesirable behavior | Following undesirable behavior, see that there is NOT an abundance of:<br>  Material rewards<br>  Social recognition<br>  Positive activities<br>  Attention and approval<br>  Affection |

*"LOVE" is not to be a consequence, although acceptance of behaviors may be given. It is the basic element of the positive growth climate and should never be removed. Love is a name for a way of life and relating. Consequences are momentary.

to develop slowly or differently, and no amount of nagging, scolding, punishment, or consequence manipulation will alter the child's progress to match a parent's expectations.

2. Improve the home's positive climate. Parents considering this option often ask, "Is there something else that I can do?" "Is my child not getting something needed at home?"

3. If the home climate seems positive and any higher ratio of undesirable actions cannot be accepted, then the third option is to wait. Sometimes a parent knows that all that can be done has been attempted. Without letting up, this parent may simply have to wait it out. Personal experiences have shown to these authors the value of having patience. Sometimes as adults we don't remember that youth is a difficult period of time. Changes will continually occur, although not necessarily according to a schedule based on parental desire. Often, it is necessary for a child to work out his or her own problems.

4. There comes a time when something must be done. This is the last option, and the word to describe the required action is "intervention." Subsequent chapters of this book describe how to intervene. In these chapters, the most basic and documented ways to intervene and facilitate behavior changes are discussed.

Part III has stressed what we feel to be two of the most important aspects of successful and enjoyable child rearing: a positive and organized home environment. When studying these two aspects it appears that, in general, child rearing is at its best when the home climate is one of openness, acceptance, warmth, structure, and guidance. Notice that it should ideally be neither too permissive nor too controlling. Recall that in Chapter 2's discussion on the warmth-vs.-hostility and restrictiveness-vs.-permissiveness parent dimensions, it was similarly concluded that desirable child behaviors were most likely to occur if parents were warm and neither too restrictive nor permissive. Indeed, our discussion of the home climate theory is consonant with these ideas.

# SELF-CHECK

1. Though similar to demands, _____ are more conducive to the development of freedom and trust.
   a. expectations
   b. stringent rules
   c. specific rules
   d. all of the above
2. One psychologist, when reviewing studies on moral development of children, concluded that one of the most effective ways to engender moral maturity is to
   a. make few demands; rely on expectations.
   b. enforce authoritative rules.
   c. assign work and responsibility.
   d. do none of the above.
3. In our modern, technologically advanced culture
   a. it is impossible to provide proper work experiences for children.
   b. children can be taught to appreciate hard work.
   c. play is an activity that is equally important to a child's psychological and social development.
   d. b and c above are both true.
4. In a popular book on child psychology, Vander Zanden (1981) states all but which one of the following about play?
   a. It is a vehicle for cognitive stimulation.
   b. Although beneficial, it does not help a child build his or her own sense of identity.
   c. It provides opportunities for rehearsing adult roles.
   d. It allows for both reality and fantasy.
5. Having adequate knowledge and truth about oneself and the world around us is a basis for
   a. visual–motor coordination.
   b. personal confidence.
   c. honesty.
   d. physical capacity.
6. Improper and adverse housing conditions have been shown to
   a. have no adverse psychological effects on children.
   b. have adverse psychological effects on children.
   c. affect only children of racial minorities.
   d. affect those who let them affect them.
7. Leo Tolstoy, Gordon Allport, and Victor Frankl all expounded on the importance of knowing or experiencing _____ in one's life.
   a. aggression
   b. nourishment
   c. friendship
   d. meaning

8. Abraham Maslow stated the following about needs:
   a. People begin their lives by satisfying basic needs and then moving to higher needs.
   b. Before a person can meet higher needs, lower needs must have been adequately satisfied.
   c. An indication of a child's need for safety is a preference for orderliness.
   d. All of the above are true.
9. Which of the following has been shown to affect psychological and/or physiological functioning?
   a. Crowded living conditions
   b. Sleep deprivation
   c. Malnutrition
   d. b and c are both true.
   e. All of the above are true.
10. _____ in a home has been called different names: rules, expectations, limits, standards, encouragement, guidelines, and laws.
   a. Meaning
   b. Predictability
   c. Parenting
   d. Structure

KEY: 1–a; 2–c; 3–d; 4–b; 5–b; 6–b; 7–d; 8–d; 9–e; 10–d

# PART
## ◦ IV ▫
# Parental Influence

Many concerned parents try their best to provide homes of warmth, acceptance, organization, and structure. Yet, situations still arise when children's behaviors are inappropriate and very trying. The situation of a child not wanting to go to bed and becoming very obnoxious when bedtime arrives is all too familiar to most of us.

Similar examples could be given by many parents. Becoming occasionally frustrated with children, and wondering what form of discipline or influence would be most effective, is an inevitable part of the parenting role. Part IV is a collection of various ways parents can influence their children's behavior.

Chapters 7 and 8 elaborate further on behavior modification theory as introduced in Chapter 3. These chapters provide instructions and examples of how to strengthen or weaken certain specified behaviors using behavior modification principles. Recall that in Chapter 1, behavioral theory was pointed out as a major influence in producing a restrictive parenting trend. Behavior modification principles are based upon strict control of rewards and punishments—for this reason the term *high-power techniques* is used, signifying a greater amount of parental control in relation to orientations presented in Chapters 9 and 10.

Chapter 9, "Moderate-Power Techniques to Produce or Lessen Behavior," is less focused on strict parental control, but nevertheless emphasizes proper usage of natural, logical consequences of behavior and rational approaches to teaching children the consequences of their actions. Chapter 10, "Low-Power Techniques to Produce or Lessen Behavior," suggests that very little parental power is necessary to influence children's behavior. Rather, children can be taught through dialectical exchanges to understand other people's emotions and how their own behaviors influence other people's thoughts and feelings.

The ideas in Chapters 7 through 10 are presented as guides. The actual techniques parents use will vary according to their child's age, maturity, and behavior problems. No one orientation is encompassing enough to effectively deal with all types of problems. The parent's task is to ingeniously and creatively apply them.

Chapter 11 then discusses additional ways parents may influence the development of appropriate behaviors—through example.

# CHAPTER 7

# HIGH-POWER TECHNIQUES TO PRODUCE AND DEVELOP BEHAVIOR

Most psychologists agree that the environment can strengthen existing actions or produce new behavior. Behaviors that the environment reinforces will tend to recur. As mentioned in Chapter 3, the behavioral theorist relies heavily on environmental contingencies to explain the origin and maintenance of behavior. This chapter focuses on behavior modification principles that produce and sustain adaptive behavior in children.

## Modifying Behavior through Rewards

One of the most historic descriptions of behavior modification is B. F. Skinner's book *Science and Human Behavior* (Skinner, 1953). According to this approach, human behavior can best be understood by analyzing the environment, while simultaneously avoiding speculation about psychological causes. Beliefs about drives, needs, mind, will, abilities, desires, motives, ids, egos, and superegos are superfluous; the focus is more appropriately placed on *external events* that can be controlled by parents.

Behavior modification can be used with a wide range of problems. One popular personal adjustment book enumerates a surprisingly large list of problems that have been successfully treated with this approach (Watson & Tharp, 1972). The list includes alcoholism, cheating, drug abuse, unethical behaviors, impulsivity, rational and irrational fears, self-abusive behaviors such as hair pulling and scratching, lack of persistence in obtaining goals, knuckle cracking, neurotic and psychotic symptoms, overeating, aggressiveness, laziness, low self-esteem, numerous sexual problems, smoking, and poor study habits. It would appear that if behavior modification isn't the answer to the world's problems, it at least deals with many of them.

Many realize that causes of behavior problems include broken homes, poverty, poor housing conditions, physical and mental disabilities, norms derived from deviant groups, and drugs. However, even an idealist knows all these causes cannot be eliminated in time to benefit children today. These ills were with us yesterday, continue with us today, and will be present or replaced by similar problems in the future. So, rather than trying to delineate and eradicate underlying psychological and sociological causes behind inappropriate behaviors or the absence of appropriate ones, the behaviors themselves should be dealt with directly.

Simply put, behavior modification creates or strengthens desirable behavior by giving the child rewards. Positive techniques are recommended and punishment is often avoided because of numerous practical problems. (A discussion on punishment will be presented in Chapter 8.)

# Rewards—Reinforcements

Behavior modification theory is a reward–punishment model, although emphasis is usually on rewards. Behaviors followed by a reward are strengthened. For example, if a child is courteous with a group of friends but not at home, courtesy has probably been rewarded with friends, but not at home. However, environmental consequences can do more than just strengthen or weaken existing behavior. Positive consequences can also create new responses. For example, when a child practices a skill, he or she will occasionally make responses that depart from usual performance. If these departures are followed by positive consequences, these new responses are strengthened and eventually become habitual.

Many individuals use the terms *reward* and *reinforcement* interchangeably, but there are important differences between the two terms. Sometimes a negative event increases behavior even when the event is considered undesirable. For example, Alfred, age eight, is told by his mother, "I'm going to leave for a while. When I come back, I don't want you to have played in the kitchen or else you'll get a spanking." The moment his mother closes the door, Alfred goes straight to the kitchen and gets everything out. When she returns, the kitchen is a mess, and Alfred gets spanked. The same thing happens on the second and third day. What's happening? If the theory is true, Alfred ought to stop messing up the kitchen because he's not getting any reward; in fact, he's being punished! However, in this case, the so-called punishment is actually *reinforcing* the unwanted behavior. This may be the only time poor Alfred receives any attention.

Accordingly, all events that strengthen subsequent behaviors are called reinforcers, whether they appear rewarding or not. A *reinforcer* is any event following a response that increases the probability that that type of response will be repeated, regardless of whether it appears rewarding or not. We will refer to any events strengthening subsequent behaviors as reinforcing.

## Steps in Using Behavior Modification

Behavior modification is easily applied once the manipulator of environmental reinforcers, in this case the parent, understands the basic steps involved. Although in this chapter increasing and developing desirable behaviors is the primary focus, examples of decreasing undesirable behaviors will be given occasionally, as the principles are similar. In addition, reinforcing desirable behaviors and punishing undesirable behaviors often occur simultaneously.

### SPECIFY THE DESIRED BEHAVIOR

First, the parent *specifies the behavior* he or she wants to increase. Concern is not with labeling the behavior (e.g., obedience, cooperation, etc.) but rather with describing what the child is doing. Describe the behavior in as much detail as possible. If it is social interaction, then define exactly what the child does during an episode. Does she approach others, talk to them, face them? Must she be within so many feet of someone else before she is considered to be interacting? The time, frequency, and dates of the behavior may all be relevant. The more precisely the behavior is described, the more easily it can be measured.

## MEASURE THE BEHAVIOR

Measurement is the second step. Measuring the behavior is usually accomplished by establishing a *baseline,* the frequency of a response prior to treatment administration. In other words, it is important to identify how often a behavior occurs, so that post-treatment changes can be validly assessed. Again, if the target behavior is a child's prosocial behavior, the date of the first observation is put on a graph, and the number of times the child interacts positively is recorded. Psychologists usually continue the baseline for one week to ensure that the baseline period is stable. Each observation period correlates with the behavior frequency. For example: "day 2," 1 time; "day 3," 2 times; "day 4," 1 time; "day 5," 2 times (see Figure 7.1). For the psychologist, no treatment is begun until the baseline is established. Parents

Figure 7.1   Behavior Frequency Graph

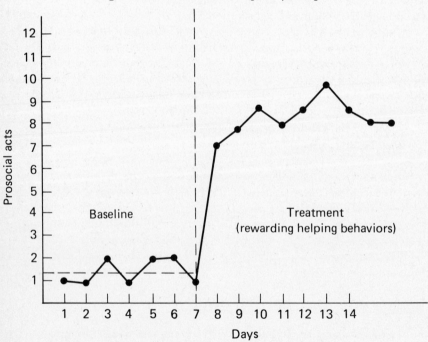

may skip this step, although it is helpful in determining whether progress has occurred.

Ironically, having the child monitor, or count, the specified behavior can produce some change by itself. If a child, for example, tabulates herself whenever she is nice to a sibling, she may show an increase in prosocial behavior before reinforcements are even begun. Inappropriate behavior can be decreased in the same manner. Christie, Hiss, and Lozanoff (1984) decreased a child's inattentiveness in the classroom by having him record his own misbehavior.

## CATALOG THE REINFORCERS

While a baseline is being established, a list of reinforcers for the person being studied should be cataloged. As mentioned earlier, the frequency of a behavior is controlled by reinforcers. Although diverse, reinforcers can be roughly divided into three major categories: (1) physical, (2) social–emotional, and (3) activity (see Table 7.1). A child performs a behavior so that he or she can obtain a reinforcer. It may be *physical,* like food; or, it may be *social,* such as verbal praise or affection. These are probably the most common types of reinforcers. Receiving more turns at bat or going to recess earlier are examples of reinforcing *activities.*

A psychologist named Premack (1965) illustrated the importance of activity as a reinforcer. He found that a specified behavior occurred more frequently if it was followed by an opportunity to engage in a behavior that was desirable to the person. Money, candy, or affection was not necessary as a reinforcer. For example, a class was requested to be quiet. After a desired interval of silence, the nursery-school teacher said, "Now, everybody run and scream!" The children ran and screamed. After many such experiences, when asked to be quiet the children complied. Teachers use this Premack principle when they say, "After you do your arithmetic, you can go to recess." The child works hard to complete a disliked classroom assignment for the reinforcement of going to recess—something more desirable.

### Table 7.1  Possible Reinforcers

| Physical | Social–Emotional | Activity |
|---|---|---|
| Candy | Praise | Movie |
| Gum | Hug | Stay up late |
| Marbles | Kiss | Free time |
| Food | Smile | Play outside |
| Money | | Read a story |
| Puzzle | | |
| Cookies | | |
| Soft drink | | |
| Toys | | |

Before commencing a behavior modification program with children, a listing of reinforcers is desirable. Parents can establish just what reinforcers will work for a particular child and then control those reinforcers. Control over obtaining money or candy will insure that the child receives these *only* when producing the desired behavior. It may also be important to eliminate other sources of reinforcement that would increase competing behaviors.

## OBTAIN AND DEVELOP REINFORCERS

Still another important consideration is the supply of reinforcers. If parents determine that money is a good reinforcer, it will not be helpful if money is quite limited. A large supply of the reinforcer should be available. One way to avoid a concern about reinforcer supply is to implement social and emotional reinforcers. These reinforcers are more convenient and economical. They include kisses and hugs, a pat on the back, and praise such as "I'm proud of you," or "You did a good job." If a child will work for a simple verbal compliment then wages are low. Compliments are both efficient and cheap.

However, before social reinforcers can become effective, the parent must be liked, respected, or held in high esteem by the child. Parents normally have an advantage here because young children especially look up to them, if only from their position of dependence. Therefore, parents can use rewards of praise and affection freely. Another positive aspect of social and emotional reinforcers is that, unlike M&Ms and other physical reinforcers, a child is rarely saturated or "full" of praise and affection. Rarely does a child receive too much praise, affection, or companionship. Therefore, parents have access to an almost inexhaustible supply of rewards or reinforcements.

Unfortunately, parents do not often cultivate or employ these kinds of reinforcers. Even when they have the power to educationally control reinforcers such as attention and affection, they freely and indiscriminately give them away or fail to use them when appropriate. In some families, when a child brings home a school project no one says, "I'm proud of you." So, the child neglects to take home projects in the future, because it does not produce a desired reinforcer. Frequently, parents object by saying such a program is bribery. "I don't want to give my child an M&M each time I ask him to empty the garbage." On the other hand, these same parents often say, "You can get your allowance by doing your share of the work!"

## USE THE REINFORCER

Once the behavior is *specified* and *measured,* and the *reinforcers are cataloged* and *controlled,* the desired behavior can then be reinforced. When an undesirable behavior occurs, ignore it. Some have advocated rewarding desired responses and punishing undesired ones. However, when punishment is introduced, a new set of problems, such as frustration or resentment, must be anticipated. In many cases, it is just as effective to reinforce the correct and ignore the incorrect behavior. Only when inappropriate behaviors are potentially dangerous and destructive or severely disrupting, need punishment be a regular part of the treatment program.

Reinforcement programs have also been shown to be effective in whole groups of individuals. In fact, having group reinforcement contingent on everybody's efforts adds a component of peer observation, which may increase the program's effectiveness. For example, excessive lunchroom noise was decreased at an inpatient facility for emotionally disturbed and learning disabled children (Michelson, DiLorenzo, & Calpin, 1981). If the decibel level decreased to a previously specified level, everyone received ice cream.

## EVALUATE THE PROGRAM

Many times when learning behavior modification techniques the program may not progress as planned. This is not to suggest that behavior modification does not work, but merely that something has not been properly carried out. Perhaps what was thought to be initially reinforcing turned out not to be. Or, even if it was reinforcing, perhaps the reinforcement value was not strong enough to effect a change.

Other reasons for failure are also possible. Some parents fail to reinforce the desired behavior immediately, and the child fails to associate the desired behavior with the reinforcement. Sometimes the desired behavior may not be reinforced consistently during the initial stages, and the child feels that the probability of being reinforced for his or her behavior is not great enough. These are just a few of the many possible snags when learning to use behavior modification principles in child rearing.

## Developing and Maintaining New Behaviors

Difficulty arises when attempting to increase a child's behavior repertoire. How can a parent reward a child for a behavior that the child cannot or does not perform? In this situation a procedure called *shaping* is used. Shaping occurs when the parent first reinforces only a small part of the total desired response. As this small part is mastered, more of the complete response must next be made by the child before a reinforcer is given. The child is expected to make "successive approximations" of the final response and to gradually master more and more of the desired result. For example, when teaching a very young child to learn to say "water," a parent might first reinforce a partial response. The child is rewarded when he or she says "wah." Later the conscientious mother expects more, so she responds only when the child says "wah-wah." As the child progresses she will not give any water until he says "whata." Each time, the child must progress further toward a perfect response, making a successive approximation each time, while the parent is careful not to expect more than the child can produce. This example, however, does not suggest that small children of any age can be taught various sounds and words through a simple shaping procedure. Speech development is determined, in part, by neurological and biological development and influences.

In summary, the sequence of events so far discussed is:

1. Specify the behavior.
2. Measure the behavior.
3. Make a list of the reinforcers.
4. Obtain and develop reinforcers.
5. Reward the desired behavior, ignoring the undesired behavior, and, if necessary, shape the correct response.
6. Evaluate the results.

## REDUCE REINFORCERS

To promote rapid and efficient learning, a response should be reinforced each time it occurs. Once a response is brought to a high level of occurence, however, the frequency of reinforcement can be reduced. It is not necessary to reward every response. Responses can be maintained on a surprisingly intermittent reinforcement schedule, often only one reward for every 6 to 10 acts.

It has been thoroughly demonstrated that children who don't receive a reward each time a response is emitted retain the behavior longer than those who are reinforced after every response. Once a response is learned, children do not need to be reinforced each time they do something correctly. In fact, natural life situations rarely show reinforcement each time children make correct responses.

## MOVE TO A NATURAL ENVIRONMENT

An extension of the above discussion leads to the eighth step. As soon as possible, the child should be moved from an artificial laboratory environment (if such was the case) and into a natural environment, removing all contrived reinforcers. For example, suppose a behavior modification program has been started at a comprehensive clinic, and an encopretic child (a child who defecates in his or her pants) is given a poker chip each time he reports an accident-free day during the past week. A previously agreed upon number of chips can be traded for a fishing trip with the therapist.

However, it is obvious that children will need to eventually acclimate themselves to reinforcement by individuals other than the therapist, and to reinforcers other than poker chips. The therapist could aid the parents in effectively using physical, social, and emotional reinforcers in a more "natural" setting. If children have been taught correctly, there should be enough natural reinforcements in the environment to keep them accident-free. For example, friends and relatives can verbally praise children for their progress.

When a child is placed in a natural environment, a check on training effectiveness should be made by establishing a new baseline and comparing it with the baseline plotted before the program. Of course, moving to a natural environment is simplified if the training program begins in a somewhat natural setting.

## CONTROLLING A DISRUPTIVE CHILD

Frank was a likable second-grade child with a record of disruptive behavior in the classroom. He manifested antisocial activities around his teacher and extreme aggressiveness on the playground. The teacher would constantly catch him out of his seat, as he talked to other children. He would not respond to any form of discipline. In fact, when disciplined for doing something wrong, he would then be sure to do the same thing again. Frank was intelligent: He had an IQ of 106, and at the beginning of the school year his academic achievements were adequate.

The school psychologist found Frank's mother to be courteous and warm, but unable to discipline her son. His father was serving in the Air Force away from home. Frank was placed in an experimental program at his school, and the psychologist suggested that three things might be done.

1. Provide explicit rules (e.g., no object will be thrown in class; you may not leave your seat without permission, etc.).
2. Ignore inappropriate behavior.
3. Provide praise for desired behavior.

While physical restraint may be necessary at times to control disruptive behavior, in general, ignoring inappropriate behavior and praising desired behavior can by itself be very influential.

After Frank had been observed and his behavior recorded for one week, the teacher applied the first two elements: (1) a statement to the child describing desired behavior and (2) the ignoring of misbehavior. Praise for following the rules was given during the next week while inappropriate behavior continued to be ignored. Not surprisingly, during the next week the percent of time intervals in which misbehavior occured decreased to less than 5 percent as compared with previous highs of 70 to 80 percent. In this case, praise appears to have been the important ingredient (Madsen, Becker, & Thomas, 1968, p. 143). As can be expected, it would not be too difficult for Frank's mother to continue a similar program at home.

Parents often take good behavior for granted and pay attention only when a child misbehaves. Praise and attention are needed when the child is doing what is desired. Shape the desired behavior through successive approximations by giving praise and attention. Start "small" and work toward greater goals. When the child begins to behave appropriately, give adequate praise such as "You're doing a fine job."

## CONTROLLING CLASSROOM NOISE

Consider the simplicity of the next experiment to bring classroom noise under control by reinforcing the group (Schmidt & Ulrich, 1969). While noise may seem to be a socially insignificant misbehavior to some people, there is probably no single factor more discouraging to a teacher. In this experiment, a fourth-grade classroom consisting of 14 boys and 15 girls was

Bringing a noisy classroom under control is not as difficult once behavior modification techniques are consistently and correctly applied.

told that a timer would be set for 10 minutes. If no disturbing noise occurred during the 10-minute interval, a buzzer would sound and the class would receive a reward of two extra minutes during their gym period. Also included was a two-minute break for the children to do whatever they wanted to do before another 10-minute period was set on the timer. Whenever the noise in the class reached 42 decibels, a whistle would be blown and the timer reset to 10 minutes.

This procedure resulted in a rapid decibel decrease. It was found that the noise level which initially exceeded 50 decibels could be brought to a level almost equal to that of an empty classroom. In a further elaboration of this experiment, individual children who created noise in excess of 42 decibels by yelling and slamming doors were required to write their name on a blackboard. They then lost five minutes of their gym time. To control getting-out-of-seat behavior, a timer would randomly ring a bell, and any students out of their seat when the bell rang were also required to write their names on the board. Children with names on the blackboard had to forfeit five minutes of enjoyable gym time. The results were similarly striking. Out-of-seat behavior dropped from a record of between 150 and 250 instances during a 45-minute period to a level approaching 10 or 15. It was also found that the number of teacher-initiated reprimands could be reduced by using similar procedures.

## Behavior Modification Techniques: Practical Suggestions

1. Identify the problem in specific behavioral terms: exactly what behavior is to be reinforced or changed, and how it can be counted.
2. Initially, immediately following the desired response, reinforce all such behaviors.
3. Avoid frustration and punishments.
4. Use social and emotional reinforcers found in the natural world instead of artificial or contrived ones. Or, at least pair social and emotional with artificial reinforcers, so that the contrived ones can later be phased out.
5. Use patience in administering reinforcements. Frequently, a child will not perform as well as he or she did the previous day. This necessitates going back and *finding* a level of performance that does not frustrate the child. When words and other aids are not used, learning will probably be slow and gradual, and improvement will occur in very small steps.
6. Use short training sessions rather than long, extended periods of time. Ironically, B. F. Skinner wrote an article reviewing what psychologists could learn from animal trainers. Dog trainers find that 10 or 15 minutes of learning or training is long enough, and the same time period seems best for children (Skinner, 1951).
7. If possible, structure the training in natural settings rather than

artificial environments such as laboratories, churches, etc. If the parent is concerned with aggression on the playground, then training should be attempted on the playground. For speech training, the child should be trained in a situation where he can talk with others in a natural context. If individuals are trained in social assertiveness, then they should be able to learn in actual social settings, even if contrived. They will not perform at the same level if all training occurs in the therapist's office.

The process of acquiring complex behaviors such as sharing, kindness, and altruism is a slow process begun by reinforcing only rudimentary elements of the final response. One gradually expects more complete behaviors at older ages.

## Reasoning and Language

The reader may notice that little has been said about thought, reason, language, or logic, although they are associated with what is ordinarily considered behavior. What role do they have? Contemporary behavioral theory is beginning to put an emphasis on cognitions, realizing that internal and external language and reason are potential mediators of environmental stimulus–response chains.

Verbal statements may serve as cues or discriminative stimuli. A *discriminative stimulus* is an event that signals when a response is now appropriate. For example, O'Leary (1968) taught first-grade boys to press a telegraph key. Whenever the key was pressed the boys were to obtain a marble; but the key was to be pressed only when a signal was present. Half of the boys were told they were to state the rule aloud—the key is to be pressed only when the signal is present. The other half did not state the rule aloud. The boys who stated the rule aloud were more successful in following that condition repetitively. Similar experiments document that language does play an influencing role in producing behavior.

In an experiment by Hartig and Kanfer (1973) several types of self-instruction were compared. The experimenters wanted to see how successfully children could refrain from playing with forbidden but attractive toys when left alone in a tempting situation. The children were four through seven years of age, attending a private school in Cincinnati. After being brought into a room, the children were told that toys on a table behind them were not to be looked at. The experimenter then stated that she had forgotten her paper and pencil and that she would have to return to the classroom to get them. She told the children not to turn around and look at the toys until she returned, because looking at the toys would spoil the surprise. Different groups of children were then told to repeat the following sentences aloud during the experimenter's absence.

*Group 1 (verbalization positive):* "I must not turn around and look at the toy. If I do not look at the toy, I will be a good boy (girl)."

*Group 2 (verbalization negative):* "I must not turn around and look at the toy. If I look at the toy, I will be a bad boy (girl)."

*Group 3 (verbalization instruction):* "I must not turn around and look at the toy."

*Group 4 (verbalization control):* "Hickory Dickory dock, the mouse went up the clock."

*Group 5 (no verbalization control):* The child was not given any instructions to verbalize aloud.

It was found that the first three groups did better resisting a peek at the toys than the last two groups (Hartig & Kanfer, 1973).

## The Withdrawn Child: A Detailed Example

Paul Robinson (1981), an experimental psychologist, reports a carefully managed and successful program to treat a withdrawn child. The following illustrates many of the principles presented in this chapter.

A school principal expressed concern about a child, who for several years seemed to be withdrawing socially from her classmates. He had referred her to the school psychologist three years ago because of poor interpersonal and reading skills, but she was not making progress. Dr. Robinson suggested some behavior modification therapy, and the principal stated he did not believe such approaches were effective, but added, "Although I don't believe it would work, I would certainly be willing to give it a try if I could find someone to do it." Robinson agreed to do it, but stipulated one condition: "You must agree to let me carry out the investigation in such a manner that we may determine what it was that changed her behavior; assuming that it changes, of course." Robinson's purpose was twofold: to help the girl and to show that behavior modification is an effective therapeutic approach.

Mary was a 15-year-old girl from a middle-class family, enrolled in a special education class, homogeneous in chronological age (14–16) and mental age (80–85). Her teacher's report said, "Mary does not mix with any of her peers, just reads and does her work alone. . . . She has good art skills and shows a definite respect and friendliness to her art teacher. . . ." Robinson decided to work with Mary 30 minutes every day during art period. First, a baseline was taken. Every 30 seconds he marked on a data sheet whether she was socializing (talking to or with other students, or even looking at them) or not socializing (working alone). These data were then converted into percentage of time spent socializing and recorded on a chart.

After seven days a baseline was obtained, and Treatment B was begun. Seeing that Mary enjoyed interaction with her art teacher, it was decided that a reward for socializing with classmates would be attention from him. Each time Mary socialized with classmates, the teacher would go over to Mary, smile, verbally interact with her for 15 seconds, and then move away. This was done for the next two weeks and the percentage of socializing was again recorded.

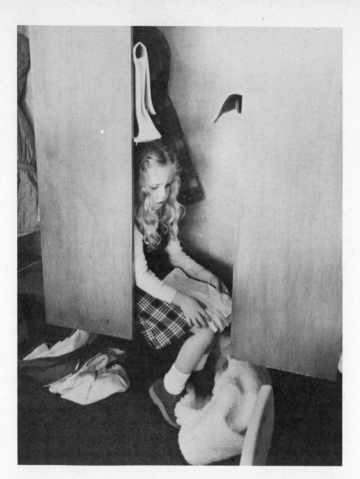

If a withdrawn child's social behaviors are reinforced, the tendency to seek isolation should diminish.

At the end of the second week of reinforcing Mary for socializing, she was spending 95 percent of her time socializing with classmates. Robinson concluded, after speaking with Mary's parents who told him that she was not withdrawn at home, that Mary's asociability was not a deeply ingrained personality problem, but was being specifically controlled by something at the school. Seeing that Mary was getting attention from teachers when she was antisocial, he hypothesized that the extra attention from teachers was actually producing her problem.

Robinson then told the principal that teacher attention was the determining factor and, by removing the reward of attention for socializing, she would return to prior antisocial ways. The principal was astonished that Robinson should even suggest such a thing, but Robinson reminded him of his promise and told him not to worry.

For the next three sessions Mary was no longer given teacher attention when mingling with her peers. Rather, she was attended to when exhibiting antisocial behavior, and social behavior dropped. Later, the reward for social interaction was reinstated and the behavior climbed again.

## Summary

Identifying and controlling environmental or contrived reinforcers is one of the most effective ways parents can provoke and develop desired behaviors in their children. In fact, this component of behavior modification is perhaps implemented in some fashion by most parents, whether they realize it or not. Yet, when it is not effective, a few of the steps identified in this chapter have probably been left out or improperly used. It would benefit most parents to review these eight simple steps.

First, specify in observable, measurable terms exactly what behavior is desired. Second, measure the frequency of that behavior to establish a baseline prior to implementing the treatment. Third, identify those rewards that are reinforcing. If physical or contrived rewards are decided upon, social and emotional reinforcers could be simultaneously paired to facilitate later generalization and stability of the behavior. Fourth, be sure that the chosen reinforcers are adequate in value to produce the desired behavior, and that enough reinforcers are available. Fifth, reinforce the desired behavior each time it occurs. Sixth, evaluate the program's effectiveness to determine if the desired results are being obtained. If not, reconsider the value and use of the chosen reinforcers.

After the desired behavior has been produced, phase out reinforcers gradually, while reinforcing the behavior at infrequent ratios. At the same time, a move to a more natural environment can be made, if necessary, to ensure generalizability of behavior change.

A parent's imagination is the limit when devising behavior modification programs, as long as the above steps are followed. Rosen and Rosen (1983), for example, eliminated stealing in a seven-year-old schoolboy by marking all his personal items with green circles. Every fifteen minutes his desk was checked; he received points if marked items appeared in his possession and fines if unmarked items were present.

# S E L F - C H E C K

1. Which of the following is true of behavior modification theory?
   a. Behavior modification creates or strengthens desirable behavior by giving the child a reward.
   b. Human behavior can best be understood by analyzing the environment.
   c. Speculation about psychological causes of behavior should be avoided.
   d. a and b are both true.
   e. a, b, and c are all true.
2. All events that strengthen a subsequent behavior are called
   a. rewards.
   b. reinforcers.

c. negative punishers.

d. response contingencies.

3. Behavior modification is easily applied once the parent understands the basic steps involved. Consider the following steps and then answer the question that follows.

1. Measure the behavior.
2. Obtain and develop reinforcers.
3. Specify the behavior that is to be changed.
4. Catalog the reinforcers.
5. Use the reinforcers.

In which order should these steps be carried out?

a. 1, 2, 3, 4, 5
b. 3, 1, 4, 2, 5
c. 3, 1, 2, 4, 5
d. 1, 3, 4, 2, 5

4. Measuring behavior is usually accomplished by establishing a baseline. What is a baseline?

a. The frequency of a response for about a week prior to treatment administration
b. A line graph connecting pre- and post-treatment response averages
c. The difference between Day 1 and Day 2 response frequency
d. An average of a response one day prior to treatment

5. How can a parent reward a child for a behavior that the child cannot or does not perform?

a. Punish all undesirable behaviors.
b. Be patient until the child performs the behavior desired and then reinforce immediately.
c. Perform a "shaping" process.
d. Tell the child exactly what you want done and ignore incompatible responses.

6. After a behavior has been learned by using the steps in Question 3 it is important that

a. the behavior not be reinforced further once it is learned.
b. the child be moved to a natural environment, removing all contrived reinforcers.
c. the frequency of reinforcers be reduced.
d. b and c above are both important.

7. Several practical suggestions have evolved from the use of behavior modification programs. Which of the following is not a practical suggestion?

a. Identify the problem in specific behavioral terms.
b. Avoid frustration and punishment.
c. Use social and emotional reinforcers found in the natural world.
d. Use long, thorough training sessions.
e. All of the above are practical.

8. Contemporary behavioral theory is beginning to put an emphasis on _____ and their role in learning.

a. cognitions
b. infantile psychosexual stages
c. unresolved Oedipal complexes
d. unconscious thought processes

9. What would probably be the most effective method of treating a young girl who had withdrawn socially from her classmates?
   a. Punish antisocial behaviors.
   b. Reward antisocial behaviors.
   c. Use a process of shaping—reward responses that are compatible with socializing behaviors.
   d. All of the above are equally effective.
10. Behavior modification can be used with a wide range of problems. Which of the following would you expect to not be effectively treated using behavior modification principles?
   a. Rational and irrational fears
   b. Neurotic and psychotic symptoms
   c. Numerous sexual problems
   d. Smoking
   e. All of the above could be effectively treated using behavior modification.

KEY: 1–e; 2–b; 3–b; 4–a; 5–c; 6–d; 7–d; 8–a; 9–c; 10–e

# CHAPTER 8

# HIGH-POWER TECHNIQUES TO LESSEN BEHAVIOR

Chapter 7 focused primarily on using behavior modification principles to increase desirable behaviors. However, perhaps one of a parent's greatest concerns is how to control a child's inappropriate behavior. How can I discipline without turning my child away from me? Is physical punishment detrimental? Is it possible to eliminate unwanted behavior by nonpunitive methods? Issues such as these will be discussed in this chapter.

A variety of commonly used techniques to change behavior will be described. Physical punishment, withdrawal of privileges, and verbal punishment will first be discussed. Special considerations when using these forms of punishment are enumerated. We will then consider the use of guilt, fear, and shame as a control—how these emotional feelings felt by others or fostered from within can influence a child's behavior. However, the dangers of this style of discipline will also be discussed to help parents realize how excessive guilt, fear, or shame can endanger a child's self-concept and autonomous functioning.

In many cases, special techniques for eliminating behavior can be used instead of punishment. Borrowing from behavior modification, these techniques are often more appropriate for effective discipline and preservation of positive family relationships.

## Punishment

Punishment comes so naturally. "I'll teach her," or "He won't get away with that," are common expressions preceding punishment. It is so simple to inflict pain on others if they are not doing what you want. Historically, we see this in the paddle, the whip, and even torture instruments, which were devised to stop others from deviating. Compassionate, tender-minded mothers find themselves hitting the hands or seats of their toddlers. Some parents who deplore physical punishment find themselves using social, emotional, or psychological punishment. The origin of this tendency to punish one another is elusive, but the reason for punishment's persistence is simple. When we punish, something happens! Punishment does have an immediate effect. Even if it doesn't permanently stop undesirable behavior, it disrupts the pattern. Some psychologists maintain that punishment simply suppresses behavior or causes punished children to disguise their actions so they won't be detected. Even so, this temporary suppression or disguise is more preferable than having the action blatantly continued. There is solid evidence that punishment can weaken, eliminate, and/or suppress behavior (Walters & Grusec, 1977). Punishment also dissipates tension for both the parent and child.

*Punishment* is here defined as deliberately presenting an unpleasant stimulus or taking something positive away. There is nothing mysterious about this definition. If in doubt, ask someone being punished. Sometimes children will call punishment something else, but rarely will they err in knowing when someone is deliberately presenting an aversive stimulus or removing something positive. It may be beneficial, however, to differentiate positive punishment from negative punishment. Generally, *positive punishment* involves *adding* something to *decrease* a behavior (e.g., spanking to decrease foul language). Conversely, *negative punishment* involves *withdrawing* something to *decrease* a behavior (e.g., taking away the car keys to decrease coming in late at night). It is apparent, then, that punishment includes more than just physical contact. Spanking is punishment, but so is sending a disruptive child to her room, taking away toys if they are being improperly used, and withholding dessert when vegetables are not eaten. All serve to decrease a behavior—disruptiveness, carelessness, and wastefulness. Ironically, however, presenting an aversive stimulus is called positive punishment, whereas removing something is called negative punishment.

## GOOD OR BAD?

While most psychologists are very hesitant to advocate the use of harsh punishment, there are some occasions when it seems appropriate. Krumboltz and Krumboltz (1972) suggest three such occasions:

1. When teaching small children what *no* means, mild punishment may be necessary. Most young children learn the meaning of *no* by having it spoken in a gruff voice, or simultaneously with a slap on the hand, for example.

2. Punishment may be necessary in dangerous situations where other forms of discipline would fail to avert an emergency. For example, if a young child runs into the street a forceful approach such as a spanking may be required. Lower-power techniques discussed in subsequent chapters would not deal with the immediate danger of getting hit by a car.

3. At times, punishment is the only way to provoke children into alternative behavior. Undesirable behavior patterns often become so entrenched that simple reinforcement of alternative behavior does not produce change (p. 186).

However, these same psychologists list some clear dangers in using punishment.

1. Attempted punishment may actually serve as reinforcement. A teacher who punishes a child by making him sit in front next to her desk or by writing his name on the blackboard calls attention to the child. Other children notice him. Such attention may actually be reinforcing, thereby increasing rather than reducing his undesired behavior.

2. Punishment may produce intense fears and anxieties which may last a lifetime.

3. When a child receives frequent punishment and sees no course of action that will enable him to escape that punishment, a foundation is laid for later neurotic behavior.

4. Children tend to resist punishment by fighting back, by actively escaping, or by withdrawing into passive apathy. Vandalism, truancy, and uncooperativeness are names frequently given such forms of resistance when they occur in school. They are the direct result of the punishment adults mete out to children.

5. The child tends to avoid the punisher whenever he can. A child who has constantly been punished by his parents does not want to be near them any more than he has to be. . . . In families where punishment is frequently used, the children, when they grow up, may feel uncomfortable near their parents. Children can develop severe feelings of guilt if they have been taught that they should love their parents but in fact do not. When you love someone, you want to be near him. But you do not want to be near someone who punishes you. You cannot want to be near a person . . . [who punishes you] without undergoing some kind of inner conflict. Parents and teachers who want their children to love them should maximize the opportunities to use positive reinforcement and minimize the use of punishment (Krumboltz and Krumboltz, 1972, pp. 185–186).

This chapter has thus far provided brief recommendations for when punishment seems to be appropriate, and dangers involved with punishing children. Let's look more closely at circumstances that are likely to make punishment most effective. Following this short discussion, a brief outline of punishment techniques is presented.

## EFFECTIVE PUNISHMENT

Perhaps no factor is more important when using punishment than *timing*. Generally, punishment will be most effective if it occurs at the beginning of, or during, a deviant act, rather than after the act is completed. If punishment occurs following inappropriate behavior, the longer the time interval between the behavior and punishment, the less effective is the punishment (Liebert, Poulos, & Marmor, 1977). Two basic ideas support this reasoning.

First, a young child is especially prone to confusion when punished at times other than during or immediately following a punishable act. An animal trainer follows this assumption, knowing that the animal is limited in associating certain temporally separated events. Punishing the animal for breaking a rule is likely to be effective only when performed immediately following misbehavior. A small child is similarly rationally handicapped. If a child mistreats his or her baby brother, but isn't dealt with until "your father gets home," the child might associate the punishment with the father alone, or with acceptable behavior occurring prior to the father's discipline.

A second reason for timing punishment has to do with the reinforcing qualities of misbehavior itself. Unacceptable behavior generally produces immediate reinforcement. The child who sneaks cookies is reinforced by the enjoyment of the cookies; the child throwing a tantrum might get his or her way. The longer children are allowed to enjoy these reinforcements, the more likely the reinforcements will outweigh negative aspects of punishment.

A number of experiments during the 1960s attempted to assess this relationship between timing and punishment (Aronfreed & Reber, 1965; Walters, Parke, & Cane, 1965). In these studies, children were punished for reaching for the more attractive of various toys. Punishment consisted of a loud "no," an unpleasant buzzer noise, or losing a piece of candy from a pile given to them prior to the experiment. Some of the children were punished as they reached for the forbidden toy; others were punished only after the toy was taken. After this procedure, each child was left alone in a room with the attractive toys and instructed not to touch them. Those children who had previously been punished as they reached for the forbidden toy were more likely to resist the temptation of touching the toys when alone.

Another principle affecting punishment is a *child's understanding* of why a certain behavior is forbidden. If children are told why they shouldn't run around the house, throw rocks at other children, or sneak cookies before lunch-time, the timing of punishment is no longer as relevant. However, a combination of rationale and punishment is most effective (Parke, 1974). Naturally, a child's ability to comprehend such rationales depends on cognitive development (see Chapter 4).

*Intensity* of punishment is also influential. If a child is required to sit in his room three minutes for neglecting assigned Saturday chores, he probably won't do them the following week either. "The overall findings from field and laboratory studies generally support the expectation that high-intensity . . . punishment in most circumstances more effectively inhibits the punished behavior than does punishment that is less intense" (Parke, 1979, p. 86). A good rule to remember is the recommendation cited below by Norton (1977)—"Punishment should match the behavior."

Finally, the *relationship between child and adult* influences punishment effectiveness. Punishment from a predominantly rewarding and nurturant parent is more likely to be effective than punishment from a cold and distant parent (Parke, 1969).

Researchers have found that certain procedures make punishment more effective. They are:

1. Punishment should be arranged so that escape from it is impossible.
2. Punishment should be as intense as possible.
3. Ideally, each response should be punished.
4. Punishment should be immediate.
5. Punishment should not be increased gradually but introduced at maximum intensity.

The researchers compiling this list of five procedures also listed eight more practices that increase punishment's effectiveness (Azrin & Holz, 1966).

For practical and humane reasons, it would be impossible to always meet and comply with these procedures. However, when these and other conditions are not present, punishment has been shown to be quite ineffective in weakening behavior. In an attempt to identify practical and humane punishment procedures for children, one author recommended the following:

1. Do not use physical punishment when emotionally upset.
2. Consider using nonphysical methods of punishment such as removing privileges or verbal punishment.
3. Be sure to provide clear instructions as to what is an acceptable alternative when using punishment.
4. Avoid time lags between the time one threatens punishment and actually delivers the consequences.
5. Punishment should match the misbehavior; a behavior that has important consequences should be punished more severely than a behavior of less importance.
6. Tell the child precisely what he is being punished for (Norton, 1977).

## TYPES OF PUNISHMENT

Three broad classes of punishment are generally discussed in parenting literature: physical punishment, privilege removal, and verbal punishment. In deciding how to punish a child, reference to the present problem and situation is necessary; it is, however, usually advisable to implement nonphysical punishment, especially if you are angry at the time.

**Physical punishment.** One of the major arguments against physical punishment is summarized by Bandura.

If a parent punishes a child physically for having struck a neighbor's child, the intended outcome of the training is that the child should refrain from

One of the major arguments against physical punishment is that it teaches children to become physically aggressive when frustrated by another's actions.

hitting others. Concurrently with the intentional training, however, the parent is providing a model of the very behavior he is attempting to inhibit in the child. Consequently, when the child is thwarted in subsequent social interactions, he may be more, rather than less, likely to respond in a physically aggressive manner (Bandura & Walters, 1963, p. 69).

Physical punishment is often attractive to a parent because it achieves immediate, though often temporary, results. As stated by Bandura, however, long-term effects of modeling need to be considered. Another argument against physical punishment is the social distance often created between child and adult. As this social distance increases, the ability to constructively influence the child's behavior decreases.

Physical punishment may also "interfere with the development of a child's conscience" (Ginott, 1965, p. 107). Spanking, for example, relieves guilt easily, and the child feels free of past misbehavior; repetition of the act is, therefore, likely to occur. A child may "go into debt on one side of the ledger" and then pay for the behavior with weekly spankings. Some parents are frustrated by this process, claiming that their child seemingly asks for punishment.

**Privilege withdrawal.** Privilege withdrawal, the second type of punishment, typically involves removing the child from a particular situation or depriving the child of a desired privilege. For example, the child may be sent to her room for misbehaving at the dinner table, or she may be deprived of watching television for the evening.

Norton (1977, pp. 48–50) comments briefly on ways this technique is misused. Removing a child from a particular situation (isolation) is not likely to be effective if, for example, the child is sent to his room for refusing to eat something he doesn't like. Removing a child from the situation in this case is not punishing; the child is probably relieved by not having to eat "those vegetables" anyway. In this instance, a removal of privileges might be more appropriate.

Norton (1977) also feels that long periods of isolation only serve to produce bad feelings rather than effectively change behavior. Isolation generally should not extend past 10 to 15 minutes. It is advisable, after this brief period, to require a correction of the punished act. "If a child's behavior was such that it should have been punished in the first place, then it is probably important enough to request the child to correct it after he has been removed from isolation."

**Verbal punishment.** The third punishment technique commonly used is verbal punishment. A child learns to associate physical punishment, or some other form of punishment, with a verbal response such as "Don't do

Privilege withdrawal typically involves removing the child from a particular situation—sending the child to a corner, for example.

that." In time, the verbal response alone may be enough to terminate the behavior. However, parents often unintentionally rely on verbal punishment too heavily. One mother unknowingly said "no" to her child 250 times before noonday. In addition, we often use negative comments as part of verbal punishment. For example, a parent might say, "How many times have I told you not to play with that stick? You don't listen! You are so stupid!" This statement, intended to verbally punish the child, may do nothing other than injure the child's self-esteem. A more appropriate statement might be, "Stop doing that; it's dangerous. If I have to tell you again, I'll take that stick away."

Each of these forms of punishment must be carefully and appropriately used. The parent continually risks negative side-effects if punishment is used extensively, inappropriately, or punitively. Consider the following examples provided by students:

> All through my childhood years I was punished by my mother, not only physically but also verbally . . . she did use punishment quite a bit. As I grew older, I realized that no matter what I did, whether it be a small "wrong-doing" or a large one, I would be punished for it. My defense against this was lying. At first I would lie only a little because I knew it was wrong and it hurt, but gradually I learned the "art" of telling half-truths to escape punishment.

> As a child I had a friend who was one of four children living with a punishing mother. Her mother seldom spoke to her other than to yell about something she did or did not do. She and her brothers and sisters were spanked in front of their friends for little things like getting dirty, much to their embarrassment. By the time we were in the fourth grade, this friend all but lived at my house. When I was in the fifth grade, my family moved to another city; Joan vowed that she would not live at home anymore.

> I was sixteen and had recently received my driver's license. I loved to drive as much as my parents would let me use the car. One time during the school year, I caught a bad cold. I was very busy and didn't let this slow me down. But for some reason my parents decided that I caught the cold because I wasn't getting to bed early enough, and so they decided to remove my driving privileges until I could get to bed by 10 P.M. every night for a week. . . . It was like they were punishing me for catching a cold.

Consider how the above examples illustrate inappropriate punishment techniques.

## CONSIDERATIONS WHEN USING PUNISHMENT

Parents should be made aware of additional considerations when punishment is used. Punishment does not help the child know what positive behavior is expected. It says "stop," but does not in itself say what is acceptable. Punishment may only produce a temporary suppression of responses, so when the punishment is removed, the response will reappear. As a result, parents should not only simultaneously provide the child with appropriate behavioral alternatives but reinforce them when they do occur. The use and control of human behavior through punishment is bound to be temporary, as punishment assumes a position of continuous power on the part of the punisher. However, teachers and parents must recognize that as children grow, they will not control all environmental events that can be used for punishment. The child may simply avoid the punisher, and/or punishment. If parents rely exclusively on punishment to control behavior, they will not gain the optimal relationship that enables them to use other influential methods. Appropriate alternative behaviors need to also be taught.

With human beings, punishment also elicits other unpredictable behaviors. Although not specifying the many types of unpredictable possibilities, let us mention two. First, there is *elicited aggression*—reflective, seemingly unlearned aggression aroused when a person is punished. This aggression is directed toward another person or an object that may be entirely unrelated to the punishment. Rats placed in a box with an electrified floor will fight one another even though the other rat has nothing to do with the punishment.

Second, when a punisher administers punishment, an aggressive reaction or retaliation by the "punishee" will sometimes reduce the amount of punishment being administered. In this case an aggressive counterresponse is strengthened because it is rewarded or, in other words, counteraggression reduces the amount of punishment. Children who scream or hit parents back are sometimes successful at diminishing punishment intensity.

Some say, "Spare the rod and spoil the child." Others respond by saying that using a "rod" (physical punishment) is not a necessary component of discipline, but that children can be effectively disciplined by other methods, and still remain unspoiled. We feel the same way. At three different universities one of the authors has asked students to indicate by show of hands how often they were physically punished by their parents. It is surprising that a substantial majority of students in each setting do not remember ever receiving physical punishment, and the rest usually report little or no incidences. By most standards these students are well-socialized, have no criminal records, are responsible in meeting academic requirements, and are generally socially and emotionally effective members of society.

On the other hand, a visit to a state penitentiary or a home for delinquent youth reveals many more residents who report they received an excessive amount of punishment from their caretakers during childhood. Although many variables inside and outside the family are involved, and although various studies have shown different parental patterns behind conduct disorders in children, studies do report that overly restrictive, punitive, and rejecting parents are often found in families with aggressive and antisocial children (Bugenthal, Love, Kaswan, & April, 1971; Kogan & Wimberger, 1971; McCord, & Howard, 1961; Sears, Maccoby, & Levin, 1957; Sears, Whiting, Nowlis, & Sears, 1953). It appears that heavy reliance upon the "rod" is not a very effective way to socialize children.

## Anxiety, Guilt, Fear, and Shame

The words *anxiety, fear, guilt,* and *shame* strike a cold, frightening response. They are especially distasteful when heaped on the young child. However, we cannot ignore them for they are part of emotional life, and are powerful motivators of behavior. The differences between anxiety, fear, guilt, and shame are not clear. For our purposes, fine distinctions are not needed as the dynamics of each are similar. They are uncomfortable feelings, and anything a child can do to reduce or eliminate this uneasiness will be rewarding. A response is voluntarily emitted so that fear, for example, is reduced; this is rewarding. But to understand the processes, some knowledge about social-learning principles is needed. Consider the following description of escape and avoidance responses.

## AVOIDANCE

A dog is placed in a box having two compartments. A gate separating the two compartments is removed, and a light in the compartment on the side where the dog is standing is turned off. If the dog fails to move into the other side by jumping a small hurdle, he will be shocked within a few seconds. When the dog jumps to the other side, the light comes back on and the shock is terminated (escape). At first, the typical dog will not immediately respond

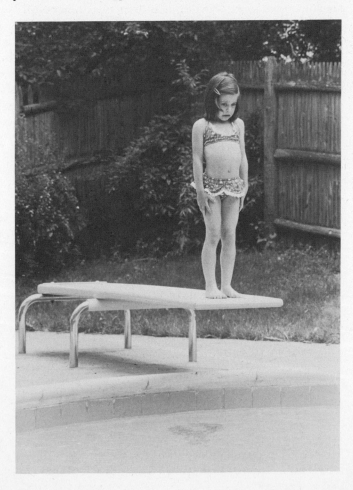

Children tend to avoid situations that create fear.

when the light goes out, or when any signal is presented, but when the shock occurs the animal will jump, turn, defecate, or show other signs of general excitement. Eventually, he will jump from the shocked compartment to the other side to escape the shock. This is called *escape learning*. After a few trials, the dog will jump immediately when the light goes out.

After regular escape behavior is established, the experimenters can turn off the electric shock, for when the light disappears, the dog will continue to jump, even though from this point on he will never again be shocked *(avoidance learning)*. The dog will maintain this behavior to the point of exhaustion; fear reduction is all that is needed to continue the response (Solomon & Wynn, 1954).

A similar case is a child who initially found playing with matches enjoyable. During one episode, she burned herself badly. Initially, the matches were a neutral stimulus (i.e., not eliciting a particularly strong emotional response). However, after being paired with pain, even the sight of matches elicited a conditioned fear response. Thereupon, any response that the child made to reduce this fear was strengthened by the reward of fear reduction. The child soon learned that if she turned away from the matches, no longer seeing them reduced her fear. She may find that her fear is reduced even more by turning and walking out of a room where matches are present.

In the above examples, the animal or human has learned that avoiding a specific anxiety-producing stimulus decreases the anxiety. The stimulus may be inherently anxiety-provoking (e.g., a loud noise) or may have taken on distressing properties through a cond.tioning process. In any event, the anxiety can be avoided if withdrawal from or avoidance of the stimulus occurs.

## AVERSIVE EMOTIONS

As described above, any action can come to produce fear or anxiety by being paired with pain (Stage I). Because anxiety is an unpleasant state, any response that reduces or eliminates the fear is a response simultaneously reinforced by fear reduction (Stage II). Accordingly, many children who have been disciplined for lying feel anxious when they lie, and when they later tell the truth, they feel better. Consider the following account about a young girl who changed her behavior after guilt feelings were aroused by her mother:

*My fifth-grade daughter's teacher called to ask if I had seen and signed her math test. "No," I said, I hadn't. "Because," replied the teacher, "she told me you had signed it and had accidentally thrown it away." I was a little surprised though not alarmed that my daughter had lied to her teacher. I told the teacher I would speak to my daughter and asked the teacher to talk to her also.*

*I then talked carefully with my daughter, asking her to think of how she should feel and make amends (after she admitted she had been dishonest). The next day my daughter approached me quietly.*

*"Mom, I wrote a note and said I was sorry to Mrs. Daly. I told her in the note that I would take the test over again."*

*"Thanks, Dana."* I put my arm around her. *"You handled it well."*

◑

In a gentle way, this mother created an unpleasant emotional state, motivating an apology and a change of attitude and behavior.

Aversive emotions can be developed through ways other than physical punishment or pain, thereby avoiding some of the disadvantages of physical punishment. Many years ago a psychologist concluded: "Experiencing distress when another is in distress seems primitive, naïve, and reasonably universal" (Murphy, 1937). Children have empathic responses when viewing slides of other children in emotional situations (Feshback & Roe, 1968). Physiological measures indicate that emotional responses occur when one

If disciplined for disobeying parental wishes, a child may then become anxious when disobeying in the future. If strong enough, this anxiety prevents misbehavior.

observes another person being shocked, failing in a task, experiencing extreme heat, or even someone in a wheelchair (Berger, 1962; Clore & Jeffrey, 1972; Craig & Weinstein, 1965; Tomes, 1964; Weiss, Roger, Lombardo, & Stick, 1973). Aronfreed and Paskal (1968) proposed that empathic responses often result from observing another's distress.

Therefore, situations producing negative emotions for one individual are likely distressing to other children. This would produce the recommendation of allowing children to face a wide range of emotional experiences, enabling them eventually to be present in a social context where others are distressed. Accordingly, as adults they would likely feel distress when observing another's distress, and learn to be charitable, helpful, or unselfish in an effort to reduce that person's discomfort—thereupon alleviating their own. Another common source of distress or anxiety among humans is eye-to-eye contact. A steady gaze maintained longer than 10 seconds usually arouses anxiety (Argyle & Dean, 1965). This anxiety is sufficient to produce avoidance behavior. Ellsworth, Carlsmith, and Hensen (1972) found that when drivers who were stopped at an intersection for a red light were stared at by a person standing on the corner, they would drive through the intersection more rapidly when the light changed than would drivers who were ignored. In a later replication of this study it was found that female drivers crossed the intersection more slowly when a male observer smiled at them (Bakken & Bromley, 1972).

To recapitulate, parents help children learn appropriate emotional responses for social and interpersonal situations. It is mature to feel remorse, anxiety, or regret after having inflicted pain and suffering on others, or after failing to meet responsibilities. However, it is also necessary to teach children the correct responses following these emotions and how to avoid these feelings in the future.

How does a parent engender emotions in a child? Fortunately, it is not necessary to create emotions, as they occur readily in a natural environment. However, if a child appears insensitive to others, feels no remorse when knowingly disregarding parents' wishes, or violates his or her own accepted rules or agreements with no apparent regret, then a parent must help the child develop appropriate emotions. One such method is described below.

## APPROVAL WITHDRAWAL

"We are not going to punish you; we accept you as our child and love you, but we cannot approve of what you have done." Through approval withdrawal, children understand that parents are unhappy about inappropriate actions. They must not be sheltered from their parents' valuing process. Feeling a lack of approval from *loving parents* is often sufficient to motivate corrective behavior. It must be emphasized, however, that care should be taken to make sure children know they are always loved and accepted as people. Some parents say, "I love you, but I don't like your behavior." A parent need not always express love and concern verbally, however; a child is sensitive to nonverbal clues. Perhaps simpler and yet amply powerful words are, "Your father and I do not approve of dishonesty." These words from loving and valued parents have great emotional impact.

Two undesirable methods of communicating disapproval when teaching emotions should be distinguished from the simple approval withdrawal mentioned above: "I'll beat the hell out of him so he'll know the feeling of fear the next time he does that," or "I can't accept her as a daughter if she is going to do that." The first is punishment and the second is love withdrawal. Both will likely produce more serious problems rather than teach the child. A good indicator of whether parents have used approval withdrawal or love withdrawal is how willingly and frequently their children will come to them when they make mistakes. If love is not withdrawn, children will still come to their parents to discuss inadequacies and mistakes.

## HEALTHY GUILT

Events and circumstances producing emotional responses such as anxiety are sometimes similar to those eliciting guilt and shame. *Shame* usually refers to negative emotional feelings about self as a result of ridicule and censorship by others; *guilt* results from violation of personal standards, self-held beliefs, or values. However, both are effective catalysts of behavior change.

A distinction should be made between healthy and unhealthy guilt (see Knight, 1969). For healthy, acceptable guilt to occur three conditions must be satisfied. First, the child must have previously accepted the values he or she has violated. It does not matter where or from whom these values were acquired, as long as the child personally adopts them. Before reaching adolescence, a child generally amasses a great many standards into what can be called a "framework of values." From these standards, the child defines which violations produce guilt, and which do not. If the child refuses to accept these standards, guilt will not occur when they are trespassed. For example, if a child takes his brother's toy without asking and has not adopted a "personal property" value, he will probably not feel guilty.

Second, the child must feel an obligation to abide by the values he or she has selected. Obligation connotes responsibility. People must feel responsible for their actions and know that they control the consequences of their behavior, or guilt will not be experienced. The child must be able to voluntarily start or stop the behavior. If a child believes she has been forced into violating standards, she will not feel guilty. Obligation implies choice, and choice implies freedom of action.

Third, the child must have the ability to be self-critical, to look at his or her actions and decide whether or not an accepted value has been violated. This requires that children have at least a minimal amount of intellectual maturity. At the same time that they are able to undergo self-scrutiny, they are often able to verbalize these feelings. A little boy might say "no, no" as he takes a cookie from the cookie jar, or "bad boy" as he splashes water out of the sink. These attempts to analyze actions and put feeling into words signal that the child is beginning to acquire essential elements necessary for the development of genuine guilt. This capacity to accept moral values, feel personal obligation, and engage in self-analysis corresponds to what most people call *conscience*. Parents can assist this developmental process.

One mother helped her daughter feel the implications of her inappropriate behavior in a religious context:

> I received a call from a mother with a first-grade son in my daughter's classroom. My daughter, according to her son Jeremy, had taken his Mickey Mouse watch. I investigated and found the accusation true. Yes, she said, she had taken the watch.
> We talked about her knowing it was wrong to take other people's things, and then I asked "What can we do now?"
> "Well, we can give it back."
> "Sherrie," I looked at her carefully, "will you give it back?"
> "But Mom, I'm scared."
> "Is it the right thing to do?"
> "Yes."
> "Then we must not be too afraid to do the right thing. When a person knows he's done something wrong, he must feel sorry. That also means to change and do the right thing. Then you will feel happy inside."
> I knelt down beside Sherrie and said a simple prayer. Then I asked her to pray that she would not be afraid to choose the right. We then went to Jeremy's home together, returned the watch, and apologized.

## POSITIVE OUTCOMES

When considering the process of healthy guilt, and how it can be effective in stimulating appropriate behaviors, the following process results: First, a negative emotion such as guilt is experienced, which motivates the child to perform a good act. As the good act is performed, guilt is reduced or eliminated and relief is experienced. This feeling of relief is perceived as a positive emotional state; similar positive feelings for behaving morally are soon expected. The child acts in anticipation of the positive emotional state as well as out of a desire to eliminate guilt feelings.

These recommendations are relatively simple after the complex rationale is understood. Parents, teachers, and caretakers must lay the emotional base for behavior, including both positive and negative emotions, by introducing emotions children can handle for their age. Emotional experiences should not be restricted to home life, church, or school, but rather encountered in a wide variety of natural contexts. The emotion to be encountered is not the parent's; it is the emotion that the child experiences that is essential.

A child should be allowed to experience emotion at an early age, and to attach appropriate responses to each of these emotions. Appropriate responses are those that are socially desirable and can be enacted by children.

## NEGATIVE EFFECTS OF UNHEALTHY AND OBSESSIVE GUILT

Symptoms resulting from obsessive or unhealthy guilt include oversensitivity, withdrawal, and lowered self-esteem. The child may become emotionally constricted and fearful of responding and making changes or mistakes. Other symptoms include moodiness and sulkiness. The child with too much "bottled-up" emotion may strike out angrily at other children, parents, or inanimate objects, sometimes appearing cruel; or, the child may regress to earlier, safer childhood behaviors because he or she knows what to expect and is not worried about taking chances and failing.

A child must learn to reduce guilt feelings in a socially acceptable manner. For example, confession of and restitution for the guilt-producing behavior, if possible, are desirable responses. In some cases, a realistic and accurate self-evaluation is appropriate, avoiding the common error of viewing oneself as worthless or bad. Once learning to reduce guilt through appropriate action, the child may not need guilt in the future to provide impetus for appropriate behaviors. Actions originally motivated to reduce guilt now produce their own rewards, sustaining moral behavior.

A parent may also be instrumental in helping a child reduce unnecessary guilt by providing logical explanations of the child's actions and their effects on other people. Such clarification helps the child distinguish and identify which guilt feelings result from the child's own acts and which come from other sources. The child should not feel guilty about acts and events beyond his or her control.

## SUMMARY OF USING EMOTIONS AS CONSEQUENCES

Eliciting feelings is much more simple in young children than adults; their emotions are fewer and less intricate. A number of approaches have been shown to elicit these feelings. In addition to the most obvious—external punishment, reward, and the manipulation of love—other ways are not only available but preferable. The human being—an extremely intelligent, sensitive creature—will react emotionally to different combinations of words. Some are in the form of story or reason, others are simply "help" or "please."

Emotions can also be elicited by facial expression, viewing the distress or delight of another, staring, and listening to sounds other than words; both positive and negative emotions can be produced. If a parent is patient, difficulty should not be encountered in helping the child experience feelings that can be easily associated with specific acts, thoughts, and ideas—particularly in relation to the child's own behavior. A child should be provided with feedback about his or her own behavior and information about values, attitudes, and truth.

A mature morality is often the outcome of first-hand encounters with choice situations. Provide the child with experiences, beginning with simple choices and expanding to encounters with a full range of feelings. People who have not received this training are often referred to as sheltered, naïve, or weak. A life so structured and supervised that a person need not make difficult personal choices is inadvisable. A crucial element of experiencing is decision making. The risk, of course, is that choices may be wrong. It is because of this risk that the best time to provide experience and choices is during youth, when poor choices do not result in catastrophic or irreversible damage.

Allowing freedom implies both freedom from external control, and freedom from more subtle social and emotional controls. For example, a child may be given a "choice," but emotional pressures of guilt, shame, and social expectations are so strong that she feels she cannot do as she wishes. When letting children make personal decisions, the wise parent then allows the child to proceed, letting her know that love or positive regard will not be withdrawn should she choose an option contrary to the parent's wishes.

## Special Techniques for Eliminating Behavior

What do you do when you don't want to physically punish or use guilt, fear, and shame to eliminate undesirable behavior? Unfortunately, punishment and fear sometimes appear to be necessary. Sometimes behaviors must be stopped immediately to prevent injury or harm to the child or other individuals.

However, a price will be paid if punishment and fear are relied upon extensively. When administered, punishment causes stress and later requires policing. Children will resist by screaming and trying to pull away during physical punishment, or arguing and making counterthreats during nonphysical punishment. As mentioned earlier, frequent use of punishment hurts the parent–child relationship. After extensive punishment, children might "come around," but it would have been better if the time had been spent nurturing positive feelings.

Another negative consequence of punishment is what it might do to the child; the effects are variable. A never-failing illustration of this occurs when asking students in child psychology classes how they reacted when punished. Typical answers include, "I would just wait until they couldn't catch me and do it anyway," "I'd go to my room and wouldn't talk," and "I felt rebellious and tried to fight back." Reactions of withdrawing, lying, sneaking around, and fighting back are often worse than the behavior being punished. These unpredictable side-effects require additional discipline, and unpleasant emotions convince most experienced parents that punishment is a last resort technique.

Relying extensively on emotions such as anxiety, fear, and guilt can also be detrimental, as children may begin to experience excessive and unhealthy guilt, and may begin to feel less sure of themselves. However, parents know that some behaviors cannot be tolerated. They justifiably ask, "What can I do?" Several excellent alternatives are listed below.

## EXTINCTION

Clearly, the simplest established way to eliminate negative behavior is to see that the behavior is not rewarded. In many cases it is surprising to notice the great variety of rewards actually following a behavior. Attention, for example, is given to many misbehaving children—exactly what they want.

An example of eliminating behavior through extinction took place with an emotionally disturbed 11-year-old boy. In a special English class the boy frequently threw tantrums involving crying, kicking, and screaming. It was a common occurrence to see attendants drag the kicking and screaming boy out of class, thereby attracting a large audience of staff members. Most onlookers believed the tantrums occurred when the boy was frustrated or teased. The teacher noticed, however, that the tantrums were not temporally associated with the child being teased or frustrated. Instead, she saw the tremendous amount of attention given to him at these times. She decided to eliminate the tantrum behavior through an extinction process.

The next time a tantrum occurred, the teacher asked the attendants to bring the boy to her desk. The attendants placed the boy at her desk and left the room. The teacher closed the door and waited. She told the boy that when he had finished crying, they could start working. The boy cried for approximately eight minutes and then said he was ready to work. The teacher then went to her desk to help him with his English exercises, and the boy was cooperative for the remainder of the class period. After several weeks of this extinction procedure the tantrums disappeared completely (Zimmerman & Zimmerman, 1962).

Consider another example. At a nursery school a four-year-old boy continually and persistently cried when attending school in the morning. His crying was observed and recorded. An average of eight episodes occurred each morning. It was discovered that his crying and whining resulted in immediate attention from the teachers, who hurried to comfort him until he stopped. In this situation, Bill cried because he was being rewarded with attention by the nursery-school teachers. An extinction program consisted of ignoring Bill whenever he cried without cause. He was still given a share of attention and affection by the nursery-school teachers, but never when crying. This technique was carried out for 10 days. The number of crying episodes fell to almost zero (Whaley & Malott, 1971, p. 10).

If ignored, tantrums and crying fits often extinguish.

In theory, extinction should be the most effective way of eliminating behavior, for no behavior continues unless it is reinforced. The key to using this intervention technique is identifying when and where the reinforcement for undesirable behaviors occurs. Once these reinforcers have been identified, it is usually easy to eliminate them. Within a matter of days behavior should weaken and then disappear.

## SATIATION AND NEGATIVE PRACTICE

Sometimes we hear the expression, "Too much of a good thing." A child may say, "I'm tired of it," "We do that all the time," or "Let's do something else." It is similar to the youth who loved pizzas but after having worked in a pizza shop eating all the pizza he wanted, he now orders hamburgers. Reinforcing properties are often lost through repetition, and satiation occurs. For example, a child beginning to play with matches may be required to light four boxes while he is watched by his father. The initial reinforcing quality of watching the match burn is soon satiated, and its future occurrence is reduced.

Closely related to satiation is *negative practice,* which is often used to reduce the frequency of motor tics and other habit disorders. When this method is used, a person is asked to practice or perform the annoying, unwanted behavior again and again. A child with an annoying tic may be asked to perform the tic over and over. As she does so, fatigue builds up, and the tic becomes aversive; it takes on negative properties. In addition, when the negative practice session terminates, the rest period (absence of the tic) becomes reinforcing. Recall that satiation involves performing a reinforcing behavior over and over until it loses its reinforcing value. Somewhat differently, negative practice involves repeating a neutral or even annoying behavior until fatigue makes it aversive, and stopping it is reinforcing. Negative practice could apply to nail-biting, stammering, thumb-sucking, and swearing.

A teacher asked a psychologist what she could do to eliminate the behavior of a third-grade boy who always performed imitations of animal sounds to her annoyance. The psychologist asked the teacher to place the child in an empty room and direct him to make the imitations for 10 minutes. When the child stopped making the noises the teacher was instructed to have the child continue by directing him, "Please continue." After a series of 10-minute periods, the teacher reported no more difficulty with animal imitations in the classroom. The fun of imitating sounds had been satiated.

One young lady reported how she came to dislike an activity as a result of satiation:

*I was a tomboy while in grade school. I wanted a Johnny Bench Pitchback for elementary-school graduation. My parents didn't want to get it for me because they thought it would foster my boyish characteristics, but they got it for me nevertheless. I soon stopped using it as much but my mother would always say, "You complained to get it, now use it." After being forced to play with it day after day, I had only one solution—I broke it.*

An example of negative practice was eliminating an elementary-school child's habit of foul language. He cursed continuously, especially when riding the bus to and from school. The bus driver, unable to tolerate the crude language any longer, took the boy into a vacant room upon arriving at school.

He instructed the boy to say all the dirty words he knew. He insisted that the boy shout them as loudly as he could for at least five minutes. The boy was ready to quit after two or three minutes, but was ordered to continue for five minutes. Even several days after the incident the boy did not curse in the driver's presence, apparently with no negative side-effects (Blackham & Silberman, 1971, pp. 67–68).

## STIMULUS CONTROL

Certain conditions seem to be present when certain responses occur. To eliminate or reduce those responses one needs simply to change the eliciting stimuli. If reading comic books is followed by nightmares, the mother can eliminate these frightening dreams by making sure the child does not read comic books before going to bed. Although sounding absurd, this illustration nevertheless suggests that in less obvious situations we may punish when a response could be eliminated simply by taking away the circumstances producing the response. For example, aggression and fighting are frequently punished, but it may be that the response could be better eliminated by removing competing, crowded, and frustrating situations. Similarly, it is discouraging to observe a mother continually scolding her child for getting into certain things, when all that is necessary is to remove them from the child's reach.

Another common procedure used by parents who want to eliminate undesirable behaviors in their children is to notice when, where, and with whom the child was playing prior to observing the inappropriate behavior. Sometimes restricting certain books, TV programs, or friends is all that is needed to eliminate obnoxious behavior. In more extreme forms, parents have been known to send their children to summer camp or to visit grandparents as a means of removing them from an unhealthy environment that elicits undesirable behavior.

## TIME OUT

Mark and James Wood, ages 10 and 11, are brothers. One summer their father noticed they argued every night after supper when playing together. Mr. Wood found he was not able to get them to stop by merely telling them to or by threatening them. He particularly disliked threatening them since it seemed to ruin the whole atmosphere. Therefore, he substituted an immediate, mandatory 10-minute (minimum) conference in which the boys let each other speak without interruption in front of their father. When they settled on a mutually agreeable solution to the conflict, they returned to their activity. Each confrontation produced a conference until the boys finally learned to solve problems without losing 10 minutes of playing time. Mr. Wood reported that for the first three nights, the boys were in conferences continually and finally realized that it was best to "conference quietly" without getting Dad involved (Abidin, 1976, p. 81).

Another frustrated father described a successful solution to a conflict with his son:

*When I was watching a basketball game two Sundays ago my little boy was making a fuss about eating his dinner. He was arguing loudly with my wife so I asked him to be quiet and finish. He continued to howl so I quickly and unceremoniously took him to his time-out area (his room) and told him when he could be quiet he could join us again. It worked.*

When using a time-out procedure, the child is removed from the environment or activity in which the undesirable behavior is occurring. This procedure is not considered positive punishment in the sense that an aversive stimulus is administered to stop the behavior. Rather, it involves removing all positive reinforcers of the behavior, and placing the child in a "time-out" room or setting void of attention, toys, and other positive stimuli; this is negative punishment.

Many institutional settings have designated time-out rooms where people are placed for specified periods of time until they can return and manage their behavior properly. It is important that (1) the original environment be shown to be reinforcing, thus discontinuing the inappropriate behavior when the child is removed; and (2) the time-out room not provide reinforcing opportunities for children to amuse themselves, distracting from the original intent.

## OMISSION TRAINING

In omission training the child is expected to discontinue a response for a period of time before receiving a desired reward. For example, a child can be told, "If I don't hear any arguing for the next half hour, then we will all go to town and have a treat." Consider the disruptive behavior of one class of elementary-school children. The teacher reinforced nondisruptive behavior by delaying recess until no disruption occurred for 10 minutes. If disruptive behavior occurred, the children had to wait another 10 minutes.

An extreme example of omission training was used to eliminate self-injurious behavior of institutionalized retarded children. Behaviors to be omitted included face-scratching, eye-poking, and head-banging. While several procedures were used, omission training was effective in eliminating injurious behaviors by depriving food, and then reinforcing with food when the behavior did not take place. It should be noted, however, that using electric shock as a punishment was still more effective in this experiment, illustrating how tempting it is to use the more immediate and dramatic technique of positive punishment (Corte, Wolfe, & Locke, 1971).

The following also illustrates the successful but simple application of omission training:

*I was a mother's helper for six months last year for a newborn baby and a 4½-year-old. The 4½-year-old would mess in his pants on purpose. We had the doctor check him out, but there was nothing physiologically wrong with him. He would do it for attention, so his mother and I promised him that if he went for a week without messing in his pants, we could go to the zoo. Using this procedure, he immediately learned to handle the problem.*

This omission procedure is frequently used by parents. Mother may say that if there is no loud talk or disruptive noise at the dinner table, she will serve a special dessert. Father may say, "If we get our work done this morning, then we'll go to the park this afternoon."

## REINFORCEMENT OF AN INCOMPATIBLE RESPONSE

In the authors' opinion, the most effective way of eliminating a behavior is to teach and strengthen incompatible responses. The success of this method depends on increasing the occurrence of a desirable behavior through positive reinforcement, making it impossible to perform the undesired behavior.

To employ this technique, a summer-camp counselor rewarded cooperative behavior rather than punishing aggressive behavior:

*During the summer, I worked at a summer camp for kids from low-income groups in the Los Angeles area. Many of the boys who came to camp were quite aggressive and often started fights with other boys in the cabins. It was invariably very hot throughout the day, so a favorite activity was to go swimming in the pool. When a boy did something nice for one of the other boys, like doing his clean-up duty, I gave him extra time in the pool while everyone else stood there in the heat watching him. Helping behaviors were positively reinforced, and it's amazing how fast the other kids caught on and stopped fighting.*

The key to eliminating undesirable behavior is to reinforce desirable behaviors incompatible with the undesirable one. Smiling is incompatible with frowning. Laughing is incompatible with crying. Telling the truth is incompatible with lying, sharing is incompatible with selfishness, and courtesy is incompatible with rudeness. To select an incompatible desirable behavior, ask the following questions:

1. Is there a behavior that is the opposite of the undesired response? Can it be reinforced?
2. When he or she performs this preferred behavior, will it be impossible to perform the undesired behavior?

In a preschool classroom a four-year-old girl isolated herself from the other children and received adult attention for this behavior. The incompatible response in this case is obvious. Instead of trying to eliminate withdrawal, the teacher should attempt to increase her social interaction. In this case the teacher ignored any isolated behavior and rewarded her when peer play was initiated. Since peer interactions did not occur frequently, anything close to a peer interaction had to be initially reinforced; even standing near or playing beside another child was reinforced. Gradually, social interaction began to occur. This child acquired an acceptable level of social interaction within one month (Allen, Hart, Buell, Harris, & Wolfe, 1964, pp. 511–518).

Many of these techniques can be combined to increase a parent's intervention effectiveness. For example, Kolko (1983) combined negative practice with "corrective consequences" and reinforcement of an incompatible response to eliminate the fire-setting behavior of a six-year- old boy. Each day the boy had to light a fire in his mother's presence. He had to collect matches, paper, basin, pail of water, water hose, scrub brush, and dishwashing liquid. After lighting the fire and putting it out he had to wash the basin thoroughly. Each time this entire process was repeated, his mother provided "corrective" fire-safety precautions and questioned his understanding of the precautions. The boy was also rewarded for performing appropriate non-fire-setting behaviors like playing with his sister.

## Summary

Undesirable behaviors will often need to be eliminated. A natural tendency is to use positive punishment, as it seems to be the quickest in suppressing behavior. Punishment, when used efficiently, can be effective. However, alternate ways of eliminating undesired behavior are often preferable. Excessive use of punishment and emotions such as fear and guilt can be problematic for the child, as well as for the relationship between parent and child. Many parents use punishment only as a last resort. In this section, several safer and more effective procedures to eliminate undesirable behavior have been given. Below is a listing of the methods discussed.

1. *Punishment*—the use of threats, inflicting physical pain, and tearing down the social, emotional, or psychological perception of another person are all common methods of punishment. Punishment may be defined as deliberately presenting negative stimuli or removing positive stimuli to reduce a behavior. Punishment is often used simply because it is easy to use and brings about immediate results.

However, evidence indicates that frequent punishment commonly does not necessarily weaken, eliminate, or suppress behavior over an extended period of time.

2. *Extinction*—simply ensuring that a behavior is not followed by a reward. The key is to identify when and where reinforcement for undesirable behavior occurs, and to then eliminate that reinforcement.

3. *Satiation and Negative Practice*—based on the idea that repeating a behavior over and over will result in its end. A person may be required to repeat an undesirable behavior continuously for an extended period of time until the behavior becomes aversive.

4. *Stimulus Control*—requiring a change in the eliciting stimuli to eliminate or reduce undesired responses. For example, if a child shows a great deal of hyperactive behavior after eating large amounts of sweets, the behavior can be changed by not permitting the child to eat so many high-sugar foods.

5. *Time out*—behavior is eliminated by removing the child from an activity when the undesirable behavior is displayed. For example, if the boys fight, although they know they shouldn't, each must spend 15 minutes in his bedroom alone.

6. *Omission Training*—accomplished by letting the child know that if he refrains from undesirable behavior he will be reinforced. This is usually specified in terms of time (e.g., "Billy, if you don't fight with Susie all week you can go roller skating").

7. *Reinforcement of Incompatible Responses*—involves increasing a desirable behavior, through positive reinforcement, making it impossible to perform the undesired behavior. If Tommy is constantly beating up his little brother Willy, Mother may offer Tommy a penny for every time she sees him playing nicely with Willy.

# S E L F - C H E C K

1. Which of the following is *not* true of effective punishment?
   a. Punishment should be immediate.
   b. Punishment should be increased gradually.
   c. Avoid time lags between punishment threats and actual delivering of consequences.
   d. Do not use physical punishment when emotionally upset.
   e. All of the above are true of effective punishment.
2. While most psychologists are hesitant to advocate the use of punishment, there are some occasions when it seems appropriate. Which of the following is *not* an appropriate reason?
   a. To save a child from a greater danger
   b. To get a child to try some alternative behavior that can then be reinforced
   c. To teach a child what *no* means
   d. To ensure that punishment is not reinforcing
   e. All of the above are appropriate reasons.
3. Which of the following is a danger of using punishment?
   a. Children often resist punishment by fighting back.
   b. The child tends to avoid the punisher.
   c. Punishment may produce lifelong fears and anxieties.
   d. A punishment may be reinforcing.
   e. All of the above are dangers.
4. Three broad classes of punishment are generally discussed in parenting literature. Which of the following is not included?
   a. Privilege removal

b. Ignoring inappropriate behavior
c. Verbal punishment
d. Physical punishment
5. Guilt can be used as a behavior modification technique if used correctly. Which of the following conditions is *not* necessary for healthy guilt to occur?
a. The child must experience love withdrawal.
b. The child must feel an obligation to abide by the values he or she has selected.
c. The child must have previously accepted the values he or she has violated.
d. The child must have the ability to be self-critical.
6. The simplest way to eliminate negative behavior is to see that the behavior is not rewarded. This process is called
a. stimulus change.
b. extinction.
c. negative practice.
d. time out.
7. Time out is a behavior modification technique that falls under the following class of punishment:
a. Privilege removal.
b. Ignoring inappropriate behavior.
c. Verbal punishment.
d. Physical punishment.
8. If a child is told, "If I don't hear any arguing for the next half hour then we will all go to town and have a treat," what behavioral technique is being used?
a. Negative practice
b. Omission training
c. Time out
d. Extinction
e. None of the above is correct.
9. If a child continually isolates himself socially, the behavior might most effectively be changed by reinforcing social behavior, rather than punishing antisocial behavior. Which technique is this?
a. Reinforcement of an incompatible response
b. Negative practice
c. Stimulus change
d. Extinction
10. Aversive emotions can be developed through ways other than physical punishment or pain. Which of the following is one of those methods?
a. Viewing other people in distress
b. Steady eye-to-eye contact
c. Neither of the above is correct.
d. Both a and b above are correct.

KEY: 1–b; 2–d; 3–e; 4–b; 5–a; 6–b; 7–a; 8–b; 9–a; 10–d

# CHAPTER 9

# MODERATE-POWER TECHNIQUES TO PRODUCE OR LESSEN BEHAVIOR

Strict control of a child's behavior through skillful manipulation of reinforcements and punishments is not always desirable or feasible. Especially with older children free of significant behavior or "acting-out" difficulties, and not under as much immediate control or supervision, it would be advantageous if they could respond to other forms of discipline. It would be helpful, for example, if children could be assisted and encouraged through more verbal forms of parenting, by considering their motives, reasoning with them, helping them internalize their controls, rather than having to rely on environmental manipulation of consequences. Or, they could be instructed by helping them become cognizant of natural, logical consequences of their behaviors, rather than contrived ones. For example, rather than punish a child for not coming to the dinner table on time by using a time-out procedure, why not let the child suffer the natural consequence—no dinner? Such is the reasoning of viewpoints to be presented in this chapter, and in Chapter 10 as well.

However, psychologists espousing the above ideas and those supporting behavior modification theory are often critical of each other. According to behavior modification experts, if verbal forms of praise and disapproval are paired with contrived reinforcers and punishment, they will begin to act as reinforcers and punishers themselves. Children will learn to behave appropriately without necessitating constant reinforcement as their reinforcers become internalized. Additionally, variable reinforcement schedules do not require constant parental supervision.

Also, with regard to natural and logical consequences, it is impossible to rely solely on natural forms of punishment. It is unwise, for example, to let baby brother learn to leave his older brother's toys alone by letting him be physically abused by his brother every time. Other forms of intervention would be necessary to prevent physical harm or injury.

Yet, these and similar arguments are often semantic, and such is not the focus of this text. We attempt to present differing viewpoints and to allow parents to glean from their study and develop what for them is effective. We will call these next approaches "moderate-power techniques to produce or lessen behavior" because of their reduced emphasis on strict control of environmental circumstances. Rather, consequences are more natural and focus on dealing with children on a more rational level, as opposed to just focusing on observable behaviors and controlling reinforcers and punishers.

## Rudolph Dreikurs

The Constitution of the United States was framed to provide a democratic form of government for its citizens. This type of government system provided new challenges, for it was based on the idea that all human beings are created equal and must be equally represented. Rudolph Dreikurs, in his theoretical ideas about behavior, believes that the democratic way of life affects not only society, but family life and children within the family circle as well. Within this framework, Dreikurs analyzed children's behavior and offered a theory to help parents teach children to live in a society allowing equal opportunity and representation.

Dreikurs is a disciple of the Adlerian school of psychoanalysis. Alfred Adler maintained that the basic need of humans is to *belong,* and that they are continually striving to find a prominent place within their group. Another assumption is that they are affected by stimuli from inside and outside the body. Dreikurs considers it irrelevant to discuss whether heredity and environment or internal states are more important influences on behavior. Both affect the child; what is important is how the child acts within this framework. Consider a handicapped child. One might say, "The child has this handicap and will, therefore, become this particular type of child," but children with the same handicap do not always develop similarly. Some see their handicaps as a burden—they see themselves as inferior or unacceptable to others. Others have learned to deal positively with their impediment, often developing spectacular abilities. It is the attitude about the handicap, not the handicap itself, that is more important in many instances.

Another premise of Adlerian theory is that all behavior or action is *goal-directed.* A person never acts without reason. We may not be consciously aware of a goal at the time we are pursuing something, but all behavior is goal-directed, and our basic goal is to belong. Two children, for example, may both strive to gain attention. One child may find that aggressive behavior obtains the desired results. The other child, however, may find that giggling or running through the house causes parents to take notice.

Children often develop such attitudes and orientations while quite young, experimenting with their behavior on a trial-and-error basis. If one technique doesn't work, others will be tried until a behavior is found that brings about the desired goal. When certain behaviors are found to gain attention, they may be repeated whenever attention is desired. Most children experiment in this manner up to age four or five, at which time they begin to consolidate their attitudes and establish a definite lifestyle.

## DETERMINANTS OF CHILDREN'S ATTITUDES

Several events have a significant influence on a person's lifestyle. While these events alone do not determine a child's attitudes, they have great impact.

**Family atmosphere.**   The first significant influence is the *family atmosphere*—the tone or quality of action and interaction within the family. If parents are very competitive with each other in their interpersonal encounters, then children will consider competitiveness to be the natural way of life. Sim-

Family atmosphere has a significant influence on children's attitudes. If positive, child attitudes are similarly beneficially influenced.

ilarly, if parents are punitive and use physical punishment, a child may also learn to be physical and punitive in his or her relationships with others.

**Family constellation.**   The second important influence is *family constellation,* which includes birth order of the child. Significant psychological differences often exist between younger and older children, as they have different experiences. The following paragraphs suggest possible characterizations of children in different ordinal positions.

*The First-Born:*  This child is often called *the dethroned child.* A first and only child who has had love and attention lavished by a first-time mother, the first-born has the experience for two or three years of being the major object of concern and care, when suddenly a younger sibling arrives. The mother's affections and concerns are sharply shifted, and the first-born must now learn to share attention with someone else. The new baby becomes a rival. Because of this sudden loss of involvement with Mother, the eldest often goes through life semiconsciously feeling that this kind of thing can happen again. The feeling often continues as an adult and influences the way he or she functions on the job and in social relationships, including marriage.

If experiencing a lot of pampering or undue attention as an only child, the eldest often develops hostile feelings toward the second. Eldest children tend to be past-oriented, looking on the past with favor because it was then they experienced their greatest happiness. They also tend to be protective of others who are suffering, for they identify with them because they feel that they, also, are hurt and suffering. First-borns tend to be conservative and oriented toward rules and authority, because they see in them a protection of their position. They do not care to take chances in life for fear that they might once again be hurt.

*The Middle Child:*   If the oldest child tends to be active, the middle child will tend to be less active. Or, the middle may be more active than the oldest. Whatever the situation, the first and second children tend to be dissimilar in personality. Middle children tend to feel that they have to make up for lost time, as if they were in a race and moving under full steam. Often, middle children in competitive families will feel slighted or abused. They will feel that people are unfair to them, for they do not have the rights of the older child nor the privileges of the younger. Sometimes they set their goals so high that it is impossible to achieve them and, therefore, suffer for the rest of their lives with feelings of incapability.

The middle child tends to be revolutionary, subtle, and liberal, stemming from a conviction that he or she will find a place only through change and revolution (i.e., by overthrowing the first-born). Perhaps having a tendency to slander others or to cut them down, the middle may, on the other hand, praise them so highly that they cannot possibly meet her expressed expectations. Through subtlety, then, this child is able to throw someone off the pedestal he or she has set them on.

*The Youngest Child:*   The youngest seems to be the favored child in history books and fairy tales. It is the youngest who overcomes older brothers, who rides the white horse, and is the good son. We also find this tendency in religious history as portrayed in the stories of Joseph and David.

Typically, youngest children are the most pampered, and become adroit in

Ordinal position affects siblings differently, depending on their respective birth order.

manipulating others. They are often courageous, for they see others ahead of them fail; therefore, failure is not such a traumatic event.

However, because they are the smallest and most incapable, youngest children may suffer from inferiority feelings. They may have the urge to put themselves forward, to advance and outdo other people. They become adroit and inventive, and often develop a repertoire of tricks to mask their situation of being the smallest and most incompetent family member. Their tricks typically revolve around getting other people to give them service, making them feel important. They may learn to be charmers and to attract others through cuteness.

Although a number of other factors affect children's behavior, family atmosphere and constellation seem most important to Dreikurs. These two variables will affect children's strategy in their efforts to feel that they belong.

## THE BASIC GOALS OF MISBEHAVIOR

Dreikurs' analysis of children's misbehavior is one aspect of this theory that parents and teachers find most helpful. As indicated above, a child's behaviors are goal-directed—to have a place in his or her group, to belong. A well-behaved and well-adjusted child will generally find ways to obtain this goal through acceptable means. The misbehaving child, however, is still trying, in a mistaken way, to gain social status. One of four goals may be adopted: attention-seeking, power, revenge, and assuming inadequacy. Children are usually unaware of these goals, but their behavior will be consistent with their particular orientation.

**Attention.**   The first goal of misbehavior, attention-seeking, is usually very easy to identify. For example, if Father sits down to write a letter, an attention-seeking child might start crawling on his lap. The child seems to assume he is important only when attended to. Yielding to these demands increases the child's belief that his assumption is true.

Attention can be constructively or destructively gained. Children actively seeking attention through constructive channels are often viewed as successful yet somewhat obnoxious children. Their only measuring stick for success is the amount of attention and praise they receive for a particular act. In other words, the activity is successful only when attention from a significant source (parent, teacher, etc.) accompanies the activity.

The child actively seeking attention through destructive channels is labeled a nuisance. Such a child leaves messes, fights, and makes noise—anything to keep the parent or teacher attentive. As long as these destructive activities gain the goal of attention the child will persist.

Some children find passive attention-seeking mechanisms more successful. The *passive-constructive* attention-seeking child is the charmer, who doesn't necessarily act constructively, but just sits there being charming and cute. The *passive-destructive* child gains attention through laziness, finding that activity does not bring attention. However, when the child is not doing what he or she is supposed to, Mother and Father are constantly trying to entice and encourage (or they criticize and/or punish). Either way the child gets the desired attention. Generally, parents can identify if their child's goal is attention-seeking because they feel annoyed. They find themselves reprimanding or coaxing the child.

**Power.** The second goal of misbehavior is power—wanting to be the boss. If attention-seeking behavior is not productive for the child, he or she may resort to a power struggle. The child looks at Mother and Father and thinks, "What really makes Mom and Dad what they are is that they have power over me. Power is what I need to be accepted." The child then attempts to exert power over parents, as when the parents say, "You *will*," and the child retorts, "I *won't*." Parents can usually recognize when they are engaged in a power struggle because they feel provoked and angry toward the child.

If parents finally give up, they have yielded to the child's power and the child feels successful. On the other hand, parents may become upset with the child and exert their power by "beating" the child. In this case the child has lost the struggle, but has gained respect for the importance of power and thinks, "Wait 'til I get older!"

Power is evident in active- and passive-destructive methods. A child actively seeking power through destructive tactics is a "rebel" and does the opposite of what is expected. The passive-destructive power seeker is not the "rebel" type, but rather shows power by being "stubborn" and refusing to submit to others.

**Revenge.** The third goal of misbehavior is revenge. A revenging child is one who has lost in the power game and feels humiliated. Seeing that he or she is not strong enough to compete with more powerful parents or teacher, this child feels that to belong he or she must hurt the parents or teacher in parallel fashion. Revenging children do not concern themselves with consequences of their actions—they are only interested in hurting.

Active-destructive children seeking revenge will usually retaliate physically. They break Mother's cherished music box, cut the curtains, or poke holes in the couch, while being oblivious to the possible consequences. The passive-destructive "revengers" employ less physical means. They no longer hope for attention or power, but feel that finding their place in the family

**Table 9.1  The Basic Goals of Misbehavior**

| Goal | Parent's Reaction | Inappropriate Parental Reaction |
|---|---|---|
| Attention | Annoyance | Reprimanding or coaxing |
| Power | Anger | Giving in or exerting their own power |
| Revenge | Hurt | Trying to get even |
| Assuming inadequacy | Despair | Punishment, ignoring |

means making themselves hated. They know how to hurt and to take advantage of others' vulnerabilities, embarrassment, or shame. Parents experiencing this type of misbehavior generally feel hurt, and may even want to get even.

**Assuming inadequacy.** If none of the above strategies gives the child a sense of belonging, and power is continually forced upon the child, he or she will eventually feel helpless. At this point the child becomes so discouraged that he or she feels it is probably better not to do anything other than just face the possible consequences of failing or losing; anything he or she does will probably be met by criticism and ridicule. Such a child wants to be left alone. At this point, parents feel despair and often do not know what to do.

What many parents don't understand is that children displaying these types of misbehavior are the most in need of understanding and encouragement. What generally happens, however, is that they are most likely to be punished and ignored.

## DEALING WITH MISBEHAVIOR

Dreikurs advises parents (1) to use encouragement to help prevent misbehavior; and (2) to use the method of natural and logical consequences to correct misbehavior.

**Encouragement.** To prevent misbehavior, children can be provided with many encouraging experiences: The first rule for providing encouragement is to eliminate discouragement. Suppose Mother walks into young Mary's bedroom and the child announces she has made her own bed this morning. However, Mother only sees a pile of sheets covered by a not-so-neatly-placed bedspread. She says, "That bed isn't made. You've piled everything up. You go outside and play and I'll make this bed for you." In this case the mother has discouraged her daughter and neglected giving credit where credit was due. She subtly told her daughter that she couldn't perform the task she had proudly presented for approval. It is more important to praise the child for the good or the task attempted, than to point out negative aspects of the performance in a discouraging manner. Through encouragement, a child will practice and improve in the tasks performed. If criticized and discouraged, the child will see no reason to attempt the task on subsequent occasions.

Four general rules should be considered when giving encouragement to children:

1. *Encouragement should be focused on the child.* Phrases like "*I'm* so proud of you," "*I* like the way you did that," and "That makes *me* happy" should be replaced by "I'll bet that makes *you* feel good" and "*You* do very good work."
2. *Accentuate the positive and eliminate the negative.* Instead of saying, "Don't get water on the car," say, "Keep the water on the grass." To a timid child, say, "It is nice

that you are going to visit Aunt Hilda. She likes to talk with you and wants to hear what you have to say," not "People won't like you unless you talk with them; don't be shy or whisper, but speak out loud."

3. *Try to get the child to express feelings.* Ask the child, "How does that make you feel?" or "What do you think about that?" This encourages the child to evaluate his or her own performance.

4. *Be sincere.* Sometimes a quick "That's nice, dear" is more discouraging than no comment at all.

In summary, Dreikurs feels that heredity, environment, and internal states are equally important in determining behavior; all behavior is goal-directed; family atmosphere and family constellation are significant influences on a person's lifestyle; misbehavior has a goal; and children should be given encouragement to help prevent misbehavior. As suggested above, he also expands his theoretical position to include disciplinary techniques (Dreikurs, 1948, 1968; Dreikurs & Grey, 1968; Dreikurs & Soltz, 1967). His approach, unlike physical punishment, focuses on natural and logical consequences.

**Natural and logical consequences.**   If a person steps off the top of a tall building, the consequence is obvious; this is a *natural consequence.* Obedience to natural laws is compulsory. Given opportunity and freedom, children will learn to successfully comply with natural laws. Dreikurs recommends using natural consequences when training children, as long as they will not hurt the child. For example, if young Bobby does not come for dinner at the appropriate time, he can eat cold food. Having a cold meal usually won't hurt a child. Consider the following story of a child who would not take care of his toys:

●

*My little brother was destructive when he was small. He would take Tonka toys and roll them down the big avenue gutters, soon to be lost forever. He would find ways to tear apart stuffed dolls and animals, or throw balls and other objects on buildings. One day he demolished his tricycle with a hammer. After much money was spent on toys, my parents decided not to replace them. My brother became somewhat distressed because his toys were slowly declining in number. He finally ended up not having any playthings. My parents didn't buy him toys until six months later, when they bought him a brand new bike with training wheels. To this day (15 years later) that bike is still in the family.*

●

If natural consequences are too dangerous, then *logical consequences* should be devised (i.e., a consequence that relates to the act but is not dangerous). Natural consequences usually occur without intrusion by parents or caretakers, whereas logical consequences are calculated beforehand. For

Sometimes children have to learn lessons involving unwanted risks on their own.

example, if Kathy is continually running out into the street, a parent could not risk letting the natural consequences occur. A parent cannot let her run into the street, get hit by a car, and then say, "Now let that be a lesson to you!" Logical consequences are necessary in this case: "You may either play in the back yard or come in the house." A three-year-old child, for example, is not mature enough to assume responsibility for playing in the front yard unsupervised, so a choice is given between the back yard or the house.

This approach takes some of the responsibility of enforcement away from parents, allowing children to often learn something on their own. It is often difficult to let children discover things for themselves, but sometimes a child has to learn a lesson involving an unwanted risk. The parents of the following child allowed him to learn for himself the consequences of his actions:

*When I was in high school my parents were quite protective of my inappropriate behavior (i.e., bailing me out of jail when I was in trouble, seeing that I was cared for when I got drunk, or making sure I was OK when I arrived home late). They had come to the detention home several times to rescue me from the law. One day, without any warning, my parents didn't come to my rescue when I got into trouble. I spent several nights in detention. I suffered and felt somewhat rejected. I decided the so-called "good times" I was having weren't worth the consequences.*

Trying to find a balance between expecting too much and expecting too little requires sensitivity on a parent's part. Parents can be helpful, but children should be allowed the privilege of failure. If a child is trying to climb up onto a chair and it doesn't look like she's going to make it, parents shouldn't run over and help her up. She should be allowed the experience of failure, though being encouraged at the same time—"You almost made it that time; maybe you can do it next time." With that kind of approach a child is going to go back and try again by herself, because she has been told she might be able to accomplish the task. (For further information see Allred, 1968; Dreikurs, 1948, 1968; Dreikurs & Grey, 1968; Dreikurs & Soltz, 1967).

A parent must help the child realize that consequences are a result of the child's misbehavior, not the parent's wishes. When enforcing the consequence, a parent can remain friendly and undisturbed. For example, one child was given the assignment of cleaning the kitchen before going to the beach. The child wandered off and did not attend to his chore. As the child repeatedly came back and asked when they were going to leave for the beach, the father calmly replied, "As soon as we get the work done, we can go." This child never completed the work and as a result the trip was cancelled.

**Logical consequences or punishment?**    To work best, logical consequences must be related to what the child has done. Punishment, on the other hand, may have no relationship to the child's behavior. For example, spankings rarely have a logical relationship to anything the child has done. A child does not do assigned chores and gets spanked—the relationship between neglect of duties and spanking is not natural, but contrived, and the child fails to learn natural and logical connections between events. If, however, chores must be done before fun and games, the connection between failure to do work and deprivation of privileges fits together more logically.

Natural and logical consequences do not ridicule or pass moral judgment on the child. The child pays a price, but the parent is not a judge meting out a sentence. The word "wrong" need not even be used, and it is better if parents do not emphasize the consequences, but let them take place with as little involvement on their part as possible. In a parenting book recommending this disciplinary procedure, the author provides five guidelines when using logical consequences. They are:

1. Consequences are a reasonable result of the misbehavior and are not retaliation or punishment on the parent's part to get even with or humiliate the child.
2. Choices are provided (e.g., telling the little boy who insists on running out to the busy street that he has the choice of staying in the back yard or coming in the house). This way the child determines what will happen to him, within limits set down by the parent, of course.
3. Results of consequences should be logical and understandable to the child.
4. Parents should watch their tone of voice. There is a tendency, when disturbed by a child, to be angry. The tone of voice should be calm.
5. Empathize with the child. Know and understand how the child feels; however, do not pity or sympathize with him, for this may weaken a parent's resolve and firmness in dealing with the child (Allred, 1968, p. 61).

It may appear that using natural and logical consequences is simply another form of punishment. Dreikurs adamantly maintains that this is not the case. Consider some of his statements about the differences between punishment and natural or logical consequences:

> Consequences must have an inner logic understandable to the child. Telling him he cannot go to the movies if he does not eat his dinner has no logic; but if he does not come home from the movie on time, it is reasonable that he be told he may not go next week. . . .
> Consequences are a natural result of misbehavior—but they are not retaliations. Consequences are, rather, an invitation: "As long as you misbehave, it will be impossible for you to . . ."
> If you speak in a harsh, angry voice then you punish. If you maintain a friendly attitude, you emphasize that it is the order which has to be observed, not your personal desire or your power. In the first case, you take a stand against the child and consequently he feels rejected. In the second case, you object only to the child's behavior and his personal value is not threatened (Dreikurs, 1972, pp. 30–31).

Dreikurs points out that this type of discipline requires parents to demonstrate they have respect for their children. To show respect for a child, one has to appreicate that the child is an individual. Each has his or her own personality and thoughts and deserves the right to receive the same amount of respect given an adult.

In some instances, the difference between punishment (as defined by behavior modification theory) and Dreikurs' natural and logical consequences appears to be one of semantics. For example, when defining logical consequences, Dreikurs (1967, p. 81) provides an example of a child who refused to stay out of the street when playing in the front yard. Rather than let natural consequences—being hit by a car—teach the child about improper behavior, a contrived or logical consequence was necessary. In this case, the mother carries the child into the house, stating "Since you do not feel like playing in the yard, you may not go out. When you are ready, you may try again."

Yet, this same process could be explained as follows: Because the child has not done what was expected or what he or she was told to do, a negative punishment technique is used. Recall that negative punishment involves removing something to decrease a behavior. In this case, removing the child from the yard is taking away the reinforcing properties of playing outside. This is done to decrease "playing in the street" behavior. In fact, Dreikurs appears to have implemented a time-out procedure.

Similarly, to suggest that the family will go to the beach when the chores are done, and that the consequence of not doing chores is a cancelled trip, is the same as suggesting a positive reinforcement of going to the beach to elicit helping behavior. If chores are not done, the opportunity of going to the beach is taken away to reduce "not helping" behavior in the future—negative punishment.

However, Dreikurs' approach does teach parents some important principles not found in other orientations. By attempting to use natural and logical consequences, parents are not arbitrarily imposing power to force compliance. Rather, the consequences apply to everyone living in a similar environment. As such, the child learns more about how his or her actions result in certain consequences. For example, coming home late to dinner need not be "punished." The child instead faces the consequence of cold food or preparing his or her own meal. The parent need not step in and administer or remove something to decrease the behavior. This approach would appear less susceptible to strained parent–child relations, which are found when punishment is used excessively.

Also important is Dreikurs' emphasis that instead of being vindictive, parents can be compassionate, kind, and supportive in helping children face consequences of their behaviors. The parent need not be in the position of "serving justice," which in behavioral theory would be confounding if parents were simultaneously warm and supportive—this would be reinforcing. Rather, having the consequence follow naturally, children see more clearly their responsibility in the behavior–consequence chain, and the focus is not upon the parent. As a result, parents can be warm and compassionate when consequences follow, and the learning process is not retarded.

## William Glasser
## RATIONAL CONFRONTATION

*Jimmy must have had a long day in Ms. Carson's first-grade classroom. At any rate the teacher's repeated reminders to be quiet were to no avail. In desperation she sent him out.*

*I was the student teacher of the classroom and was asked to check on Jimmy. He was sitting on a bench with his chin resting on his hand as I sat down beside him.*

*"Jimmy, do you know why you're here?"*

*"Yes."*

*"Can you tell me?"*

*"I wasn't quiet."*

*"That's right, and it was disrupting to the class, wasn't it?"*

*"Yes."*

*"Well, what can we do about it?"*

*"Be quiet, I guess."*

*"Can you do that?"*

*"Yes."*

*"For the rest of the day?"*

*"Yes."*

*"Great, Jimmy. Let's shake on it." We shook. Jimmy smiled and was great the rest of the day. Periodically I remembered to pass by him and whisper encouragements and compliments on his improved conduct.*

This successful confrontation was reported by a student when completing her student teaching experience in a small rural school. Consider the next illustration:

*A mother of two young boys found them fighting one afternoon. Apparently, one had taken a toy that belonged to his brother. The brother had just found out and wanted his toy back. Here's how the mother handled the situation:*

| | |
|---|---|
| Mother: | *"What are you doing?"* |
| 1st son: | *"Fighting."* |
| 2nd son: | *"Fighting. He took my toy."* |
| | *[The children identify their behavior.]* |
| Mother: | *"Does fighting make you feel good?"* |
| 2nd son: | *"No, but he took my toy."* |
| 1st son: | *"No, but I wanted to play with his truck."* |
| | *[The children make a decision about their behavior.]* |
| Mother: | *"What are some other things that you could do so you wouldn't have to fight about your toys?"* |
| | *After some discussion the children reply:* |
| 1st son: | *"I could let him have his truck back."* |
| 2nd son: | *"Let him play with mine, just this once."* |
| Mother: | *"Yes, you could. Why don't we make a rule that your brother can play with one of your toys if you aren't playing with it. Is that okay?"* |
| | *[The adult provides a plan of behavior if the child cannot think of one.]* |

| | |
|---|---|
| 1st son: | *"Okay."* |
| 2nd son: | *[Nods]* |
| Mother: | *"Now, will you follow the rule?"* |
| Sons: | *"Yes."* |
| | *[The children make a commitment.]* |

The above examples outline an approach recommended by William Glasser, a psychiatrist who has proposed a practical way to deal with children using rational confrontation, which he calls "reality therapy" (Glasser, 1965, 1969). While Glasser has proposed an entire approach to therapy, we have selected the heart of his program to illustrate how direct confrontation can be used to influence children's future behavior.

The object of a confrontation is to help a child make a value judgment about his or her behavior and a commitment to improve. Glasser asks parents to first confront the child with his or her behavior and ask if that behavior is going to be satisfying or not. The parent then asks the child to identify future results of this behavior and asks if it is going to be satisfying to the child or to others. This rational approach of pointing out consequences and having

Rational confrontation requires that parents use a verbal, didactic approach to discipline.

the child evaluate those consequences helps bring him or her to the point of accepting responsibility.

Second, after present behavior is examined in terms of consequences, a child is given the opportunity to formulate several alternative plans of behavior to bring about more desirable results; a decision is then made as to which is the best plan of action to follow. Third, if a child makes a responsible decision, Glasser then asks the child to make a commitment. He maintains that commitment is essential for the development of maturity and feelings of self-worth, eventually leading to a stable self-identity. Parents should accept no excuses for not following through once a commitment is made; previously decided-upon consequences need to follow if the commitment is not upheld. A child will then learn to recognize his or her own responsibility for actions taken, including assuming the consequences of misbehavior. Glasser assures parents that if they exact these standards, they will not alienate their children from them. Instead, as children successfully comply with or meet these standards, they will gain in self-respect, closeness, and love for their parents.

This description of discipline by Glasser may give the impression that parents should not allow freedom. However, Glasser asserts that necessary freedom for individual growth is granted to people by allowing them to make decisions and to then receive the consequences of their behavior. If, on the other hand, an individual is mentally impaired and unaware that he or she will receive either a natural reward or punishment for actions taken, that person should not be given the freedom to make such decisions.

## EMPHASIS ON RELATIONSHIP

Glasser's approach is an active approach, but its success depends on a positive relationship between child and parent. Parents must build firm, personal, and emotional relationships with their children. This is particularly true for those who have failed to develop such a relationship in the past. Parents should be responsive to their children and yet at the same time objective and rational. They should be patient enough to listen to a child's request for sympathy, but strong enough to not condone the child's misbehavior or to place responsibility on anyone other than the child.

Also, parents should be willing to accept a wide range of behavior, even sharing and recognizing their own shortcomings. Being uncritical and understanding is essential. This implies not becoming frightened or defensive, when confused about how to deal with a child, but having a genuine emotional involvement with the child receiving guidance. This type of relationship is oriented toward helping the child recognize and become aware of his or her own potential and strength. Consider the following example:

*Shaune was teasing her sisters and being hard to live with as they were trying to get ready for school.*

*"Shaune, come and sit on the couch with me for a minute." She ran over and sat down.*
*"What's happening?"*
*"You know, Mom."*
*"You tell me."*
*"I was just teasing!"*
*"Does that make our home happy?"*
*"No."*
*"What can we do about it?"*
*"I can stop."*
*"Will you?"*
*"Yes."*
*"Promise?"*
*"Yes."*
*As she left for school after an amazing turnabout in actions, she hugged her mother and said, "I love you, Mom" and ran off happily to school.*

In summary, Glasser's reality therapy technique is a process of helping children to accept responsibility for their own behavior, which will, in turn, help them to fulfill their own needs. The child is confronted with his or her behavior and helped to see the consequences of actions taken. Assisted in choosing alternative behaviors, the child is then asked to make a commitment. This approach relies on a positive, warm relationship between parent and child.

## Summary

Dreikurs' and Glasser's approaches, when taken together, are somewhat different than behavior modification. Whereas behavior modification techniques (high-power techniques to influence behavior) focus only on observable behavior, these moderate-power techniques emphasize respecting the child for his or her own individuality; needs and thoughts are of primary focus. Understanding a child's behavior (misbehavior) and the change process must both consider these more subjective events. Through this process, the child's self-understanding and self-responsibility increase.

After reading Chapters 8 and 9, it is more apparent why Dreikurs' and Glasser's ideas have been termed *moderate-power techniques*. Parents using these approaches exercise less power and control over their children's environments. Rather than being the controller of reinforcers, they attempt to let children grow by making mistakes, and by helping them understand their environment, the consequences of their actions, and how their actions impact other individuals.

# SELF-CHECK

1. Rudolph Dreikurs is a disciple of the Adlerian school of psychoanalysis, a basic assumption of which is
   a. that human beings are affected by stimuli from inside and outside the body.
   b. that the nature of the human being is to belong.
   c. the importance of heredity over environmental influences.
   d. a and b above are both correct.

2. The following events, according to Dreikurs, have a significant influence on a person's lifestyle:
   a. Family atmosphere
   b. Family constellation
   c. Age of the parents
   d. a and b above are both correct.

3. Dreikurs stated several goals of misbehavior. Which goal might be present if a parent experiences anger toward the child?
   a. Attention-seeking
   b. Power
   c. Revenge
   d. None of the above is correct.

4. When giving encouragement to a child, the following general rule applies:
   a. Encouragement should be focused on the child.
   b. Be sincere.
   c. Try to get the child to express his or her feelings.
   d. All of the above are correct.

5. Dreikurs' approach to discipline focuses on
   a. physical punishment.
   b. contrived circumstances.
   c. natural and logical consequences.
   d. nonverbal communication.

6. Which of the following is true about the use of natural and logical consequences?
   a. Natural and logical consequences do not ridicule or pass moral judgment.
   b. Natural consequences could be used at any time.
   c. Logical consequences need not always be related to what the child has done.
   d. None of the above is correct.

7. William Glasser's rational confrontation approach to child rearing and discipline is called
   a. natural and logical consequences.
   b. objectifications.
   c. reality therapy.
   d. motive therapy.

8. The object of Glasser's approach is
   a. to help a child make a value judgment about his or her behavior and then commit to improve.
   b. to help parents identify future results of their child's behavior.
   c. to help the parent accept responsibility.
   d. to help the child understand a parent's rationale.

9. The key to making Glasser's approach work is
   a. a restrictive parenting pattern.
   b. the child being above 10 years old.

c. an above-average intelligence and ability to reason.

d. a positive relationship between parent and child.

10. When using natural and logical consequences

a. parents should watch their tone of voice.

b. results of consequences should be logical and understandable to the child.

c. empathy with the child is important.

d. All of the above are true.

KEY: 1–d; 2–d; 3–b; 4–d; 5–c; 6–a; 7–c; 8–a; 9–d; 10–d

# LOW-POWER TECHNIQUES TO PRODUCE OR LESSEN BEHAVIOR

Low-power techniques to influence behavior will be discussed in this chapter. The orientation begun in Chapter 9—the shift away from a focus on observable behaviors and control of reinforcers and punishers—is continued here. Parents can interact with their children to help them understand others' feelings and their own, and how their feelings and behaviors affect those around them. The work and ideas of Thomas Gordon will be heavily cited to present this orientation toward influencing children's behaviors, because his approach reflects nicely our purpose in this chapter.

## As Little Power as Possible

Thirty-five kindergarten boys were asked to rank five toys in order of preference and then promised either an attractive flashlight or two "so-so" marbles. Next, the boys were left alone with the toys but told that if they played with their second favorite toy, they would not receive the promised gift.

As you might expect, the boys did not play with the forbidden toy, but that was not the point of the experiment. What is interesting is that when the boys ranked the toys a second time, the rating of the second toy changed. Those threatened with the loss of two marbles lowered the attractiveness of the toy, while those threatened with the loss of the flashlight now thought the toy was more attractive. Many ranked it first!

Using a more powerful incentive to deter or stop an action actually *increased* the desire, whereas a mild threat (loss of two unimportant marbles) *lowered* motivation to play with the forbidden toy (Pepitone, McCauley, & Hammond, 1967).

A similar experiment was performed by Lepper (1973). One group of children received a strong threat to keep them from playing with attractive toys, a second group received a mild threat, and a third received no threat at all. Three weeks later the experimenter returned and asked all children to play a game to obtain attractive prizes. The catch was this: Only by falsifying their scores and being dishonest could the children win a prize. The experimenter correctly predicted from his theory that subjects who received only a mild threat would falsify their scores the least, while those receiving a strong threat would be most dishonest. He reasoned that if subjects did not play with the forbidden toys when receiving a mild threat, they would conclude that they refrained because they were good children. Those who had received a strong threat would reason differently, concluding that they were being bad because a strong threat was necessary to keep them from deviating.

As mentioned throughout this text, there is no one "best way" to raise children, but these two experiments represent a body of studies that has produced at least one important principle for effective child rearing. The prin-

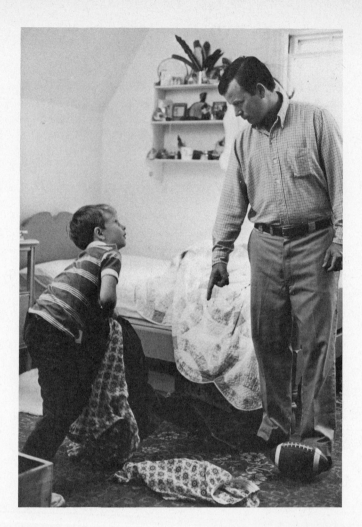

Severe punishment may in some cases less effectively reduce inappropriate behavior than less powerful techniques.

ciple can be simply stated: Use as little power as possible. It would seem that severe punishment (high-power consequences) may in some cases be less effective in reducing inappropriate behavior than less powerful techniques. Yet, parents often underestimate just how much power they use when dealing with young children. A listing of just some elements parents control includes:

1. Food and water
2. Activities and opportunities
3. Money and other socially attractive incentives
4. Possession of information and knowledge
5. Affection
6. Love
7. Pain

When parents use one or more of these elements to control or influence their children, they are using power. The disadvantages of controlling children through high reward power however, are shown in several phenomena:

1. Children come to expect a payoff for their behavior.
2. Children stop behaving when rewards stop, sometimes with a strong negative reaction.
3. Parents eventually lose ability to compete with other sources of reward (e.g., clubs, peers, etc.).
4. Children develop the feeling that external causes (the rewards) rather than internal elements control their actions.

However, the above disadvantages are not always present when using high-reward-power child-rearing techniques. Using high reward power is sometimes not too bad an approach. Research indicates that if parents want to raise obedient children, the high-power approaches can be used. If you want children who are compliant, obedient, submissive, courteous and proper, with the least parental effort in the shortest time, then judiciously control and administer these powerful rewards. Dispense rewards only when the child acts appropriately. In fact, it is almost impossible to avoid using high reward power during the first two years of life when children's communication skills are less developed and their comprehension limited.

One might ask, "If high reward power is so effective, why not use it?" You might say, "I'll settle for a child like that!" However, upon further reflection, you will likely conclude that you want more for your children; that instead of just obedience during childhood, a higher goal is sought.

## Facilitating a Child's Growth Toward Maturity

Low-power techniques may better facilitate the development of personal growth. While obedience during childhood may be compatible with personal growth toward maturity, there are reasons to believe that in many cases quickly obtained obedience works against long-term growth. The children being reared with low-power techniques, for example, do not experience a powerful parent controlling all rewards and punishments. Instead, they perceive expectations from a warm, affectionate adult who not only trusts them, but is also ready to help. The parent becomes a helper, growth facilitator, and partner in growing, rather than a domineering authority assuming total responsibility for the child's growth. Children raised in such conditions are different. Findings from investigations of homes where parents use low-power techniques suggest independent, self-sufficient, assertive, creative, and problem-solving children.

It is often asserted that the primary advantage of low-power discipline is that it facilitates independence and maturity. Upon comparison, 21-year-old individuals from homes using low power will probably be more indepen-

Using low-power techniques may not be as imme- diately success- ful, or may be more frustrating initially, than higher-power approaches. However, a higher goal is being sought— not just obedience.

dent and mature than those from high-power homes. It is also probably true that when parents use low-power techniques, children may not always come as promptly when called; they may not persist as long on a tiring, boring task; and they may make more mistakes in carrying out assignments. Also, the par- ent may at times feel more frustrated, and not as much in control or receiving of respect. However, when reared with low-power techniques, children are likely to show behavior that is more genuine and more enduring. The moti- vation is different. In this chapter some low-power methods will be described.

## Gordon's Parent-Training Model

Thomas Gordon (1970, 1980) has developed a program of parent edu- cation called "Parent Effectiveness Training." In addition to publishing a nontechnical book of the same name that describes his program, he has insti- tuted small training centers in several states. Beginning as a consulting clinical psychologist in California, he developed his program to teach parents how to more effectively deal with their children. Gordon begins by pointing out that parents are frequently accused of being the source of their children's prob- lems. Too much attention is given to blaming parents and not enough to training them. He maintains that his program is a complete system, sufficient to train parents to effectively deal with their children.

### ACCEPTANCE

Gordon points out the natural and inevitable fallibility of parents. Since parents are human, acknowledging this fallibility should not lessen their effectiveness. Understanding that parents can and do make mistakes is a realistic and honest beginning point for rearing children.

**Acceptance is not absolute.** The theory upon which Gordon bases his recommendations focuses largely on learning how to accept children's behavior. However, it is unreasonable to expect parents to accept all their children's behaviors. Some behavior is acceptable; some is unacceptable. For example, breaking a bottle of catsup in the living room is unacceptable. However, effective parents accept more of their children's behavior than ineffective parents.

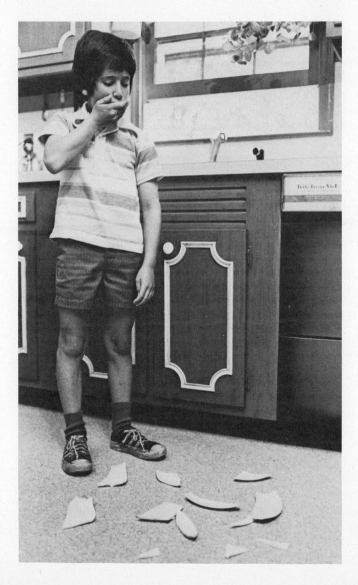

It is unreasonable to expect parents to accept all their children's behaviors.

Parents should strive to be as accepting as possible, although amount of acceptance may change from one child to the next. For example, parents may find much of the behavior of an extremely active or energetic child unacceptable to them. A quieter child, however, might find his or her interest in books and music fully accepted by the same parents.

Children's behaviors are also often differentially accepted by the same parents, based on how they feel about themselves. If parents feel self-confident or good about themselves, more behaviors are accepted. However, when the parent is tired or feeling unstable, the level of unacceptable behavior is raised. Thus, how a parent feels is going to raise or lower the amount of behavior that is acceptable.

**Inconsistency.** Notorious among parents is the willingness to accept poor table manners at home when company is not present, but to sharply criticize the same manners in public. This inevitable change varies from child to child, parent to parent, and from situation to situation. Gordon states, "Inevitably, then, parents will be inconsistent. How could there be anything else when their feelings change from day to day, from child to child, and from situation to situation?" A parent tells one son to study harder when sent off to the university, but another is counseled to take some time out for relaxation and fun. One son was not loved more than the other, but parents can and will be inconsistent. There is likely to be a difference between parents' understanding of male and female acceptable behaviors as well. Fathers, for example, tend to react differently toward their daughters than mothers do.

**Genuineness.** When trying to be an accepting parent, false acceptance should be avoided. For example, a parent may say, "All right, you may stay out after dark and play," although not wanting to accept the behavior and feeling uncomfortable about the child staying out late. The little girl soon discovers that staying out and playing after dark is really not acceptable, even though her parents consented. By their attitude and poorly disguised feelings, the parents rejected both their decision and the girl's behavior. When discovering this false acceptance, the child begins wondering whether she can trust other forms of acceptance coming from her parents; she has doubts about the parents' genuineness or honesty, and learns that her parents may say one thing and actually feel or mean something else.

Gordon maintains that parents can be human and need not maintain artificial attitudes. They need not always be consistent, nor need they accept everything a child does. As a result, if parents acknowledge their human characteristics, children will actually prefer this and be able to relate to them more honestly and openly.

When parents are able to accept children for what they are, they become genuine, helping parents. Some parents falsely believe that if children are accepted as they are, they will remain the same and not improve; they believe that their nonacceptance can push their offspring to further achievement. Actually, the opposite is true. When children are accepted, they are free to grow and develop; when not accepted, they become defensive to protect themselves, thus prohibiting change.

**Communicating acceptance nonverbally.** Communication can be relayed through nonintervention. Suppose a child is learning to clean up the kitchen and is making numerous mistakes. The parent can say, "Here, let me show you how to do it right," which tends to imply rejection. If the child is allowed to complete the task, however, then acceptance—a sign of confidence—is communicated. Nonintervention is viewed by the child as acceptance.

Another method of acceptance is *passive listening:* silently listening to the child while saying nothing. Suppose a child comes home and tells her parents she had a fight during school, and then describes what she did to solve the problem. Her parents may be able to suggest more appropriate methods of handling the situation, but they should continue to sit and listen. If the child knows that she is really being listened to, acceptance is conveyed.

## ACTIVE LISTENING

Acceptance cannot be continually projected nonverbally. Children require dialectical interchanges to build healthy relationships with their parents. However, many parents fail to respond verbally to their children in accepting, relationship-building ways. Instead, they make negative responses that Gordon says usually communicate something *about* the child. For example, if judged, criticized, warned, lectured, advised, or ordered, the child may receive the message that he or she is perceived as incapable. Rather than provide the child with negative messages, active listening constructively responds to children's feeling-messages or problem-messages.

Active listening begins when the child has a need. The child takes this need and codes it into a message, thereupon sending the message to the parent. The parent decodes the message, interprets it, then encodes the same message and sends it back to the child. For example, if the child asks, "When do we go home?" he may actually be trying to express that he is bored or sleepy. The parent receives the message and decodes it: "He is bored or wants to go to sleep." The parent then encodes the message and returns it by asking, "Are you getting sleepy?" In this fashion, the child feels he is understood. Outcomes of active listing include the following:

1. It provides a child with a cathartic outlet to open up and get feelings out.
2. It helps the child accept his or her own feelings.
3. It promotes warmth and understanding between child and parent.
4. It facilitates a problem-solving attitude in the child.
5. It will eventually help the child to be more aware and to listen to parents' thoughts and ideas.

Children try to communicate with parents who listen. Active listening helps children think about the problem, solve it, and handle it themselves.

The parent can be empathetic and understanding, yet still allow the child to retain responsibility for the problem. The child grows through this process in the above-mentioned ways, without being ordered, criticized, or lectured.

**Potential problems with active listening.** Parents must want to hear what children have to say and accept their feelings when they are sent. For example, if a child sends the message "I think that Ms. Gray should be hung," a parent might say, "So you want to hang Ms. Gray." However, that is not what was meant in the original message. When correctly deciphered, the message says, "I don't like Ms. Gray." In addition, parents must trust children's abilities to eventually handle the problem, realizing that feelings are transitory, not permanent. For example, how many of us have heard children say to their parents, "I hate you!" The feeling may last another hour or so but that's all. Likewise, the way a child feels about Ms. Gray is going to change.

Active listening should not be used with the intent of manipulating the child and calling it guidance. "Active listening" implies sending a message back and letting the child solve his or her own problem. If a parent changes the message so as to solve the problem for the child by giving solutions or suggestions, active listening has not occurred.

Parents often fall into the habit of parroting a child's statements—of not recoding the child's message to show the child that he or she is understood. Rather, the very same words are used, reflecting back the message without feeling and understanding, and the child remains confused as to whether the parent really understands. Another frequent error is listening without empathy. Accurate listening and recoding can occur, but fail in their purpose if no real concern or caring is present. Children easily detect this attitude.

Still another problem occurs when active listening is used inappropriately. Instances arise, for example, in which other forms of communication are more appropriate. Active listening works only when the problem belongs to the child, that is, when *the child* has a need that is not satisfied. If, however, when attempting to satisfy personal needs, the child's actions interfere with parents' needs, then it also becomes the parent's problem. Active listening is not useful when both parent and child share the problem. Remember that a child's need is sent in message form to parents; the parent decodes the message, interprets it, encodes it, and sends it back to the child without attempting to solve anything. If a problem is going to be solved, the child will have to solve it.

Suppose a child comes home concerned about a run-in he had with a friend. The child owns the problem; a parent can implement active listening to help the child express his feelings, state the problem, and develop some solutions. However, what if the child is presently arguing with a sister, and the noise and bickering are interfering with a parent's ability to hear a news program? The child's problem is now interfering with the parent's needs and has become his or her problem as well. Active listening is inappropriate in this instance. A different communicative technique is necessary when a parent shares the problem. Gordon calls this an "I" message. In essence, "I" messages help parents share their feelings with children rather than ordering, lecturing, preaching, advising, or warning.

## SHARING FEELINGS

> Mrs. H. reported an incident during their family vacation. Their small children had been very loud and boisterous in the back of the station wagon. Mrs. H. and her husband had been resentfully enduring the racket, but finally Mr. H. could stand no more. He braked the car abruptly, pulled off the road, and announced, "I just can't stand all this noise and jumping around in the back. I want to enjoy my vacation and I want to have fun when I'm driving. But, damn it, when there is noise back there, I get nervous and I hate to drive. I feel I have a right to enjoy this vacation, too" (Gordon, 1970, p. 130).

In this example, Mr. H. simply shared his feelings, and as a result the children settled down. They had not realized how their behavior was affecting Father. When this was pointed out to them, they were willing to act so that Father would not experience additional distress. In life, we all alter behavior because of its potential impact on others; this is also true of children. If used properly, sending "I" messages, or sharing feelings, will teach children how their behaviors affect other people.

Unfortunately, parents often underestimate children's willingness and ability to change behavior that is annoying to others. Instead, these parents send solution messages to their children as mentioned before, such as: (1) ordering and directing; (2) warning and admonishing; (3) preaching and moralizing; and, (4) advising and giving suggestions. Three things are wrong with these messages. First, children don't like being told what to do. Second, they communicate that the child is incapable or not trusted. Third, they convey that you think your needs are more important than theirs.

**"I" messages.** Statements such as *"You* do this," or *"You're* this way," are "You" messages and differ from "I" messages such as "I'm distressed when that happens," "I'm worried about you at night," or "I'm afraid you're going to fall." Mr. H. shared his feelings about the children's noise in the back of the car by sending a string of "I" messages. Thomas Gordon believes "I" messages to be more effective for four reasons:

1. They are less likely to provoke resistance and rebellion. When a child hears a parent say, "I'm worried," resistance and rebellion are not usually engendered.
2. They place responsibility with the child. Parents identify how the child's behavior is making them feel.
3. They help the child assume responsibility for his or her own behavior. When a "You" message is sent, the parent is assuming responsibility for the child's behavior through ordering, lecturing, or judging.
4. Because they are honest, they tend to encourage honest messages in return, thus facilitating communication.

In her book *The Process of Parenting,* Jane Brooks (1981) states the following about sharing feelings in the form of "I" messages:

> The "I" message, as this is called, contains three parts: 1) a clear statement of how the parent feels, 2) the child's behavior that has caused the parent to feel that way, and 3) why the behavior is upsetting to the parent. For example, a parent who is frustrated with a teenager's messy room might say, "I feel upset and frustrated when I look at your messy room, because the family works hard to make the house look clean and neat, and your room spoils all our effort (p. 55).

Brooks (1981) recommends "I" messages because: (1) parents become more aware of their own needs; (2) children discover parents' feelings and reactions; and (3) children are taught to problem-solve.

Even young children are sensitive to other people's feelings, and Gordon (1970) feels that parents can use nonverbal signals to share feelings with them. He gives the following examples:

> Rob is squirming while Mother is putting his clothes on. Mother gently but firmly restrains him and continues to dress him. (Message: "I can't dress you when you are squirming.")
>      Mary is jumping up and down on the couch and Mother fears she will hit the lamp on the end table. Mother gently but firmly removes Mary from the couch and jumps up and down with her on the floor. (Message: "I don't like to have you jump on the couch, but I don't mind if you jump on the floor.") (p. 234)

"I" messages do require great skill on the parent's part. When first used they will sometimes fail to produce results because children have been so accustomed to other methods and have not learned to be sensitive and considerate of their parents. However, with continued use, this technique of sharing feelings will begin to yield success.

**Possible pitfalls.**  When a parent sends "I" messages, some traps need to be avoided. First, don't always send negative "I" messages. For example, Gordon points out that when a child is out late at night, the parent can use positive statements, or at least include positive elements in the statement, such as "I'm so glad to see you return." Gordon also explains that "I" messages are often insufficiently stated. For example, if a child is playing in a dangerous area, the parent wouldn't say, "I'm worried." An "I" message should convey true feelings ("I was so worried that I just couldn't . . ." or "I am extremely scared . . ."). Emphasize the true strength of feelings, rather than sending weak messages.

Also, too many "I" messages may overwhelm the child. If the child continually hears, "I was worried," "I was unhappy," "I was afraid," "I'm concerned," "I'm questioning," day after day, he or she will become emotionally exhausted. Parents must learn to use this technique appropriately, in the right circumstances, and in the right "dosage."

**How "I" messages work.** The essential element making sharing of feelings effective is trust—a belief that children, when they are aware they are disturbing, irritating, or annoying to other people, will self-correct their behavior. If they are never given the opportunity to self-correct, children will not learn consideration and responsibility. Sharing feelings provides the opportunity for a child to act responsibly for the welfare of others.

The parent does not directly show the consequences of an action to either self or others, but in an even more removed fashion simply shares positive and negative feelings with the child, assuming and believing that even young children have sufficient intelligence and sensitivity to alter their behaviors so that others are not hurt, distressed, or made unhappy.

It is important to remember that "I" messages may also be used when sharing positive feelings, not just when portraying a problem. Parents should express even positive feelings to children, explaining what they did to make them feel that way. For example, "It feels so good to come home each day, because the house always looks so good and you children are always so thoughtful and kind to me." Without question, it is better to have an abundance of positive feelings rather than negative, even though "I" messages may be used effectively in negative situations.

## THE NO-LOSE METHOD

Thomas Gordon (1970) describes an additional problem-solving technique when confrontation between parent and child occurs. Called the "No-Lose Method," it comprises six steps:

1. Identify and define the conflict.
2. Generate possible alternative solutions. At this point, don't try to decide which is the best solution. Attempt to list as many solutions as possible. All solutions should be written out so they won't be lost.
3. Evaluate the alternative solutions.
4. Decide which is the best acceptable solution.
5. Work out a way to implement the solution to put it into practice.
6. Follow up and continuously evaluate how this solution works.

In each of these steps, parent and child have equal input and evaluation. The first solution agreed upon may not be the best. If it doesn't work, admit it is poor and try again; or, children may send a message that they don't like the original solution—try another. Life becomes a process of mutual problem solving between adult and child. Together, they generate possible solutions, evaluate alternative solutions, follow up, implement, and evaluate.

Gordon believes that the No-Lose Method is effective because: (1) the child is motivated to carry out the solution; (2) a greater chance of finding a quality solution exists; (3) it develops children's thinking skills; (4) less hostility results; (5) it requires less enforcement; (6) it eliminates the need for power techniques; (7) the real problem is exposed rather than just skirting the issues; (8) it helps children become more mature because they are treated more like adults; and (9) it is therapeutic for the child, helping him or her to develop psychologically and overcome problems associated with growing up.

Gordon points out that parents generally have some concerns about using the No-Lose Method, worrying that it may be interpreted as weakness. He refutes this notion and feels that children won't view their parents as weaker, but rather as supporters or consultants—people they can rely on. Another criticism of this method is that using it takes too much time. Actually, parents will eventually spend less time because policing, checking, and enforcing are reduced. If honestly approached, children will come to accept and trust the No-Lose Method.

According to Gordon, penalties for noncompliance should not be included in the decision-making process—a proposal contrary to Dreikurs' suggestions in the previous chapter. If possible, penalties and punishments for noncompliance should be eliminated. When agreements are acceptable to all parties but are then broken, the approach should be "let's take a look and see why this happened." Instead of enforcing a penalty the family should try to set up a new agreement.

## Induction

Induction describes a technique used to develop desirable and lessen antisocial behavior. Parents using this method attempt to induce in the child an awareness of how his or her actions influence both self and others. However, central to this method is the assumption that children are aware of other people's perspectives and care about them. Is this true?

In the past, psychologists have noted that children see things primarily from their own point of view. Recently, however, psychologists have come to believe that children are actually somewhat person-oriented and concerned about others. Consider the following examples given by a researcher. After a two-year-old boy hits a small girl on the head, he looks afraid and says, "I hurt your hair. Please don't cry." An 18-month-old sees her grandmother lying down to rest. She goes over to her crib, picks up her own blanket, and covers her grandmother (Pines, 1979). Is it possible that these children actually cared for the comfort of another?

It has also been shown that even two-year-old children share with each other.

In showing an object to another person, the children demonstrate not only that they know that other people can see what they see but also that others will look at what they point to or hold up. We can surmise that they also know that what they see may be remarkable in some way and therefore worthy of another's attention. . . . That children so young share contradicts the egocentricity so often ascribed to them and reveals them instead as already able contributors to social life (Rheingold, Hay, & West, 1976, p. 1157).

If, as suggested above, young children can perceive others' perspectives and are not necessarily so egocentric, parents need not artificially produce such feelings to help children acquire healthy negative feelings toward inappropriate behaviors; induction can be advantageously implemented.

**Two types of induction.** Induction techniques can be subdivided into two major categories: self-oriented and other-oriented. *Self-oriented induction* involves pointing out consequences of a person's behavior on him- or herself. *Other-oriented induction* can be accomplished by directly pointing out or explaining the nature of consequences in general, or on other individuals specifically—for example, "If you throw snow on their walk, they have to clean it up all over again," "pulling the leash like that hurts the dog's neck," or "that hurts my feelings." The basic element in induction is to cause or induce in children ideas and feelings concerning the consequences of their

Induction helps children understand how their behaviors influence others.

behaviors. A parent can provide reasons for both engaging in appropriate behavior and refraining from undesirable behavior. One student remembered how his mother used induction:

> *My mom consistently used feelings to communicate herself to me when I was an adolescent. On one particular occasion I teased my youngest sister until she began to cry. My mom took me aside and gently told me that my teasing bothered her as well, and that she thought my teasing might cause tension in the home because I wasn't showing respect to my sister as I should. What touched me the most about my mom's messages was the feeling she conveyed to me. I had no desire to see her feelings hurt from my misbehavior, so I improved my actions considerably. Though the temptation to tease still exists, I would rather maintain peace and harmony in the home.*

Consider some additional examples of inductive statements:

When you forget to feed the dog he will be hungry during the night.

If you wear your sister's clothes she won't have anything clean to wear when she comes home from school.

I have been waiting here for one hour and am very bored. You said you would meet me at two o'clock and it's already three.

These statements are intended to produce either an understanding or an emotional response for the act being discussed. However, they need not always focus on the negative. For example, a parent might say:

Look at your brother now that you let him ride your bicycle; see how happy he is.

Don't you feel better now that you have completed your assignment?

## INDUCTION VS. PRODUCING GUILT

Some may suggest that induction elicits guilt or self-condemnation. For example, when saying, "I have been waiting here for an hour and am very bored," some say it is difficult for a child to clearly separate withdrawal of love and rejection from merely indicating your disappointment, or implying that the child ought to feel bad. However, induction is a parental behavior indicating that others are hurt or disappointed, without suggesting that love and respect are being withdrawn. Induction involves drawing generalizations from acts rather than blaming the child. In addition, induction need not occur after a behavior, but may occur in advance through discussion or vicarious experience.

## WHY INDUCTION IS EFFECTIVE

The induction technique is effective because it explains consequences of the child's behavior. Attention is directed away from a personal evaluation and is concerned with action rather than judgment of the child. In addition, induction teaches how to produce positive reactions or acts such as reparations or apologies, and it helps motivate children to become more mature in the use of reasoning and discussion. It also communicates to the child that he or she is an individual capable of understanding more mature concepts, having the ability to give up personal satisfaction to help others. Finally, induction benefits the development of empathy.

The use of induction relies on the assumptions that: (1) children have a need to engage in approved social or moral actions; (2) they have a motivation toward maturity; and (3) they can understand others' viewpoints and feelings.

There is evidence that induction as a disciplinary technique is superior. Hoffman and Saltzstein (1967), using interviews with middle-class parents, discussed four situations in family life. They asked parents what they would do if their child delayed when asked to do something, if the child was careless and broke something of value, if the child talked back, and if the child did poorly in school. The child's level of moral development was then studied to see if he or she manifested mature guilt, made internal moral judgments, confessed after a mistake, accepted responsibility, and was considerate of other children. Hoffman and Saltzstein found that parents who used induction and affection had children who were more mature, had higher internal moral judgments, were more willing to confess, accepted responsibility, and were more considerate of others. The mother's use of induction was most significant. In later studies, Hoffman (1970) continued to find induction to be superior to either withdrawal of love or power and punishment as disciplinary techniques.

## Summary

Parents using low-power techniques do not manipulate environmental events, or mete out reinforcements and punishments to control their children's behavior. They do not overlook the idea that their children's behavior is prompted by needs, desires, and thoughts. Similarly, parents using low-power techniques do not directly show their children the consequences of their actions. Rather, in a more removed and noncontrolling fashion, they share positive and negative feelings with children, and assume that they have sufficient sensitivity and intelligence to perceive how they influence others. As a result, the child autonomously alters his or her behavior in a responsible, mature manner.

In this chapter children are considered more than respondents of carefully controlled environmental reinforcements and punishments. They are thinking, feeling beings capable of growing by being perceptive of how they influence others. Through active listening, sharing feelings, and helping their children through dialogue to induce the consequences of their actions, parents are able to assist them in becoming responsible, mature human beings. Strict control is not necessary.

To suggest that using low-power techniques to deal with children's behavior is "better than" using high-power techniques is not necessarily accurate. High-, moderate-, and low-power techniques all have their place in child rearing, and may be more effectively used interchangeably, depending upon the child's cognitive development, emotional and social maturity, and past learning history.

As children develop, cognitive and intellectual changes occur. They are able to store more bits of information in short-term memory. A two-and-a-half-year-old child, for example, can store approximately two bits of information; the six-year-old can store three to four; the average adult stores six or seven. As children grow, higher cortical functions also develop. They begin to leave a concrete world, and develop abilities to reason abstractly and complexly. Abilities to selectively attend to isolated aspects of their environment and to broaden behavioral alternatives increase. Emotional controls dampen labile, impulsive tendencies.

This developmental process requires that parents change parenting techniques as their children grow. Very young children lack sufficient cognitive abilities to reason abstractly, to remember complex messages, to communicate efficiently, and to autonomously develop alternatives to inappropriate behavior. As a result, low-power techniques such as Gordon's model or induction training may be largely ineffective. Even moderate-power techniques may be ineffective with the very young child, who has difficulty making abstract connections between behavior and consequences. However, the same child is able to learn through classical and operant conditioning (see Chapter 3). Indeed, animal trainers base their training techniques upon these principles; young children have much less difficulty learning adaptive behavior by these same processes. Stricter parental control of environmental reinforcements and punishments seems most appropriate, and often necessary, when teaching young children.

However, many parents make the mistake of trying to retain strict control as their children grow. The child's abilities invite a shift to "lesser-power" techniques. They are able to reason and problem-solve with parental assistance, but the parent retains a tight rein. These children often rebel and become more difficult to handle.

In addition to cognitive development, emotional and social maturity determines how parents effectively discipline their children. Hyperactive, extremely introverted, and emotionally disturbed children necessitate stricter controls if behavior change is to occur. These children often lack sufficient interpersonal skills and behavioral and/or emotional controls to respond appropriately to "lesser-power" techniques. As the child progresses, parenting techniques may progress from higher- to lower-power techniques.

A third consideration is the child's past learning history. Teachers, foster parents, stepparents, and adopting parents often acquire children whose previous environments were not conducive to the development of "normal," mature ways of responding. For example, a physically abused child may learn to consider physical punishment as reinforcing, if that is the only time attention is paid. Or, at least the abuse loses some of its normally punishing qualities. Similarly, coming from a home void of warm, interpersonal contact and dialogue, the child may not respond to parenting techniques incorporating active child involvement in problem solving and the sharing of feelings. Even parents whose natural children have grown up being strictly controlled may be at a loss if power becomes suddenly low. In each of these cases, as with the previous two considerations, parenting techniques may follow an evolutionary progression from high- to low-power techniques.

It is certainly our experience as parents that high-, moderate-, *and* low-power techniques for influencing behavior have all been beneficial in raising our own children. Yet, we still maintain that, ideally, a progression of sorts would occur. As children mature and develop, and as relationships develop in a loving and organized home climate, parental influence would require less power and control.

# S E L F - C H E C K

1. According to Thomas Gordon, parents should:
    a. acknowledge their fallibilty.
    b. not accept everything their children do.
    c. strive to be as accepting as possible.
    d. do all except b.
    e. a, b, and c are all correct.
2. Acceptance can be communicated through the following methods *except* for:
    a. active listening.
    b. nonintervention.
    c. being a parent who always accepts a child's behaviors.
    d. passive listening.
3. Gordon maintains that moralizing, judging, correcting, and so forth are poor responses to children's messages because:
    a. they are nonjudgmental and therefore leave the child unsure as to where he or she stands.
    b. they usually communicate something negative about the child.
    c. they all tend to be some sort of praise, which is unhealthy in excess.
    d. None of the above is correct.
4. Gordon listed five outcomes of active listening. Which one of the following is not an outcome?
    a. It helps the child accept his or her feelings.
    b. It facilitates a child's problem-solving skills.
    c. It promotes warmth and understanding between parent and child.
    d. All of the above are outcomes.
5. Which of the following is *not* a potential problem with active listening?
    a. Active listening will be inappropriately used if the child "owns" the problem.

b. Active listening may be used with the intent to manipulate.

c. Parents may fall into the habit of parroting a child's statements.

d. Listening may occur without empathy.

6. If a parent owns the problem, what technique does Gordon suggest to solve the problem?

a. Nonintervention

b. Active listening

c. "I" messages

d. Passive listening

7. Gordon talked about "I" messages; Jane Brooks (1981) said these messages contain the following parts *except* for:

a. encoding of the child's decoded message.

b. a clear statement of how the parent feels.

c. why the behavior is upsetting to the parent.

d. the child's behavior that has caused the parent to feel that way.

8. Place the following steps of the No-Lose Method in their proper order in the blank below.

a. Evaluate the alternative solutions.

b. Work out a way to implement the solution to put it into practice.

c. Identify and define the conflict.

d. Generate possible alternative solutions.

e. Decide which is the best acceptable solution.

f. Follow up and evaluate how the solution works.

---

9. _____ is the method to cause the child to have an awareness of how his or her actions influence both self and others.

a. Passive listening

b. Rational confrontation

c. Active listening

d. Induction

10. The method described in question 9 can be divided into two types:

a. self-oriented and other-oriented.

b. self-oriented and interpersonal-oriented.

c. other-oriented and interpersonal-oriented.

KEY: 1–e; 2–c; 3–b; 4–d; 5–a; 6–c; 7–a; 8–c,d,a,e,b, f; 9–d; 10–a

# MODELING AND IDENTIFICATION: SETTING THE EXAMPLE

Chapters 7 through 10 discussed ways parents influence children's behaviors in an active way. That is, certain techniques (varying from high to low in power) are actively carried out by parents or caretakers to help guide their children's behavior. This is largely a conscious process. Parents discuss how to discipline their children. They read books, attend lectures, take classes, and listen to more experienced parents, all in an effort to increase their effectiveness and help facilitate positive growth. Although some parents do discipline their children in a haphazard, "nonthinking" manner, their actions are, nevertheless, deliberate, and are often consciously reconsidered.

Another aspect of parental influence is not as heavily considered or discussed by parents. This is the passive influence they have on their children—the not-so-deliberate effects of their examples. We have all heard the phrase "Do what I say, not what I do." Yet, the repercussions of having our children watch us in our roles as parents are not as visible. The effects are not always as immediate. As a result, parents may continue acting in maladaptive, selfish, and inappropriate ways, hoping that their disciplinary and teaching techniques will enable their children to be different. The assumption is that children, with help from their parents, will see their parents' weaknesses and steer away from the same vices. Such is not necessarily true, however. In fact, a parent's passive influence may outweigh what he or she is actively trying to develop in his or her child through low-, moderate-, and high-power disciplinary methods.

This chapter considers how a parent's example, or model, affects a child's behavior and why it works. (A large portion of the discussion on modeling is adapted from the work of Albert Bandura, 1967, 1969, 1971.) This learning occurs on a conscious level through imitation, but also on a more unconscious, developmental level through identification. In addition, we will consider the influence television may have in a child's life.

## Modeling and Imitation

In the film *Being There,* Peter Sellers portrayed an intellectually limited man who copied what he watched on TV. Considered a genius, he became a celebrity because of what he said and how he acted. In a way, many children considered mature and precocious are merely acting out what is modeled for them. Children naturally imitate parents and other adults whom they admire and respect. The extent of this imitation may be humorous, as seen in the following account written by a student in one of our classes. It concerns a young child watching a hostess in a well-to-do, family:

Children naturally imitate parents and other adults whom they admire and respect.

When I was 17 I attended a dinner party with my parents at the home of a very proper and wealthy couple from the suburbs of Boston. Our neighbors also attended the party with their 6-year-old son, William.

The hostess of the party was very proper and closely followed established rules of etiquette. She frequently instructed her butler and waiter Charles to announce the so-and-so's, or to go to the kitchen for the such and such, all the time speaking with a proper Boston accent.

William was fascinated by the hostess. He followed her everywhere, listening to her every word, and watching her every action. It was amazing—he never left her side. Finally, as the guests began to leave, she greeted each one as they approached the door. William watched for a few moments and then went out to the porch and stopped each of the guests to tell them goodbye as the hostess had *done. He imitated her perfectly in his soprano voice with a Boston accent. "Good night, Jerry and Vivian—it was so-o-o delightful to see you again. Do give my love to Jenny. . . ."*

*Imitation* will be defined here as the tendency for a person to reproduce actions, attitudes, or emotional responses exhibited by live or symbolic models. *Modeling* refers to what one person does in front of another person: what the grown-up does in front of the child; what the teacher does in front of the student; what the minister does in front of the congregation.

## WHY MODELING WORKS

There are several possible explanations for the effectiveness of models. For instance, it is possible that a model, under some conditions, serves to remind observers of norms for social conduct to which they subsequently conform. At other times, a child may simply be engaged in the act of imitative pleasing; having never performed the act before, he or she performs simply to please the adult. The following sections deal more specifically with some of the common interpretations of why imitative behavior occurs.

**A model is a reminder of what is right.**   Consider the following account:

*A major rule in my home stated that shoes were not to be worn in the house. A violation would bring severe discomfort to my hind-end. Growing up, I was always reminded by the example of my parents that shoes were to be left at the door. When coming home alone, I'd see their shoes sitting by the doorway, reminding me to take off my shoes before entering.*

Models work because they are reminders of internalized behavioral norms: social responsibility, giving, charity, helping others in distress. Having previously learned these social norms, a child may need only be reminded of them in order to comply willingly. Under normal circumstances adults and children at times need to be reminded of proper behavior.

For example, in one large family with young children, the mother faced the problem of having her children just drop what they carried into the house. As the children entered the front door, coats, instead of being hung up, were simply pitched on the couch or chair. Soon the entryway was piled with books, sacks, and coats. To eliminate this problem the mother asked her husband to model what should be done. He acted out his part with excellence; upon entering the house, he would say aloud, "I'd better hang up my coat and take this sack into the kitchen." He kept this up for a few weeks and soon, with the help of a few discussions, the children just accepted the idea that items were to be put away.

This same family used a similar approach to model courtesy when talking to each other. To halt disrespect and anger in conversation, the parents resolved to model respect for one another and a positive attitude for their children. They found that this, in conjunction with verbally stating their expectations, immediately improved the quality of language and attitudes in the home.

**Models reveal socially acceptable rewards.** In another family a visitor was able to observe modeling, imitation, and reward of a small child.

◐

*The other night I was visiting my girlfriend when her married sister and brother-in-law dropped in with their cute little 1½-year-old girl named Ashley. Everyone was delighted because playing with Ashley is considered to be a rare treat. As I watched each person interact with Ashley, I noticed how often Ashley was expected to model certain behaviors—of course, under the unspoken rule that if she would imitate certain behaviors, she would be showered with love and affection (and sometimes even candy) for her responsiveness. I watched Ryan, her 11-year-old uncle, teach her how to fall to the ground whenever she was shot by an imaginary pistol. I watched Grandma show her how to give "loves" and kisses, and then expect "loves" and kisses in return.*

*Finally, the ritual of saying goodbye was something to behold. First, Ashley was expected to give everyone "loves" after which she was prodded to wink. After winking, they would have Ashley "show her teeth" by opening her mouth wide. Last of all, Ashley was expected to wave her hand in the air and say "bye" while everyone else mimicked this behavior. I realize now more fully how children are taught through modeling and then rewarded when they imitate properly.*

◑

This view depicts the child's active effort to seek rewards via the model. When the modeled behavior is imitated, rewards follow. Rewards, or reinforcements, can be verbal "pats on the back" or material, such as candy.

**A model increases pressure for conformity.** Demand characteristics are perceived pressures to conform to another's expectations, or to respond appropriately to situational cues. Children sometimes have an uncanny ability to conform to the desires and wishes of important others. If the child's motivation is to please the parent, then he or she may do whatever it is thought would please the adult. They may not necessarily be motivated to obtain a pat

Models reveal socially acceptable rewards.

on the back, but do it instead because it may be discomforting to not feel they had pleased a parent or teacher.

In one family a child was exceptionally negative about life. She didn't like her food, the games other children played, or the activities and shows her friends participated in or saw. The parents handled this problem by acting before the child would bring up criticism. They quickly asked another child a question they knew would be answered positively. For instance, "How do you like the salad tonight?" "Did you have fun while we were gone?" "Are the kids at school nice?" Over the weeks, it soon became clear to the one child that the negative attitudes she held were clearly out of line with those of all her brothers and sisters, and she started to be more positive. In a nonforceful way, the modeling of other family members effectively exerted a pressure or demand on her to be more positive.

**A model shows ways to relieve distress.** How do you feel at seeing a dog straining at a leash, or a blind person trying to put a coin in a vending machine? Most of us can imagine how we would feel in similar circumstances causing distress or discomfort. To relieve that distress, we can ignore the matter, quickly forget it, or rationalize it away. Occasionally, however, we might obtain relief by aiding the person (or animal) in need of help. By relieving their distress, we relieve our own. Many acts of kindness no doubt result from such feelings.

The role of a model in facilitating this type of response is to provide examples of acts that the observer comes to recognize as relieving distress for both the distressed party and the observer. For instance, suppose a preschool boy sees a girl fall from her chair and hurt herself. Will the boy act by trying to comfort the girl who fell, or by trying to clean any scratches? Perhaps, on this occasion, an adult (model) appears and proceeds to comfort the hurt child, whereupon she ceases crying and begins to smile. After seeing this, the boy will probably also be relieved and will come to associate the modeled behavior with relief of his own distress. In future instances, he will have a tool at his disposal for relieving uncomfortable feelings he experiences when seeing another person hurt.

Consider the following account provided by a student.

*Whenever my family would go to friends' houses, I was never sure what to expect; and I was always afraid that I wouldn't fit in with everyone else. To relieve this stress, I would just watch my parents, and then act in ways they did; or, if other children were there, I would follow their examples. By doing this I felt like I fit in.*

**A model is an example of desirable or undesirable behavior.**   This explanation assumes a desire in adults and children to do the correct thing. Usually, as people mature, they become more aware of community rules and conventions, which prescribe what is proper. How often, for example, does one call up and ask a friend what she is wearing tonight, or look around at what others (models) are wearing as a confirmation of what attire is appropriate?

The younger children are, the fewer rules they know and understand, and the more they need a mature example as a model. Sometimes, mere expression of a rule may be sufficient: "When sister cries, comfort her." More often, however, such verbal exhortations and expressions alone will not be enough. Children, as well as adults, quickly forget the meaning of such platitudes. What is needed is the opportunity to observe what is advocated. Although children may be motivated to do the right thing, unless they have the chance to actually mimic, duplicate, or emulate the behavioral implications of rules they learn, they may remain unable to do what is appropriate.

**A model can demonstrate self-rewards.**   How much people learn by observing others often depends on consequences that the model receives. If the model is rewarded by his or her behavior (whether external or internal rewards) this behavior is more likely to be imitated. Consider the following example, which also illustrates how siblings and peers can be effective models:

*In our family I have grown up getting basically good grades. My younger brother John could see this. John began to see how much eas-*

*ier things were for me as a result of getting good grades. I was happier and more content with my studies as well as my position in the home. Seeing the self-reward I was getting, this impressed upon John that he might be a happier person by getting good grades.*

Models often pattern behavior that is self-reinforcing. A mother may give to charity and afterward smile and say how good it made her feel. A child picks up on these consequences and may then emulate the behavior as long as it makes him or her feel good also; if it does not, the child will stop. One may find verbal exhortations to share toys, for instance, noneffective because children will not feel good letting someone else share what they want themselves. However, if they see an adult derive pleasure from sharing, such self-sacrificing behavior will more likely bring joy to the child. Modeling is, therefore, a way to prime children for pleasant emotional experiences when acting in an altruistic manner. Once acquired, the altruistic act will be repeated as long as people can give themselves a pat on the back for doing it.

In keeping with our philosophy on a natural progression from high- to low-power techniques (see Chapter 10, Summary), modeling influences similarly become more important as children grow. They become more cognizant of, and able to understand, an adult's social behavior. Parents, then, should not only realize how much more influential their own behaviors are to older children, but should rely more on teaching them through example.

> According to the social learning view, people vary in what they teach, model, and reinforce with children of differing ages. At first, control is necessarily external. In attempting to discourage hazardous conduct in children who have not learned to talk, parents must resort to physical intervention. As children mature, social sanctions should increasingly replace physical ones. Parents cannot always be present to guide their children's behavior. Successful socialization requires gradual substitution of symbolic and internal controls for external sanction and demands. After moral standards of conduct are established by imitation and modeling, self-evaluative consequences serve as deterrents to transgressive acts (Bandura, 1967, p. 43).

**A natural desire to imitate exists.**   Any parent can attest to the fact that small children sometimes imitate behaviors for no apparent reason. One of the author's children saw his dad doing push-ups one morning. Although only 15 months of age, unable to comprehend what his dad was up to, and unable to motorically copy the behavior exactly, he nevertheless started squatting up and down to mimic his father. There was no rightness or wrongness to the push-up; it was not rewarded; it carried no pressure for conformity; it did not relieve distress. Nevertheless, an attempt at imitation occurred.

We have saved this explanation until last, as it may be the most refreshing way to view the effects of modeling. Simply stated, children emulate parents because they like to imitate. It is a natural response, maybe even genetically determined. A sociobiologist would suggest that infants and children imitate because imitative behavior is selectively adaptive, in an evolutionary sense, to the preservation of species. A subhuman primate who was able to imitate food gathering, for example, would live longer than one who did not.

Children parrot their peers, and echo their parents, often being referred to as "chips off the old block." When we look at children, we often look at mirrors of parental behaviors. As they mature, some of these attributes stick and become part of their own personality.

## HOW TO INCREASE IMITATION

According to Bandura (1969), the first step in imitation is perceiving or attending to the model. The observer identifies distinctive features of the model's behavior, and develops an internal image of the behavior.

After the image is transformed into a verbal description and coded, another process, *retention,* can occur. Retention is necessary for reproducing the behavior when the model is no longer present. Following retention, *motoric reproduction* involves retrieving the behavior from memory and performing it. Before reproducing the behavior, however, the person must have some indication that it will produce positive consequences.

The above description is fairly simple and limited. A number of other variables, however, also affect whether a modeled behavior is noticed, retained, and reproduced. A description of these 10 variables appears below, and follows from the work of Bandura (1969).

**Reward the imitator.** Positive reinforcement of specific imitated responses may not only increase performance of the rewarded behavior, but can also develop a generalized imitative response tendency. This tendency can be enhanced by having various persons reinforce different types of copying responses in a variety of situations. In fact, even severely emotionally and socially impaired children can be taught appropriate behaviors through modeling and reinforcement of imitated behaviors (Van Hasselt, Griest, Kazdin, Esveldt-Dawson, & Unis, 1984).

**Reward the model.** *Vicarious reward* (seeing rewards given to a model by someone else) affects learning in essentially the same manner as when reward is applied directly to the performer. Children who witness a peer model transgress with rewarding consequences deviate more readily and more often than those who see peers punished for engaging in socially disapproved behavior. Through repeated exposure to the outcomes of others' behaviors, an observer not only acquires knowledge of rewards but may also discern cues for the model's actions. A preschool teacher wrote the following:

*At the preschool where I teach, we reward the children for certain behaviors by giving them stickers—the scratch-and-sniff kind. We put*

*them on the back of the child's hand or on a certain piece or work. As a child receives a sticker, we encourage all other children to behave as so-and-so did so they can get a sticker, too. One example of this is working quietly and carefully during activity time. The children are allowed to choose a game or activity, work with it, and then return it neatly to the shelf. A child who does especially well will receive a sticker and, therefore, acts as a model. This technique has worked very well for us.*

◑

**Use language with modeling.** Modeled behaviors should be translated into words to facilitate imitation. Verbal modeling makes it possible to transmit an almost infinite variety of values and response patterns that would otherwise be exceedingly difficult and time-consuming to portray behaviorally. For example, 60 children displaying a marked preference for immediate as opposed to delayed reward were exposed to one of three conditions (Bandura, 1969). In the first group, with a live model, an adult entered the room shortly after the child was seated and introduced himself to the already present experimenter, acting as if he had come to take a test. The adult then selected either immediate rewards (plastic chess figures now) or delayed rewards (wooden chess figures later), while simultaneously verbally expressing his reasoning while choosing. For example, a model selecting an immediate reward would say, "Chess figures are chess figures. I can get just as much use out of the plastic ones right away." A model selecting delayed rewards would say, "The wooden chess figures are of a much better quality, are more attractive, and will last longer. I'll wait two weeks for better ones."

In the second group, the experimenter explained to children that an adult had come in and made a choice, but, since they were so busy, he had made a choice and gone. The child was then allowed to see the answer book and to read the adult's comments, who behaved as the models in group one. In the third group no modeling occurred.

As expected, both live-model situations in condition one increased preferences. Children tended to prefer what the model had chosen. Such was not the case in the other conditions. After adequate language development is achieved, children rely extensively upon verbal modeling cues for guiding their behavior.

**Provide opportunity for practice or rehearsal.** Imitation can be enhanced through overt practice or rehearsal. There is also evidence that cognitive, covert rehearsals enhance retention. This principle is used by some coaches, who find that mastering a feat is enhanced by showing films and asking athletes to imagine themselves performing the skill.

**Build new behaviors on old behaviors.** Modeling outcomes are best achieved when they involve the integration of previously learned behavioral elements into new patterns. For example, imitating sharing of candy is more

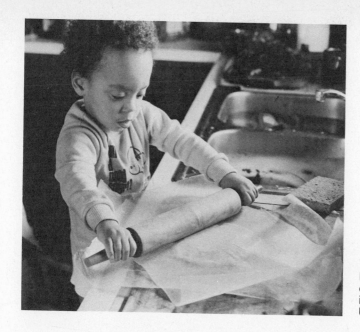

Practice helps children perfect imitated behaviors.

likely to occur when the child's ability to communicate, divide portions, and empathize is already established. Even on occasions when children attend closely, reproduction of an adult's behavior may be deficient because required components of the behavioral pattern are lacking.

**Provide other models.**   Peers often replace parental figures as principal models and agents of socialization. The process becomes complicated when children are exposed to parental and peer models displaying conflicting standards. However, the selection of peer models is greatly influenced by values prevailing in the home. Children tend to choose friends who share similar values and who are, therefore, more likely to reinforce familiar standards of conduct than to serve as sources of conflict.

During later periods of development, people draw extensively from a variety of nonfamiliar models in preparing themselves for vocational, professional, and social roles that cannot be transmitted within the family. Imitation should, therefore, be viewed as a continuous process involving multiple models rather than as occurring just in familial relationships. In fact, models portrayed in films or through the media can be as influential as real-life models.

When a child is exposed to many models, he or she will not reproduce all elements of any one model's actions. Rather, the child typically displays novel patterns of behavior made up of a combination of different models' behaviors.

**Be competent and powerful.**   For half the boys and girls in one experiment, a male model controlled rewarding resources (to simulate the husband-dominant family), but for the remaining children, a female model controlled positive resources (to simulate the wife-dominant home) (Bandura, 1969). Following these experimental operations, the two adults performed several tasks in the children's presence using different movements and verbal patterns. The children then performed the same tasks in the adults' absence. The children copied the model that was perceived by them as the more powerful—the one that controlled rewards.

Children often imitate aggressive models presented on film; yet, the success of the model's behavior is a crucial factor in determining whether an aggressive behavior is reproduced. When the aggressor's behavior fails to gain power and control, or produces punishment, imitation does not occur.

**Be warm and loving.** A warm and loving adult elicits considerably more imitative behavior than a model lacking these qualities. However, these characteristics may be only facilitating and not necessary conditions for imitation. Children who had a highly nurturant adult model were more inclined to accept low standards set by the model than high standards or expectations. Adult nurturance may facilitate modeling only under some conditions.

**Be prestigious.** Imitation is influenced not only by immediate consequences to the model, but also by distinctive status symbols, such as prestige, power, competence, and socioeconomic status. Models who are experts, or celebrities, are imitated more often. The effect of this prestige carries over from one area to another, as imitative responses even generalize to unfamiliar persons if they are similar to past reward-producing models. Even deviant models, if possessing prestige, can produce imitation of socially disapproved behavior.

A model's prestigious qualities may not only increase the probability of imitative behavior, but may also produce stable value changes, as is demonstrated in the following story by a young girl influenced by her father's accomplishments.

*Because my dad is a very successful and competent person in his business, I believe I have tried to model some of his behaviors, particularly his trait of being generous. I've seen him pay for others' dinners, treat people to things, give gifts, and take time out to listen to others. Consequently, I try to do the same. It comes naturally now, but as I grew up it seemed that I'd do things because I saw my dad do them.*

**Be similar.** Persons told they have qualities in common with a model are more inclined to imitate responses portrayed by the model than subjects who initially share no common characteristics. The mother who says, "You're lazy just like your dad" is unwittingly likely to increase the child's laziness.

Although many parents don't generally think about the complex ramifications of their behavioral examples on children, the fact remains that modeling can produce significant change in children. As shown above, a parent can change and control many variables to increase his or her effectiveness as a model. Of course, the converse is also true. Parents not following many of these principles may be ineffective models to their children.

As mentioned earlier in this chapter, children must attend to, retain, and then reproduce modeled behaviors before imitation can occur. However, not all behaviors that resemble parents' actions are imitated. Sometimes, these similarities occur through the process of identification.

## Identification and Gender Role Acquisition

Suppose that upon entering college, a person were required to take a test that presented four pictures—a dog, a snake, a monkey, and a human being—and then asked to identify which species was *Homo sapiens*. Usually, there would be no difficulty selecting the correct picture. If the person was then given pictures of a man and a woman, and asked to choose the picture representing him- or herself, the person would also be successful.

These questions would seem ridiculous to ask a mature adult. If, however, the questions were changed somewhat, the difficulty would be increased. For example, when and how did you learn to act like a human being? How and when did you learn your appropriate gender role? Because of the fundamental importance of these questions, psychologists have been particularly intrigued with this aspect of human development.

Babies have a nonsexual role. Developmentally speaking, initial role behavior is not heavily influenced by gender; babies are babies. Yet, development of gender identity begins very early. Before children even learn that two different genders exist, parents begin to treat them differently. Little girls are dressed in pink, and baby boys in blue. Toys given the child and play activities initiated by the adult may be different. Rubin, Provenzano, and Luria (1974), for example, compared first-time parents' descriptions of sons with first-time parents' descriptions of daughters. All children were equal in length, weight, and Apgar scores; yet, the girls were more likely to be described as little, beautiful, cute, and pretty than were the boys. Similarly, Lewis (1972) determined that during the first six months of life, boys received more physical contact (e.g., touching, holding) and less nonphysical contact (e.g., looking at, talking to) than girls. Finally, Maccoby and Jacklin (1975) concluded that parents *elicit* more gross motor behaviors from sons than daughters, a difference many still attribute strictly to innate differences in motor development. This type of differential treatment leads to what is known as gender-typing or gender-role differentiation—the process of learning those behaviors appropriate to one's gender.

By about 18 months, children are expected to begin showing this differentiation in their behavior. Parents teach attitudes such as "Big boys don't

Different treatment of boys and girls by adults leads to gender-typing; children become accustomed to "gender-appropriate" behavior.

cry" and "Nice girls don't talk like that." In addition, in more subtle ways, parents often set up a reward and punishment system that encourages children to reflect parental attitudes. By early preschool years many signs of gender-typing have appeared. Boys tend to prefer wheeled toys, rough games, and guns. Girls tend to play more quietly, often with dolls, and usually prefer playing house over the more rugged and masculine play of cowboys and Indians. Research has even found that first-, third-, and fifth-grade children do not know that the pronoun "he" in gender-neutral contexts refers to both males and females (Hyde, 1984). Rather, they believe that the typical person is "he" and "he" refers only to males.

A comprehensive study by Nemerowicz (1979) looked at children's perceptions of gender and work roles, finding that children generally learn the traditional ideology, although not necessarily perceiving an inequality between the sexes. For example, children in general see men as working outside the home and as being limited by their ignorance from cooking and housekeeping. Women, on the other hand, are perceived as working inside the home and as being restricted by their fears, ignorance, and weaker physiques from participation in various occupational pursuits. These traditional roles are perceived more strongly by younger than by older children.

The classic example of how differential treatment of boys and girls leads to gender-appropriate behavior comes from the writing of Money and Ehrhardt (1975), who recount a case study of two identical biologically male twins. Through a surgical error the penis of one of the infants was removed, and at 17 months of age it was decided to rear the child as a girl. The child's clothing, hairstyle, and name were changed, along with completion of sex-reassignment surgery. The child's mother began rearing the child as a girl and she remarked how the daughter by the age of 5 preferred traditional female clothing and activities, was very neat and tidy, and copied her mother's behaviors. The boy, by comparison, was messy, was active, disdained housework, and tended to copy the father.

Parental behaviors are not the only source of differential treatment of the sexes. Schools, peer groups, toys, the media, literature, art, music, and humor all differentiate male from female behavior (Weitz, 1977).

Other than differential treatment, children learn gender-typical behaviors through the processes of imitation and identification. Imitation as previously discussed refers to a child's behavior on a conscious level. The child may be reminded of what is right; perceive rewards; feel a pressure to conform; want to relieve distress; or simply have the desire to imitate. In any case, it is a voluntary decision and conscious process. The child *chooses* to imitate, because of a desire to have his or her behaviors be similar to someone else's.

*Identification*, on the other hand, refers to a more unconscious, involuntary process leading a child to think, feel, and behave as though the characteristics of another person were his or her own. Young children usually identify with the same-sex parent. A child can learn to say a word or tie a shoe by imitating or copying a model, but a boy, for example, who exhibits characteristics "in the mirror image of his father" probably does so through this unconscious identification process. Identification is described by Sears, Rau, and Alpert (1966) as developing early in life, occurring spontaneously without apparent reward, and becoming strongly established and resistant to change, even in the model's subsequent absence. In addition, identification is an unrestricted process; many of the model's behaviors are reproduced.

However, the two processes of imitation and identification are not necessarily mutually exclusive. A child may learn many gender-appropriate responses through a combination of both identification and imitation.

Models available for a child to either identify with or imitate are constantly changing. For the first two years of life, a child is influenced by the immediate family, especially the mother. From ages two through five, most influence is still within the family, but is spread more evenly between parents. As the child begins school, teachers often become significant figures, but parents still have a dominant influence on the child's identification and imitative processes. During adolescence, time spent away from home is greatly increased. Appropriate adult gender-role behavior learned during the formative years through identification and imitation is tested in actual performance, and parents and peers vie for the sphere of influence.

Although identification and imitation processes occur simultaneously, the influence of identification changes as children grow. A person's identification process is strongest for his or her parents during the earlier years and gradually diminishes as the child grows older. Imitation, on the other hand, occurs throughout the individual's life, and involves numerous individuals.

## THEORIES OF IDENTIFICATION

Three basic theories of identification will be discussed: (1) developmental-identification theory, (2) social-power identification theory, and (3) anxiety-reducing identification theory.

**Developmental-identification theory.** The developmental-identification theory requires seven conditions for identification to take place:

1. Parents are warm and nurturant.
2. Children depend on the parents' warmth and nurturance.
3. Parents are physically present and interact with their children.
4. Parents use some degree of "love withdrawal" when a child's behavior is inappropriate.
5. Parents' model of appropriate behavior is clear and consistent.
6. Parents' expectations of the child are consistent.
7. Parents accept their role as models for their children.

The most significant factor of this theory is nurturance. Children will strongly identify with warm and loving parents who provide clear and consistent expectations.

**Social-power identification theory.** Social-power identification theory accepts many antecedents of developmental identification theory, but adds the following:

1. Parents are capable of a degree of "power" in that they control most items that satisfy a child's needs.
2. Parents exhibit power as they relate to each other, and as they relate to other persons outside the family.
3. Power that a parent is capable of exerting is often related to the gender of the parent, and to the role of the parent in the family.
4. Parents exhibit power as they control the child's behavior and resources.
5. Parents control both positive reinforcers (sources of pleasure) and negative reinforcers (sources of pain, deprivation, or discomfort).

An example of this notion is provided by the following:

An extremely domineering mother brought her seven-year-old son to a clinic for counseling. She believed he had many girlish tendencies and was, therefore, concerned. The psychiatrist observed the child and agreed with the mother; the boy did have many girlish tendencies. But he also observed that the child was not the only one who needed help. The mother had, in fact, helped create the problem. She dominated the father in a criticizing and belittling fashion. The son saw his mother as the power figure and identified with her.

According to this theory the child will identify with the model in power. The more the child envies the model's control over resources and gratification, the more the child will identify with him or her.

**Anxiety-reducing identification theory.** The oldest theory, anxiety-reducing identification theory, stems from the psychoanalytic orientation. While the other two theories consider identification to be a general disposition to be like parents, psychoanalytic theory conceives of identification as a total "introjection" or "incorporation" of the parent into the child's personality. Furthermore, identification is viewed as a defense mechanism. A boy "identifies" to reduce anxiety during the "Oedipus complex," when he falls in love with Mother and finds he is unable to compete with Father. The boy fears reprisals and tries to be like his father in order to reduce anxiety. ("If you can't beat 'em, join 'em.") Rather than fight the enemy (Father), he joins forces to reduce feelings of perceived threat. In addition, if he becomes enough like Father he might be able to win Mother's affection.

**Combining theories of identification.** From the outline of the three theories presented, certain generalizations about the development of identification become clear. First, identification is one of the most basic processes in socialization. Second, the adult model must have at least some of the following attributes when interacting with the child:

1. Warmth
2. Mastery or power over the environment
3. Proximity (physical nearness)
4. Some amount of status or esteem
5. Perceived similarity

It is conceivable that parents lacking some of these attributes may still become objects of identification. The abusive parent, for example, although hostile, rejecting, and not a source of many rewards, may nevertheless possess power and some status in the child's eyes. In addition, the parent may be frequently at home or near the child and may be perceived as familiar. As a result the child identifies with the abusive parent and may later exhibit some of the same inappropriate behavior.

Because some parents lack these characteristics, or some families lack one parent, it is necessary to consider how such children can identify with the appropriate gender and learn gender-appropriate behaviors. For example: Mark, age eight, lives with his mother and younger sister. When Mark was three his father was killed in a car accident. Mark's mother worries that Mark won't grow up being as "manly" as he should because he doesn't have an appropriate male model to follow. What should Mark's mother do?

When more closely examining Mark's situation, it was found that his mother is already doing many things to provide an appropriate male model. Mark's mother has a picture of his father in the living room, and she often speaks fondly of him. In addition, Mark's uncle lives nearby, and they are able to associate frequently.

If a father is absent for a few years while serving in the armed services, the mother can place a picture of him in a conspicuous location and refer to him frequently in her conversation. Substitute models are also available. A mature female elementary-school teacher may serve as model for a number of young girls whose mothers are inadequate or absent. For the boy, male teachers, pastors, coaches, club leaders, or even older boys can function as identification figures. Even without specific individuals to model, a culture often pushes numerous real or symbolic figures upon the child with insistent demands that they be copied. Children's literature and folklore, and the media, continually present gender roles.

While identification can be used as an explanation for learning gender roles, there exists in today's society an additional complication as children acquire gender-role behavior. A contemporary trend is the relatively fluid, ambiguous state of gender roles; traditional attitudes about masculinity and femininity have changed significantly, and role expectations are becoming more difficult to define. Proponents of this trend maintain that it provides greater freedom of individual choice, activity, and emotion. This reasoning is evident in studies looking at the effects of maternal employment on children (Baruch, 1972; Hoffman & Nye, 1974; Miller, 1975; Nemerowicz, 1979). In general, sons and daughters of working mothers were less stereotyped in their perceptions of male and female roles. They saw their mothers as less restricted to the home and their fathers as helping out more in the home. Daughters of working mothers described women as more competent and effective, and were themselves more career oriented. Sons of working mothers saw their fathers as warmer and more expressive. The opposition states, on the other hand, that firm role expectations are necessary to help individuals know the "rules," so they do not need to think through each action or reaction in their changing environment. In any case, concerned parents with either orientation need to understand that they will be the major influence in their children's lives, especially during elementary-school years. Whatever their beliefs and ideas about proper gender-role behavior, their children will tend to imitate and identify what they themselves model.

It may seem appropriate to have the chapter end here; however, one other important influence in the lives of many children warrants discussion— the family TV. With the amount of television many children watch, the modeling power it possesses cannot be merely dismissed.

# Television and Children's Development

The American Broadcasting Company's "Sunday Night Movie" on September 30, 1973, was "Fuzz," which depicted thrill-seeking delinquents who doused waterfront tramps with gasoline and set them afire. Two days later, 25-year-old Evelyn Wagler ran out of gas while driving through a Boston slum. She was carrying a two-gallon can from a nearby filling station when six young men surrounded her, dragged her to a vacant lot, and beat her until she followed their orders and poured the gasoline over herself. Then they set her ablaze and left her . . . Evelyn Wagler died. . . . On September 10, 1974, [the film] "Born Innocent," a drama . . . in which a gang of inmates corner a young girl in a shower and sexually violate her with a plumber's tool [was shown]. Four days later . . . four children, ages 9 to 15, seized two little girls on a public beach and replayed the scene with beer bottles. Three of the perpetrators told police that they had seen the "Born Innocent" telecast (Methvin, 1975, pp. 185–186).

The 1970 census estimated that almost all American homes have at least one television set. Some researchers have pointed out that a child born today will, by the age of 18, have spent more of his or her life watching television than in any other activity except sleep (Liebert, Sprafkin, & Davidson, 1982). During the last 25 years there have been literally hundreds of studies focusing upon the particular effects of television on children. However, until recently there has been little evidence to support the notion that television viewing is to any degree responsible for either prosocial or antisocial behavior.

## PARENTAL CONCERNS

Many parents resent television because they have so little control over its content. Recently, parents have become more vocal in their criticism, giving support to Action for Children's Television and the Parent–Teacher Association's drive to improve television programming. However, even if these positive group efforts were successful, the change in programming, format, and content would be gradual—far too slow for today's children.

Instead of waiting and hoping for change, some definite steps can be taken to make television a positive, not a negative influence. However, before considering these steps, a summary of parental objections to television is in order. For example, parents normally fear that television captures too much of their children's time. They would like to see their children physically active, reading, and developing talents and skills instead of hunched before a TV set.

Another parental concern, supported by research, is that television directly influences and teaches undesirable actions, especially aggression. In early 1969, at the request of Congress, the Surgeon General's Advisory Committee on Television and Social Behavior began serious investigation into numerous aspects and effects of television viewing. It was determined in a

By the age of 18, the average child will have spent more time watching television than in any other activity except sleep.

report later prepared by the committee (1972) that a relationship does exist between viewing violence on television and subsequent aggressive behaviors in children. However, these effects were not necessarily uniform. Those children more predisposed to be aggressive (e.g., those already more aggressive due to other environmental influences) were affected the most.

This report inspired further research on television violence and behavior (see Parke, Berkowitz, Leyens, West, & Sebastian, 1977; Eron & Huesmann, 1980; Singer & Singer, 1980). In general, these studies support the advisory committee's conclusions. More recent research continues to delineate this relationship between violence on television and children's aggressive behaviors. Boys, for instance, have been shown to exhibit more imitative aggression after viewing violent films (Day & Ghandour, 1984; Hall & Cairns, 1984). One study involving 758 United States and 220 Finnish children similarly found positive relationships between TV-violence viewing and aggression (Huesmann, Lagerspetz, & Evon, 1984). In addition, the effect of violence viewing on aggression was exacerbated by: (1) boys identifying with the TV characters; (2) higher levels of violence in a show; and (3) more frequent viewing. The child's perception of the violence as unrealistic did not reduce aggression.

Other effects on children of extensive television watching include: (1)

decreased imagination (Singer, Singer, & Rapaczynski, 1984); (2) lowered involvement and concentration when reading (Winn, 1980, p. 59); and (3) slightly twisted perceptions of reality (Winn, 1980, p. 69).

The amount and type of advertising directed toward children is also objectionable. Unnecessary needs and appetites are intentionally created in young children. Toys, candies, and sweet foods do not guarantee happiness as children are pressured to believe. Pressure is then put on parents by children to buy unnecessary toys and games. Twenty-five percent of the television broadcasting industry's profit comes from programming directed at children.

Also, parents are not satisfied with role models appearing on TV. In too many shows the villain is successful for 50 minutes, only to be exposed and apprehended in the last scenes. With the airing of more realistic movies, the examples set by heroes or heroines are especially disconcerting. An unshaven, whiskey-drinking, crude, and callous hero in a movie is vindicated when he brutally kills evil men. The value of this social model for children is questionable and difficult for them to forget.

Experience with televised violence can desensitize children to the suffering of others. Research has shown that children exposed to violent TV shows will react with less emotion than children who have been exposed to less violent TV programming (Cline, 1972). Is there a danger that the content of our TV programs may develop a generation of children who are less sensitive to others' suffering?

Most people know their own values, and recognize that many views presented on television are contrary. And it is realistic to recognize that in our pluralistic society children need to confront opposing points of view. However, parents become upset when values appearing in most programs are different from their own. For example, many interpret the casual and light treatment of promiscuous sexuality as tacit approval.

Finally, the type and level of moral reasoning are overly simplistic. Again and again the same plot appears. Evil is pitted against good; for a time, evil has the upper hand, but then good conquers evil by using power and violence. Rather than differences being solved through reason, the bad people are destroyed by being pushed off cliffs or exploding inside their cars. The message is that resolving human conflict is best accomplished by power and violence.

## WHAT PARENTS CAN DO

What can parents do? How can they counteract excessive violence, unjustified advertisements, antisocial actions, negative models, conflicting values, and low-level moral reasoning? These objectionable elements will not just disappear despite commendable efforts of parent groups to get rid of them. However, the following five steps can be beneficial to parents when working with children within their own home.

*Step 1: Recognize what it is you don't like.* Perhaps one of the preceding criticisms is of particular concern to you. If so, identify its objectionable influence, and identify specific programs that are particularly undesirable. When these have been identified, go to Step 2.

*Step 2: Guide and help children in program selection.* It may be helpful if young children understand that television is a guest invited into the family, and that parents are involved in determining program selection. It is not difficult for them to understand that parents control use of automobiles, washing machines, and most appliances. If parents obtain a programming guide at the beginning of the week, and sit down with their children to work out a viewing program, then children will learn to manage television. Establishing this approach when the child is young is ideal but the arrangement can be initiated with older children if open, democratic discussion about program selection exists.

Program selection need not be a negative, "should not" process. Parents and children can get together to determine what good programs to watch among the many positive alternatives. There is evidence that some programs are definitely beneficial. Drs. William Meyer and Jerome Dusek (1979) of Syracuse University write in their child psychology textbook, "Children who observed prosocial programs also showed an increased ability to persist at tasks, were better able to delay gratification, and obeyed rules and followed commands better." They were referring to research on programs such as "Mister Rogers' Neighborhood," "Sesame Street," and "Fat Albert and the Cosby Kids." These programs are actually designed to increase cooperation, sharing, helping, persistence, understanding feelings, delaying gratification, and valuing individuality.

Other types of highly beneficial programs include documentaries and nature programs. Recently, one parent insisted on viewing an educational telecast of a science series. He found that his children, who at first were not interested, became involved as they watched the program. They began asking questions about our universe. Without his enthusiasm and advance planning, the children would never have watched this program.

One father was surprised to find that his nine-year-old son enjoyed the half-hour national news. At that time the child was interested in the Iranian hostage crisis and in who was to become president. Viewing sports can also be a positive experience for both boys and girls. Children often identify with teams. Sportscasters, to create interest, dramatize personality and character in both teams and players. Young children can view actual accounts of stamina, patience, persistence, and hard work in the sportscasters' commentaries.

*Step 3: Provide discussion and counteropinion.* In addition to program selection, a parent can watch TV with the child and then discuss program highlights. The importance of discussion and counteropinion becomes apparent when viewing programs known to have negative content. Commercial breaks are often ideal to discuss what is going on in the program. If the material is too volatile and controversial, it may be better to wait a day or two. At the appropriate time refer back to the program you watched together.

Even commercials can be discussed. As early as the first grade children are able to laugh, joke, and satirize ads for perfumes, shampoos, and make-

Ideally, television should be a second alternative to other family activities.

ups that are said to transform the homely into the beautiful. A healthy skepticism can be cultivated early.

*Step 4: Provide alternative activities.* Adults as well as children will catch themselves turning on the TV when they have nothing to do. How many times have you watched a mediocre program out of habit? Too often we say, "If nothing is worth watching, then I'll do something else." Reverse the process by saying, "If there isn't something worth doing, then I'll watch TV."

By providing games, family outings, athletic events, reading hours, or even a night of cooking in the kitchen, parents can reduce the need for TV watching. Scheduling a study hour with children early in the evening is often a positive experience. Magazines, books, and newspapers can be read, or children can be helped with school assignments. By scheduling this activity during hours when undesirable programs are on TV, a double benefit is achieved.

*Step 5: Share television experiences.* In today's world, parents and children spend less and less time together. Children go to school, and parents work and attend to home responsibilities. There is often little time for sharing. Television can provide these much-needed experiences upon which to base discussion and opinion. However, for this to work, parents and children often need to compromise their own preferences and watch TV together.

There is merit in having only one TV set in the home. The advantages of compromising and sharing within the family will far outweigh the pleasures of viewing only according to one's preferences. By watching common programs, questions will be asked and conversations sparked. These conversations can develop communication skills and thinking ability, as well as clarify beliefs and values. Children can be asked to discuss their own lives in light of what they have watched on television or the news of the day. Some of the content may prove to be so controversial or interesting that the family may want to read more about it.

It may be well to apply the old phrase "If you can't beat 'em, join 'em." Television programming will not change drastically in the near future. So, instead of developing a hopeless or resentful attitude, use the preceding steps to help develop a positive approach to television. Television can be a beneficial influence, and can be used to bring parents and children closer together, and help children become informed about today's world.

## Summary

Children's behaviors are often a product of imitation and identification. Through identification, children unconsciously take on characteristics of parents who are warm, close, esteemed, and powerful. This influence lessens as children grow older. However, imitation occurs throughout childhood and adolescence, as they "copy" parents, peers, and other significant figures. Imitation is facilitated by rewards; the use of language as a mediator; opportunities for rehearsal; multiple models; and competent, prestigious, and warm models. Imitation occurs because modeling is a reminder of what is right; increases pressure for conformity; reveals socially acceptable rewards; shows ways to relieve distress; is an example of desirable and undesirable behavior; and demonstrates self-rewards.

These influences, combined with the disciplinary techniques described in earlier chapters, contribute to the child's total personality. A parent's influence is passively (imitation, identification) and actively (high- to low-power techniques) transmitted. Parents do well to evaluate their own behaviors and the degree to which they conform to what they are trying to teach through their control of environmental consequences.

Television can also influence a child's development in social, emotional, and cognitive ways. Although these effects may be detrimental, the wise parent could monitor more closely a child's television viewing to take advantage of television's positive possibilities.

# SELF-CHECK

1. _____ is defined as the tendency for a person to consciously reproduce actions, attitudes, or emotional responses exhibited by live or symbolic models.

a. Modeling
b. Imitation
c. Identification
d. Attachment
2. Which of the following is not a reason why modeling works?
   a. A model shows ways to relieve distress.
   b. A model increases pressure for conformity.
   c. A model is a reminder of what is right.
   d. A model always portrays rewarded behavior.
   e. All of the above are reasons.
3. If a brother notices that his older sister has good feelings after sharing, and he subsequently starts to share, the following reason for the modeled behavior is probably responsible:
   a. A natural desire to imitate exists.
   b. A model can demonstrate self-rewards.
   c. A model increases pressure for conformity.
   d. A model shows ways to relieve distress.
4. If you wanted to increase the imitative "clean room" behavior of your small daughter, you could
   a. let her witness a sibling being rewarded for cleaning up her room.
   b. verbally suggest the behavior to be imitated and its reward.
   c. be warm and loving.
   d. provide opportunities for practice.
   e. do all of the above.
5. Imitation is also influenced by:
   a. the model's prestige and power.
   b. multiple models.
   c. the model's similarity with the observer.
   d. all of the above.
6. Society usually starts gender-typing
   a. upon birth.
   b. after two years of age.
   c. during childhood.
   d. during adolescence.
7. Which of the following is true of identification?
   a. It is an unconscious process.
   b. It is essentially the same thing as imitation.
   c. It usually occurs between a child and the opposite-sex parent.
   d. It is maintained by rewards.
8. Identification with others is strongest during:
   a. early life
   b. adolescence
   c. adulthood
   d. the first 18 years
9. If a boy's father was totally paralyzed throughout the child's growth years, which theory of identification might predict that the child would probably identify with the mother?
   a. Developmental-identification theory
   b. Social-power identification theory

c. Anxiety-reducing identification theory

d. Proximity-identification theory

10. Today's changing, ambiguous sex roles may result in which of the following?

a. Boys developing some traditionally feminine traits

b. Confusion

c. Both of the above may result.

d. Neither of the above will result.

KEY: 1–b; 2–d; 3–b; 4–e; 5–d; 6–a; 7–a; 8–a; 9–b; 10–c

# PART
## ○ V ▫
# Special Parenting Situations

Part IV discussed high-, moderate-, and low-power techniques to produce or weaken children's behavior. We suggested that parents use a mixture of these techniques in rearing their children, as each approach is valuable in its own right. Additionally, we recommended that parents follow a progression from high- to low-power techniques. As children grow and develop, their cognitive, emotional, and social skills allow parents to change parenting techniques. Parental influence becomes less direct and controlling, and nonverbal manipulation of environmental reinforcers gives way to democratic dialogue. Children become less talked *to* and more conversed *with*. They are given more and more freedom with fewer restrictions.

Very young children, and cognitively, emotionally, and socially impaired children may require predominantly high-power techniques. Because these children lack the necessary understanding, skills, and self-restraint, their parents must take more control. Yet, raising these children is not that simple. Manipulating environmental reinforcers and punishers is not all that is required. Rather, a deeper understanding of special parenting situations can help parents deal more effectively with children who do not respond at the time to lesser-power techniques.

Part V now deals with these "special" situations in more depth. Parenting of infants will first be discussed, followed by a chapter dealing with physically, mentally, and emotionally handicapped children. Finally, in every child's life, normal development and environmental crises occur to create emotional obstacles. These obstacles are more effectively overcome if parents understand more than the use of techniques alone.

# CHAPTER 12

# INFANCY AND EARLY CHILDHOOD

Many of the ideas presented in previous chapters apply to children who are old enough to interact and communicate with parents in some fashion. Even though, for instance, one-and-a-half-year-olds may not be able to verbally communicate much with parents, they can nevertheless usually make their needs known. Yet, how do parents know what to do with infants and toddlers? And how are things like feeding, weaning, and toilet-training handled? These situations are especially anxiety-provoking to many first-time parents.

Many parents-to-be are given the following advice: "Don't worry, it'll come to you; you pick up parenting skills as you go; it won't affect the baby at all." Although there is a certain amount of truth to this statement—that parents do pick up skills as they go—much uncertainty and anxiety may be alleviated if parents read and learn about infancy and childhood prior to the actual experience. This chapter is written as a type of "informative brief" to help alleviate some of the early parenthood anxieties that many adults encounter. The topics of feeding, weaning, crying, and toilet training will be considered.

## The Transition to Parenthood

When a child enters the family unit, especially the first child, parents experience a variety of new problems and changes. The postpartum period, in particular, although a time of pleasure, often brings considerable stress (Grossman, Eichler, & Winickoff, 1980). Sollie and Miller (1980) identified the following general classes of problems that first-time parents often face:

1. *Physical demands:* loss of sleep, extra work, fatigue
2. *Strain on the husband–wife relationship:* less time together, changes in sexual relationship
3. *Emotional costs:* new responsibilities, doubts of one's competence as a parent
4. *Opportunity costs and restrictions:* less freedom to travel and go out on short notice, loss of income and career opportunites

LaRossa and LaRossa (1981) also conclude that during this transition to parenthood, the probability of misunderstandings and conflicts of interest between spouses is increased. However, Hobbs (1968) concluded that with the arrival of a couple's first child, the idea that the transition to parenthood is a severe crisis appears to be false. Rather, it seems to be marked with only moderate difficulty for most parents. It is true that marital adjustment and satisfaction tend to decline with the arrival of children into the family (Burgess & Wallin, 1953; Rollins & Feldman, 1970). This decline may be due to the many changes taking place as responsibilities of child rearing are added to those already existing. Nevertheless, most parents would agree that this decline is more than compensated for by the joys obtained by raising children.

These differences in how the transition to parenthood is perceived are due, in part, to different research methodologies. In addition, variables other than simply having a new infant combine to make the transition less or more difficult. The transition appears to be more difficult if: (1) parents are younger (Hobbs & Wimbish, 1977); (2) the child is more temperamental (see section on "Individual Differences" in this chapter); (3) the child's health is poor (Gath, 1978); (4) parental expectations are unrealistic (Kach & McGhee, 1982); (5) husbands are less cooperative and do not share responsibilities of caring for the infant (Belsky, Lerner, & Spanier, 1984); and (6) postpartum depression and anxiety are present (Grossman, Eichler, & Winickoff, 1980).

Furthermore, postpartum depression and anxiety appear to be inversely correlated with: (1) less anxiety and depression early in the pregnancy; (2) a higher motivation for the pregnancy; (3) easier labor and delivery; (4) financial security and higher education; and (5) most important, previous and current marital satisfaction (Grossman, Eichler, & Winickoff, 1980).

The transition to parenthood is made easier if parents (1) develop appropriate coping strategies; and (2) are informed. Myers-Walls (1984), for example, found that mothers adjusting best to parenthood implement the following coping strategies:

1. Role conflict between parenthood and other demands (e.g., career, social life, marital relationship, housekeeping) is favorably defined. That is, the conflict appears manageable to the mother.
2. Future mothers decide before child bearing which role will dominate when conflict arises.
3. Mothers are able to separate the roles and disregard one when involved in another.
4. Mothers are willing to compromise commitment to competing roles.

In addition to developing proper coping strategies, first-time parents reduce their anxieties by educating themselves about infancy and early childhood. Education can be obtained through dialogue with experienced parents, attendance at seminars, and learning from books in the field.

## Early Physical Development

While most parents find the birth and first few months of an infant's life memorable and enjoyable, at the same time they find this period anxiety-provoking. "Is my child developing normally?" "Shouldn't she be sitting up by now?" "My friends' baby can support his head now; why can't mine at the same age?" These questions and many like them can be fielded by pediatricians, and it is quite wise to have regular baby check-ups while the child is young. Neurological and skeletal abnormalities can usually be detected early by the trained eye.

Additionally, many paperback books are on the market to help educate parents about their child's early development (see, for example, *The First Three Years of Life* by Burton L. White; *Baby and Child Care* by Benjamin Spock). Most child development textbooks describe physical as well as cognitive, intellectual, social, perceptual, emotional, and language developments from birth on. For lack of space, this text will not focus on this aspect of infancy and early childhood.

## Feeding

Even before birth, nourishment is an important consideration for an infant's health. Mothers-to-be are counseled by doctors to eat regular, well-balanced meals to assure the fetus the necessary nutrients. They are instructed to limit, if not completely cease alcohol intake and to stop smoking. Smoking to any degree has been claimed to reduce birthweight (Meredith, 1975), increase perinatal and neonatal mortality (Goujard, Rumeau, & Schwartz, 1975; Meyer, Jonas & Tonascia, 1976), and even produce long-term deficiencies in cognitive abilites and social adjustment (Davie, Butler, & Goldstein, 1972; Dunn, McBurner, Ingram, & Hunter, 1977). Similarly, chronically alcoholic mothers are known to give birth to infants with physical, mental, and growth deficiencies (Streissguth, 1982). Mothers are also asked to be cautious about any medications not prescribed or cleared by their obstetrician. Prenatal vitamin supplements are routine prescriptions provided by many doctors. The saying "Your baby is what you eat" is adamantly believed by many individuals.

Prenatal nourishment is unique in that only one source exists, the mother's placenta. The placenta serves as the vehicle for oxygen-, nutrient-, and waste-product exchange—the only one of its kind. Upon birth, however, nourishment is not as easily decided. A common controversy centers around the question that many mothers with newborns face, "Do I breast-feed or bottle-feed my baby?" The question is not whether breast-feeding is good or bad but whether bottle-fed babies are just as healthy and emotionally attached to their mothers as breast-fed infants.

A number of decades ago it was expected that infants were to be nourished from breast milk. In those instances where the biological mother was unable or unwilling to breast-feed due to disease, physical restrictions, or social ideas that breast-feeding was debasing and improper, a wet-nurse was employed. Some wet-nurses fed many infants simultaneously.

With the advancement of sterilization techniques and nutritional supplements, bottle-feeding began to be popular. This popularity reached a point where nursing mothers were a minority, and were considered nonconforming. To many mothers, breast-feeding was embarrassing and unnatural. If it wasn't necessary, why do it? Many doctors even discouraged mothers from breast-feeding, saying things such as, "Your milk is too thin," "Your breasts are too small," or simply, "There is no difference between breast milk and other nutritional sources, as far as the baby's health is concerned." One author noted this widespread neglect concerning breast-feeding—"fewer than 25 percent of the babies born in this country are nursed even for the five days of the usual hospital stay" (Pryor, 1973). Developers and marketers of infant formulas were eager to advertise their products as perfect substitutes.

In spite of this trend away from breast-feeding, the tide seems to have changed. Major producers of infant formulas have even begun to publicly recognize the superiority of human milk. Although favoring commercial infant formula as the best alternative for breast milk, the importance of human milk is nevertheless often appropriately emphasized.

Reasons for this trend reversal are many and varied. We will provide a brief overview of some advantages and disadvantages to nursing and bottle-feeding. It must be noted, however, that strict reliance on any one literature source may be misleading. Scientific discovery is advancing rapidly, and some past findings have been based on inconclusive evidence. Other sources emphasize a particular person's understanding, which may or may not be accurate. For these reasons, it should not be too disconcerting for the mother-to-be to discover that what she heard or read from one source has been discounted by another. Rather, an objective literature review will help a mother make an informed, comfortable decision, regardless of whether that decision is to breast-feed or bottle-feed her baby.

## BOTTLE- VS. BREAST-FEEDING

**Attachment and closeness.** A frequent argument supporting breast-feeding regards the psychological attachment that results as mother and child engage in close, physical contact during feeding time. This contact provides the mother with a sense of fulfillment as she perceives her child's dependency and the fact that she alone is providing for her child's physical needs.

> The most convincing evidence of the value of breast-feeding comes from mothers who have done it. They tell of the tremendous satisfaction they experience from knowing that they are providing the baby with something no one else can give him, from seeing his devotion to the breast, from feeling his closeness . . . A woman doesn't get to feel like a mother, or come to enjoy being a mother, or feel the full motherly love for her child just from the fact that a baby has been born to her. With her first infant particularly, she becomes a real mother only as she takes care of her child. . . . In this sense breast feeding does wonders for a young mother and for her relationship with her baby (Spock, 1968, pp. 72–73).

Like Dr. Spock, many authors also assert that the closeness and warmth felt between mother and infant during feeding time are important considerations. This closeness is necessary for the infant to develop a sense of security and well-being. John Montgomery, a physician, suggested that the abrupt, disrupting experience of leaving the sheltered, comfortable, and soothing environment of the mother's womb is made easier if the infant "can feel that he is not completely separated from the body that bore him" (Montgomery, 1951, pp. 33–34). This is accomplished during the close cuddling of breast-feeding.

The closeness experienced by infant and mother is important; breast-feeding is instrumental in this process. However, no mother should feel that the bottle-fed infant will necessarily be deprived of such a relationship. Some mothers have diseases or physical problems that preclude breast-feeding. Others must work and are not able to breast-feed their baby at regular intervals throughout the day. This does not mean close relationships and attachment will not develop between mother and child. Indeed, the most frequently given reason for bonding is physical closeness and loving acceptance. This can be experienced during bottle-feeding also, as long as the baby is held close to the mother and comforted in a fashion similar to that of breast-feeding.

Psychological growth would seem to depend on the relationship between developing infant and mother, not the feeding technique. "A baby raised in a loving home can grow up to be a healthy, psychologically secure

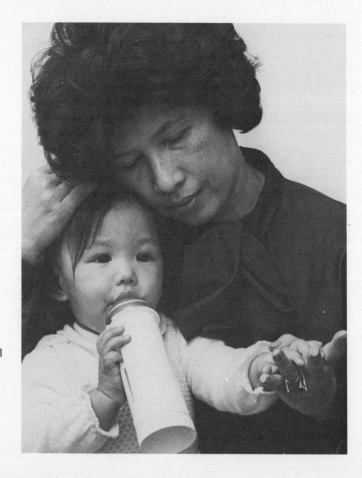

Parent–child bonding, facilitated by physical closeness and loving acceptance during breast-feeding, can be experienced during bottle-feeding also.

individual no matter how he receives his nourishment" (Olds & Eiger, 1973, p. 18). However, bottle-feeding comes under criticism when mothers rely too heavily on the bottle and forget the importance of holding and cuddling their feeding babies. It frees the mother somewhat, and she often tries to do other things while the baby is feeding. As a result the infant doesn't receive her full attention.

This inattentiveness is adequately displayed when a mother props the bottle up in a bassinet or crib so that she can sweep the floor during feeding. Bottle-propping has also been discouraged due to the danger that arises if the baby chokes on the milk, or if the bottle falls out of its mouth and it swallows too much air. However, the negative effect most salient to this discussion is the lack of attention and contact. Indeed, as one pamphlet put it so nicely, "It's hard to prop a breast."

**Nutrition.** Another important reason given for breast-feeding, and perhaps the most difficult to refute, concerns nutrition and infant health. A mother's milk, without controversy, is designed for babies.

> Breast milk contains more whey proteins providing essential acids than cow's milk; is free from bacteria; and is easier to digest. Milk formulas are satisfactory and adequate, but cow's milk proteins may cause allergies. Cow's milk contains 40% less iron and vitamins A and D than human milk. Vitamin C is adequate in human milk but is insufficient in cow's milk (Hafen, Thygerson, & Rhodes, 1976).

Kathleen Berger (1980) enumerated nutritional benefits similar to those above, and even maintained that bottle-fed babies given well-prepared formulas have more allergies and digestive problems than breast-fed babies. Other authors, however, conclude that bottle-feeding can be safe, satisfactory, and convenient (Smart & Smart, 1978). Nonetheless, digestive problems are clearly evident in babies who are fed cow's milk. The solubility of fat is different from human milk and is problematic for many infants. Undissolved fats contribute to digestive disturbance and can produce colic, constipation, or irritability.

Chances of allergies and illness are often increased in non-breast-fed infants. A thick, yellowish liquid called *colostrum* is present in the breasts from before birth until a few days after nursing has started. Doctors have identified colostrum as a carrier of antibodies present in the mother. These antibodies help protect the baby against certain diseases during the first six months of life, whether breast-feeding is continued or not (Pryor, 1973). The child is protected against pathogens such as polio, Coxsackie B virus, several staphylococci, and *E. coli,* an adult intestinal bacterium. An infant's gastrointestinal tract is immature and unable to provide protection from many of these viruses without the colostrum's help. Cow's milk and infant formulas do not equal the immunological strengths of human milk.

Some doctors have even cited findings that breast milk itself is "a suspension of immune system cells in a highly nutritive medium" (Beer, in Winter, 1980). These immune-system cells give protection through the infant's intestines, which, as stated above, are open to invasion from viruses, bacteria, and undigested proteins. As a result, breast-fed babies have fewer allergies and digestive upsets than even formula-fed babies.

**Weight gain.** Formula-fed babies tend to gain weight faster. This faster gain rate is not necessarily due to abnormally large amounts of fat and calories in comparison to human milk. Rather, feeding practices themselves tend to be different. When fed by bottle, infants are more often overfed; mothers often see to it that the bottle is emptied. Contrariwise, a breast-feeding mother tends to allow feeding until the infant is satisfied. Fomon, Filer, Thomas, Rogers, and Proksch (1969) experimentally changed the caloric count of infant formulas and found that infants would increase or decrease their intake volume to compensate for the change. After receiving sufficient calories for their needs, they would stop feeding. There appears to be no need to push babies to finish a bottle.

Many counsel against excess weight gain during infancy because of the obesity precedent that may be set for later life. Fat-cell division is greatest during the last trimester of pregnancy, throughout infancy, and then in early adolescence. Overeating during these periods stimulates growth of a greater number of fat cells, leading to an increased incidence of obesity as an adult (Hafen, 1981; Knittle, 1975; Mayer, 1975; Winnick, 1975). "In general, the six-month-old period seems to be the critical point at which chubby infants are more likely to become overweight or obese adults than normal or light-weight infants will" (Isenberg, 1982, p. 59). It has been suggested that breast-feeding may be the best prevention of obesity during a child's first year (Flynn, 1975). Giving infants solid foods too early also contributes to infant obesity.

**Additional arguments.** Breast- versus bottle-feeding has even become a debate among some dentists, who suggest that breast-feeding promotes better jaw development (Smart & Smart, 1978). "The breast requires a complicated coordination of biting and sucking, whereas the bottle instigates simpler, relatively passive movements."

In addition to the advantages cited above, other advantages given for breast-feeding include the following:

1. Breast-feeding helps the mother's uterus return to its normal prepregnant state.
2. Breast milk is always at the proper temperature and, under normal conditions, is sterile. Preparation time is, therefore, minimal as well as convenient when traveling and away from home.
3. Breast-feeding is economical in comparison with prepared formula.
4. Breast-fed babies have fewer problems with constipation and, as many mothers maintain, a breast-fed baby's bowel movement odor is less undesirable.

**Disadvantages of breast-feeding.** Although advantages to breast-feeding are many, disadvantages also exist. A mother must maintain a proper diet to ensure that her baby receives necessary nutrients and to be healthy herself. Although the body is remarkably adept at producing a sufficient quantity and quality of milk, nursing mothers will be less tired and irritable and have a more adequate supply of milk if nutrition is improved. Strict dieting is not recommended following pregnancy. In addition, mothers who breast-feed must control their own ingestion of substances potentially harmful to the infant when passed through the milk in large quantities—nicotine, caffeine, hormones present in oral contraceptives (McCall, 1979).

Restrictions on a lactating mother are also disadvantageous. She may feel tied down because wherever she is, when feeding time comes she must respond. Some mothers restrict their social activities to avoid awkward moments in public. No one else can do the feeding; it is the mother's sole responsibility. Nursing may be especially problematic if the mother is working outside of the home. If she attempts to have a babysitter feed the baby formula during the day, while waiting to nurse in the mornings and evenings, she will face the pain of engorged breasts and possible cessation of milk production. To avoid this, she may have to manually express milk during the day. If one feeding rather than two or three is missed, this displeasure may be bearable. Milk pumps can be bought or rented to allow storing of milk in the refrigerator until that feeding time comes when she is away. One mother manually expressed her milk into small plastic nursing bottles and put them in the freezer so that one could be taken to a public event. When feeding time came, the milk had thawed and she was able to feed her child unobtrusively.

In general, advantages of breast-feeding seem to be the baby's advantages, while advantages of bottle-feeding seem to be the mother's. A mother who makes an informed decision, weighing costs and benefits for her and the baby, will feel better about that decision. Many other factors will also enter into this decision—style of life, community customs, attitudes of doctors and husband (some parents opt for bottle-feeding so the father can be involved in the feeding process), and a mother's personality and feelings about mothering. Of utmost importance is that the decision be a comfortable one.

## FEEDING SCHEDULES

Opinions on feeding schedules vary on the continuum between strict scheduling and feeding on demand. Keeping a strict schedule implies that the infant will adjust to a set routine if the mother enforces her schedule. After she gets to know how much the infant takes at each feeding and how long the nourishment satisfies, she can set up a rigid schedule that might mean, for example, the infant is fed every four hours. On the other hand, feeding on demand implies that whenever the child gets hungry and cries, it is feeding time.

Some babies will have problems adjusting to a regular feeding schedule. Their stomachs may not be able to hold four hours' worth of milk, which would be problematic if the mother felt that a four-hour feeding schedule was appropriate. A baby may be extra tired and go to sleep halfway through a feeding; or the baby may be colicky or sick and not eat as much one time. Sometimes a mother who is nursing her baby may be tired, anxious, or ill, resulting in a temporary decrease of milk production. In any of these cases, waiting for four hours to elapse before the next feeding is not recommended. To ascertain hunger, the parent may let the child fuss for 10 to 15 minutes. Allowing extended periods of crying, however, is not desirable. Obviously, strict scheduling will not always work.

However, some parents misunderstand this statement to mean that the other extreme is the answer—that they must feed their baby any time it wakes up and never wake it up for a feeding. This might be well for the pleasant, peaceful baby with good digestion, and for parents whose own schedules are flexible and who don't mind being available on demand. But, for fretful babies who cry frequently, and for parents whose schedules or demeanors are such that make unpredictable attending to the child very frustrating, irritating days and restless nights may be the result. In addition, allowing the child to eat whenever he or she is suspected of being hungry prolongs the dropping out of feeding times when the child should be able to go longer in between feedings.

If we were to continue supposing that both rigid and feeding-on-demand schedules are extremes, it seems that an ideal—depending, of course, on each individual child—is somewhere in the middle of the continuum. An example of such a schedule is given in Dr. Spock's book *Baby and Child Care* (1976).

A relaxed baby girl who weighed 7 or 8 pounds at birth usually is able to last 3½ to 4 hours on a full stomach and wants 6 or 7 feedings in the 24 hours at the start. The parents can keep in mind, as a rough guide, a 4-hour schedule (6 A.M., 10 A.M., 2 P.M., 6 P.M., 10 P.M., 2 A.M.), but be quite willing to feed her early if she really seems hungry—1 hour early if she is taking good amounts from the bottle; as much as 2 hours early if she is breast-fed and the supply is not yet well established.

If your baby is still asleep when one of these regular feeding hours comes around, you can wake her up. You won't have to urge her to eat. A baby who is woken up 4 hours after her last feeding will usually be starving hungry in a few minutes. But suppose she wakes up an hour early for her next feeding. You don't have to feed her the first minute she whimpers. She's not sure herself she's hungry. But if in 10 or 15 minutes she's crying hard with hunger, I wouldn't wait any longer. What happens to the 4-hour schedule? She may make up the difference and sleep long enough before the next feeding to get back on schedule. If she doesn't make up the time during the day, she may make it up at night. If she's always waking early, nearer to every 3 hours, maybe she isn't getting enough to last 4 hours. If she is being breast-fed, let her nurse more

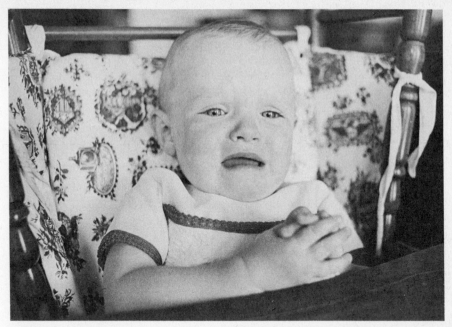

The hungry infant has only one way to communicate need—crying.

often—even after 2 hours if she seems very hungry—expecting that the more frequent emptying of the breast will stimulate it to supply more milk in the next few days. When she gets a larger amount, she will be able to last longer. If she is on the bottle, draining every one, and regularly waking early, consult the doctor about increasing the formula (p. 84).

From a psychological perspective, infants are learning to react with their environments upon birth. When they are hungry, they cry. This is their way of having their needs met, and eating is their primary means of satisfaction. When hunger is satisifed, they are happier; when hungry again, they let the environment know by crying. How others respond to pleas will teach them something about how they fit in with their environments, and how to have subsequent needs met. A sense of trust or distrust is developed. The infant on a rigid, nonchangeable feeding schedule learns he or she has no control over what happens. Communicating with the environment does not seem to do any good. Children whose needs are not met promptly have been shown to later be less secure, less attached to parents, and more fretful (McCall, 1979). At the other end of the continuum, it was once thought that children who are always fed on demand not only learn that they have control over their environment, but expect that all their needs will be met immediately. However, McCall (1979) suggests that "most contemporary opinion is that self-demand feeding per se does not produce spoiled children" (p. 38).

The example provided by Spock (1976), then, may need to be modified to allow parents more flexibility in attending to their child's demands. It has been suggested, for example, that the majority of two-week-old infants prefer a two-hour feeding schedule (McCall, 1979). Both the child's and the parents' needs are important considerations when setting up feeding schedules. Parents need not think that being good parents means having rigid control over all their children's demands. Indeed, they should adapt feeding schedules to the child's own needs (MacKieth & Wood, 1977). On the other hand, they need not ignore their own convenience. Order is desirable, but flexibility is a necessity.

## Weaning

Weaning also varies from baby to baby. Many pediatricians have slightly different opinions on: when an infant can begin to take solid foods; which foods should be started out first; when breast-feeding or bottle-feeding should be stopped altogether; or, if the mother is nursing, when the baby should be weaned to a bottle or cup. Generally, a doctor's advice is good and should be considered. Despite small differences in personal opinions, the doctor will consider personal knowledge and each baby's progress and unique differences.

Often, a breast-fed baby does not need any solid foods until five or six months old. No matter how big the infant might be, the mother's milk provides necessary nutrients and calories for adequate growth. A bottle-fed baby, however, may need early supplements. The breast-fed child may signal the need for additional nourishment if he or she begins getting hungrier between feedings; this may occur between two and four months of age.

Parents usually start babies on cereal first. The parent may try giving the infant a little cereal prior to the regular feeding; if the baby refuses, it should not be forced. Quite a few rejections may be necessary before the baby starts to take cereal. It is new, and the baby is not accustomed to passing food from the front to the back of the mouth by using his tongue—it's not like sucking, and cereals may taste pretty bland. Instead of trying solids before feeding, they may be offered during milk feedings. It might be a while before the infant associates solid food with feeding time and the reduction of hunger.

Many suggest that fruits be offered next because so many infants take them enthusiastically due to their pleasing sweet taste. Yet, it is exactly for this reason that other doctors prefer to start vegetables before fruits. A child starting on fruits will find it harder to begin taking vegetables, which are not as sweet and often more uniquely strong and different. Vegetables are also harder to digest and may cause gastrointestinal distress when given too early.

When weaning the child from the breast, many wait until the child is old enough to become familiar with drinking from a cup. This generally occurs around six months, though individual babies differ. Whether weaning the child from the breast to a cup or bottle, or weaning from the bottle to a cup, the switch is preferably done in a slow, trial-and-error fashion. Choose the one feeding during the day toward which the infant has developed a little disinterest and introduce the new stimulus at this time. If the infant rejects it, that's fine, try again the next day. If this procedure does not appear to be effective, that particular feeding can be eliminated altogether. Being hungry increases the incentive to try something new. After the infant is consistently taking the bottle or cup at this feeding, another feeding may be chosen for the switch-over. Unless the parent is constrained to perform the entire change in a very rapid manner, the slow-and-easy approach is easier on both parent and child.

Setting an appropriate age for weaning from the breast or bottle cannot be done. The exact time is dependent on doctor's advice, mother's wishes, child's needs, and a host of other variables. An occasional mother will continue nursing, along with supplemental nourishment, even after her baby has reached one-and-a-half years of age.

## Crying

An infant's cry is a very powerful attention-getter. Even total strangers respond to an infant's strained, helpless cries, and many individuals feel uncomfortable when hearing such crying. First-time parents are especially prone to confusion, upset, and discomfort by an infant's often excessive crying. Perhaps the most frequently asked question of physicians by new mothers concerning crying is "Do I always try to comfort my crying child, or are there times when he or she should be left alone?" The answer is not short and simple. In a very general sense, "It all depends. . . . " It depends on why the child is crying, how old the child is, and even on a doctor's particular orientation.

### WHY DOES A NEWBORN CRY?

Crying is a newborn's only way of communicating its needs to the outside world. It has no concept of itself or other people as individuals, and no means of communication other than crying. So, whenever discomfort is felt, crying results. An infant cries for a variety of reasons: for relief from hunger, for relief from a wet or full diaper, from pain, from being too cold or too hot, from wanting to be held or cuddled, from discomfort due to fatigue, sickness, or indigestion. Consider the following account given by a mother:

*One morning about 2 A.M.* our little daughter woke up crying. My husband Jim went into her room and checked her diaper to see if it needed changing. He then tried giving her a bottle, which she would not take. He came back to bed and she continued to cry for some time after that. I then got up to recheck her. Jim got up also, and we looked to see if the diaper pins were sticking her or if the bottle Jim gave her had been clogged. We couldn't discover anything wrong and finally brought her into our bed hoping we could comfort her better. Well, *this did not help either. Jim tried rubbing her stomach and, as he did, he loosened her pajamas. She was wearing pajamas that were somewhat big. While loosening them, he found that her little toe was caught in the elastic around the ankle of the pajamas. Jim freed her toe, and she immediately went to sleep—it took us 1½ hours to find that out.*

## ATTENDING TO CRYING

Many parents are worried about "spoiling" the child, feeling that always running to pick it up when it begins to cry is a reinforcement for crying, thus causing more crying in the future. Burton White, author of *The First Three Years of Life* (1975), does not believe that a child can be spoiled in the first seven months of life. Unrelenting crying is difficult to endure, and a child should not be left to cry it out. White states further that "prompt response to an infant's crying leads to a better quality of attachment between caretaker and baby" (White, 1975, p. 29). From this viewpoint, crying is a natural expression of distress and should not be ignored lest the child's trust in his or her caretaker and environment be greatly reduced. And, immediate

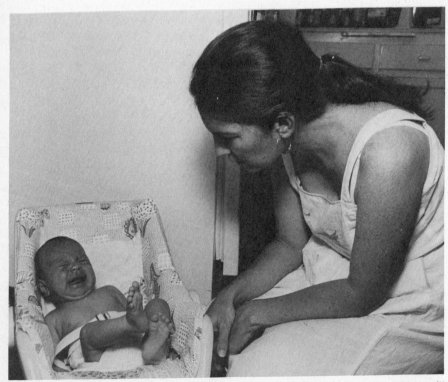

Many parents are overly concerned that always attending to a crying infant will spoil the child.

responding does not necessarily cause the child to become manipulative with its crying.

Bell and Ainsworth (1972) focused on crying patterns during the first year of life and found that although a mother's behavior (how often she ignored crying) remained consistent throughout the year, the baby's crying was not consistent until the last half of the year. In general, those mothers who responded immediately to crying had babies that cried less later on. On the other hand, ignoring a baby's cries tended to increase the frequency and duration of crying during months 7 to 12. Promptness in responding was the most important factor in stopping crying. In addition, responding was most effective if it involved picking up and holding the baby. Montgomery (1951), author of *America's Baby Book,* states quite emphatically that babies allowed to cry it out tend to grow up frustrated, resentful, and uncooperative. Allowing babies to cry for long periods before being attended to often causes them to continue crying after needs have been satisfied.

It must be pointed out, however, that many authors with the above opinion also state that there are times when no amount of feeding, diaper-changing, and holding will quiet a frustrated, crying baby. If not explicitly stated, it is implied that crying cannot always be halted by immediate attention giving. The experienced parent will become familiar with different types of crying and be able to determine whether the baby is crying because it is hungry, tired, or uncomfortable; with such knowledge, crying can and should be attended to without making the child cry for long time periods. However, the same parent would become attuned to cries signaling the need for only attention. Most parents would agree that attention is important for a baby, and that close physical contact is important in relationship building. On the other hand, the parent's needs are also to be considered, and a baby that is very demanding of attention may need to learn early that life is not always so "self" oriented. One mother of a small baby related the following story:

*When our first child was about three months old and not sleeping through the night, I consulted our physician to see if the situation could be remedied. He suggested that we make sure he was not crying for a particular reason (other than habit) and then just let him cry until he cried himself to sleep. He cautioned us not to let him see us while checking on him or he might feel rejected. The first night he cried for approximately 45 minutes, and that was hard on us. The second night he cried for about half an hour and the third night for only about 15 minutes. On the fourth night he slept peacefully through the night— and so did we.*

The key seems to be for the parent to recognize the purpose of crying. A child's needs can be appropriately met when the cause is known. If the parent is aware, for example, that his or her child is demanding too much attention for no particular reason other than just wanting to be held or played with, crying may need to be responded to in a little less servile fashion. Babies will soon learn that they cannot always be held or paid direct attention. Such knowledge may even be advantageous, as they will learn ways to amuse themselves rather than being amused by someone else. Consider the following experience:

*This past summer my family, namely my mother, baby-sat my nephew off and on at our house. When he first came, he wanted to be held constantly. Every time he was set on the floor with his toys he cried or screamed. He was 15 to 16 months old, and my mom felt it was time he got adjusted to not having someone come running every single time he cried. She began by setting him in the living room a lot of the time, and we would all stop to play with him a little, then go on to other things that we were doing. He screamed several times within the first hour of this. The interesting thing to watch was how he would take a breath and peer around to see if any of us were very concerned about his crying. We ignored it, but not him. No one picked him up, but Mom would say, "What's the matter, Scott, don't you like your toys?" My dad talked to him and my sisters and I would say something to him as we went through the room. Soon he was playing happily with his toys by himself. Eventually he even crawled over to where my dad was reading the paper and babbled on and on about something.*

*We continued the treatment every time we baby-sat him. When he's at our home he doesn't throw temper tantrums anymore; he gets toys to play with or drums up companionship from some of us. He's really quite pleasant to be around.*

## INDIVIDUAL DIFFERENCES

Elsewhere in this text we pointed out that even during the first few weeks of life, humans differ. In one study, Thomas, Chess, and Birch (1970) were able to classify infants into the following categories: difficult babies, slow-to-warm-up babies, and easy babies. Difficult babies wail and cry a great deal, often throw tantrums, will not take food, twist and scream, and have irregular sleep patterns. Little the parent does seems to make them comfortable. Slow-to-warm-up babies tend to be withdrawn, negative, and less responsive to eye gazes than other children. The last group, easy babies, are the most responsive, pleasant ones we typically see and write about in the popular media. They make up approximately 40 percent of all children. Thomas and his associates have some advice for parents of the more difficult babies:

[T]he recognition that a child's behavioral disturbance is not necessarily the direct result of maternal pathology should do much to prevent the deep feelings of guilt and inadequacy with which innumerable mothers have been unjustly burdened as a result of being held entirely responsible for their children's problems (Thomas, Chess, & Birch, 1968, p. 202–203).

Research indicates that not only do parents influence infant behavior, but that babies also influence parenting styles (Dion, 1974; Marcus, 1975; Osofsky & Danzger, 1974; Yarrow, Waxler, & Scott, 1971). Two researchers, Mary D. Salter Ainsworth and Sylvia M. Bell (1969), expressed this finding as follows:

> Whatever role may be played by the baby's constitutional characteristics in establishing the initial pattern of mother–infant interaction, it seems quite clear that the mother's contribution to the interaction and the baby's contribution are caught up in an interacting spiral. It is because of these spiral effects—some "vicious" and some "virtuous"—that the variables are so confounded [and it is difficult to untangle them] (p. 160).

It is easiest to love babies who smile in return, cuddle and snuggle up when they are ready to go to sleep, sleep through the night, take naps, and enjoy their food. With the difficult, crying, colicky baby, however, parents often feel rejected and failures. In some cases they may become angry and abusive. To these parents, success seems unattainable and their frustration may turn into rage. Even with the best of intentions, these parents will not raise their children as they would intend. Differences between how two children were raised are seen in the following quote:

> *My brother was generally restless as a child, which caused my parents to try to force certain controls upon him, causing him to be insecure or paranoid when he did something wrong. When I was young, I was of mild temperament, and my parents were not as restrictive with me as with my brother. My brother and I are very near to the same age but have been raised very differently.*

For these reasons, we as authors feel it unwise to prescribe one way to raise children—the methods used must be adapted to the child's personality as well as the parents'.

## DEALING WITH CRYING

Without debating the pros and cons, this section will list some techniques parents have used to reduce crying. Regardless of whether crying is good or bad, most parents find at one time or another that they are working very hard to reduce crying episodes. The most common methods include:

gentle rocking; touching; cuddling; holding; a pacifier; additional feeding; a warm, comfortable bath; humming; or supporting the child on the parent's shoulder (Birns, Blank, & Bridger, 1966; Korner & Thoman, 1972; Pederson, Champagne, & Pederson, 1969; Smart & Smart, 1978; Thoman, Korner, and Beason-Williams, 1977). Most of these methods involve diverting the child's attention to something else, or simply making the child more comfortable. In our parenting classes we have asked mothers to tell us about unusual ways they have discovered to soothe and comfort crying children.

One mother found that if she could distract her baby with novel and fascinating stimuli, he would stop crying. For example, she whistled when he cried, and he would become distracted and listen to the whistles. Occasionally, she also sang to him. Another mother noticed that riding in a car tended to comfort her child and put her to sleep. When the child became especially irritable during the day, she took advantage of the time by running errands or going to the store, which would settle her child down. Other times, the best thing to do would be for the mother to take a little break. One mother became so upset she started fearing she might physically harm the baby. As a result, she called a sitter for a quick half-hour to let her cool down a bit. Family members who are home can also assist in caring for the child.

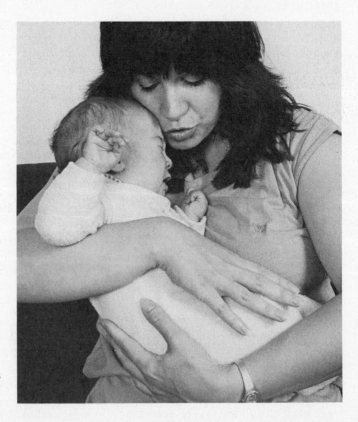

Parents often find special ways of soothing their crying infants.

One inventor decided that the reason infants cry initially is because they are taken out of the environment they are accustomed to, the womb, which makes them feel insecure. So, he recorded the sounds inside a pregnant woman's womb and placed the tape inside a teddy bear. The teddy bear would then be placed in the baby's crib as a comfort. (This commercial venture was reported to have met with some success by one of our students.)

Parents often learn special ways of caressing and stroking the child. One such case illustrates the unique ways parents learn to comfort their children.

When my little brother was born, my mother was in bed for three months. I took care of him, and had to deal with his crying. Mom used to say, "Let him cry . . . he'll stop when he realizes no one is going to pick him up." For some reason he never stopped. However, from day one, he had a soft blanket that he slept with constantly. It was edged in a satin-like material. I found that if I picked him up and laid him on his back on top of my legs, then stroked his cheeks and tummy with the satin-like material, he'd stop crying and fall asleep.

Sometimes these individualized techniques develop into elaborate rituals:

When my little brother was born, he had the attention he wanted almost all of the time. However, when he was tired and needed a nap, it seemed he could be soothed in only one way. My mother had to rock him over her shoulder until he relaxed and then had to put him face down on a pillow on her lap and continue to rock him until he fell asleep. If my mother held him on her shoulder without ever putting him on her lap, he would not go to sleep. If she tried to put him on the pillow first, he would squirm until she held him up to her shoulder and rocked him.

The idea of snugly wrapping a child in a blanket has been suggested by many parents. One young girl soon discovered the success of this method:

When my last sister was born my mother was working quite a bit so I, being the oldest, ended up taking care of her. During this time I learned little tricks to soothe her. One that worked really well, especially when she was just a newborn, was to wrap her up really snug in a receiving blanket. The snug wrapping seemed to give her a sense of security, which is very important to an infant. It seemed that once she was *wrapped up well with her other needs being met, we could lay her in her bassinet on her stomach and she would go right to sleep.*

◑

Children respond well to differences in tone and are capable of detecting very faint tones. Thus, it is not surprising that they respond well to singing and lullabies. Although he didn't sing lullabies, one young attorney noticed by chance that his newborn twins quieted down when the vacuum was on. He tape-recorded the vacuum, and when all else failed he could turn on this tape-recording to settle the twins.

## CRYING TANTRUMS

For older children, where crying could often be more accurately called tantrums, using extinction and other methods for eliminating undesirable behavior is appropriate (see Chapter 8). In discussing how to eliminate the crying of an older child, students in our classes were able to suggest some novel techniques. One mother found that when her three-year-old engaged in a tantrum, her best method was simply to place the child in front of a mirror. The child quickly ceased crying as he did not like the sound and the sight of his own crying. An eight-year-old child who cried to get her own way quit crying when her family screamed and cried in unison with her. She soon saw the inappropriateness and childishness of her actions. (Note that these techniques are more appropriate for the older child and really have no relevance for the infant, the focus of this chapter.)

## COLIC

Colic refers to a condition in which the baby's abdomen fills up with gas and becomes distended. This is very uncomfortable, causing the baby to scream piercingly and pull up or stiffen its legs (Spock, 1976, p. 219). Colic commonly begins between two and four weeks of age. In many cases, the mother may be distraught because the baby was fine in the hospital, only to become colicky after coming home. She may think she is doing something wrong—that her milk supply is insufficient or, if bottle-feeding, that the formula is not being properly digested. One indicator of colic is the pattern of crying. Colic can be differentiated from "hungry" crying as it occurs after feeding and not before. Moreover, colic does not occur after every feeding; rather, it is usually most noticeable between 6 P.M. and 12 P.M. or between 2 P.M. and 6 P.M. At other times, and after other feedings, the baby may be quite happy and quiet. Spock (1976) describes a typical case of colic:

> The baby was said to be well behaved and quiet in the hospital, but a few days after going home she suddenly has a crying spell that lasts for 3 or 4 hours straight. The parents change her, turn her over, give her a drink of water, but nothing works for long. After a couple of hours, the parents

wonder if she is hungry ahead of time, because she seems to be trying to get everything into her mouth. The parents warm up a bottle and she takes it eagerly at first, but before it's finished she lets go and cries again. The screaming often continues for the full 4-hour interval between feedings. After she has finished her next regular bottle, she may be miraculously relieved (p. 219).

Perhaps most important for parents to understand is that colic is not abnormal—nothing they have done and nothing the baby has done have caused the problem. With this understanding, parents' whole approach to dealing with a fretful, crying baby will be different.

Although the occurrence of colic may be beyond parents' control, they may find that doing certain things help subdue or pacify the child somewhat. Specific methods may be unique to a particular child; in other cases, suggestions such as the following may help in a large number of cases: use a pacifier; burp sufficiently after feedings; lay the infant on its stomach; rub the infant's back; lay the infant on a hot water bottle; and provide company and cuddling in a calm and gentle manner.

## Toilet Training (Bowel and Bladder Training)

As with infant feeding, methods of toilet training vary, and even if one method were applied to a number of children, individual differences would result in varying degrees of cooperation, resistance, and success. With this in mind, and a reminder that children develop socially and neuromuscularly at differing rates, a word of caution is in order—parents should not become blinded by popular techniques that specify a set age at which toilet training should occur, how fast it should occur, or exactly how it should be implemented. Preconceived ideas can lead to frustration for both parent and child if strictly followed. Attempting to train too early could lead to psychological distress or be simply a waste of time. Improper training could promote resistance, dependency, or even refusal and delay in toilet training.

In addition to remaining flexible, parents may glean valuable information from some of the more popular training techniques, as they are based on fundamental learning principles such as modeling and reinforcement. Behavioral modification techniques like those discussed earlier are effective in promoting dryness and continence. Some of these ideas may not be directly applicable to a particular child, but should provide parents with an adequate knowledge of how similar methods may be tailored to their children's personalities.

### Determining Readiness

Most children do not have the neuromuscular maturation necessary for anal and bladder sphincter muscle control until about two years of age. Train-

Attempts to begin toilet training before neuromuscular control is somewhat developed will probably be futile.

ing attempts before this control is at least somewhat developed will probably prove futile. Again, it must be noted that children are different. Some are ready for training at 18 months of age; others are not successfully trained until 28 months or older. However, if complete bladder control has not been obtained by the third or fourth year, especially if leaking or wetting occurs during both day and night, consultation with a urologist is recommended to rule out slow maturation, small bladder capacity, allergies, anatomical defects, or other organic factors. Azrin and Foxx (1974) suggest that parents consider three questions to help determine if bladder control is sufficient for toilet-training procedures to begin:

1. Does [the] child urinate a good deal at one time rather than dribbling throughout the day?
2. Does he stay dry for several hours?
3. Does he appear to know he is about to urinate as indicated by his facial expressions or by special postures he adopts (p. 36)?

An affirmative answer to these three questions indicates the child is sufficiently aware of bladder sensations and able to control the bladder for training.

Another consideration is the child's own readiness—his or her willingness to respond to training, and the ability to follow instructions. The latter of these two is necessarily a requirement for the first. The child must be able to understand and carry out instructions before being considered socially and intellectually responsive to training. Obviously, broad language capabilities are not necessary. However, if the child can understand simple instructions, can point to the potty chair, can sit down, or walk into a particular room when told, can point to parts of his or her body, and can indicate somehow the need to go "potty" or "poo-poo," communication skills may be sufficient.

In addition to communication skills, readiness is also indicated by an interest in the process. If children are stubborn, refuse to follow simple commands, or otherwise show disinterest in the toilet-training process, they should not be pushed. Training should be postponed for weeks before another attempt is made. Indeed, many authors recommend that children be trained at their own pace, when they are ready and practically train themselves.

Brazelton (1962), for example, emphasizes a child-oriented approach in which parents implement a relaxed, nonpressured technique. When the child achieves physiological and intellectual-psychological readiness, training is begun. The child is first presented with a potty chair, which is verbally associated with the parents' toilet. For approximately a week, the fully clothed child is taken to sit on the potty seat. The parent sits with the child, may read aloud, but does not force the child to sit there. If the child wants to get up to leave, he or she is allowed to do so. After this initial step, the same procedure is performed, only this time with the child's diapers off. The next step involves placing the child on the "potty" twice a day. One of these times may be during diaper change itself. The soiled diapers could then be dropped into the potty, helping the child understand the eventual function of this new chair. Once this understanding is achieved, the child can be taken to the chair several times a day, providing an opportunity to actually use the potty chair. Throughout the process, parents should be encouraging and rewarding when the child succeeds at using the potty.

Brazelton's process is not forceful, enabling the child to approach potty training at his own pace. If not ready, or stubbornly refusing to cooperate, the child should not be pushed. The parent backs off and makes another attempt later. Practically all approaches stress the importance of not being forceful and punishing when toilet training. However, some authors feel that approaching training in a more rapid, time-efficient manner can be highly successful without being pushy or punishing. Nathan Azrin and Richard Foxx (1974) have sold close to a million copies of their paperback *Toilet Training in Less than a Day*, which outlines such a procedure.

Before discussing this procedure, we must point out an additional sign of readiness that Azrin and Foxx (1974) feel is important for completion of their procedure—physical readiness. Physical readiness is accomplished if the child has enough finger and hand coordination to pick up objects easily, and if he or she is easily able to walk from room to room without assistance. Physical readiness is important for Azrin and Foxx's method because the child is expected to take an active part in the training process. Active participation involves pulling down and pulling up one's own pants and emptying the potty chair oneself. For this reason, physiological, intellectual-psychological, and physical readiness are all important considerations.

## TOILET TRAINING IN LESS THAN A DAY

Prior to training, the child needs to be prepared in four ways. This preparation can take place before the decision to train has been made, for it is not part of the training procedure itself.

1. The child should be taught to assist in dressing and undressing himself. Perhaps most simple is to teach him to lower and raise his pants. This may be the only thing a child can do, but it is a beginning.
2. Allow the child to watch others go to the bathroom.
3. Teach the child words that will be used later on during the training process such as "pee-pee" and "poo-poo."
4. Teach the child to cooperatively follow instructions. This of course can refer to instructions asking the child to do anything he is capable of doing. It is important that parents not allow their instructions to go unfulfilled (Azrin & Foxx, 1974, pp. 48–49).

Toilet training can begin by helping the child instruct a doll or other appropriate toy to use the potty chair.

Training begins by letting the child watch his or her mother, or some other trainer who is close to the child, demonstrate the whole procedure with a doll that wets. For example, the trainer can give the doll some water, lower the doll's pants and then place it on the potty chair. Praise should be used as the doll wets in the potty. Dryness of the doll's "training pants" should be noticed and emphasized.

After the child has seen the doll taken through the procedure, he or she is aided in teaching the doll to use the potty chair. Encouraged to praise the doll when it goes in the potty, the child offers the doll a treat—one that the child enjoys and that will later be offered in his or her own training. The child can then be instructed to remove the doll from the chair, pull the doll's pants back up, empty the potty into the toilet, and then flush the toilet. You will recognize the procedure of *imitation*—the child learns the whole training routine by imitating what he or she has just taught the doll. As part of training with the doll, the parent may spill some water on the doll's pants when the child is not looking. As pants inspection occurs, the child notices the wet pants and is instructed to tell the doll of his or her displeasure—"No, Dolly, big girls (boys) don't wet their pants."

Working with the doll should continue until the child clearly understands the steps in toilet training. Azrin and Foxx maintain that "no more than one hour is normally needed for this understanding."

As a first step in the child's own training, the child's pants are inspected every few minutes for dryness. If dry, the child is praised and is offered something pleasurable to drink. This serves as a reward for dry pants and also helps the child drink lots of liquid to facilitate the teaching process. The child is then instructed to go to the potty, lower his or her pants, and sit down for several minutes. These prompted trials should occur about ever 15 minutes, decreasing in frequency as training progresses. Through praise and approval, children eventually learn that they are expected to urinate in the potty, to pull up their pants when finished, to empty the potty into the household toilet, and to then flush it.

This method draws heavily on behavioral techniques such as providing rewards and vicarious learning through the doll, and has proven highly successful. However, the quickness with which training is accomplished should not lead a mother to thinking it simple to perform. She should plan on spending four to five uninterrupted hours with the child. It requires patience, and a good knowledge of the procedure and why it works.

Before we leave Azrin and Foxx's rapid toilet-training method, it is important to emphasize that individual differences must be considered in starting time and length of training. Azrin and Foxx acknowledge this fact; however, it may be easily overlooked by the anxious parent. Specific steps may need to be altered or sequentially changed, or training delayed altogether if unforeseen events disrupt the process. As mentioned earlier, stubbornness may preclude effective training. If a mother, for example, is not able to perform training without interruption (if she works during the day, for example, and at night she and the child cannot be alone), she will need to use ideas acquired through reading to develop her own program. This is perhaps the most important aspect of a technique such as Azrin and Foxx's—it is heavily based on behavioral techniques, which, when learned and understood by the parent, enable parents to effectively toilet-train in ways nicely tailored to a particular child's temperament. In fact, strict adherence to one technique may be detrimental if modifications are not made, or if the parent does not fully understand the procedure. Matson (1975) and Butler (1976) found a number of parents who read only the book and were unsuccessful at training.

## SUMMARY OF TOILET TRAINING

Charles Schaefer (1979), after reviewing and summarizing a number of toilet-training procedures, developed a list of positive and negative practices for parents or professionals working with children. The following is a summary of these practices.

*Accentuate the positives.*
1. Teach children words that indicate a need to eliminate, such as "go potty."
2. Provide a potty chair for training.
3. Use praise and immediate food rewards for successful elimination on the potty. Incentives such as books or toys may be used when the child is on the potty. However, these incentives should not be overly distracting. If the child insists on getting off the toilet and playing, the incentives should be removed.
4. Motivation may be increased by emphasizing dryness and being clean, and associating these emphases with "being grown up."
5. Toilet training may be started only when the child seems eager and willing.
6. Follow a regular schedule and use verbal encouragement at appointed times to establish regularity—such as after meals or before and after naps.
7. Try to anticipate elimination by being observant of cues such as squirming, grunting, or facial expressions. When noticing such signs, take the child to the potty.
8. Gently ask the child at regular intervals if he has to go to the bathroom.
9. Use training pants as a sign of progress to the child. Training pants also aid in the training process as the child can pull them up or down by himself. Training pants should be loose enough so that this isn't too difficult.
10. Do not begin training too early; postpone training if the child does not seem ready.
11. Allow the child to see other family members use the toilet.
12. Remain calm and patient during the training process and expect "accidents" to occur even after training is almost completed.
13. Avoid being too harsh or too lenient and "remember that toilet-training difficulty is a common problem in childhood and is usually not a sign of deep-seated personality problems in the child."

*Minimize the negatives.*
1. Do not punish harshly if the child has an "accident."
2. Do not blame, shame, threaten, or moralize to the child.
3. Parents should not insist that the child remain on the potty seat longer than five to 10 minutes.

4. Fluids should be restricted before bedtime.
5. After a child is trained during the day, do not worry about night-time training. Nocturnal wetting may continue in a child until four or five years of age.

These do's and don'ts reflect a theme occurring in most toilet training methods—it is important that the parent not be premature or harsh in implementing these procedures. In addition, sound behavioral principles can be used to train children when they are ready, although specifics may vary from child to child.

## Attachment: The Foundation of Healthy Parent–Child Relationships

For the remainder of this chapter we will discuss how parent–infant attachment may facilitate later parent–child relationships. Psychologists define *attachment* as a relatively enduring, emotional tie to a specific person or thing. To determine whether attachment has occurred, psychologists look for a number of signs. For example, once attachment is established, distress will be shown upon separation from the caretaker. In addition to separation distress, the child actively seeks to be near the caretaker, and experiences joy or pleasure upon reunion. A child who is attached to a parent will look for and orient toward the parent even when the parent is not present. Attachment behavior between parent and child is also indicated through holding, touching, looking at, and talking to each other. The intensity of attachment is described by one prominent child psychologist:

> Children's attachment to their parents is a passionate thing. When a two-year-old is frightened, the child's small arms cling to the parent's body with surprising strength. When the parent has been away and the two are reunited, the child's smiles and enthusiastic hugs are among the unalloyed pleasures of parenthood, signaling that the child returns the parent's love. On occasion, children will protest with all the vigor at their command a separation from their parents. Yet, the quality of a child's affection is not the same as an adult's—it is more demanding and less giving, and it is built on the child's needs and the parent's ability to gratify the needs (Maccoby, 1980, p. 47).

The formation of infant attachment can be seen in almost all mammals. It is particularly pronounced among monkeys, where prolonged disruption of attachment during the early weeks of life results in permanent inability to form healthy adult relationships.

## TYPES OF ATTACHMENT

Ainsworth (1967) and Sroufe and Waters (1977) identified three types of attachment behavior in infants: avoidant, securely attached, and resistant.

**Avoidant.** In the avoidant type of attachment behavior, a mother who reappears after separation is usually ignored or avoided by the infant. This infant is not particularly distressed by separation from the mother and is easily comforted by a stranger.

**Securely attached.** Before a mother leaves, the securely attached infant will play comfortably with toys and react positively with strangers. However, when the mother is absent, play will be considerably reduced as the child's distress becomes obvious. Upon Mother's return, the child goes immediately to her, may seek contact, and calms down after being in her arms.

**Resistant.** The resistant child is not as content prior to its mother leaving. When the mother returns, the infant will seek contact with the mother, but simultaneously will resist contact and show anger. This child may reach to be picked up but struggle to be put down almost immediately. Even with the mother present this child does not play contentedly.

In the opinion of these researchers, it is desirable and natural for children to show a strong attachment to their mothers, show distress when mothers leave, seek to be near them, miss them when they are gone, and show joy upon reunion. Researchers found that children who were *securely attached* during the first year and a half of life were more competent later in childhood. Securely attached children tend to be social leaders. Other children follow them and teachers rate these children as more forceful, self-directed, and eager to learn. Insecurely attached children are more withdrawn and do not like to participate in activities. They are less curious about novel stimuli, and do not pursue goals as well. Most child psychologists infer that effects of secure attachment are seen in older children and even in adults, believing that healthy relationships as adults stem from this attachment (Main, 1973; Matas, Arend, & Sroufe, 1978; Waters, Whippman, & Sroufe, 1979).

## CAUSES OF ATTACHMENT

A review of psychological literature reveals a number of explanations for attachment. The most popular explanation, and perhaps the oldest, is that children become attached to adults because they are fed. Warmth and nourishment during nursing cause the infant to "love" the mother. Since Freud's early emphasis on the oral stage of development, pediatricians, psychiatrists, and child psychologists have pointed out the importance of nursing.

The most dramatic evidence to explain how infants attach to their mothers comes from a study with monkeys (Harlow & Harlow, 1969). Harlow and Harlow found that soft, contact comfort was the most critical variable in infant attachment. More attachment occurred between young monkeys and a makeshift terry-cloth mother that did *not* feed them than with a wire mother that fed with a nursing bottle. Monkeys reared in isolation suffered like those reared with wire mothers in that both groups were unable to form healthy adult relationships. Warm bodily contact was the critical variable in forming attachments; failure to form attachments resulted in unnatural adult relationships. For example, monkeys who have not had these adequate attachments during infancy are later unable to care for their own offspring.

Play and stimulation also foster attachment. Even during the first five months of life, children will come to prefer adults who talk to them (Roedell & Slaby, 1977; Ross & Goldman, 1977). Infants prefer those adults who play with them and provide stimulation.

Familiarity, security, and control facilitate attachment. If a child can feel secure in a familiar situation, he or she will come to be attached to adults providing that security. Children are born into the world highly dependent and helpless; with the aid of adults they can feel secure and safe in a new environment. If the child can control the parent—know how to cause the parent to bring aid when he or she is in distress—the child will feel more secure with that parent. Thus, parents who respond to cries or learn to communicate with the child will engender positive attachment.

In addition to feeding, contact comfort, play, security, control, and familiarity, Ainsworth, Bell, and Stayton (1971) provided additional insight into maternal characteristics that facilitate strong and healthy parent-child attachment. These mothers: (1) were sensitive to their babies' needs, able to interpret their babies' signals correctly, and quick to respond; (2) accepted their often-restricting parenting responsibilities cheerfully and showed little irritation over their babies' bad moods; (3) respected their babies' autonomy and tried not to interrupt their activities or exert direct control; and (4) quickly noticed their babies' distress signals, even at a distance, and willingly responded.

Nowhere in the above discussion on attachment is it suggested that a critical period for attachment exists, and that failure to provide close physical contact during this period produces irreversible emotional and/or social deficits. Although some research (e.g., Kennell, Jerauld, Wolfe, Chester, Kreger, McAlpine, Steffa, & Klaus, 1974) claims to have shown that extra mother–child contact after birth (e.g., in the hospital) can positively influence mother–child relationships for a year or more, other research does not support this conclusion. For example, Leifer and his colleagues (Leifer, Leiderman, Barnett, & Williams, 1972) compared mother–child attachment of full-term and premature babies who spent little or no time with their mothers during the first days of life. After one month little difference in attachment behaviors between the groups appeared.

Sluckin, Herbert, and Sluckin's (1983) conclusions are similar to the above. Essentially, they maintain that little conclusive evidence exists to suggest that adequate attachment requires extra contact following birth, or that a child's later emotional, psychological, or social difficulties can be realistically attributed to a lack of bonding. In addition, they maintain that short-term advantages of increased mother–infant contact following birth are attributable to the mother having learned caretaking skills earlier and faster, and that if these short-term advantages are postponed due to prematurity or Cesarean birth, irreversible negative effects are not the result.

From the research it can be seen that a number of concrete parental behaviors facilitate attachment. There is also good evidence that the securely attached child has a better chance of developing healthy relationships *with others* at an older age. Thus, the first elements of good parenting probably begin in infancy and involve the characteristics identified above: dealing with feeding, toilet training, and crying. The need for attachment will gradually lessen during later years of childhood as the environment becomes less frightening, as the child acquires language skills and friends, and as the child becomes more capable of meeting his or her own needs. In addition, the failure to develop healthy attachment bonds during the first days or months of a child's life does not preclude establishment of positive relationships at later ages.

## Summary

It has probably become apparent to the reader upon reading the previous sections on feeding, toilet training, and crying that we advocate the following:

1. *An informed parent is an efficient parent.* Studies on infant and child development do have a purpose. One of the aims of research is to advance human understanding. If everyone were to rely totally on his or her own experience, a lot of mistakes would be made in ignorance. Man's ability to code and relay knowledge and understanding by written and spoken language, however, allows progress over the foundation of previous generations' discoveries. Parents need not be totally lost with their first child. Even advice from other individuals increases a future parent's understanding and, therefore, confidence. However, not all advice is good advice; a parent must be informed enough to sift sound suggestions and council from hasty, unfounded conclusions.
2. *A "middle-of-the-road" policy is often the best.* Parents who are too lenient or too strict in their feeding and toilet-training programs, or who are unresponsive or react punitively to a baby's crying, will sow problems for later childhood and adolescence. Overly strict and punitive parents inhibit the growth of autonomy, creativity, trust, independence, and decision-making capabilities. Overly lenient and unresponsive parents do not provide sufficient structure, guidance, and feelings of acceptance for their children.
3. *Parents need to be flexible.* After digesting advice and qualified, professional findings, parents need to realize that no two children are exactly the same. Children of a particular study or in a particular family are different than your own. For this reason, "sound" advice and "fool-proof" methods may need to be altered slightly to meet your child's own personal needs.
4. *Patience is important.* Children mature at different rates, even within the same family. It is not advisable to make strict comparisons of ages at which feeding and toilet-training steps occur. General indicators are used by doctors to pinpoint neurological, emotional, or familial-sociological problems. However, just because one child

is wearing training pants two months earlier than another, no conclusions can be drawn.

# SELF-CHECK

1. The present trend in infant nourishment is
   a. away from breast-feeding.
   b. toward breast-feeding.
   c. at a standstill.
   d. to let the poor creatures fend for themselves.
2. According to recent literature, the following statements are true of breast-feeding *except* for:
   a. Breast-fed babies will become more attached to their mothers, even if bottle propping is avoided.
   b. Breast-fed babies, it is believed, will have increased immunological benefits.
   c. Breast-fed babies gain weight more slowly than bottle-fed babies.
   d. a and b are not true.
3. The following feeding schedule is probably best for most infants:
   a. strict schedule according to set time intervals
   b. feeding on demand
   c. somewhat in the middle of a and b
   d. none of the above is best
4. Doctors usually start babies on
   a. fruits.
   b. vegetables.
   c. cereal.
   d. meat and eggs.
5. All of the following child traits are suggested before beginning toilet training *except* for
   a. the ability to understand instructions and communicate minimal desires.
   b. neuromuscular maturation of anal and bladder sphincter muscles.
   c. ending of the "terrible two's."
   d. the child's readiness.
6. Which of the following is a unique aspect of Azrin and Foxx's procedure, "Toilet Training in Less than a Day"?
   a. The child must know words such as "pee-pee" and "poo-poo."
   b. The child is taught to assist in toilet-training a doll.
   c. The child is taught to follow instructions cooperatively.
   d. Rewards are used to reinforce using the toilet.
7. Recent literature suggests that
   a. mothers who responded immediately to crying had babies who cried less later on.
   b. mothers who responded immediately to crying had babies who cried more later on.
   c. promptness was not an important factor in stopping crying.
   d. there are never times when babies should be left crying.
8. Which of the following items helps differentiate colic crying from hunger crying?
   a. whether the baby is breast-fed or bottle-fed
   b. whether the baby quiets immediately upon being fed

c. whether crying occurs after every feeding or only at certain times

d. whether crying occurs before or after feeding

e. c and d are both correct

9. Four suggestions on infant care were given toward the end of the chapter. Which of the following is *not* one of those suggestions?

a. A "middle-of-the-road" policy is often best.

b. An informed parent is an efficient parent.

c. Parents need to be strict in adhering to infant care routines.

d. Patience is important.

10. Which of the following types of attachment is most desirable?

a. avoidant

b. securely attached

c. resistant

d. comfortable independence

KEY: 1–b; 2–a; 3–c; 4–c; 5–c; 6–b; 7–a; 8–e; 9–c; 10–b

# CHAPTER 13

# SPECIAL CHILDREN AND PARENTING

This chapter focuses on instances when parenting becomes especially difficult—when children are emotionally, mentally, and/or physically handicapped. Specifically, children with physical handicaps, hyperactivity, mental retardation, and childhood psychosis will be briefly discussed. It must be understood that most of these cases require professional medical and/or psychological consultation and guidance. This chapter is not meant to be a substitute for professional care. Rather, it is an introduction with three major purposes: (1) to provide parents of these children with some additional understanding; (2) to help any adult working and interacting with these children (e.g., teachers, neighbors, friends) to understand the child's disorder and limitations; and (3) to enlighten individuals as to the obstacles parents with handicapped children face.

## Handicapped Children

"Of all the burdens parents carry, the heaviest is that of having a child who is handicapped" (Wentworth, 1974, p. 3). Approximately 250,000 babies are born with birth defects each year in the United States. Defects are manifested through mental retardation, physical deformities and inabilities, and emotional disturbances. This chapter begins with the more general discussion of handicapped children and their families. An effort is made to increase the reader's understanding of struggles a family faces upon birth of a handicapped child.

## REACTIONS TO THE BIRTH OF A HANDICAPPED CHILD

Most parents expect to have a normal child. For many of the same reasons parents have children (see Chapter 1), they anticipate a healthy, viable infant. However, for some parents, these dreams are temporarily upset and often modified, as their child is born with a handicapping condition. When this occurs, a number of reactions surface. A discussion of these reactions, below, is taken from the works of Wentworth (1974) and Kew (1975).

It must be noted that considerable variations exist among researchers regarding parental adjustment to the birth of a handicapped child. Although most research suggests that family members progress through stages, the number, names, and components of these stages vary (Blacher, 1984; Fortier & Wanlass, 1984). Progression of adjustment might not be in the order specified below, nor might it include all of the stages. Nevertheless, families of handicapped children experience many of these feelings identified in each stage.

**Shock.**  Shock describes accurately the emotional numbing that takes place when knowledge of a handicapped child reaches parents. It is a temporary anesthetic, so to speak, protecting the parent until stronger emotional defenses are erected. Shock may occur slowly, as when parents begin suspecting an intellectually handicapping condition in a young toddler. Or, as it usually happens, the shock occurs rapidly—immediately following delivery, when a medical diagnosis is made. This stage may be accompanied by much tension, anxiety, and disorganization in the family. Perhaps most important at this point is that friends and physicians take time to listen.

**Denial.**  Following the initial impact, denial often occurs. The parent refuses to accept the fact that his or her child is really handicapped. Consider the following example cited by Kew (1975):

> All the doctors told us that our little girl is mongoloid and that she will never grow mentally, but we just can't believe they are right. She does have a look about her eyes though, that kind of worries us, they're slanty like. And sometimes we even think she may be blind, because she doesn't respond or smile like most babies of her age. There is something we feel, but we pray that the doctors are wrong (p. 40).

Denial is initially a normal reaction. Parents fear for the child's future, and for their own feelings of inadequacy to raise such a child properly. With such a blow, denial is somewhat protective. Parents may refuse to see a deformed newborn, or may shop around for another diagnosis. Yet, if denial is not resolved, the child is later denied adequate love, treatment, and education. One parent entered a community mental health clinic complaining that her son was becoming too withdrawn socially. Her boy, age 14, had been in special education classes since first grade, and testing suggested he was mentally retarded. But he was "normal in appearance and could be very sweet around the house." His mother refused to believe the school's reports and felt he was being improperly labeled. Her own expectations of him were clearly unrealistic, and the boy gradually felt more inferior as the message he was getting at home was that he was lazy, inadequate, and irresponsible. Cognitive deficits were disregarded. As a result, the unfortunate child became more and more withdrawn to prevent failure.

Fathers tend to set the tone (Love, 1970). If they accept the handicap and do not deny the child's disabilities, the rest of the family tends to do so also, and expectations toward the child become more realistic.

**Grief.**  After accepting the fact they have a handicapped child, many parents grieve for themselves. Why did it have to be us? It will be so difficult! I feel so heartbroken! Again, such feelings are normal if they do not persist and disrupt present and future family relationships. Parents must be allowed to grieve, although it may take many months before they can become fully attached to the handicapped child (Bristor, 1984). However, parents must eventually understand how each other feels, how other family members feel, and even how the handicapped child must be struggling. Involving grandparents and other family members in the grief process can only bring everybody closer together. It is often the case that those who suffer and feel for the child most develop the strongest emotional bonds to the infant.

**Guilt.** Most women carrying a child wonder about their health. Should I be smoking? Am I getting proper nourishment? Should I have sex during the last trimester? Am I getting enough exercise? Imagine the guilt if some of these fears are suddenly followed by a child with birth defects.

If parents fail to realize that the exact influence of all these factors on neonatal development is uncertain, and that some birth defects cannot be reliably traced to any definite external cause, other than random genetic miscombination, they may carry this guilt around for some time. As a result, the child may become spoiled as parents spend a lifetime making up for their mistake.

**Hostility.** Many parents tend to go through a hostile stage, aggressively blaming everybody for their plight. God is blamed for His injustice, the spouse is blamed for bad genes, teachers and therapists are blamed for not doing better with their child, doctors are blamed for not helping to prevent the problem. Even the child is blamed for causing such a drastic change in their lifestyle.

Uncontained hostility prevents the child from receiving adequate medical and educational care, as well as the necessary love and warmth from a realistically concerned parent.

**Withdrawal.** As parents face despair and fear caused by the handicap, they may withdraw. A mother who remains at home and cares for the child is especially vulnerable to withdrawal. She may stay at home more often, not take the child out into public, and refuse social interaction. A husband out working must be cognizant of his spouse's needs, and enable her to get out by herself to pursue personal interests.

**Rejection.** Rejecting the child is "one final effort on the parents' part in their fight against having to believe that their child's deficiency will prevent his leading a normal life" (Wentworth, 1974, p. 73). The parent may be embarrassed, be ashamed that his or her child is not a source of social pride, resent the additional burden, despise the child's lack of accomplishment, or fear the future. In any event, the child is rejected—his or her needs may be ignored and affection is not communicated.

**Acceptance.** Only when the child is accepted, and when grief, denial, guilt, hostility, withdrawal, and rejection are overcome, is a period of adjustment reached. At this point, parents learn more about the handicap, pursue special training and therapy for the child, and solidify family relationships.

## EFFECTS UPON SIBLINGS

> The relationships of the mother with her other children often become distorted, at times severely, because of the extra time and attention the handicapped child requires. Understandably, the other children tend to interpret this as meaning that they are less favored and loved (Poznanski, 1969, p. 234).

The most common disturbance among siblings is attention-seeking behavior. They may become disruptive or clinging, develop tantrums or psychosomatic pains, or turn to promiscuity or stealing—all in an effort to divert some attention back toward themselves. Additionally, siblings may become resentful of their handicapped brother or sister—jealous of the attention he or she receives, and hostile at the same time. For example:

> Mr. and Mrs. B. could not understand how their little daughter, Susie, could have scratched and bruised her legs so badly. She was nearly three years old, but because her cerebral palsied condition was so severe, she could not even turn from her back to her stomach—much less sit alone or move about enough to have hurt herself—or move her arms enough to reach her legs. The bruises and scratches increased over the next few days, and the distraught parents began to fear that the mild cold Susie was recovering from wasn't just a cold after all, but something serious. Then the mystery was solved. One day Mrs. B. was hanging up clothes in Susie's room while she was napping in her crib; suddenly Susie screamed. Mrs. B. looked around the door and saw their six-year-old, Mary, standing by the crib, "That's right—cry! I hate you! Just because you got sick, I couldn't have my birthday party. I wish you'd die!" (Wentworth, 1974, p. 213)

Siblings of the handicapped need attention too. They also need to feel certain that they are loved and are important. They too need special rights and privileges. Siblings also need to understand what is wrong with their handicapped brother or sister so as to better understand the excess attention directed his or her way. In general, children who adjust best to handicapped siblings have parents who have adjusted. Parents clearly have a responsibility to work through their own difficulties to insure that their handicapped and nonhandicapped children receive the necessary attention, love, and consideration.

Long-term effects of handicapped children on siblings are not definitive. Some studies suggest that handicapped children may have deleterious effects on siblings' adjustment (Cairns, Clark, Smith, & Lansky, 1979; Gath, 1972; Harvey & Greenway, 1984; Tew & Laurence, 1973). Other studies, however, claim that siblings of handicapped children are no more at risk for maladjustment than other children (Caldwell & Guze, 1960; Cleveland & Miller, 1977; Lavigne & Ryan, 1979).

## ADDITIONAL FAMILY IMPLICATIONS

Goffman (1963) has determined that persons without handicaps generally feel uneasy around handicapped individuals; they are unfamiliar with the handicapped person's problems. What do I talk about? Should I try to do favors for her, or will she feel I am condescending? What if I don't know how to help him down the stairs?

This uneasiness is definitely detected by handicapped individuals and their families. Combined with the additional logistical difficulties of getting out in public, it is no wonder that 45 percent of families with mentally retarded children have limited social contacts (Tizard & Grad, 1961), and that 50 percent of families felt that the handicap impeded their ability to visit other homes (Schonell & Watts, 1957).

Parents are able to keep their parenting roles happy and relatively satisfying despite the added strain and challenge of a handicapped child.

Nevertheless, a study by Darling (1979) indicates that the data as a whole do not suggest that social stigma and labeling necessarily produce maladjustment and a low self-esteem: "Parents remain the major, most significant definers of self- and adjustment-related attitudes that these children encounter" (p. 43). Again, we are reminded of the importance of a warm, organized home climate. Although families may experience temporary disruption upon the birth of a handicapped child, a home based on love and organization is perhaps more readily equilibrated. After reviewing much of the research, Longo and Bond (1984) found that couples were able to keep marriages intact and relatively satisfying despite the added strain and challenge of parenting a handicapped child.

## Hyperactive Children

Perhaps no handicap is as problematic to so many parents as hyperactivity. It has been estimated that as high as one in 20 children may be hyperactive to some degree (Ross & Ross, 1976). In the text *Abnormal Psychology and Modern Life* the authors state:

> Hyperactive children tend to be overactive, restless, and easily distractable. They . . . tend to talk incessantly and to be socially uninhibited and immature. Usually they do poorly in school, commonly showing specific learning disabilities, such as a difficulty in learning to read or in mastering other basic school subjects (Coleman, Butcher, & Carson, 1980, pp. 492–493).

The term *hyperactivity* refers to the condition of a child who is excessively active. Restlessness, distractability, impulsivity, and inattentiveness are behaviors supposedly related to motor overactivity. *The Diagnostic and Statistical Manual of Mental Disorders,* third edition, called DSM-III, is published by the American Psychiatric Association (1980). A standard reference of classification, it has *redefined* hyperactivity as "attention-deficit disorder with hyperactivity," because hyperactive children usually exhibit deficits in attention span, concentration, and delay of impulse expression. DSM-III provides the following diagnostic criteria for attention-deficit disorder with hyperactivity:

**Inattentiveness.** At least three of the following must be present to characterize the child as inattentive:

1. Often fails to finish things he/she starts.
2. Often doesn't seem to listen.
3. Is often easily distracted.
4. Has difficulty concentrating on school work or other tasks requiring sustained attention.
5. Has difficulty sticking to a play activity.

**Impulsivity.** To classify the child as impulsive at least three of the following must be present:

1. Often acts before thinking.
2. Shifts excessively from one activity to another.
3. Has difficulty organizing work.
4. Needs a lot of supervision.
5. Frequently calls out in class.
6. Has difficulty waiting turn in games or group situations.

The above two characteristics—inattentiveness and impulsivity—are necessary for a diagnosis of attention deficit disorder without hyperactivity. For a diagnosis of attention-deficit disorder *with* hyperactivity, the following is *also* necessary.

**Hyperactivity.** At least two of the following behaviors must be present:

1. Runs about or climbs on things excessively.
2. Has difficulty sitting still or fidgets excessively.
3. Has difficulty staying seated.
4. Moves about excessively during sleep.
5. Is always "on the go" or acts as if "driven by a motor."

In addition, these children generally exhibit behavior problems such as aggressiveness and disobedience. However, controversy exists as to whether such behavior and hyperactivity are separate or dependent dimensions. For example, Stewart and his colleagues (Stewart, Cummings, Singer, & DeBlois, 1981) reject the notion that a definition of hyperactivity should include aggressiveness, disobedience, and antisocial behavior.

Werry (1979), on the other hand, concludes that evidence is not strong enough to suggest convincingly that hyperactivity and aggressiveness and antisocial behavior are independent problems. Hyperactive children often behave in a fashion contrary to major age-appropriate norms (e.g., stealing, lying, destruction of property). Conversely, children behaving antisocially often exhibit signs of hyperactivity. Whether antisocial behavior is a part of hyperactivity, or is precipitated by the social difficulties that hyperactivity causes, is debatable.

Some parents may be baffled by teacher reports of a child's inattentiveness, impulsivity, and hyperactivity. In their interaction with the child at home, the child may appear quite normal. However, hyperactive behavior occurs more often in situations requiring sustained attention and intense social interaction (e.g., work and play), and may, therefore, be somewhat hidden from a parent's view (Zentall, 1984).

It must also be pointed out that many parents have children who, at one time or another, or quite frequently, exhibit "hyperactive" signs such as excessive activity, inattentiveness, and impulsiveness. However, the presence of hyperactivity is determined by the number and severity of symptoms, while taking into consideration the child's developmental level. It is, for example, more common for younger children (three to four years old) to exhibit some hyperactive symptoms than older children (six to seven years old). Younger children, in general, have less impulse control and less ability to sustain attention. Yet, if symptoms persist as a child grows older, or if a young child exhibits a severity, frequency, and number of symptoms in excess of what is developmentally appropriate for that age group, attention-deficit disorder may be present. Behavior problems, although sometimes present in young children, do not begin to show a relationship with future psychological difficulties until the behaviorally disordered child is six or seven (Robins, 1979).

## ETIOLOGY

Theories on the etiology of hyperactivity range from strictly reproductive and genetic to an interaction between these and environmental factors. Reproductive and genetic theories suggest that the child is born hyperactive—nothing can be done to alter its emergence. Interactionist ideas, however, suppose that because of various reproductive, genetic, or other perinatal factors, a child may be predisposed to hyperactivity. Yet, the child's psychological environment will determine the severity of its expression.

**Perinatal and genetic influences.** Perinatal influences such as prematurity; short, sharp labor; full or partial placenta previa; anoxia at birth; and bleeding during pregnancy have all been hypothesized to produce hyperactivity (Knobloch & Pasamanick, 1974; Werner, 1971). Something apparently went wrong during development and/or birth that affected the child's neurological system and subsequent functioning.

Other theories suggest that hyperactivity is genetic. If a parent was hyperactive as a child, he or she is carrying the gene for the disorder, and will pass it on to the child. The child may or may not exhibit hyperactivity, depending on the genotypic requirements for hyperactivity to occur. Wender, Reimherr, and Wood (1981), for example, found that 41 percent of parents with a history of hyperactivity had children who were similarly affected.

**Other biological influences.** Another condition hypothesized to lead to hyperactivity is an inability in some children to tolerate and assimilate glucose. Many parents have seen the effects that a candy bar or other high-sugar food can have on a child prior to bedtime. For some children, this tendency may be exacerbated whenever moderate to high amounts of sugar are ingested.

Glandular problems, lead or carbon monoxide poisoning, and brain lesions have also been proposed as possible causes. In each case, a biological abnormality leads to hyperactive behavior. Consider the following example.

Take the case of D., a five-year-old girl whose parents brought her to me because she had difficulties in school, threw tantrums, and was generally hyperactive. A neurologist had diagnosed this child as schizophrenic. . . .

Because I suspected poor oxygenation due to a heart problem, I sent her to a cardiologist. He determined that she had an extra vessel between the heart and the lung which was preventing a normal flow of oxygen to the brain. D. underwent surgery to correct this defect, and her hyperactivity, fatigue, rages, and tantrums disappeared. She began to participate in normal school activities, and is progressing well without medication (Walker, 1974, p. 44).

**Allergies.**   One case study (Trites, Tryphonas, & Ferguson, 1980) described a six-year-old boy who, beginning at 12 months, became increasingly active, aggressive toward his brother, and more prone to temper tantrums. Eventually, he could no longer be left unsupervised. He was diagnosed as hyperactive and placed on medication. However, his behavior only worsened.

Later, this boy was examined for the presence of food allergies and it was determined that he was allergic to foods containing oats and rye. Removal of these foods from his diet significantly reduced his so-called hyperactive behaviors. Trites, Tryphonas, and Ferguson (1980) maintain that 20 percent of hyperactive children improve when controlled for foods to which they are allergic.

**Interactive approach.**   Wender (1971) demonstrates the interaction between a child's internal biology and external environment in bringing out hyperactive behaviors. The child may through perinatal and genetic influences be predisposed to hyperactivity. Suppose this predisposition were "moderate." If, then, the child's familial and societal environment were warm, supportive, and nonstressful, the hyperactivity might be only mildly exhibited. However, an aberrant, rejecting, hostile, and extremely stressful environment may produce a marked hyperactive syndrome.

# BATTLING HYPERACTIVITY

**Outgrowing hyperactivity.**   One optimistic finding is that children commonly outgrow hyperactivity. Actually, this is an oversimplification, for although hyperactivity may decrease, inattentiveness and impulsivity generally persist, as do the secondary symptoms that have resulted from the disorder (e.g., academic problems, social and peer difficulties, aggressiveness). The restlessness, hyperactivity, and distractability make academic activities somewhat difficult. Although hyperactivity may decline during adolescence, academic difficulties have a history, and often persist (Keogh, 1971). Because of their sometimes aggressive behaviors, hyperactive children are often disliked by their peers (Bryan, 1978; Paulauskas & Campbell, 1979), so social and interpersonal difficulties can persist into adolescence. Low self-esteem is also a secondary problem, as are delinquent behaviors, which are sometimes a result of continued academic and social frustrations (Cantwell, 1975). However, the severity of secondary symptoms and their persistence into adolescence are determined, in part, by whether hyperactivity was successfully identified and treated while the child was growing up. Treatment is necessary.

**Treatment with stimulant drugs.**   Drug intervention is the most commonly used treatment for hyperactivity. It has been estimated that about 2½ percent of all elementary-school children in the United States receive stimulant medication to treat behavioral disorders and learning disabilities (Weiss & Hechtman, 1979). The use of stimulants is paradoxical, since amphetamines normally *increase* behavioral activity in adults. However, with hyperactive children, disruptive behaviors decrease and attentiveness increases. The most popular stimulant, Ritalin, is claimed to work becasue it filters out distractions and enables hyperactive children to attend more closely to what they are doing (Reid & Borkowski, 1984).

However, stimulants appear to simply mask symptoms without providing a cure. Improvement lasts only as long as medication is administered (Ross & Pelham, 1981). In addition, medication does not tend to produce short-term or long-term improvements in academic performance, or lasting

Medication often reduces hyperactive, distracting behaviors, enabling the hyperactive child to attend more effectively in the classroom.

changes in social behavior (Barkley & Cunningham, 1978; Rie & Rie, 1977; Weiss, Kruger, Danielson, & Elman, 1975).

**Behavioral intervention.**   Behavior modification is the principle alternative to pharmacological intervention and has proven effective. Treatment involves teacher and parent training in contingency management (the use of reinforcers and consequences as discussed earlier in this text), "including the contingent use of attention, consistency of response, incentive systems, daily report cards, and time out from positive reinforcement" (Ross & Pelham, 1981). More specifically, high-power techniques (as described in Chapter 7 and 8) can be very beneficial. Reinforcing attentive, controlled behavior and punishing inattentive, impulsive, and "running around" behavior would have to be individualized to the child. Because the child has less internal control over his or her behavior, lower-power techniques would probably fail. However, when using behavior modification, parents must: (1) be consistent, and (2) be sure to reinforce positive behavior, not just punish the negative. Hyperactive children, for example, learn a task better when provided continuous contingent positive feedback as opposed to noncontingent negative reinforcement (Rosen & Baker, 1984).

However, as with the use of stimulants, behavior modification rarely brings the child into the normal behavior range. In addition, treatment requires intensive efforts by those working with the child, and often does not generalize (transfer) to environmental situations in which the teacher or parent is not present.

**Diet.**   The role of foods in determining certain behavior patterns has received attention in hyperactive research. In discusssing behavior chemistry one author writes:

> The human brain has a high metabolic rate which must be satisifed with a continuous supply of glucose—not an amount that varies from 150 milligram percent down to 60 milligram percent in the space of an hour or two. (It is estimated that the glucose requirement of an infant or child's brain is about double that of an adult.) The suddenness of this drop is a threat to the body, and stimulates the adrenal glands to secrete adrenaline and other hormones that release glucose from glycogen stores within the body, chiefly the liver.
>
> This may be the explanation for the apparent increase in incidence of hyperactivity. It is no secret that we are eating more sugar than we did just a few years ago. (Indeed, the salt of sugary breakfast foods has increased seventeen percent in the last year.) It may be that children with sensitive nervous systems cannot handle sudden rises in quick sugar. Their bodies overreact to the sudden increase by excreting extra insulin. The resulting sudden drop in the sugar level in the bloodstream may be the stress that triggers frantic, purposeless muscular activity (Smith, 1976, pp. 47–48).

This quote introduces the idea many physicians hold, that hyperactivity can be effectively treated through close monitoring of diet. If excessive sugar intake were hypothesized to be the cause, then lowering sugar levels should effectively reduce hyperactivity. In a similar vein, Feingold (1975) hypothesizes that hyperactivity is caused by an inherent hypersensitivity to artificial colors and flavorings, the preservatives BHA and BHT, and naturally occurring salicylates. Eliminating these substances, therefore, should help control hyperactivity. Feingold's hypothesis has not held up well to experiment and testing, however, and it has been suggested that only 5 to 10 percent of hyperactive children are hypersensitive to artificial colorings, for example (Ross & Pelham, 1981).

## SUMMARY OF HYPERACTIVITY

That hyperactivity is a complex and frequently misunderstood behavior problem is evident. One expert's conclusions are presented as a summary:

> From the information available on hyperactivity, the accepted viewpoint here is that the term hyperactivity refers to a set of symptoms that reflect a variety of possible causes. The symptoms—inattentiveness, impulsivity, physical overactivity, excitability, and distractibility—are often present in early childhood, thereby giving credence to the concept of a developmentally based, constitutional hyperactivity. But, the symptoms may also appear after age four or five, thereby offering support for the view of a psychologically based hyperactivity. Some experts still believe that there is an organic basis to hyperactivity (i.e., brain damage, cerebral dysfunction, neurological impairment, etc.); however, there is limited data, via neurological study, to support this position among the majority of children labeled hyperactive. . . . [D]iet factors have been presented as a possible cause of hyperactivity. The scientific literature, however, remains inconclusive as to the incidence and degree of food substance related hyperactivity. Diet, as with the other possible etiological factors, needs to be considered seriously, but may or may not be relevant with a given child. While the condition tends to diminish in severity by adolescence, residuals persist (i.e., poor grades, and personal and social adjustment difficulties). Intervention, rather than a "let's wait until he outgrows it" attitude, seems merited. The most prevalent form of intervention is medication, typically methylphenidate hydrochloride (Ritalin). . . . [T]hese stimulant medications can produce a seemingly paradoxical effect in calming down a child (Fine, 1980, p. 233–234).

## Mental Retardation

If asked to describe the appearance and capabilities of mentally retarded individuals, many people picture odd-looking characters with uncoordinated, jerky gaits who would not know how to take care of themselves if they had to. Dependent on others for all their needs, the mentally retarded have the intellect of a small child.

In actuality, the above description fits only about 9 percent of retarded individuals. Different levels of mental retardation according to severity have been identified, and the least severe level contains the majority of mentally retarded individuals. Many of these people function quite well in society and appear normal to the average observer. Only a minority of the mentally deficient fit the "incapable" stereotype of being severely handicapped, both mentally and physically.

## DEFINITION

The American Association on Mental Deficiency (AAMD) defines mental retardation as "significantly subaverage general intellectual functioning existing concurrently with deficits in adaptive behavior, and manifested during the developmental period" (Grossman, 1973, p. 11).

"Significantly subaverage general intellectual functioning" refers to intellectual ability that is lower than 95 percent of the general population. This does not appear to include a lot of individuals; in reality, however, about 6,850,000 individuals (3 percent of the total population) fit into this category (Robinson & Robinson, 1976, p. 37). "Intellectual functioning" refers to performance on a standardized intelligence test. The most commonly used tests in assessing this general cognitive ability are the Stanford-Binet and Wechsler scales.

"Adaptive behavior" is defined as individuals' ability to provide and care for themselves independently, and the degree to which they meet demands of personal and social responsibility. Are they able to provide for part if not all of their financial needs? Can they adequately perform self-sustaining tasks such as buying and preparing food, watching out for their safety, and sufficiently caring for their hygiene so as to avoid social ostracism as well as illness and disease? Are they able to interact adaptively and have their needs communicated and met in appropriate ways? Can they make sufficient academic progress to permit the development of marketable skills?

Determining whether behavior is satisfactorily adaptive is often difficult. What may be satisfactory personal and social responsibility in one culture might not be satisfactory in another. In addition, adaptive behavior is evaluated in relation to the individual's age. During infancy and childhood, sensory-motor, communication, and self-help skills are considered when evaluating deficits. During childhood and early adolescence the focus is on academic skills and appropriate interaction with the environment. Later in life, an individual's ability to assume vocational and social responsibility is considered.

## CLASSIFICATION

Using intellectual functioning and adaptive behavior as criteria, the AAMD classifies mental retardation into four categories—mild, moderate, severe, and profound.

*Mild mental retardation* includes the IQ range 50 to 70, based on the Stanford-Binet. Adults in this category have intellectual abilities approximating those of an 8- to 11-year-old child. Social adjustment approximates that of an adolescent. According to DSM-III, "individuals with this level of mental retardation can develop social and communication skills during the preschool period (ages 0–5), have minimal impairment in sensorimotor areas, and often are not distinguishable from normal children until a later age" (American Psychiatric Association, 1980). Due to these minor deficits, mildy retarded individuals can learn social and vocational skills that would enable a minimum of self-support. Although guidance and close supervision may be necessary, these individuals can learn various labor skills and be gainfully employed. As mentioned earlier, the majority of mentally retarded individuals fit this classification—about 80 percent are mildly mentally retarded.

*Moderate mental retardation* characterizes about 12 percent of the entire population of mentally retarded individuals. They are considered "trainable" in that they may profit from vocational training, being able to perform unskilled or semi-skilled work when closely supervised. They can learn to talk or communicate, but, even when given special education, rarely progress beyond academic abilities approximating those of the fourth grade. The IQ range of this category is 35 to 49. Unlike the mild retardate, these individuals would rarely be able to live and function independently with very little supervision; they require close supervision and guidance when under mild social or economic stress (Sloan & Birch, 1955).

*Severely mentally retarded* individuals make up about 7 percent of all

Being able to perform unskilled or semi-skilled work when closely supervised, moderately retarded individuals may profit from vocational training.

**Table 13.1 Levels of Mental Retardation**

| Level | Approximate IQ | Adaptive Functioning |
|---|---|---|
| Mild retardation | 50–70 | Can learn: to communicate and interact socially; academic skills up to about sixth grade; to perform vocational tasks |
| Moderate retardation | 35–49 | Can learn: to communicate although social interaction is poor; academic skills up to about fourth grade; to perform semi-skilled labor under close supervision |
| Severe retardation | 20–34 | Poor motor development; minimal speech; no academic abilities; self-support abilities are minimal although can perform simple health and hygiene tasks |
| Profound retardation | Below 20 | Little motor and speech development; needs total supervision and care |

retarded individuals. Having an IQ of 20 to 34, they approximate the stereotype presented earlier. DSM-III states, "During the preschool period there is evidence of poor motor development and they develop little or no communicative speech. During the school-age period, they may learn to talk and can be trained in elementary hygiene skills" (American Psychiatric Association, 1980).

*Profound mental retardation* includes those individuals who have IQs below 20, and characterizes 1 percent of individuals with mental retardation. These individuals require constant care, as they remain unable to develop self-maintenance and self-care skills. Although some motor and speech development may occur at later ages, it is minimal. It is these individuals who most frequently exhibit gross physical abnormalities and "appear" retarded to the observer just by physical features. (See Table 13.1 for a summary of these levels.)

## THEORIES OF MENTAL RETARDATION

Causes of retardation may be grouped into two major categories: organic and sociocultural. Organic causes include genetic defects, chromosomal abnormalities, and brain damage. For example, Down's syndrome, phenylketonuria (PKU), Tay-Sachs disease, and severe head trauma may all produce mental retardation. Organic or biologically induced retardation usually includes those individuals who are moderately, severely, or profoundly retarded.

The majority of mildly retarded individuals have performance and social deficits that seem to reflect sociocultural deprivation—a lack of intellectual stimulation and social-skills learning. It would be inappropriate to assume that all mild retardates are a result of deprived environments; a combination of genetic predisposition and environmental influences may exist. However, a correlation between mild retardation and environment has been found. The President's Task Force on Manpower Conservation (1964), for example, found the families of draftees rejected for intellectual deficits to be predominantly impoverished and poorly educated. Liebert, Poulos, and Marmor (1977), summarizing a number of studies, found low achievement-motivation of parents, father's absence, lack of appropriate gender-role models, impoverished financial status, and low emphasis on education to be related to retardation (Chilman, 1965; Robinson, 1967; Robinson & Robinson, 1976).

## WORKING WITH RETARDED INDIVIDUALS

Retarded children are often placed in institutions or community residential facilities due to the constant care and supervision necessary. The number of community residential facilities in the United States has increased from 611 in 1974, to 3686 in 1977, to 5700 in 1983 ( Janicki, Mayeda, & Eppel, 1983). While cared for in this manner, however, behavior modification principles are often successfully used to improve self-help skills and to reduce antisocial behaviors. Even severely retarded individuals can be trained in self-help skills such as grocery shopping, social skills, and appropriate sexual behavior (Foxx, McMorrow, Storey, & Rogers, 1984; Heal, Colson, & Gross, 1984). Because parents whose children are severely intellectually and adaptively impaired often transfer care to professional facilities, we will not focus on these conditions here.

Consider what Sattler (1982) says about working with mildly retarded individuals:

> Preschool and school-aged children functioning in the mild range of retardation can benefit from programs offered in regular schools, either in special education programs or, when appropriate, in regular classes. Much, too, can be done to help those families that are not able to take advantage of opportunities to help their children develop properly. Intervention strategies for those families include better incomes, better housing, preschool education for their children, further education for the parents, and effective family planning (p. 430).

There has long been a question of whether placing "educable" mentally retarded (EMR) individuals in special education programs is more desirable and advantageous than leaving them in regular classes. It has been debated that placing these individuals in special classes further segregates them from peer group norms, which widens the gap between their education and the education received in regular classes. Bauer (1967, in Liebert et al., 1977) studied numerous special class curricula and concluded that they were inferior copies of what was taught in normal classes. Goldstein, Moss, and Jordan (1965) compared academic accomplishments of retarded children placed in regular and EMR classes, and found no significant difference in IQ or general knowledge.

However, supporters of special classes maintain that it is inappropriate to expect EMR students to catch up with, or even close the gap between, them and their peers. Rather, the emphasis should be on teaching social competence and occupational and practical skills. Such an approach is not easily compared with regular class instruction to determine its effectiveness. In addition, removing EMR students from the regular curriculum helps prevent further rejection by peers. Goodman, Gottlieb, and Harrison (1972) found that EMR children integrated into a nongraded school were rejected significantly more than a comparable group of children placed in a special class.

Parents who have mentally retarded children should be aware that many of the high-power and moderate-power techniques to weaken or produce behavior presented earlier (see Chapters 7–9) can also be appropriately used. In addition, parents can benefit by training in how to deal with their own personal difficulties in meeting everyday problems (Intagliata & Doyle, 1984). When doing so, they focus less on their children's problems, see more accurately how they contribute to their own difficulties, and broaden social support networks among relatives and friends.

## Childhood Psychosis

*Childhood psychosis* is a conglomerate term referring to a variety of emotional disorders among young children. The major categories into which these disorders are classified are *childhood schizophrenia* and *early infantile autism*. This section will characterize the behaviors associated with these disorders, consider some of the most prominent theories concerning their origins, and take a look at each disorder's probable course. Following this review, some considerations for dealing with childhood psychosis will be covered.

### VIEWS ABOUT PSYCHOSIS

Psychosis means different things to different individuals. Some see it as a disease, contagious and to be avoided. Others view psychopathology as evidence of an evil spirit's presence. Though not as prevalent today, this demoniacal perspective was pervasive several centuries ago. During the Middle Ages, for example, mental illness was evidence of the devil's presence. The victim was thought either to have made a pact with the devil or to have been seized by the devil as punishment from God for his or her sins. This possession was, of course, presumed perilous to the community, necessitating that the victim be removed from it. The "possessed" were tortured and "witches" were hunted, burned at the stake, and drowned. Some individuals were housed in dungeons and jails; asylums were later built to rid society of their influence.

With the advancement of medicine, scientific thought, and humanitarian values, the mentally deranged were later considered ill and in need of aid.

During the Middle Ages mental illness was considered evidence of witchcraft or presence of the devil.

Help involved adequate care, supervision, nutrition, and cleanliness in a medical environment. However, placement in mental hospitals essentially perpetuated the idea that mentally ill persons must be removed from the mainstream of society. Typically built on the city's outskirts, mental hospitals were far removed from contact with the population.

Although contemporary views about mental illness are, in general, more humanitarian, mental illness is nevertheless a very forceful, intimidating term. When finding out, for example, that someone's child is "psychotic" or "autistic," most individuals prefer to avoid an encounter with the child—they do not know what to expect and therefore prefer to avoid the unknown. Parents of psychologically disturbed, mentally retarded, or otherwise handicapped children have experienced this passive rejection from friends and neighbors. An inability to predict or adequately deal with unknown situations leads to avoidance. A better understanding of what mental illness is, how it is manifested, and how it can be dealt with may help many individuals to be more accepting of these children.

## CHARACTERISTICS

Children who have been termed schizophrenic, autistic, or merely psychotic tend to show marked deviations or abnormalities in the following: (1) relationships to people and the environment, (2) emotional maturation, and (3) acquisition and integration of perceptual, motor, and cognitive skills (Sattler, 1982). Yet, specific characteristics may change with age. For example, the psychotic infant will experience deficiencies in the mother–infant relationship due to an unresponsiveness to Mother's overtures of affection. An older child may experience social difficulties in school, behavioral problems at home, speech and language difficulties, or visual hallucinations. Symptomatology will also differ according to the disorder present—autism or schizophrenia.

Not many children suffer from childhood psychoses, however. In one study, 2 in 10,000 children were found to be autistic; the same was true of other childhood psychoses (Gillberg, 1984). However, the numerous difficulties a family of a psychotic child experiences warrant special attention in this chapter.

## EARLY INFANTILE AUTISM

*Autism* is defined, in part, as appearing during the child's first 30 months. Childhood psychoses appearing after this time tend to have different symptomatologies. Autistic children exhibit severe language deficiencies, and many do not develop speech at all. In fact, 50 percent of all autistic children fail to learn to speak (Rutter, 1966). Severe problems in understanding spoken language are also evident. Many simply repeat phrases that are spoken to them *(echolalia)*, or fail to use pronouns correctly *(pronoun reversal)*. Examples of these communication problems follow.

> *Question:* How are you today, Jimmy?
> *Echolalic response:* How are you today, Jimmy?
> *Pronoun reversal:* He is fine.

Echolalia and pronoun reversal are often closely related. The child refers to himself as he has heard others talk to him. In other words, echolalic responses result in the child referring to himself in the third person, which is often the case with pronoun reversal. When speech in autistic children occurs, these and other grammatical errors evidence a lack of communicative ability, which is directly related to intellectual functioning and later adjustment. DeMyer and his associates (DeMyer, Barton, Alpern, Kimberlin, Allen, Yange, & Steele, 1974), for example, found that IQs exhibited by autistic children are higher if they have adequate conversational abilities.

From the beginning, an inability to respond socially is noticed. A mother's first suspicion of something being wrong often occurs when the child appears cold and aloof, and won't respond to cuddling or other affectional advances. When picked up and cuddled, the child arches his or her back and does not return Mother's gaze. Autistic children may be content to be by themselves for long periods of time, and occupy themselves with mechanical objects and rhythmic movements such as endless rocking back and forth. Some autistic children may perform self-injurious behaviors such as hitting themselves in the face. A resistance to change may cause the child to throw a tantrum if familiar surroundings are altered in any way.

Autistic children may be content to play by themselves for long periods of time—even if other children are present—as if nobody else were in the room.

A beautiful girl of five, with autism, finally made contact with her teacher. Each morning she had to be greeted with the set phrase, "Good morning, Lilly. I am very, very, glad to see you." If even one of the very's was omitted or another added, she would start to scream wildly (Diamond, Baldwin, & Diamond, 1963, p. 304; in Davison & Neale, 1978).

Other signs of autism may include difficulties in abstract thought, and problems with learning to walk or in bowel training.

Aside from these characteristics, Rimland (1964) claims that autistic children are unique in some of the following ways:

1. Autistic children are usually attractive and healthy.
2. Some have exceptional capabilities. For example, Rimland (1964) cited the case of one child who could recite a complete aria of Don Giovanni at 17 months of age.
3. Most autistic children come from families in which parents are generally high in intelligence, education, and occupational level.
4. Autistic children are often described as graceful and dexterous.

The following case, taken from the *Diagnostic and Statistical Manual of Mental Disorders Case Book* (Spitzer, Skodal, Gibbon, & Williams, 1981), provides an excellent example of an autistic child.

Richard, age three and a half, a firstborn child, was referred at the request of his parents because of his uneven development and abnormal behavior. Delivery had been difficult, and he had needed oxygen at birth. His physical appearance, motor development, and self-help skills were all age appropriate, but his parents had been uneasy about him from the first few months of life because of his lack of response to social contact and the usual baby games. Comparison with their second child, who, unlike Richard, enjoyed social communication from early infancy, confirmed their fears.

Richard had appeared to be self-sufficient and aloof from others. He did not greet his mother in the mornings, or his father when he returned from work, though if left with a baby-sitter, he tended to scream much of the time. He had no interest in other children and ignored his younger brother. His babbling had no conversational intonation. At three years he could understand simple practical instructions. His speech consisted of echoing some words and phrases he had heard in the past, with the original speaker's accent and intonation; but he could use one or two phrases to indicate his simple needs. For example, if he said "Do you want a drink?" he meant he was thirsty. He did not communicate by facial expression or use gesture or mime, except for pulling someone along and placing his or her hand on an object he wanted.

He was fascinated by bright lights and spinning objects, and would stare at them while laughing, flapping his hands, and dancing on tiptoe. He also displayed the same movements while listening to music, which he liked from infancy. He was intensely attracted to a miniature car, which he held in his hand, day and night; but he had no imaginative, pretend play with this or any other toy. He could assemble jigsaw puzzles rapidly (with one hand because of the car held in the other), whether the picture side was exposed or hidden. From age two he had collected kitchen utensils and arranged them in repetitive patterns all over the floors of the house. These pursuits, together with occasional periods of aimless running around, made up his whole repertoire of spontaneous activities.

The major management problem was Richard's intense resistance to any attempt to change or extend his interests. Removing his toy car, disturbing his puzzles or patterns, or even trying to make him look at a picture book precipitated temper tantrums that could last an hour or more with screaming, kicking, and biting himself or others. These tantrums could be cut short be restoring the "status quo." Otherwise, playing his favorite music or a long car ride were sometimes effective.

His parents had wondered if Richard could be deaf, but his love of music, his accurate echoing, and his sensitivity to some very soft sounds, such as that made by unwrapping a chocolate in the next room, convinced them that this was not the cause of his abnormal behavior. Psychological testing gave him a mental age of three years in non-language-dependent skills (fitting and assembly tasks), but only 18 months in language comprehension (pp. 125–126).

# CHILDHOOD SCHIZOPHRENIA

> Patients are described as psychotic when their mental functioning is sufficiently impaired as to interfere grossly with their capacity to meet the ordinary demands of life. . . . Deficits in perception, language, and memory may be so severe that the patient's capacity to mentally grasp a situation is effectively lost (American Psychiatric Association, 1968, p. 23).

Generally, schizophrenia first occurs during late adolescence or early adulthood, and consists of at least one of the following:

1. Bizarre delusions such as being controlled by an alien force, that one's thoughts are broadcast to the external world, that one's thoughts are not one's own, or that they are inserted into the mind by some outside force;
2. Delusions of not existing, that one's brain or body is rotting away, that one is of great importance (e.g., Jesus Christ);
3. Delusions of being persecuted by others or being delusionally jealous, if accompanied by hallucinations (it is important to understand that a delusion is a false personal belief not supported by reality);
4. Auditory hallucinations;
5. Thought disorders such as incoherence, excessive shifting of ideas from topic to topic, or statements showing no relation to each other, if accompanied by atypical affective (emotional) displays, delusions, hallucinations, or disorganized physical behavior (adapted from DSM-III, American Psychiatric Association, 1980).

Although an adolescent may fit the above diagnostic criteria, younger children very rarely experience hallucinations or bizarre delusions. For this reason, the term *childhood schizophrenia* may be misleading; DSM-III presently uses the term *childhood onset pervasive developmental disorder* to describe a "profound disturbance in social relations and multiple oddities of behavior, all developing after 30 months of age and before 12 years." Diagnostic criteria for this disorder include:

1. Extreme impairment in social relationships
2. At least three of the following:
   a. sudden, excessive anxiety
   b. constricted or inappropriate affect
   c. resistance to change in the environment
   d. motor movement oddities such as peculiar posturing and peculiar hand or finger movements
   e. abnormalities of speech
   f. hyper- or hyposensitivity to sensory stimuli
   g. self-mutilation practices such as head banging

The classification of childhood onset pervasive development disorder has similarities as well as differences with both infantile autism and schizophrenia, and is what some authors have referred to in the past as childhood schizophrenia. As stated above, children infrequently have delusions or hallucinations. DSM-III excludes these two symptoms, as well as incoherence and excessive shifting of ideas and statements, from the criteria for childhood onset pervasive developmental disorder. Otherwise, this disorder would be very similar to some forms of schizophrenia occurring among adolescents or adults.

Some similarities between early infantile autism and childhood onset pervasive developmental disorder are in resistance to environmental changes and peculiar hand or finger movements. On the other hand, aside from the age of onset, differences often occur in the areas of health and appearance, autistic aloneness, and motor performance. Autistic children are generally described as healthy and good-looking (Kanner, 1949), while schizophrenic children have many health problems. Rimland (1964) argues that the schizophrenic child does not seek isolation as the autistic child does. In addition, autistic children are often observed to have dexterous and graceful finger movements, whereas the schizophrenic child's movements are awkward and clumsy.

The following example of childhood onset pervasive developmental disorder was obtained from the DSM-III Casebook (Spitzer et al., 1981):

> Bill, age five, was brought by his mother for evaluation because she felt that he was not progressing and developing like other children. She says he speaks only in simple phrases, does not use the pronoun "I" to refer to himself, and does not say "yes" or "no" to indicate agreement; he repeats what he has been told. Upon inquiry, it turns out that the only communcation Bill has with others is repeating what he has heard (echolalia). Bill does speak to himself at times, but in a disjointed, disconnected, rambling manner.
>
> Though these were the only spontaneous complaints of the mother, questioning her revealed that Bill does not relate to other children and is totally uninterested in other youngsters. Although he seems to recognize his parents, he is not affectionate or responsive to them. His eye contact is very poor, and he is described as "looking through people." When approached affectionately, he shrinks away and screams.
>
> Bill is described as being extremely interested in music and very good at remembering songs and tunes. He spends a great deal of time listening to records while he rocks back and forth or from foot to foot. At other times, however, he grinds his teeth and stares at his hands while making motions with his fingers.
>
> His mother reports that he was fine until he was about three, when he began to change. Within a few months he began to act in company as though no one were around, and he did not seem to recognize people who were familiar to him. He started spending long periods of time staring into space, looking self-absorbed, as if he were deaf. Since then he has been remote and inaccessible (p. 275).

The examples provided for early infantile autism and childhood onset pervasive development disorders are very similar, and the two conditions are often differentiated primarily by the age of onset.

# THEORIES ON THE ORIGIN OF CHILDHOOD PSYCHOSIS

Theories concerning the etiology of childhood psychosis fall into three categories. These categories have been referred to as organic, nonorganic, and organic–experiential by Hingtgen and Bryson (1972). Similarly, Davison and Neale (1978) termed these three orientations physiological, psychological, and diathesis–stress models of autism and childhood schizophrenia. A summary of these theories, as found in Davison and Neale (1978), follows.

**Physiological theories.**  Organic or physiological theories maintain that deficiencies seen in autistic and schizophrenic children are due to organic damage or impairment in the central nervous system. Three such theories have been suggested by Bender (1955), Rimland (1964), and Moore and Shiek (1971). Bender maintains that certain children have a genetic predisposition toward childhood psychosis. This genetic disposition is precipitated by some kind of intrauterine disturbance or birth difficulty, producing a disorder in central nervous system functioning.

Rimland (1964) and Moore and Shiek (1971) both suggest that autistic children are genetically disposed to be geniuses, but that something has happened to upset that genetic inheritance. According to Rimland, damage to a central region of the brainstem causes the brain to be in a constant state of underarousal. Rimland says this produces an inability to relate present stimuli to remembered experience. Moore and Shiek, on the other hand, state that as in the development of many animals a "critical period" exists during the neonate's development. This critical period results in the infant becoming attached to a member of its own species, usually its parents. The importance of this period has been demonstrated by Konrad Lorenz (1935), who has shown baby ducklings to imprint on human beings if they were the only source of maternal care during this period. However, the autistic child's critical period occurs while the baby is still in the womb. Imprinting on an environment, rather than another human being, occurs. This environment, however, is void of much stimulation except for rhythmic sounds of pulsating blood and the baby's movements. The child becomes an isolate with deficiencies of communication and other developmental processes.

More recently, research has looked at possible biochemical or infectious factors responsible for central nervous system malfunctioning. Brain neurotransmitters may be insufficiently synthesized, released, or broken down (Ornitz & Ritro, 1976, 1977). It has also been hypothesized that autism may be due to an infectious disease process. This is suggested by findings that autistic children have abnormally high levels of white blood cells (Ornitz & Ritro, 1977).

**Psychological theories.**  Nonorganic or psychological theories assume that the child is normal at birth, but that environmental interaction—most importantly the mother–child relationship—produces personality deficits leading to psychotic behavior. Bettelheim (1967), Ferster (1961), and Rutter (1968, 1974) have proposed theories in this area.

Bettelheim (1967) hypothesizes that an autistic child's parents are negative and rejecting. The child's own actions seem to have little impact on his or her parents. This experience of helplessness causes the child to withdraw into his or her own fantasy world. Ritualistic hand movements and echolalic speech, for example, are methods of shutting out the world.

Ferster (1961) is a social-learning theorist who postulates that psychotic childhood disorders are caused by certain learning experiences. The parents of disturbed children are inattentive, neglecting the child for selfish personal desires or professional activities. As such, the child experiences inadequate forms of human reinforcers and learns to function alone. The parents are, therefore, later unable to control their child's behavior because secondary and generalized reinforcers such as praise and love have not been adequately established. Mothers of autistic children, for example, are more likely to be neurotic than mothers of normal children (Dor-Shav & Horowitz, 1984).

**Diathesis-stress theories.** These theories take into account both physiological and psychological contributors to the disorder. For example, an infant may have an inborn response to being held. Shaffer and Emerson (1964) found infants to be "cuddlers" or "noncuddlers" even before they had been held much following birth. Some infants were more resistant to close physical comfort and arched their backs when picked up and held. This is the diathesis aspect of the theory. The stress aspect results from the mother's response to the child's behavior. Inexperienced mothers may find it difficult to continue being warm and cuddly to an unresponsive child, resulting in a failure to establish social relationships.

In summary, the diathesis-stress model maintains that a child has a predisposition upon birth to act or respond in a certain way. This response style may run a negative or positive course, depending on environmental reaction. If the mother continues to be understanding, patient, and warm, the resisting child will not become autistic. Conversely, if the mother becomes frustrated and emotionally rejects the child, he or she may become more unresponsive and aloof.

Current research largely supports the organic or physiological theories, and in some cases the diathesis-stress theories. Little evidence substantiates claims that autism is due solely, or even largely, to environmental events.

## TREATMENT AND PROGNOSIS

Treatment programs for childhood psychosis vary, depending on the disorder type, the intellectual functioning of the child, the etiology behind the disorder, and psychosocial factors. Concerning autistic children, the goal is often to develop better social and language skills. In addition, self-destructive behaviors may need to be eliminated. Lovaas (1968) and his associates

(Stevens-Long & Lovaas, 1974) applied operant conditioning and modeling procedures to autistic children. Self-destructive action was reduced by isolating the child; echolalic speech was reduced by nonattention; and speech was gradually developed by rewarding the children with food when they approximated sounds verbalized by the examiner. Some of the children made great progress in responding appropriately to questions and following through on commands.

An effort was also made by Lovaas to help the children later respond to social rewards, not just tangible rewards such as food. To do this, the word *good* was paired with presentation of food when a particular act was performed properly. In many instances, the child was simultaneously hugged to express the examiner's appreciation. Later, it was hoped that praise alone would become a reinforcer.

The reader will notice that Lovaas's techniques resemble high-power techniques to produce or lessen behavior discussed in Chapters 7 and 8. Such behavioral techniques, though very powerful, require training, time, and patience. Parents, for example, would need to be trained in the use of behavior modification techniques; they would then need to spend a considerable amount of time with the child. It must also be noted that the progress obtained by such an intensive behavioral program as Lovaas's is not always permanent. Some children, for example, after being worked with for many months in a hospital or laboratory setting, regressed to previously maladaptive behaviors when returning home. This could be due to parents' inexperience or simply the fact that it would be too emotionally taxing for a parent to spend so much time and effort with the child in continuing a behavior modification program.

Although autistic children are educable, approximately 60 percent of autistic children remain severely handicapped and unable to function independently (Rutter, 1977). A study by Lotter (1974) found that the best predictors of later social adjustment, employment, and placement were the ability to communicate effectively and the child's IQ. Prognosis is also better if the child exhibits less severe behavioral disturbances and has had some good schooling and a harmonious family (Rutter, 1977).

Sattler (1982) suggests that autistic children can be helped in school if carefully structured educational programs are designed. Such programs are feasible and should begin early in life, with parents being the primary teachers.

While the therapeutic outlook has brightened considerably, the general prognosis for most childhood psychosis is still poor in terms of developing levels of normal functioning. Significant expansion of their behavioral repertoires can be achieved, but spontaneity may remain absent, especially in the area of speech. . . . What is clear at this point is that abilities vary widely from child to child, no matter what the diagnosis. Until each child's specific limitations of learning are objectively determined, all methods of proven effectiveness must be used to enable him to reach his highest level of performance. At best, these therapeutic approaches could allow the child to function well in home and school settings; at the very least, they could provide for the construction of prosthetic environments, designed for the individual child according to his maximum abilities (Hingtgen & Bryson, 1972, p. 33; in Sattler, 1982).

## Summary

Many parents experience additional strain and challenges in parenting physically, intellectually, emotionally, or otherwise handicapped children. The challenges and difficulties are different for each family, yet some generalizations can be made.

Parents first realizing their child is handicapped experience a number of emotions or tendencies, including shock, denial, grief, guilt, hostility, withdrawal, rejection, and acceptance. If allowed and able to experience and express their feelings, they will at some point resolve inner conflicts and begin coping positively with their situation. Children also need to be allowed to grieve and adjust to a handicapped sibling.

Almost one in 20 children suffers from some sort of hyperactivity syndrome. These children exhibit impulsive, inattentive, and excessively active tendencies. Although most children outgrow the hyperactive aspect of the disorder during adolescence, they may nevertheless continue to be affected by impulsiveness and inattentiveness, and the secondary effects of "growing up hyperactive" (e.g., academic and social difficulties). Possible etiologies of hyperactivity include: perinatal, genetic, and biological influences; and allergies. Treatments include stimulant medications, behavioral intervention, and diet restrictions.

With mental retardation and childhood psychoses, severely affected children are often institutionalized. Etiologies of both can be grouped into three categories: (1) physiological or organic; (2) environmental or psychological; and (3) an interaction between biological/genetic influences (stress) and environment (diathesis). Whether a child is retarded or psychotic, parents must realistically consider the child's limitations and abilities, thereby creating realistic expectations.

# SELF-CHECK

1. All of the following characterize younger psychotic children except for:
   a. inability to form adequate relationships with people.
   b. deficiencies in emotional maturation.
   c. marked visual hallucinations.
   d. perceptual, motor, and cognitive skill deficits.
2. Other than symptomatology differences, the following is most often used to distinguish autism from childhood schizophrenia:
   a. the time of occurrence (before or after 30 months of age)
   b. family configuration
   c. sex of the child
   d. None of the above is correct.

3. Autistic children often repeat exactly what was said to them. This is termed:
   a. pronoun reversal.
   b. echolalia.
   c. retarded speech.
   d. IQ deficit.
4. The following is true of autistic children according to Rimland (1964):
   a. They are usually attractive and healthy.
   b. Some have exceptional abilities.
   c. They are often described as graceful and dexterous.
   d. All of the above are true.
5. Etiological theories of childhood psychosis are varied. Some researchers hypothesize that certain infants are predisposed to emotional aloofness and it is the parents' reaction to this behavior that exacerbates the onset of psychosis. This theory fits into the
   a. physiological theories.
   b. psychological theories.
   c. diathesis–stress theories.
   d. None of the above is correct.
6. In general, the prognosis for childhood psychosis is:
   a. good.
   b. bad.
   c. better if the particular child exhibits less severe behavioral disturbances.
   d. b and c are both correct.
7. A definition of mental retardation necessitates all of the following *except* for:
   a. significantly subaverage intellectual functioning
   b. physical abnormalities
   c. deficits in adaptive behavior
   d. onset during the developmental period
8. An IQ range of 35 to 49 includes which category of mental retardation?
   a. mild
   b. moderate
   c. severe
   d. profound
9. Which category of mentally retarded individuals is considered "trainable" but not educable?
   a. mild
   b. moderate
   c. severe
   d. profound
10. The majority of retarded individuals have performance and social deficits that seem to reflect:
    a. organic or biological abnormalities.
    b. Down's syndrome.
    c. sociocultural deprivation.
    d. none of the above.

KEY: 1–c; 2–a; 3–b; 4–d; 5–c; 6–d; 7–b; 8–b; 9–b; 10–c

# C H A P T E R                    14

# EMOTIONS: DEVELOPMENT AND OBSTACLES

*We lived on a farm, and since I was the sixth of seven children, there was plenty to keep my younger brother and me busy. We played for hours in the hay or the attic in the barn. My parents were always loving, and I always wanted to please them. At the time, I suppose, I felt obligated to do what was right and make them happy, but this pressure did not stem from them but from myself. I recall being up to something all of the time. I loved to clean my brothers' rooms, to rub their backs, to vacuum. All these things made me happy. I had everything I needed and most of what I wanted.*

*Generally, I was just a happy little kid. Being out in the country is the only way to go. I hope that I can raise my kids there. I could do almost anything, go anywhere (down to the dump, up to the lake, to the railroad tracks, where we would put pennies on the track). We climbed up on the roof of the barn, had dirt clod fights. Looking back, I'm amazed that my mom let us do the things we did—we could have gotten hurt! But it was great . . . happy . . . carefree.*

Not all of us have childhoods like that described by a student above, but we all recall childhood experiences of some sort or another. Usually, those experiences we remember most are laden with emotions—not being invited to a slumber party, hitting a home run in a Little League game, the first day of school, bringing home a straight-A report card. Even parents tend to remember those experiences with their children that involve the expression of intense positive or negative emotion.

*My son would get really frustrated and angry when I didn't understand what he wanted. He knew exactly what he wanted me to do but didn't always have the ability to let me know what it was. I don't know if he was more frustrated at me or at himself for not being able to express himself very well.*

*He also got really angry when I did understand what he wanted but I didn't do it. He wanted me to play ball with him constantly, and when I didn't, he got angry.*

This chapter will consider the development and impact of a child's emotions, and then look at some problems or obstacles facing many parents when dealing with their children's emotions: crises such as divorce or death of a family member; fears; chronic illness; and sexual urges. Strong emotional expression—especially that expressed by impulsive, unhampered children—is not always easy to handle. High-, moderate-, and low-power techniques to change and influence behavior may need altering. In addition, since parents tend to get emotionally involved in the situations described in this chapter, these situations warrant special emphasis.

## Emotional Development

Emotions are often difficult to classify. Often, the same emotion is expressed differently by various individuals. Or, numerous people may observe expression of a certain emotion, yet use numerous, varying terms to describe what they saw. Fortunately, children's emotions are expressed very honestly and are usually easier to recognize.

### ORIGIN OF EMOTIONS

**Emotions are learned.** What happens in the body during the expression of various emotions? One psychologist elicited fear and anger from experimental subjects and found, surprisingly, that the majority of physiological responses were the same for both (Ax, 1953). Schachter and Singer (1962) illustrated a similar phenomenon. A university student received an injection of an unknown yet harmless drug. In truth, what the student actually received was adrenaline, a stimulating hormone. The student was then asked to step into a waiting room, where he met another student—actually a stooge, someone acting on behalf of the experiment's purpose. The stooge had been instructed to act strangely. For example, he wadded up paper and played basketball with the wastebasket. He found a hoop in the room and pretended it was a hula hoop, dancing with gaiety and recklessness. The stooge then asked the drugged student to join him in the fun. With the help of the drug, the two were soon engaged in even more exciting, boisterous behavior.

Other students received the same injections with the same instructions, but for them the stooge pretended to be angered, bitter, and aggressive. In this situation, the drugged students responded negatively. Physiological processes were the same for all the drugged students, but outward manifestations and interpretations varied from delight to bitterness.

More recently, Malatesta (1982) determined that mothers actively shape their child's emotional expressions through facial gestures and tone of voice. In this study, mothers autonomously restricted their own range of emotional expression toward their children to mostly positive emotions. They also made immediate, contingent responses to positive emotions coming from their children, while responding less immediately and contingently to more negative emotions. As a result, it was concluded, the children tended to increase their own expressions of positive emotions. Obviously, we *learn* how to act when emotions are aroused. Inevitably, children will become aroused, but how they react and interpret their feelings depends greatly on environmental learning.

**Emotions are inborn.**   On the other hand, it can be argued that the expression of emotions is innate. Facial expressions across cultures are virtually universal, especially among children. As children grow, however, cultural influence requires children to assume certain masks for their emotions. Infants and small children in any culture will probably respond similarly to frightening experiences. Yet as they grow, cultural and familial influences may create tendencies to show control and reserve, or simple surprise, in the same situations. Emde, Gaensbauer, and Harmon (1976) determined that initial levels of emotional expression in infants (crying from birth to two months, smiling, and then stranger anxiety) appear to be biologically determined and regulated by maturation. They spontaneously appear in growing infants without practice or environmental stimulation.

Thus, we conclude there are both inborn and learned components to emotional expression and development. The knowledge that emotions are innate can help parents and teachers be more accepting and tolerant of children's emotional uniqueness. The knowledge that emotions are influenced by environment can help parents realize that guidance in emotional development and control should be provided.

## DEVELOPMENTAL INFLUENCES ON EMOTIONAL EXPRESSION

In an early study, one psychologist (Bridges, 1932) observed the development of emotions from birth through two years of age. Bridges found that an infant's first emotional response is an innate excitement or agitation. As early as three weeks of age this excitement begins to differentiate into excitement and distress; negative emotional excitement may be demonstrated when the child is hungry, in pain, or uncomfortable. The differentiation of positive emotional excitement does not appear until approximately the third month of life, corresponding with smiling and the beginning of cooing. From these observations Bridges identified three general characteristics of emotional development:

1. The intensity of emotional responses gradually decreases over time.
2. Emotional responses gradually become channeled into socially approved modalities.
3. Training and social pressures produce gradual changes in the expression of emotional responses.

Generally then, emotional development proceeds from a general, undifferentiated state to higher specialization. That is, emotions proceed from the general to the specific. For a baby, crying is a total body activity: arms and legs jerk and twitch; the eyes close and open; the infant will work up a sweat. Later, emotions become more differentiated so that less of the body is involved in expressing a single emotion; the emotion becomes specialized. For instance, with crying, the arms and legs become less involved until it becomes essentially a facial activity. This differentiation process is influenced by social expectations.

All emotions seem to develop in this fashion, beginning with expressions that are relatively global, and later becoming less involved and more under the individual's control. A child's emotions are also fairly simple, definable, and pure. The child experiences very little of the mixed emotions and ambivalence that older children, adolescents, and adults find themselves facing.

Children's emotions are also very intense. Children experience few cultural inhibitors to dampen their emotions. They will become very angry and shout, "I hate you!" Fifteen minutes later, however, they may express love through warmth and endearing words. Their emotions are also quite labile. Expressions in young infants, for example, change at an average rate of every eight seconds (Malatesta, 1982). As they grow, this time period lengthens. Children's emotional reactions to the same stimulus may also change as they get older. For example, seeing parents engaged in conflict creates distress and crying among toddlers, whereas school-age children more often respond by comforting or intervening (Cummings, Zahn-Waxler, & Radke-Yarrow, 1984).

**Impulse control.** In general, the two-year-old has mastered all the basic emotions of an older child—in fact, even many emotions adults possess. However, a difference is seen in the small child's immediate, impulsive, and direct expression of these emotions. As children grow and develop, the ability to control emotions is increased (Taylor & Harris, 1984). Maccoby (1980) cited a number of related changes in the growing child:

1. The child begins to be able to delay certain actions until a time when they will fit in more appropriately with concurrent actions or will have more acceptable consequences.
2. Future consequences are weighted more heavily in the choice of present actions.
3. If the pursuit of a goal is temporarily blocked by an externally imposed barrier, the child is able to put the blocked activity on hold while attempting to find a way around the barrier.
4. When the goal activity is blocked, the child does not become so emotionally aroused that his or her behavior becomes disorganized in a tantrum episode (p. 163).

A study by Van Leishout (1975) concluded that ability to control frustration begins developing at a fairly early age, especially for females. Van Leishout let 18-month-old infants play with a small toy. The toy was then taken by their mothers and put into a clear plastic container; they could see the toy, but couldn't get at it. This same procedure was observed again at two years of age. The frequency of temper reactions declined notably for girls during this six-month span, whereas boys' frequency of anger toward their mothers remained at a high level, suggesting that girls develop control over their frustrations at a faster rate than do boys.

Exactly how children begin to develop control over their emotions is not clear, but the ability to delay gratification is easily assessed by giving a child two choices: either the smaller (less desirable) of two rewards *now*, or the larger (more desirable) of two rewards or options *later*. As expected, the

Children, experiencing few cultural inhibitors, express their emotions very intensely.

younger child picks the more immediate choice (Mischel & Metzner, 1962). Seventy-two percent of kindergarten children chose the smaller, immediate reward. This percentage declined gradually; at the fifth- and sixth-grade levels, only 38 percent chose the smaller reward.

A number of additional studies done by Mischel and his colleagues shed additional light on this change (Mischel, Coates, & Raskoff, 1968; Mischel & Grusec, 1967; Mischel & Metzner, 1962; Mischel & Staub, 1965; Mischel & Underwood, 1974; Mischel, Zeiss, & Zeiss, 1974). These studies found that children are better able to delay gratification if the wait is not too long. The frustration of waiting is also easier to handle if the adult promising the reward is trusted.

In some of Mischel's experiments, children were required to complete a boring or difficult task while they waited for the delayed reward. Older children were willing to put forth more effort on the task. However, this willingness depended in part on the child's confidence that he or she could complete the task. Confidence in one's ability to work for a delayed, more desirable reward was enhanced if the child had had prior experiences with success.

Mischel also found that another reason young children have difficulty delaying gratification is their inability to occupy themselves during the waiting period. Older children learn to occupy themselves by thinking about something. Ability to wait was increased even more if the child was able to think about irrelevant, distracting events.

From this quick review of some of Mischel's studies, it is apparent that the ability to delay gratification and, therefore, to control emotions is partly a function of the developmental process. Merely getting older is helpful. However, a parent's contribution to this process is also important. If a parent is trusted by the child, if the parent is able to add some structure to the child's difficult moments of waiting for wanted objects, if the wait is not too long, and if the child is given prior experience, emotional outbursts may not be as frequent or severe.

**Language and voluntary control of emotion.** As the child grows older, expressions and emotions come more and more under voluntary control. Language is important in this developmental process, as the child develops the ability to instruct himself through what is called "self-talk" about his or her emotions and behavior. With increased language skills comes the ability to carry on an internal dialogue about why and how one is feeling a certain emotion, and what can be done about it. The child may be less likely to react impulsively, but at the same time carries the "encoded" emotion for longer periods. Thus, emotions become more subdued and yet much more persistent. Whereas young children will react and then forget, older children are more likely to respond in a socially appropriate manner, while at the same time holding onto feelings for longer periods of time.

An additional developmentally acquired skill is the growing ability to use language to understand emotions. As children become capable of labeling emotions, they can compare their feelings with those of others. Occasionally, however, parents' dishonesty makes the labeling process a problem, as demonstrated by one couple who had very strong views about controlling their own negative emotions and teaching their children positive ones. When their daughter was approximately 18 months old, the father, obviously annoyed by the child's misbehavior, told her, "It makes me feel sad when you do that." Apparently these parents did not want to express the full strength of emotions, pretending that their feelings were of sadness, disappointment, and sorrow rather than annoyance and anger. Thus, even if the child perceived the emotion accurately, the label placed on it was not used correctly by the father. If inaccurate labeling continues, she may very likely have difficulty interpreting the labels and intensity of emotions later in life. Honestly dealing with emotions is sometimes difficult for parents; yet, dishonest labeling does not adequately help children learn to understand their own feelings.

## ENVIRONMENTAL INFLUENCES ON EMOTIONAL EXPRESSION

**Modeling of parent behavior.** Although emotional growth is partially a developmental maturation of innate tendencies, parents do influence this process. Norton (1977) provided the following description:

> If you saw a person searching through the pockets of your coat while it was on a hanger in a restaurant, you might react with anger and rush over to the person and say, "What are you doing?" If your child observed this he would be learning what he might think is the appropriate reaction to someone taking something from him without permission. In addition to your rushing forward and saying something to the person, you would also be doing other things. Because of your anger you might be breathing hard, your face might be red, and your hands might be shaking. When you finally talk to your child you might say, "That made me so mad." Look at what you have modeled for the child. First, you've shown him a series of behaviors (approaching and talking to the person), bodily changes associated with emotion (shaking hands, face reddening, and hard breathing), and finally, you've given the child a label for all of these reactions—"I'm mad" (p. 142).

Dramatic and traumatic events or intense emotional experiences may have a powerful impact upon a child's life and leave lasting impressions. Indeed, early experiences within the first three years of life may set the stage

Parents' emotional expression serves as a model to children, teaching them how various emotions are expressed.

for a child's basic emotional responses. Modifying the impact of these early experiences is generally achieved only with a great deal of effort and care.

Severe punishment, as discussed in Chapter 7, may cause increased emotionality or anxiety. The child who is continually punished for little things may become extremely shy and timid, and fearful of other people or new situations. Above all, he or she may become afraid of the punishing parent. Laughter, joy, and other positive emotions may be subdued for fear of doing something inappropriate. Or, the severely punished child may develop an aggressive, negative attitude toward his or her own peers, expressing anger and revenge. In either case, the child will develop maladaptive behaviors toward others. Close, warm relationships with other people will be difficult to develop.

**Cultural expectations.**   Cultural demands are also transmitted to children, teaching them about not only the propriety or impropriety of expressing emotions, but also situations where certain emotions are acceptable. In our Western culture, a powerful source of influence is television and other mass media. Through television, children are exposed to models who behave and react emotionally. They respond by imitation, much as they would to experiences with their parents. It is estimated that American children spend one-third of their waking hours watching television. One psychologist believes that continued exposure to violence and cruelty on television has caused American children to become insensitive to the suffering of others (Cline, 1974).

## HEALTHY EMOTIONAL DEVELOPMENT

Perhaps the most important ingredient for healthy emotional development is the ratio of positive to negative or disintegrative emotions in children's lives. Love, affection, sympathy, joy, contentment, and security should predominate over hate, hostility, despair, remorse, and fear. The importance of a positive emotional environment was related in the following description by an 18-year-old looking back on her family:

*One of the most powerful emotions in my childhood was humor, or happiness. My family has always been really fun. A lot of bantering and joking goes on and Dad used to always play with us, chasing us around the house, as we screamed and laughed. He used to chase us and stick our stocking-feet into the sink under the running water or pour red ink into our bath water. We were almost always happy and laughing. My mother always played along with Dad's pranks. Sometimes she was even the one to get an ice cube down her back!*

*I don't quite know what emotion constitutes all our playfulness, but I know without it, home life would have been very drab. My brother continues in the tradition, but now the roles have altered a bit.*

*He chases my mother around the house with a glass of water to retaliate for her spraying him with the ironing bottle. I still love to go home to this happy, loving atmosphere.*

Humor and other positive emotions are important for children to encounter. The ratio of positive to negative emotions in the home should be skewed toward the positive. However, it is important for parents to let their children experience the normal ups and downs of emotional and social life without excessively shielding them from negative experiences (Hoffman, 1976). Clinical psychologists and child development specialists generally believe that children should be given the opportunity and right to feel any emotion. Emotions are real and will ordinarily appear without the child's bidding. Parents should, however, differentiate between the child's right to feel emotions and the child's tendency to "act out" emotions. That is, even though children have a right to feel certain emotions, parents may demand that the emotion be controlled in a healthy, mature fashion. The child may feel rage, but cannot be allowed to wildly attack an infant brother. Accordingly, the child will develop self-direction in dealing with emotions.

Sometimes parents help children handle negative emotional experiences by discussing the emotion with them. Following an emotional experience, when intense emotions have subsided, parents can help children go back over the experiences in an atmosphere of trust and relaxation to learn more about the emotional aspects. Parents must be aware of some children's tendency to hide their emotions, sometimes called "stuffing" of feelings. Nail-biting, enuresis, nervous tics, and similar behaviors are indicators of possible emotional stuffing. The concerned adult can help children to "free up" and understand these feelings and experiences by talking about them.

## EMOTIONAL STABILITY

In general, a positive emotional climate in the home is the single most important influencing factor for stable emotional responding. Particularly important is the experience of being accepted by others, which produces an emotional feeling that "I belong," "I'm worthwhile," or "I'm loved and a part of this group." Sometimes extra effort is required on parents' part to bolster self-esteem when children feel inadequate.

*When I was growing up I was always taught to have a positive self-image. This created in me the knowledge that if I wanted to do something and tried hard enough I would be able to accomplish it. My parents always tried to put trust and confidence in me to assure me that I was capable of performing well. In the fourth grade my teacher was going to hold me back because of poor reading skills. She approached*

*my parents about this possibility and told my parents that unless I showed vast improvement, I would have to repeat fourth grade. My parents came to me and expressed confidence in me and told me that if I worked hard I would not have to stay back. The possibility of failing placed an extreme strain on my self-esteem. But, through my parents' reassurance, I was able to improve my skills, and by the end of the fourth grade I was at the top of my class in reading, and I felt really good about myself.*

Unfortunately, a positive climate is not always produced in some homes, nor can the intrusion of emotional crises always be avoided. In such circumstances, a child may develop an emotional rigidity, narrowing the range of emotions he or she is willing to experience. The child may also respond negatively, including negative feelings about the self, or may push feelings deep "underground." Occasionally, professional intervention may be required to assist a child in "working through" negative emotional experiences, but even here parents should not underestimate their influence.

## Emotional Tasks

Children struggle with a variety of emotional tasks as they grow and develop. These occur naturally, but appropriate steps need to be taken to help children work through their emotions, rather than expecting them to logically solve problems on their own. We will discuss dependency, fears, and sexual urges. Various techniques for reducing inappropriate and excessive fears will also be presented. The suggestions given for assisting a child through emotional tasks are examples and are not inclusive—parents are urged to be imaginative in their efforts.

### DEPENDENCY

To most adults, dependency generally means a clinging child. To the psychologist, however, dependency is an important and necessary prerequisite for personality development. From infancy, the child, being in an inferior or dependent position, must lean upon adults to help satisfy needs. This trend will continue throughout childhood and adolescence until the individual becomes a self-sufficient member of society. Because we, even as adults, are in ways dependent upon one another, we must learn to accept dependency and trust others.

The parent should be aware of dependent behaviors and expect children, even older ones, to sometimes need help. In some cases, insecurities, frustrations, and perceived inability may accentuate a child's dependence. Attempts by teachers or parents to interpret these situations from the child's point of view may help them understand why the child is excessively dependent.

Dependency on parents is an important and necessary prerequisite for personality development.

In general, children dependent upon adults seem to be more motivated and better learners (Hartup & Smothergill, 1967). It is, of course, possible that the dependent child, with a strong need for adult approval, will work hard to obtain this approval. In any case, dependency, if not at a pathological extreme, can motivate learning.

## FEARS

It is natural and adaptive for children to have fears. For example, fear of loud noises can serve as a safety mechanism, helping children escape some sudden danger. Fear of large, unknown animals may prevent the child from approaching an unfriendly dog or other animal. Childhood fears are to be expected. It has been shown that children, even those with high IQs, experience a large number of fears between the ages of two and five (Jersild & Holmes, 1935). According to some child psychologists, more intelligent children who recognize potential dangers and hazards in the environment, and who have livelier imaginations, seem to be more aware of and thoughtful about fearful events.

As children grow, fears are a natural part of their development. Small infants (0–6 months) become startled when hearing loud noses; throwing a small child high up into the air will usually produce a frightened look and immediate crying if the child is not used to such play; somewhat older infants (6–9 months) go through a stage where unfamiliar faces are frightening. One child's grandfather grew a beard, and when the child saw this previously familiar person, she began to cry. At the age of one, children begin to respond with fear upon separation from parents. At three, they fear dogs, while at four fear of the dark is prominent. Many fears are realistic and appropriate to have. Fear of dangers like being hit by a car, falling out of a tree, or being burned by fire may cause the child to proceed with caution when facing dangerous situations.

Staley and O'Donnell (1984) found age, sex, and social class correlates of childhood fears. Although the content of fears remains somewhat constant from the age of six until 16 (physical injury, animals, school, nighttime, and public places), the frequency of these fears declines in all cases except physical injury. Girls have more fears than boys in all cases except school fears. Higher social-class children have more school-related fears than lower social-class children, while the reverse is true for physical injury fears. Childhood fears, then, are to be expected.

However, intense fears may be debilitating. Kagan and Moss (1962) suggest that intense fears occurring during childhood may cause difficulties during later life. These two researchers found that boys who had intense fears about bodily harm when young were anxious about sexuality and uninvolved in traditional masculine activities as adults.

A number of approaches may be used to minimize fears. Some approaches are not beneficial. Parents who are sarcastic or criticize their children's fears succeed only in diminishing self-esteem and possibly increasing fears; and, of course, excessive fears cannot always be ignored in hopes that they will go away. We introduce below four time-tested methods to help children overcome excessive fears.

**Systematic desensitization.** Systematic desensitization is a technique many parents unknowingly implement. Take, for example, the common fear that many young children have about dogs. The fear may result from an unpleasant experience with dogs, or may simply be a fear of the "big and unknown." In any case, this fear may be reduced through a step-by-step process in which the child is gradually brought closer to actual contact with a dog. Initially, the child would be allowed to watch a dog, with the parent, from the other side of a chain link fence. As this becomes comfortable, the child's father may enter the area where a dog is playing, while holding the child. The next step might be to set the child down next to the parent while the dog is on the opposite side of the yard. The distance will be gradually reduced, and then the child is encouraged to touch the dog, with the parent nearby. Eventually, the child's fear of dogs is reduced.

It is important to note that each one of these steps is taken slowly, to ensure that the child's fear level is not excessive for desensitization. If, for example, touching the dog was too frightening, the parent might want to return to an earlier stage, or hold the child as he or she touches the dog to provide additional comfort. By systematically exposing the child to the feared stimulus—in this instance the dog—the fear is reduced.

Systematic desensitization may be used with children at very young ages also. Peter Bentler (1962) reported a case in which an 11-month-old girl's fear of water was reduced with this procedure.

The girl, like most children, enjoyed playing in her wading pool and taking baths. Then one day she slipped and fell while she was in the tub. She began screaming and was obviously very frightened. Afterwards she was not only afraid of the tub, but also of the wading pool, faucets, and water in any part of the house and being washed in the hand basin.

Treatment of the infant's fear consisted of four parts. First toys were placed in the empty bathtub and the girl was given free access to the bathroom and the toys. During this phase of treatment she would occasionally remove a toy from the tub, but would not remain near the tub. The second stage consisted of sitting the girl on the table near the sink filled with water. Toys were placed in the water and, at first, the girl began to scream, but later played with toys on the table and near the sink. These toys were moved progressively closer to the sink until she was finally entering the sink. This caused a brief bout of crying, but helped to desensitize her to water. The third step consisted of washing the child in the bathroom sink while she was playing with her favorite toy. The child began playing with the mirror and eventually with the water in the sink. During this stage she also began playing with the sprinkler in the yard. Finally, the parents began washing the child in the tub with the water running at diaper-changing time. At first the girl began to cry, but parental hugging and firmness caused her to stop crying after two days. At twelve and three-quarters months the child was fully recovered and playing normally around water (in Norton, 1972, p. 127).

How might a child be systematically desensitized to a fear of the dark at bedtime? The first step involves identifying what is causing the fear, which is not simple if the child is too young to verbally communicate. Suppose the child started screaming every night when put in bed and the light shut off. The parent might discover that leaving the light on one evening significantly reduces the crying episode. The fear—darkness—has been identified. The next step is planning out a systematic schedule to reduce the fear. The hall light might be left on and the door to the child's room left open. Each night the door is shut a little more until eventually no light is let into the room. An alternative is to buy a dimmer switch for the child's room. Each successive evening the light could be dimmed at amounts unnoticeable to the child. The child's fear about sleeping in the dark would eventually disappear.

**Observational learning.**   Observational learning, another approach to reducing fears, is based on the assumption that observing another person effectively handle and not be harmed by a feared stimulus reduces fear toward that simulus. In the example of fear of dogs, presented earlier, suppose the father approaches the dog, pets it, and begins to play with it. During this time the child is probably standing behind the father. The child would learn to not fear the dog by observing that the father was not harmed by approaching and petting the dog.

**Stories.**   Telling stories can also be used to teach children and reduce fears. Storytelling is most effective if the story presents a situation the child is familiar with, or if the story's character is someone with whom the child can identify.

> A good teaching story should do several things: it should capture the child's attention, it should center around the child's problem, it should provide a convenient way of solving the problem, and it should provide rewards to the story character who has solved the problem (Norton, 1977, p. 165).

In telling a story, perhaps the most important message given to the child should be, "I am on your side. I have confidence in you. Even if you are unable to meet this challenge right now, that doesn't change my confidence and my caring for you."

Consider the following example of a story that could be told to a young child afraid of jumping off the diving board, or, for that matter, of any task that other same-age children are performing:

*Dick was learning how to swim, but he was still afraid of the water. When his mom signed him up for swimming lessons he was both happy and worried. Have you ever had two feelings at the same time like Dick did? Dick was happy and worried. Can you remember a time when you felt two feelings like that—when you wanted to do something but at the same time you were afraid to do it? Sometimes it seems to happen that we want to be able to do something, but we're afraid to do the things that will take us there. Dick wanted to be able to swim and wanted to not be afraid of the water, but he was worried because he was afraid.*

*Every day Dick went to swimming lessons with the other children. He would watch very closely what the teacher told him to do. Then he tried harder, even if he was afraid.*

*His lessons started by getting used to the water. First, the chil-*

dren put their faces in the water; then they paddled and kicked; and then they began to swim a little. One day the teacher said, "Now it's time for you to jump off the diving board." Dick was frightened. He didn't think he could do that, but his teacher said, "I'm sure you can do it. Each of you knows how to swim—how to paddle and how to hold your breath. I'll be close to help you if you need any help, but I don't think anybody in the class will need any help."

They all lined up at the diving board. Dick waited until the very last because he was feeling frightened. Do you know what that feels like? It's a feeling of not wanting to do what someone else is doing or what you feel like you're supposed to do. You think that maybe you'll be hurt. What does your face look like? Show me, will you? That's right. When we feel frightened, our eyes are wide; sometimes our mouth is open, and sometimes we feel a bit shaky. That's what it's like to be frightened, or to have fear—which is another word for frightened.

Finally, it was Dick's turn. He climbed up on the diving board and walked out to the edge. He felt very frightened.

"Okay, Dick, now just remember what you need to do," his teacher told him. "You can close your eyes and hold your nose. Just jump off, and when you land in the water, come back up to the top and swim over to the edge."

Dick looked down at the water—it looked like a long way down. He knew the water was deep, but he said, "I'm not going to be frightened. I'm going to try very hard to be brave." His dad had talked to him about being brave, but he still didn't jump. He was still afraid. Then he said, "I'm still frightened, but I'm going to try it." He held onto his nose and jumped down into the water. He came right up to the top, and he paddled over to the side as fast as he could.

The teacher didn't need to help him at all. She smiled and said, "You were frightened, weren't you, Dick? But you did it."

Dick said, "Yes, I was frightened. I wasn't very brave."

She said, "Oh yes, you were. That's what bravery is about. Even though we're afraid to do it, we still try. That's being brave, and you have been a very brave boy today to try this new trick of jumping off the diving board. You can be afraid and brave at the same time."

Of course, her words made Dick feel very good. He said, "I want to try it again!"

She said, "Okay, good."

After climbing up on the diving board, Dick walked right out to the edge. He could feel a little bit of that fear still, but he decided he would try to jump anyway. He jumped off again.

Do you know, he did it five times that day, and by the time he stopped he wasn't frightened at all! He said to himself, "Maybe that's what bravery feels like. It's a feeling of being willing to try, even though I do feel afraid."

Think for a moment about what Dick did. Show me on your face how he felt when he first got up on the diving board. Now show me on your face how he felt the last time he jumped off the diving board after he had done it five times. Show me on your face how he looked

*as he finished his swimming lesson that day and went home. He prob-*
*ably had a big smile on his face, didn't he? He felt very happy and very*
*proud that he had been able to be brave even when he felt afraid at*
*the same time.*

◑

Stories such as this one help children understand that even parents
know what fear is like, that they have fears, and that being afraid is not indic-
ative of weakness. Naturally, the feared event, the child's reactions, and even
the sex of the child in the story could fit the child being told the story.
Through the above story, the parent was able to empathize with the child's
fears, portraying acceptance of the child, regardless of shortcomings. In addition, the story helps prepare the child for situations when these fears will be
encountered. Having it out in the open and being able to discuss and think
about it helps to alleviate some of the fear when the fearful situation does
occur.

**Prepare ahead.**   If children are not informed about what a visit to the
doctor entails prior to going, or if they are told that "it won't hurt one bit,"
they will probably distrust their parents or the doctor in the future, and be
afraid to go for subsequent visits. Fear is more effectively reduced if the child
is prepared for it a few days ahead of time. A babysitter may also be talked
about, and how he or she "will be coming over in a few days to play with you
while Mom and Dad are gone for a few hours." The parents might explain
that they understand it might be scary, but that nothing bad will happen, that
they will be back shortly.
    Dealing with fears is not strictly ameliorative, but can also be done pre-

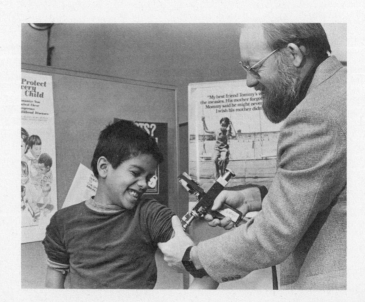

Preparing the
child before an
anxiety-provok-
ing event occurs
can help reduce
fear.

ventively. Jersild and Holmes (1935) found that a common component of many fears was a sudden or unexpected stimulus. For example, if an infant does not know what a vacuum is, and is unaware that it is about to be turned on two feet away, the infant will probably develop a fear reaction to the loud noise. It might be better to let the child see the vacuum, then go into the other room and turn it on, bringing it only gradually closer if the child doesn't become fearful. Notice the systematic desensitization and preparation occurring in this example.

## SEXUAL URGES AND CURIOSITY

Without proposing that Freud's theories are entirely correct, we can nevertheless conclude that sex and all its facets are strong motivators of human behavior. Even children as young as four and five are reported by parents and teachers to show exhibitionism, voyeurism, and curiosity about the genitals of the opposite sex.

Generally, adults in Western society are fairly puritanical about children's expression of sexual urges or curiosity. Many parents find the whole topic so uncomfortable that they refrain from ever talking to their children about sexual matters. And so, children remain in a state of conflict and anxiety regarding their sexual curiosity and feelings. True, there is not just one satisfactory way of handling such matters, but awareness of this natural motivation may help parents and teachers understand and work with it as it appears.

An essential ingredient of adequate sex education is open communication between children and adults, and the ideal teacher is a parent. However, many parents fail to communicate effectively with their children, often never touching on the topic. Result—their children pick up information, often inaccurate, from their peers. For this reason, many school systems have taken the initiative to include sex education in their curriculum.

Ideally, schools should train parents, who, in turn, educate their own children concerning human sexuality. The parent must: (1) understand and be able to explain facts of anatomy and physiology, including those of pregnancy; and (2) be able to communicate the love, commitment, and beauty behind sexual relations between married partners, without continually emphasizing the wrongness of the act in an effort to help children see societal constraints. If parents feel inadequate to discuss sex with their children, yet are concerned about what their children learn, they should feel it appropriate to seek professional counsel and education themselves, enabling them to talk more freely with their children. One youth remarks, "I can't talk to my dad about sex. He's from the old school. I think he was a lady's man, but I also think he has a fear of talking about it with me."

Besides wanting parents to be more open concerning the topic of sex, many adolescents honestly seek to know their parents' values. One of the authors talked with a youth who had had some previous morality problems. Saying he wished his parents had sat him down and explained both the functions and the moral implications of sex, he said his parents had not warned him about the consequences following certain acts. "My parents never told me what would happen so I had to find out for myself. I could have really benefited from their counsel," he said regretfully.

Speaking of the parental role in sex education values, one author wrote:

> Most people would grant that biological facts about physiology and body processes need to be made available to everyone. Accurate biological information, including charts and illustrations, is crucial and can be found in many good medical reference works and encyclopedias. Ideally, a well-informed parent could and should provide this information. But the frame of reference for this knowledge should be values like integrity, kindness, and reverence for the human body rather than a course in how to perform erotic acts. These values have everything to do with our sense of identity, or roles, and the skills we use in living with each other. Parents can and should teach these values as concepts and by the example of their relationship (Brown, 1981, p. 113).

Adolescents need to be taught the realities of sex. With today's media adolescents are continually bombarded with illusions of sexual intimacy. On television, on radio, and in the movies, different concepts of "love" are portrayed. "It is ominous for our future that a generation is being raised on television fare which teaches that a "loving" relationship can be developed in five days on an ocean liner cruising the Pacific or over a weekend while living on an island devoted to fantasy" (Brown, 1981, p. 6).

Parents must accept their roles as educators to their children. They must develop honest and open relationships with them, teaching them the realities and consequences of their sexual behavior.

## Emotional Crises

Even if children grow up in a warm, accepting environment where positive emotions outweigh the negative, where healthy emotional development has occured, and where excessive fears have been adequately overcome, situations may still arise when emotional crises need to be dealt with appropriately. Some of these instances include divorce, death of a family member, and chronic illness.

### DIVORCE

A strong statement about divorce and subsequent feelings came from a student who described her father many years after her parents' divorce:

*The strongest feeling I can remember was hating my father. My parents were separated and filed for divorce when I was nine. I hated him*

*because of the pain and misery he caused my mother. I had seen him hit her once or twice, and I couldn't stand that. He was an alcoholic and didn't care for us two kids—my sister and I. One time, on my mom's birthday he wanted to take her to a bar for a drink. He didn't tell her where they were going, and once we all got there he left my sister and me in the car alone, in the middle of the night, while they were in there for over an hour or so. He had to practically force her to go in—she didn't want to leave us alone. I remember we cried and cried. There was nothing for us to do, and we were so mad and scared we couldn't sleep.*

*He's on his fifth marriage now; Mom was his second. Unfortunately, my feelings for him haven't changed much. I hate him as a father. I even tried to get to know him as a person. I still don't like him, and I even feel sorry for him.*

◑

In Chapter 15 the topic of single parenting is discussed. Causes of single parenting and some effects on children are outlined. In this section focus is on the process of divorce itself—"What do we tell the children?" "What will be their reactions now and a few years from now?" "How can I make this transition easier for them?" These and similar questions are on the minds of approximately 1 million parents in the United States each year. In those families where children do reside, parents contemplating divorce consider very carefully the effects of separation on their children. Considerations include questions such as the following:

1. How old are the children?
2. How attached are they to each parent?
3. How important are the issues in contention, and can they be negotiated?
4. What would the children prefer? (Clayton, 1979, p. 571)

Interestingly, however, Clayton (1979) continues by saying the final decision to separate is rarely based on these considerations. "Children are seldom the reason cited for a divorce, and they are likewise seldom the sole reason given for keeping a conflict-saturated marriage intact." This statement reflects the idea that when all factors are considered, the final decision depends on responsibilities parents feel toward themselves. This is not to say that no marriage remains intact for "the sake of the children," or that parents will never make the final decision to separate because they want to remove their children from a turbulent and upsetting family situation. However, it does indicate that a lot of decisions for or against divorce, though heavily considering consequences for children, are finally made on more of a personal, rather than global, level.

**Telling the children.**   Perhaps one of the toughest obstacles during divorce is telling the children. Parents need to be honest in explaining the situation, and should refrain from keeping their children in the dark. Ilg and

Ames (1955) stated it beautifully when they suggested that parents say something similar to the following: "When people marry, they hope that they will be happy together and live together always. But that sometimes doesn't work out that way. And when it doesn't, and when they cannot live happily together, then they often feel it is better to live apart."

In spite of loving, concerted efforts to explain divorce, as in the statement above, parents should be prepared for children who blame themselves for the divorce. Parents must reassure their children that they are not to blame, and that both parents' love for them has not changed and will not change.

When explaining divorce there are also a few things that parents should not do or say. Brooks (1981) mentions the following:

1. Do not burden children with your own negative views of the other parent.
2. Do not put all the blame on the other parent.
3. Do not ask children to take sides in the matter.

Children will stay surprisingly loyal to both parents even if one of them has been abusive. In spite of the circumstances surrounding a divorce, children will often entertain hope that Mom or Dad will come back, and that their parents will love each other again and want to live together once more. Parents can accept these feelings without giving their children undue hope that things will become as they would like.

**Effects of divorce on children.**  After the question of how to tell the children has been settled, the next concern is one that does not have a simple answer, if at all. This is the issue of the immediate effects of divorce on the children. One writer examined this question relative to adolescents and their self-esteem.

> If we return to our original question, "Does the broken home have an effect upon the emotional state of the child?" the best answer would seem to be "it depends." First, it depends on religion: if the child is Catholic or Jewish, there appears to be a clear effect; if the child is Protestant, there appears to be little or no effect. Second, it depends upon the mother's age at the time of the marital rupture: if the mother was very young, there appears to be a clear effect; if the mother was older, there appears to be little effect (Rosenberg, 1965, p. 106).

It is evident that the question of whether "our divorce will negatively affect our kids" is a complicated one. Countless variables come into play; the above list is not exhaustive. The child's sex also makes a difference. Boys are more likely to become rebellious and hard to control under the stress of familial disruption than girls (Hetherington, Cox, & Cox, 1979; Rutter, 1970). Evident effects also depend somewhat on the child's age. Wallerstein and Kelly (1977), having done extensive research on the impact of divorce, found this to be the case. During preschool years, children may feel abandoned, and may regress toward bed-wetting, temper tantrums, and increased fears. Though quite often able to deny what is happening, they may still feel overwhelmed by the whole process. Similarly, Hodges, Tierney, and Buchsbaum (1984) found that, among preschoolers, with divorce came increased aggression, distractibility, and acting out toward peers. Wallerstein and Kelly (1977) maintain that parents themselves are the best intervention. They must communicate to children the reasons for the divorce, and reassure them that their needs will continue to be met. Parental comfort, love, and reassurance are most important.

Children a few years older are not as able to deny the situation. They respond with sadness and grief. One six-year-old boy's mother was called by the principal and asked if she could come pick up her son because he couldn't keep his eyes dry during class and was obviously very disturbed about something. It turned out that the little boy's father had explained to him the previous evening that he was leaving. Another frequent response of children this age is fear. They need to be reassured they will still be loved, cared for, and safe.

As children reach the age of 9 or 10, depression, anger, and worries are more readily alleviated by outside therapeutic intervention. This is not to say that parental support and concern is no longer necessary, but that older children are more likely to benefit from counseling than younger children. Counseling provides a validation of the child's feelings. Children feel better if an outside source recognizes and understands the difficulties they are facing.

Some children feel they are somehow stigmatized. It is hard to explain to friends that their father or mother doesn't live with them anymore. This feeling is partially attributable to the idea that somehow divorce reflects upon their own worth, a notion evolving from their inability to comprehend and integrate the total dynamics behind parents' decision to terminate marriage.

Following divorce, some disruption in family routine is likely to occur. Bedtime and nighttime routines, mealtime, and household duties will likely depart from the regular schedule. Relationships between children and parents may temporarily change. Parents at first make fewer demands on their children, are less likely to ask for their children's opinions or give explanations, and are less consistent with previous discipline patterns (Brooks, 1981, p. 299). However, this disorganization gravitates back toward normalcy as emotions are dealt with and order and stability are reestablished.

> The main predictor of good parent–child relationships following divorce is the parents' ability to relate to each other. When parents continue to respect each other, to agree on discipline, and to be consistent with children, children are likely to adapt well. When parents continue to be angry, bitter, and distressed with each other, it is harder to establish an organized family life that sustains the children. When other individuals like grandparents, friends, or a housekeeper contribute support, the mother's effectiveness increases. But support from outside the family is not as important as a positive relationship between the mother and father (Brooks, 1981, p. 299).

# DEATH

Dealing with a parent's death is similar to facing divorce. In both cases, breaking the news to children is difficult. As with divorce, family members must go through an adjustment period; how children react is partially a function of their age.

We will first consider the effects of death on a spouse. Although every adult responds to death in idiosyncratic ways, almost everyone experiences five stages in the bereavement process. It is advantageous for widows and widowers to be aware of these universal bereavement reactions, helping them cope better with death, and thereby enabling them to more effectively aid their own children through the adjustment period. A widow, Lynne Caine, wrote, "I am convinced that if I had known the facts of grief before I had to experience them, it would not have made my grief less intense, not have lessened my misery, minimized my loss or quieted my anger. No, none of these things. But it would have allowed me to hope. It would have given me courage. I would have known that once my grief was worked through, I would be joyful again" (Lynne Caine, 1975, p. 69; in Brooks, 1981).

The following five stages of bereavement have been identified by Clayton (1979):

1. **Numbness:** A full realization of the person's death does not occur immediately. Making funeral arrangements, switching checking accounts, and many other activities help deter reality from hitting too suddenly.
2. **Loneliness:** This stage tends to set in after the funeral. Everyone has returned home and immediate responsibilities have been taken care of. This loneliness may be very intense depending on whether the remaining spouse feels moderately to extremely helpless in taking over familial responsibilities of the deceased.
3. **Emptiness:** "A feeling in the core of one's being that part of him or her is gone," emptiness is felt by some adults for the first time as they realize just how deep their commitment level to marriage has been.
4. **Normality:** As the emptiness subsides, the person begins to understand and accept his or her new identity, that of being single. Responsibilities and lifestyle are different and are beginning to be adapted to.
5. **Adjustment to the new single identity:** Adjustment involves a resignation either to living alone as a single parent, or to beginning the search for a new partner.

Length of the bereavement process varies considerably among different subcultures. Feelings of depression, poor appetite, weight loss, and insomnia may be normal. "However, morbid preoccupations with worthlessness, prolonged and marked functional impairment, and marked psychomotor retardation are uncommon and suggest that the bereavement is complicated by the development of a major depression" (American Psychiatric Association, 1980). In such a case, professional help is warranted. In fact, many single parents find individual or group counseling to be beneficial as they adjust.

Grief reactions in children are slightly different from the adult bereavement process described above (Mahler, 1950). Following the initial sorrow that comes from separation, the child may be angry at life, or even at the

Death of a parent creates for children some intense emotional crises.

deceased parent, feeling it is unfair to be left behind. They may actually be ashamed that unlike their peers, they no longer have a mother or father. As with divorce, it is important to assure the child that his or her needs will continue to be met. It is also not uncommon for children to experience guilt, feeling that they were in some way responsible for the death. One adult therapy client carried guilt feelings around for a long time, thinking that if she had not been such a nuisance when she was a child, her mother would have paid more attention to her own deteriorating health, and her terminal cancer would have been discovered in time.

Telling children that a parent has died is not easy. Exactly what to say depends in part on the child's age. Younger children have different conceptions of death, considering it a deep sleep, which is reversible. As the child becomes older, the irreversibility of death is recognized, yet it seems to happen only to other people. For these reasons, a discussion about death may need to be somewhat tempered. However, psychologists and doctors generally agree that parents need to be honest (cf. Chess, 1979; Mahler, 1950). Children's anxiety is lessened if they know what is going on around them, and if they perceive that people are being truthful.

Preparing a child for death is important in those cases where death is not a sudden surprise. Even if an actual death is not imminent, a child's questions or observations concerning death should not be avoided. Children may not be able to comprehend everything told to them, or able to accept the finality of death, but they will be comforted by forthrightness and honesty in answers to their questions.

## CHRONIC ILLNESS

Chronic illnesses include asthma, arthritis, severe cardiac disease, sickle-cell anemia, muscular dystrophy, severe injuries, diabetes, kidney disease, leukemia, and cancer. The list could go on. And, although each one poses its special problems, they all have one similar impact upon the family of a child suffering from any of these—stress.

Stress occurs because sleep is interrupted, extra physical assistance is needed, special diets are necessary, housecleaning may be a larger chore, financial burdens increase, housing adaptations need to be made, education may need major innovations, and the parents' social isolation (as well as the child's) is increased.

As with special parenting situations (see Chapter 13), chronically ill children will require additional attention and care—attention and care that may strain parents and siblings. Ferrari (1984) found that, in the long run, siblings of chronically ill children are not at a greater risk of psychosocial impairment and maladjustment than siblings of healthy children. However, the shorter the time period following diagnosis of the chronic illness, and the older the child when first diagnosed, the harder it is for siblings to adjust. In effect, siblings require time to adjust to increased family strain and attention directed toward the ill child.

Chronically ill children may become depressed, withdrawn, or aggressive. In these cases, parents would do well to refrain from dealing with the overt behaviors (uncooperativeness, lethargy, disobedience, avoidance) but rather consider what the core of such behaviors are—feelings of helplessness, fear, anger, embarrassment, confusion. Only by doing so can the child be assisted in coping with his or her illness.

## Summary

Dealing with a child's emotions is not easy. Yet, when parents understand the development of emotions, and the innate and environmental contributors to emotional expression, dealing with various emotional tasks and crises is made easier. Parents will understand that some of their children's emotional expressions may be natural, innate responses, and therefore not justifiably punished or forbidden. At the same time, parents will understand that as their children's emotional reactions differentiate, these responses will mirror somewhat their own reactions. If a parent's emotions are fairly cool and "stuffed," the child learns to respond similarly.

Parents also do well to remember that the emotional reactions of young children are impulsive, and that delaying gratification is difficult. Punishing these tendencies can only lower self-esteem and create tendencies for children to withhold true feelings. In addition, emotional dependency, fears, and sexual curiosity and desires should be properly understood and dealt with by parents. Although a normal part of development, these emotional tasks may become problematic—as, for instance, when childhood fears become excessive. In this case, techniques such as systematic desensitization, observational learning, storytelling, and preparation can help reduce the fear.

In many children's lives, emotional crises beyond normal development require that parents take additional time and consideration in helping their children resolve internal conflicts. Divorce, death of a family member, and chronic illness may all produce emotional strain on children.

# SELF-CHECK

1. When discussing the origin of emotional expression we concluded that emotions:
   a. are inborn.
   b. are learned.
   c. are both inborn and influenced by learning.
   d. None of the above is true.
2. Babies under two years express their emotions in the following manner *except* for:
   a. simple or global expressions that are not yet specialized.
   b. intense emotional expression.
   c. impulsive emotional expression.
   d. All of the above are found in infant emotional expression.
3. Small children often lack impulse control when expressing emotions. Which of the following might be done to facilitate a child's impulse control when delaying gratification?
   a. Decrease the wait between when the reward is promised and when it is given.
   b. Help increase the child's confidence in his or her ability to acquire the reward.
   c. Don't let the child become preoccupied by thinking about something else during the waiting period.
   d. All of the above would facilitate delay of gratification.
   e. All of the above except for c would facilitate delay of gratification.
4. According to this chapter, which of the following is not an influence on emotional development?
   a. cultural demands transmitted through parents.
   b. parental example of emotional responses
   c. birth order
   d. child's physical health and intelligence
5. What does it mean to say that some children "stuff" their feelings?
   a. They hide their emotions.
   b. When asked what they are feeling, they call you a "turkey."
   c. They embellish their emotional expression.
   d. They refuse to cooperate when they are angry.
6. Which of the following is true of childhood fears?
   a. Children's fears are unrealistic and inappropriate to have.
   b. It is unnatural for children to have fears.
   c. As children develop, the object of their fears changes.
   d. Childhood fears should not be minimized by parental intervention.
7. Which of the following was *not* discussed as a method to deal with childhood fears?
   a. systematic desensitization
   b. time-out procedure
   c. observational learning
   d. storytelling

8. Sex education in the schools:
   a. should not replace parents' responsibility for teaching their own children.
   b. should always precede parent–child discussion.
   c. is not a good idea.
   d. Both a and b are correct.
9. When explaining divorce to children, Brooks (1981) recommended all *except* which of the following?
   a. Do not burden children with your own negative views of the other parent.
   b. Don't ask children to take sides.
   c. Engender some hope in the children that the marriage could work out.
   d. Do not put all the blame on the other parent.
10. How does a child's usual reaction to death differ from that of an average adult?
   a. The child may feel ashamed to be without a parent.
   b. The child may feel sorrowful.
   c. The child may feel extremely responsible for the death and therefore guilty.
   d. Both a and c are correct.

KEY: 1–c; 2–d; 3–e; 4–c; 5–a; 6–c; 7–b; 8–a; 9–c; 10–d

# PART
## ◦ VI ▫
# Changing Family Configurations

Throughout this text we have often referred to the family in a traditional manner. We have used terminology such as parents, mother and father, and brothers and sisters, all of which imply two parents and more than one child. Such a description suggests that the nuclear family predominates. However, the traditional family unit is rapidly declining and giving way to less traditional family configurations. In this section of the text we discuss different family configurations: single-parent households, teenage parenting, reconstituted or step-families, and foster parenting.

The optimal home climate and parental discipline techniques discussed prior to this point still apply: A loving, organized environment with a mixture of high- to low-power discipline techniques promotes positive child growth. However, parents in these less traditional family settings encounter unique problems. It is beneficial for such parents to become aware of and adapt to their unique situations.

# C H A P T E R 15

# SINGLE PARENTING

Single-parent households illustrate most dramatically the trend that the traditional two-parent home is shifting somewhat to other family configurations. According to the 1980 government census reports, 18 percent of all families are single-parent families—about one family in five. This figure varies across culture and ethnic group; nevertheless, single-parent families are not as atypical as many individuals would think. Estimates of the early 1980s suppose that two out of every five children born will live in a single-parent home for part of their childhood—approximately nine million American children (Vander Zanden, 1981). In a recent New Zealand study, it was found that by five years of age, about one child in eight experiences a family breakdown (Fergusson, Norwood, & Shannon, 1984).

Two-parent households, still the predominant family configuration in the United States, are not growing in number as rapidly as single-parent households. Moreover, female-headed families have grown much more rapidly than male-headed families. Of the nine million children estimated to live with only one parent, eight million are raised by mothers only—800,000 being raised by their fathers. The greatest increases in female-hardship cases have been among younger women and nonwhite families. Since 1960, nonwhite, female-headed families with children have grown twice as fast as their white counterparts (U.S. Bureau of the Census, 1974).

It is also pertinent to note the number of children in single-parent families. The same census reports estimate that 60 percent of female-headed families have children under 18, and that 25 percent have children under six. *About half the families rearing children under six are single-parent families.*

Loss of a parent, especially the father, is attributable to various causes: divorce, desertion, separation, death, and illegitimacy. The 1976 census reports on white female-headed families indicate that 32 percent were divorced, 14.6 percent were separated, 18.3 percent were not divorced though only one spouse was present, 39.4 percent were widowed, and 9.4 percent were unwed mothers. Data from seven U.S. national surveys conducted in the 1970s and 1980s indicate that some of the most significant correlates of divorce and separation are: being black, marrying young, infrequently or never attending religious services, having no religious preference, and living in large cities (Glenn & Supancic, 1984). It must also be pointed out, however, that approximately 50 percent of single parents remarry within five years; single parenthood is often a transient role for many adults.

## Problems of Single Parenthood

Being a single parent is not easy for a number of reasons. Some general difficulties pertain to both single mothers and single fathers. Others are more exclusive to one or the other. Smith (1980) states:

Single parents are often characterized as lonely and alone. This loneliness or social isolation is derived, in the first instance, from the very definition of one-parent family. The absence of one adult means limited human resources, less potential for emotional support within the household, and reduced possibilities for assistance with various household and child care tasks (p. 75).

## ROLE STRAIN

Both single mothers and single fathers experience *role strain* due to the additional responsibilities they accept. The mother is faced with duties that traditionally belonged to her husband; the father must be sure that duties his wife used to perform are taken care of—either by himself or by outside help. Needless to say, additional role strain as a parent is certainly felt.

More specifically, women find they must compensate for the absent father's child-rearing functions. Kriesberg (1970) found a shift among single-parent mothers toward a more authoritarian child-rearing pattern. These mothers felt the need to provide additional firmness and restrictiveness that was apparently her husband's function. Having no father in the home meant loss of an authoritative figure; whether the father was actually more authoritative, or whether his presence just seemed to provide that control, the now-single mother felt she needed to become more demanding and assertive with her children.

Kogelschatz, Adams, and Tucker (1972) found women to react in a variety of ways to single parenthood. Most seemed hostile and depressed about their loss (primarily due to divorce). None of the women expressed satisfaction with their daily circumstances when their husbands had been gone for more than two years. And they felt a certain dissatisfaction with frustrated dependency needs; these emotional needs were therefore directed toward their children and other immediate family to provide support and reassurance.

The single father also experiences role strain but of a different sort. He attempts to adjust to and juggle household management tasks that were previously his wife's. For many men, these are duties completely foreign to their repertoire of skills. Most often indicated as a major difficulty is meal preparation (Gasser & Taylor, 1976; Mendes, 1976). Many fathers quickly share such duties with children in the family; occasionally, the services of friends or hired help are employed. This delegating of responsibility is a possible reason that Gaylin (1977) found that although "juggling work and child care was difficult for all men, . . . most insisted that child care arrangements had not interfered with their jobs. . . . The men usually did their own housework, with help from their children."

Smith and Smith (1981) found that some fathers make the transition to single parenthood more easily than others. These are men who had actively participated in child rearing, had gained some understanding of child development, had participated in household management responsibilities, and had been involved in disciplining their children prior to becoming single.

Not all men, however, adjust as skillfully to their new circumstances. Consider the account of one widower found in Lindeman's (1976) article "Widower, Heal Thyself."

> Someone had to get a meal. That someone was me, a kitchen novice who, literally, had difficulty operating an electric can opener on his first several assaults. Someone also had to see about the laundry, do the shopping, balance the checkbook, make three sets of school lunches, drive the two younger children to school, pay the insurance, the real estate and income taxes, the mortgage, take the cat to the vet's, have the lawnmower fixed, argue with the roofer, attend the PTA meetings, sign the report cards, see about winter coats and boots, dental and doctor checkups, urge letters to grandmothers, and bedevil three children who weren't so confused and grief-stricken that they didn't know their own minds when it came to making beds, hanging up pajamas and clothes, and eating green vegetables. Given the opportunity, they would vote negative every time (p. 280).

## SOCIAL RESISTANCE

Women tend to face greater social resistance than men as they take on their new role. Orthner, Brown, and Ferguson (1976) conclude that single-parent men may seem less threatening to intact marriages than single-parent women. Men seem to generally receive a more positive social reaction. E. E. LeMasters (1977) summed up society's reaction to single mothers by stating: "They receive some sympathy, some respect, and some help, but they are also viewed as women who are not 'quite right'—they did not sustain their marriage 'until death do us part.'"

Marsden (1973) reports that single mothers feel they have little respect from neighbors. Similarly, Burgess (1970) found that many women felt out of touch with what was happening in society; their social activities declined, particularly with friends who were still married. Being single seemed to place a void between them and previous relationships. Men also experience a decline in their social activities, but tend to nevertheless report feeling satisfied and happy with their new role as single fathers. A lower degree of estrangement from society due to a more positive social opnion, as well as fewer financial problems, might be partially responsible for this difference in happiness with single-parent roles.

## FINANCIAL PROBLEMS

Finances differentially affect single-parent mothers and fathers. Esphenshade (1979) found that female-headed families had a disproportionately higher risk of being poor than male-headed families. The median income in 1977 for male-headed families was $17,517; the median income for female-headed families was $7,765. This contrast is even more powerful when one considers the fact that female-headed families comprised 14.4 percent of all families, whereas they accounted for 49.1 percent of all families in

Many single parents experience an abrupt decline in social activities and relationships.

poverty. Not only does divorce tend to reduce household income, but the drop tends to remain as long as the household is headed by a single mother (Weiss, 1984).

Some reasons why a single mother faces greater chances of poverty are more obvious than others. One not-so-obvious reason is the finding (Carter & Glick, 1970) that the probability of divorce, separation, or desertion is less likely as family income increases. This is not to suggest that poorer parents are less compatible, but family therapists have concluded that some of the strongest sources of marital conflict hinge upon inadequate communication. One major topic upon which lack of communication causes problems is financial difficulties. The lower-income family, then, is more likely to be faced with situations that cause communication problems to surface. Taking this reasoning to its conclusion means that the mother who was poor prior to divorce is more likely to be just as poor or poorer after her spouse is gone.

Child support has been built into the legal issue of divorce to prevent single-parent mothers from experiencing sudden drops in standard of living. However, many men either have no intention of keeping their agreement, or quickly find that supporting two separate households is not as easy as expected. Many men pay less than what was agreed upon during settlement,

Divorced mothers, often having had little or no prior job experience, may be forced to accept low-paying jobs with no benefits or security.

others pay nothing at all. Although ex-husbands are legally bound to continue being responsible for their families' financial welfare, the legal system lacks staffing and funds to enforce court orders for all complaints filed by divorced women. Many of these men are not to be found. Moreover, some women surprisingly refuse to report the ex-husband's negligence because of (1) fear that he might seek revenge, (2) hope that he might send the money soon, or (3) feeling that it wouldn't do any good anyway.

Women may have little or no job experience. This is especially true of women who married relatively young (out of high school) and/or have devoted their efforts to child rearing for a number of years before becoming single. They have not had as much education or practical experience as their male counterpart; many have never even considered a career. Due to this lack of specialized training or skills, they are forced to accept low-paying jobs that provide no benefits or security. "Even when women are well educated, they may be poorly prepared to earn a living" (Brooks, 1981, p. 287).

This differential emphasis on preparation and training, though changing somewhat today, is a product of the socialization process. Women have been reared to anticipate motherhood, and have not been trained, as men have, to select life goals and work toward them aggressively. In addition, a lack of independence and assertiveness makes it difficult for some to compete in the work force, or sometimes even to attempt full responsibility for the family.

## Difficulties of Single Fathers

Becoming a single parent creates some difficulties for men that are often not the case for women. Finkelstein and Rosenthal (1978) concluded that "the need to provide guidance and nurturance seemed to be more of a problem for the fathers than their entertainment and homemaking roles. Most fathers felt prepared to discipline or bathe their children but were less prepared for dealing with emotional upsets." Finkelstein and Rosenthal attributed this difficulty to the socialization process of males—that they are aided in developing instrumental skills but lack training in nurturance and child rearing. A study by Benjamin (1978) similarly reveals that a very crucial area to the welfare of children growing up in single-parent, male-headed families is the quality of emotional relationships between fathers and their children. In addition, fathers generally lack knowledge about normal child development, which becomes a difficulty when first becoming the only parent in the home.

Jody Gaylin (1977), from a set of surveys mentioned earlier, found that fathers with pre-adolescent daughters expressed concern about proper sex education. They worried about their ability to explain some of the most intimate aspects of life; they were also concerned about a lack of female role models to teach traditional feminine characteristics.

In spite of these initial difficulties dealing with the emotional aspects of their children, Gaylin reported that all of the men in her first survey reported close and affectionate rapport between themselves and their children. Two-thirds of the sample felt that their children were growing up much like children in two-parent households.

It is apparent, after considering difficulties confronting single-parent households, that the greatest burden is placed on female-headed families because of the greater financial burden they face. Although male-headed, single-parent families have inherent difficulties, the poverty-stricken, female-headed family is more likely to be scorned by society.

## Effects of Single-Parent Families on Children: Myths and Reality

Before considering possible side-effects on children of single-parent families, it is important to expose and resolve some common myths. It is commonly believed by some individuals that children growing up in such a home are necessarily psychologically and emotionally inferior. The statement of one college student whose parents have been divorced twice expresses this opinion: "Since a child derives his personality from both parents, a child with a single parent only derives half a personality." The tone of this statement is probably emotionally colored by negative experiences, not only of having one parent in the home, but also of conflict occurring before and after the process of divorce.

The authors of this text are not proposing that single-parent families are always as effective as two-parent families in meeting and dealing with problems and crises. However, we are also not maintaining that a certain psychological and/or emotional maladjustment is inherent in the single-parent family. Kempe and Kempe (1978) write that in their experience, "single parents are less abusive than couples, which is surprising because one would think that a spouse would provide support in the face of crisis. In fact, a spouse who is not supportive [may be] worse than no spouse at all when it comes to child rearing."

Dodson (1977) presents another myth which states that parents from intact homes naturally and inevitably do a better job raising their children. This myth disregards the fact that children go through the same developmental stages and create the same difficulties whether they have one or two parents in the home. Secondly, the discipline techniques presented earlier in this text apply equally well to children whether one or two parents provide that structure. In addition, researchers have found evidence to support the

Single parents need not fear that they cannot provide happy, warm environments for adequate child development just because they are single.

more realistic notion that intact families may be more effective in child rearing than single-parent families only when the intact family consists of two happily married and committed parents (Lamb, 1977; Nye, 1959; Sorosky, 1977).

With the destruction of these myths we can comfortably state that single parents need not feel all is lost. They will naturally experience unique problems; they may have to exert extra effort to prevent difficulties about which they normally would not have to worry; but they can provide adequate emotional and psychological support for their child's development.

The next half of this chapter will address possible risks to children of single-parent families, suggestions to help minimize these risks, and support systems that exist to help implement some of these suggestions.

## Father Absence and Its Effects

Many children grow up in father-absent homes, whereas few grow up with no mother substitute. The reason for this is twofold. First, the majority of divorce suits presently end up with the mother gaining child custody. Although the number of men who win custody is increasing, as is joint custody, women nonetheless end up with their children more often. Second, the single father is likely to bring in a female relative or hired help to assist in child care. Even day-care centers include predominantly female caretakers. Although these situations do not include the child's actual mother, maternal figures are present.

Perhaps one of the major issues involved in father absence is the effect it has on children. The myths we discussed previously concerning single-parent versus two-parent families have also been applied to the specific issue of father absence. In other words, many people feel that having a father in the home, no matter how inadequate he might be, is better than not having him there at all. However, children with *psychologically* absent fathers seem to be affected in much the same way as children whose fathers are *physically* absent (Blanchard & Biller, 1971; Hoffman, 1971).

Brooks (1981) mentions that preschool boys are affected more by separation from their fathers than older boys. Those separated at this early age tend to be "less aggressive, more dependent, and more feminine in interests and in self-concept" (Brooks, 1981). Rice (1979) similarly suggests that father absence removes a masculine influence and can cause difficulties for the male child. Boys have been found to be more dependent, less aggressive, and less competent in peer relationships when fathers were absent. Ostrovsky (1959) maintains that frequent absence of the father figure may be as detrimental to a daughter as it is to a son. Like the son, father absence limits her comprehension of the male role and how satisfactory emotional ties are developed with the opposite sex. It also limits her ability to compare herself with males, making her own role as a female less clear and more confusing. An adolescent girl may become anxious, shy, and inhibited; or, on the other hand, she may be too assertive, provocative, and somewhat promiscuous (Hetherington,

1972). In either case, a lack of adequate male role models may produce these difficulties.

Caution must be used in interpreting such results, however. First, negative effects on children may be due to difficulties in the home that existed prior to separation from the father. As noted before, psychological absence produces effects similar to physical absence of a father. Subsequent absence of the father might not cause dependency, shyness, or provocativeness; rather, it only appears that way. Second, the mother's attitude toward the husband and her ability to cope with being single might also be critical. Many divorced mothers are likely to be unhappy, angry toward their husbands, and have lowered self-esteem. From the child's perspective, such feelings might aid in engendering confusion and/or fear concerning the male or female roles. Third, one must not suppose that father absence cannot be compensated for—problems can be overcome and adequate male role models can be obtained. (See Chapter 11 on modeling for help in compensating for parent absence.)

## Coping with Single Parenthood

A magical set of directions for single parenting does not exist. In essence, attributes that make single parents effective are those attributes that make parents in two-parent households effective. "Good" parenting requires patience, love, empathy, and unselfishness, regardless of the family configuration.

### CONSIDERING THE CHILDREN

If loss of a parent is due to separation or divorce, it is important that children know they were not the cause of marital breakup. Small children especially, not understanding what is going on, may feel they have personally done something to cause the situation; or, they may feel personally rejected by a parent's leaving. Young children might not understand all the details, and precise explanations may not be important. They need to understand, however, in whatever way, that they are not responsible.

Many individuals have done remarkable jobs in raising their children alone. As was indicated earlier, the absence of one parent need not cause a confused gender role or inadequate emotional development. The parent may be missed, but negative side-effects are not necessary, especially if a partial substitute can be arranged. In the case of an absent father, for example, uncles, grandfathers, or mature family members may be able to provide the structure, support, and example that are lacking due to absence of the original father. "The son of separated or divorced mothers should have frequent opportunities to meet adult males. Most cities have groups like 'Fathers at Large' or Big Brothers—who enjoy taking boys on weekend outings or to sports events" (Stuart, 1981).

## CONSIDERING SELF

Single parents also need to understand that in spite of their added responsibilities, they must continue to consider their own needs. Taking time out for oneself is often overlooked by single parents, especially the single mother. Many single mothers, unlike single fathers, have not built a part of their social life and personal satisfaction around an occupation. Whereas the male has devoted much of his energy toward his job, and may have derived personal satisfaction and established relationships, the female sometimes begins work only upon becoming single. As a result, personal satisfaction and work relationships are not immediately available.

Social assertiveness is also more difficult for single women due to societal attitudes that, on the one hand, classify the male as responsible for pursuing relationships, and, on the other hand, stigmatize the single mother as being more inadequate than single fathers. It follows then, that single women may be at greater social and occupational disadvantage, both avenues of which provide a sense of belonging and accomplishment. As a result, the single mother needs to consider all the more seriously her own needs. Ricci (1980) counsels single parents to set aside "adult time" from their numerous parental responsibilities, because the renewal they receive is likewise passed on to their children.

Brooks (1981) also identified three main tasks of single parents, one of which is to re-establish an active social life with persons of the opposite sex. Social stimulation is important for single parents. Children will not regret sharing their parent a few hours each week.


## SINGLE-PARENT SKILLS

Brooks (1981) enumerated parenting techniques that single parents need to strengthen. Perhaps most obvious is the fact that previously "nontraditional" responsibilities need developing. Fathers need to develop sympathy, warmth, and patience in dealing with their children's personal problems—a skill that perhaps had been the wife's responsibility. Mothers may need to develop more authoritative attitudes to aid in discipline and settling of familial conflicts.

Single parents must also "help children develop increased competencies" (Brooks, 1981). They will need to rely more heavily on older children to help with household chores and keep the family unit functioning. Responsibility needs to be developed and distributed among all family members old enough to contribute.

Notice, however, that many of these recomendations are also desirable for two-parent families. Empathic fathers, mothers competent in disciplining, and responsible children who share household duties are considered advantageous in any family.

Single parenting can be successful and rewarding, as evidenced by this example given in one parenting class:

*I know a mother of four who had been divorced. She wanted to raise her children right. Yet, she also knew she needed to find a job so they could have the needed income. She was torn between leaving the home to work and staying with her children.*

*She did a fine job. So that the time she was at home was quality time, she set the goal to try to leave any occupational problems at work. She talked with her children about house chores, so each member of the household would help. Then she determined to have Saturdays free to do something with her children—either all at once or individually.*

*On one occasion, I asked her 15-year-old daughter what it was like to have her mother begin working. She said, "We've never been so close," and she went on to tell me all the little things her mother does that really count. She said, "I'm sure there are kids who really aren't sure if their parents love them or not. I know how much my mother loves me, and it's great to know that."*

## Support Systems for One-Parent Families

Community support systems are often helpful in assisting adults to make the transition to single parenthood. Organizations such as Parents Without Partners (PWP) exist in many large, urban settings. Robert Weiss (1973; found in Bigner, 1979) identified four types of support that PWP in particular provides.

1. PWP acts as a sustaining community. This organization accepts single parents and promotes social activities for single adults and their families. It provides an opportunity to find companionship and to draw on the experiences of others.
2. The organization brings people together who share common concerns. The friendships created provide emotional as well as situational support for single parents.
3. The organization promotes a sense of personal growth by recognizing members' service to PWP.
4. PWP also provides a means for establishing a new emotional attachment to others.

Some single parents receive support and growth from therapy groups conducted by local mental health centers or organizations similar to PWP. Such groups, if requiring any fee at all, are usually provided on sliding fee schedules, depending on a person's ability to pay.

Of course, a great percentage of support usually comes from immediate family and friends. Some single mothers live with parents or grandparents.

Some single parents receive support in therapy or other community-support groups.

Hope and Young (1976) recommend bartering services and pooling resources with friends, especially with similar single-parent families. Cooperative babysitting groups or shared apartments or homes, for example, save money and provide social and emotional support for children and parents.

One particular community-based service for single parents (Groller, 1981) illustrated below is a unique program that may serve as a blueprint for future programs.

> Warren Village, housed in an apartment building in Denver's Capitol Hill area, is a transitional community designed to help single parents like Sandy make a fresh start. The residents are primarily women with children under twelve, very little income, and not much in the way of marketable skills. The community provides inexpensive housing, day-care facilities, family and career counseling, and mutual support until residents acquire the job skills, practical know-how, and confidence they need to secure a good life for themselves and their children. There's room for 93 families at one time, and the average stay is twelve to fifteen months (p. 66).
>
> . . . In offering these programs and services the staff is careful not to cross the fine line between providing support and encouraging dependency . . . (p. 68). Of course not all problems disappear when a single parent moves to Warren Village. In spite of the community's support, Jeannine says, "It's hard being a mother and student and a housekeeper. I may be exhausted at the end of the day and then be up all night doing

the laundry. There just aren't enough hours in the day, and I never have enough energy . . ." (p. 69).

That feeling of not being alone—and therefore an oddball—is a very important aspect of life at Warren Village. "A single parent is not perceived as normal," Tria says. "Marriage is the norm, and the single parent is considered to be between marriages. Well, some of our parents have *chosen* not to be married. They're not necessarily searching for another partner. Part of what Warren Village does is to let them feel okay about that" (p. 69).

One serious concern to these authors is that, as presently constituted, the single parent is not accepted as a legitimate role in contemporary society. She or he is an abnormality who must assume the dual role of full-time home-maker and provider. This unreasonable expectation was expressed by a mother quoted in a Canadian report on single parents:

> I would like to see the pressure taken off of single parents, especially mothers, to go out and work. To my way of thinking they have, if they so desire, a very large and important job right at home. It would be more beneficial to society for them to stay at home and be a real mother to the children as in the end it is the children who lose, not having the security of either parent. However, the way our social system is arranged, one almost has no choice. It happens that we are encouraged by almost all agencies to go out and work. Make more money. Buy, buy, buy. Give lots of material things to your kids and forget all about their emotional needs. For those of us who refuse, we sacrifice even the price of a pair of shoes in order to have a house full of love, and emotional happiness. I think as well there should be some kind of 'Dr. Spock' written just for us, to help us know and understand our questionable periods (Guyatt, 1971; cited in Schlesinger, 1975, p. 22).

## Summary

Single-parent households are on the rise, and it behooves our society to become more familiar with single parenthood, its problems, effects, and pos-sibilities. First, single parents experience role strain due to the additional, and often "nontraditional," parenting duties they adopt when becoming a single parent. Single mothers, however, are more prone to this strain, as single fathers often delegate newly acquired household duties to someone else.

Social resistance is also experienced by single parents—society still regards these parents as somewhat of a failure and outcast. Again, however, single mothers face such resistance more strongly than single fathers.

A third problem of single parenthood is financial difficulties. We con-tinue to see the single mother on the bad end. Financial difficulties in the single-parent household are much more severe and prolonged if it is headed by a single female as opposed to single male.

In spite of the many myths regarding single-parent families, children from these families are not necessarily psychologically and socially inferior to children of intact, two-parent households. Effects of father absence can be overcome and improvisations within the family can be made to ensure proper growth. The conscious emphasis on the expression of love, development of organization, and appropriate use of disciplinary techniques is just as beneficial to children in one-parent as two-parent homes.

# SELF-CHECK

1. Most single mothers experience all of the following difficultues *except:*
   a. negative social reactions.
   b. inability to provide guidance and nurturance.
   c. role strain.
   d. financial problems.
2. Most single fathers experience difficulties that are slightly different from those of single mothers. Which of the following would a single father most likely experience?
   a. negative social reactions
   b. inability to provide guidance and nurturance
   c. role strain
   d. financial problems
3. Which of the following is true of single-parent families?
   a. Individuals growing up in these homes are generally psychologically and emotionally inferior.
   b. Parents from intact homes inevitably do a better job than single parents.
   c. Both of the above are true.
   d. Neither of the above is true.
4. Which of the following is *not* true concerning father-absent families?
   a. More children grow up in father-absent homes than in mother-absent homes.
   b. Not having a father is always worse on a child's development than having one.
   c. Preschool boys are affected more by father absence than older boys.
   d. a and c are not true.
5. Brooks (1981) identified several tasks of single parents. Which of the following is *not* one of these tasks?
   a. Develop parenting skills that may have previously been nontraditional.
   b. Help children increase competency in household tasks and responsibilities.
   c. Put personal interests temporarily aside to prevent family failure.
   d. Re-establish an active social life with the opposite sex.
6. Which of the following is *not* true of single-parent families?
   a. One-parent households are the predominant family configuration in the United States.
   b. Female-headed families have grown more rapidly than male-headed families.
   c. About half the families rearing children under six are single-parent families.
   d. Single parenthood is often a transient role for many adults.
7. Divorced women face financial difficulties because:
   a. they usually have more children than single fathers with children.
   b. they may have little or no prior job experience.
   c. they must pay child support.

8. Some fathers make the transition to single parenthood more easily than others because they:
   a. had previously gained some understanding of child development.
   b. had previously participated in household management responsibilities.
   c. had previously been involved in disciplining their children.
   d. All of the above are true.

Key: 1–b; 2–b; 3–d; 4–b; 5–c; 6–a; 7–b; 8–d

# CHAPTER 16

# TEENAGE PARENTING

Not only does research suggest that individuals marrying at young ages have increased difficulties and a greater chance of marital dissolution, but most individuals, when asked their personal opinion, would probably state it similarly. Unfortunately, however, too many young people marry and become parents before growing up. One of our students wrote the following about a couple she knew:

*This particular teenage couple is still growing up while trying to help their children grow and mature. The couple depends greatly on the husband's parents and family. Their two children are quite undisciplined, rarely being reprimanded for inappropriate behavior. Of course, the complicating factor is that the father works out of town during the week and is home with the children only on weekends. It also appears that this young couple does not have much patience with their children.*

*When with the father's family, whether the father is present or not, it seems they almost relinquish responsibilities of their kids to grandparents, aunts, and uncles, rarely interacting with their own children until they go home alone.*

*They have been separated but are together now trying to make their marriage work.*

## Scope of the Teenage-Parenting Problem

Between 1973 and 1978, a 13-percent increase in teenage pregnancies occurred. In 1978 alone, 1.1 million teenagers became pregnant. Of these pregnancies, only 17 percent were postmaritally conceived, 22 percent resulted in out-of-wedlock births, 10 percent were legitimated births (though premaritally conceived), 38 percent were aborted, and 13 percent miscarried. In every adolescent age group pregnancies increased, although increases were smallest for the younger age groups (under 15 years of age). Among whites, one in 11 teenagers will become pregnant, while among nonwhites the figure is one in five (Alan Guttmacher Institute, 1981).

However, this increase in teenage pregnancy and birth is slowing, and in more recent years the birthrate is declining somewhat (United States Bureau of the Census, 1984). This slowing of teenage births is believed to be due to: (1) increased abortion rates; and (2) better use of contraceptives among sexually active adolescents. Nevertheless, teenage births accounted for 39.1 percent of all live births in the United States in 1981. This figure is not merely a result of illegitimate children or pregnancies leading to marriage; studies correlating age at marriage to birth of the first child have shown that the younger a couple is upon marrying, the sooner they will have children (Rice, 1979). However, a large proportion of high-school marriages are likely the result of pregnancy.

One reason for early marriage was indicated by one couple who married because both wanted to leave stressful family environments. Wedlock to them was a way to escape arguments and to exercise independence. Similar reasons include getting married to satisfy dependency needs, or to make the desired transition to adulthood. Of course, feelings for each other are also a basis for such decisions. However, impatience and a limited understanding of one's needs may contribute to the decision to marry early.

A number of studies have investigated personal and family background variables that might be correlated with teenage pregnancy (Abernathy & Abernathy, 1974; Brunswick, 1971; Goldfarb, Mumford, Shurn, Smith, Flowers, & Shum, 1977; Gottschalk, Titchener, Piker, & Stewart, 1964; Kaplan, Smith, & Pokorny, 1974; Zongker, 1977). However, results are somewhat conflicting, possibly due to certain methodological errors in research design (Ralph, Lochman, & Thomas, 1984). Ralph and his associates subsequently performed a more controlled study by comparing pregnant and nulliparous (nonpregnant) 15- and 16-year-old black women at an adolescent clinic. They found that pregnant teenagers had less defined and optimistic vocational goals; their mothers had less education; they received later sex education; they had more brothers; and they had better family adjustment. Apparently, teenagers with (1) less knowledge of sexual behavior and (2) frequent, close contact with male peers (brothers) are less likely to avoid situations putting them at risk for pregnancy.

## Options with Teenage Pregnancy

Let's consider the most common circumstances behind teenage pregnancy—the type that is unplanned or unwanted, with the mother being single. In 1980, 43 percent of teenage births were illegitimate ("Population Trends," 1981). Three basic alternatives are available: The woman can have an abortion; she can carry the child to term and put it up for adoption; or she may raise the child herself. Each one of these alternatives has psychological costs. Many women who choose abortions under these circumstances carry with them feelings of guilt. This guilt may be self-imposed or felt as a result of societal expectations. In any case, thoughts such as, "I wonder what he/she would have been like?" or "Have I been the cause of a death?" sometimes continue for long periods of time.

A second option is to carry the child to term and then put it up for adoption. However, the actual process of giving the child away is usually much harder than earlier supposed. The young mother has experienced much during pregnancy and a certain attachment is made. Following the actual birth, seeing her baby squirming and crying often does something to change a mother's decision concerning adoption. If the woman does not change her mind about adoption, emotional loss may be felt when the child is taken. For this reason, some women prefer to not see their baby following the birth.

A third alternative is the decision to raise the child. Many factors may enter into such a decision. Steinhoff (1978) interviewed a number of pre-maritally pregnant women at the time of delivery and found that many chose to continue pregnancy and to keep the baby because they perceived parenthood as a source of direction in their lives, not as a limitation of opportunities. Becoming a mother was, to them, an attainment of adult social status. Many of the reasons for having children (discussed in Chapter 1) apply when teenagers decide to keep their own children, as is evidenced by Steinhoff's (1978) findings.

Some young mothers keep their children out of a sense of responsibility—they should be responsible for their actions; others feel they deserve the problems of raising a child; others feel that a child may be one of the few things on earth they can love. One woman who worked very closely with young, unmarried mothers found that many girls risk pregnancy because even physical comfort coming from someone else, through sex, no matter how short in duration, temporarily satisfies a deep longing to be loved and wanted. The idea of being a mother to a dependent, helpless baby might also meet such needs.

It was briefly suggested that decisions to have an abortion or to put a child up for adoption are not without psychological costs. The same is also true with the decision to keep and raise a baby. Some of the problems teenage mothers face will now be considered.

# Problems of Teenage Mothers
## LACK OF SOCIAL SUPPORT

Perhaps one of the greatest problems teenage parents face is found in this quote by Lewis and Lewis (1980): "The greatest enemy of young marriages is the fact that from the beginning we anticipate their failure. Almost no one—neither the friends of the young couple, nor their parents, teachers and employers—expect a very young marriage to grow in stability and happy mutuality."

Social ostracism is particularly evident if the teenage parent is not married. Lewis and Lewis (1980) continue by suggesting that teenage parents are pushed into a limbo state; they are no longer treated as children, yet they are also not granted full adult status.

If social rejection were not so bad, maybe the early transition to parenthood would not be as difficult. This transition to parenthood is often a troublesome one in any marriage. When children are brought into any home, adjustments in lifestyle are necessary, many of which are not anticipated. Imagine how much more difficult this transition is when, on top of the diffi-

Teenage mothers face possible social ostracism, especially if unmarried.

culties to be discussed next (psychosocial immaturity, financial problems), the teenage parent feels rejected by society.

## UNDEVELOPED PERSONAL IDENTITY

Many teenagers up to 17 and 18 are still searching for an identity. Erik Erikson's "identity crisis" is probably the most frequently quoted term when referring to adolescent development. If this stage of psychosocial development is complicated by pregnancy and possible marriage, an inability to establish stable gender and occupational roles may result. A stable identity, understanding and wisdom, maturity—or whatever it is termed—seem to be a product of certain experiences resulting, in part, from the aging process. Robert Blood (1969) in his book *Marriage* states:

> For the average person, maturity comes automatically with growing up. It is produced by socialization in the family, dating, school, and work. It is accelerated by service overseas, in the Peace Corps or in the military. But regardless of experience, age is a rough index of maturity.
>
> The later people marry, the lower the divorce rate, especially after age 21. . . . Although younger-than-average marriages do not automatically fail, they face extra hazards which make extra maturity imperative. Couples marrying earlier than usual need to be more precociously mature than their contemporaries if their marriages are to survive (pp. 163–164).

So, in a general sense, many teenage parents have not had the opportunity to develop a certain maturity that helps them endure marital and parental obstacles and difficulties. Early parenthood also interferes with completion of school and economic self-support. These interruptions can and often do produce problems concerning finances, living quarters, and child-rearing decisions.

## FINANCIAL DIFFICULTIES

Education and economic security are often closely related. A parent or couple with less education will generally experience greater financial difficulties. If the young couple is married, or if the unmarried mother is receiving some aid from the father, education is often interrupted to provide financial support. Unless the father is highly skilled in a particular trade, lack of education prevents an income substantial enough to support the three family members—perhaps one reason why statistics often show couples marrying young to have a higher divorce rate. Reduced educational attainment and subsequent work in lower-status and lower-paying jobs also characterize teenage mothers (Lowe & Witt, 1984; Roosa & Vaughan, 1984). Furstenberg (1976) has studied the effects of unscheduled teenage parenthood on the life course. His data suggest that economic strains along with disruption of the courtship process help explain these higher divorce rates.

Also contributing to financial insecurity is the "minimal time unmarried mothers have had in which to gain work experience prior to motherhood" (Presser, 1980). Presser's study focused on 69 unmarried mothers who were interviewed three times over a period of four years. Also interviewed were 241 mothers who were already married when delivering their first child. "Less than half of the unmarried mothers had ever worked for pay" (Presser, 1980). Whereas three-fourths of the married mothers were working for pay when they became pregnant with their first child, only about one-third of the unmarried mothers were doing so.

In addition to the low economic potential many young fathers possess,

Financial difficulties and inadequate housing arrangements are prevalent among teenage parents.

it was pointed out above that many unmarried mothers also have low economic potential. In their case, being unmarried is a double handicap, as they do not have a husband to share economic responsibilities. Although the father may help support the mother even though not married to her, Presser (1980) found that only 38 percent of unmarried mothers in her study received any child support at all.

Based on interviews with these mothers, two factors seemed to influence whether the father contributed financially: his desire to marry the child's mother, and whether the father had graduated from high school. If a father wanted to marry the child's mother, he was about 20 percent more likely than all other fathers to contribute to the child's support. Regarding education of the father, 45 percent of high school graduates had contributed to the child's support, whereas only 18 percent of the nongraduates had done so (Presser, 1980). Results suggest that fathers who are better able to give financial assistance are more likely to do so.

It is evident that many unmarried mothers do not receive adequate support through personal efforts and assistance from the child's father. Two additional sources of economic aid are therefore heavily used, parental and public assistance. Sixty-five percent of unmarried mothers in Presser's study reported they had received direct financial support from their parents. Teenage pregnancies also frequently involve efforts and assistance from grandparents. Public assistance is often necessary regardless of whether the mother receives economic support from the child's father or from her own parents. Again, Presser (1980) found that 86 percent of unmarried mothers in her study were residing in households receiving public assistance.

Financial difficulties are prevalent among teenage parents. When considering that financial problems may be implicated in the separation of couples in any family, it is no wonder that so many early marriages, comparatively speaking, result in divorce. And it is no wonder that so many pregnant teenagers do not get married in the first place—the father's inability to meet financial responsibilities makes marriage quite often too awesome an undertaking.

## Living Arrangements

The most common patterns of residence found among 320 young mothers (mostly blacks) were grouped into four categories: (1) those young mothers who remained with their own parents; (2) those who moved out when becoming pregnant in order to marry; (3) those who left home to establish an independent household; and (4) those who returned home after being married and subsequently divorced (Furstenberg, 1980). The percent of mothers in each of these four categories was approximately 29, 24, 15, and 11 percent, respectively. According to this study, almost half of teenage parents end up living with their own parents. When including any relatives, approximately 77 percent of the mothers were living with parents or relatives one year after delivery (Furstenberg, 1980).

One reason for the large number of teenage mothers living with relatives stems from financial difficulties, previously discussed. Too many young mothers simply cannot afford to make it on their own. This is the case even when married; 43 percent of the currently married mothers were also living with relatives one year after delivery (Furstenberg, 1980). Furstenberg found that age was not an important factor in making the decision to remain at home. Rather, the decision to continue with school was. If the mother continued her education after becoming a parent, she was significantly more likely to live with parents than those who dropped out of school.

## Raising the Child of a Teenage Parent

We have discovered that many teenage parents remain unmarried, and that mothers rely heavily on their own families for economic support and living arrangements. It might also be anticipated that relatives would participate heavily in caring for the new infant. Consider the example given by a student in a parenting class:

*Annette was 15 when she had her first baby. She wanted to raise him, but her parents wanted to adopt him instead. Her parents ended up adopting the baby, and Annette was sworn to secrecy. The baby was never to know she was his real mother. Annette lived at home during the next four years and more or less raised him with her mother. When they had disputes over discipline, Annette's mother usually got her way. She wanted to spoil the child, but Annette wanted him to learn that he couldn't always have his way.*

Although an extreme, it is not improbable that the above example might occur. A teenage parent's mother often spends considerable effort in helping to raise the child; a closeness and process of attachment are often inevitable. Referring again to Harriet Presser's study (1980), among the never-married mothers who were working or going to school, 77 percent relied primarily on relatives to watch preschool-age children. At the time of the third interview, three years later, 56 percent were still taking advantage of relatives' services. The most common helper was the teenage mother's own mother.

This assistance in child care is probably responsible for the push that some mothers feel toward living at home. Moving out of a parent's home not only reduces economic assistance in the form of room and board, but also reduces the chance that relatives are available to help care for the child (Furstenberg, 1980).

## Consequences of Teenage Parenting

What are the consequences of early parenthood? It was previously noted that early marriage more frequently leads to divorce. We also understand that early parenthood often involves only one parent, and that financial difficulties are prevalent. But what are long-term effects on the child, if any?

Various studies reveal contradictory findings on this issue. Philip Rice (1984), for example, in his text *The Adolescent: Development, Relationships, and Culture* writes:

Because both premarital pregnancy and early postmarital pregnancy are followed by a higher than average divorce rate, large numbers of children of early marriages grow up without a secure, stable family life or without both a mother and a father. Apparently, many young marrieds are simply not mature enough to assume the responsibilities of both marriage and early parenthood, so that the marriages often fail and the children suffer.

Many teenagers are still insecure, oversensitive, and somewhat tempestuous and unstable. Many are still rebelling against adult authority and seeking emotional emancipation from parents. If these youths marry, they carry their immaturities into marriage, making it difficult to adjust to living with their mate and making it harder to make decisions and solve conflicts as they arise (p. 415).

Furstenberg (1976), however, writes:

> Our results showed little variation in maternal adjustment and childrearing practices according to age at onset of parenthood, feelings about the pregnancy, socioeconomic status, and degree of maternal involvement. . . . It is also possible that the significance of these factors has been overrated somewhat and that the capacity of the young parent to respond adaptively to the challenge of parenthood has been underrated (p. 193).

One student related an experience fitting Furstenberg's results:

*Frank and I married very young—he was 18 and I was just 16. But look at us. We have a big, beautiful family that we certainly can be proud of. . . .*

Teenage parenting can be successful; it need not be disastrous although it may be difficult. The above example, while indicating that being married at a young age is not always a failure, nevertheless continues:

*And answering your question about whether or not I would choose the same course is very difficult; but I would have to say that if I had to decide again I would wait—for the simple reason that it is too risky. Knowing what I know now, I feel that it's so much better to wait until you are more emotionally mature and have a better grip on what life's all about. . . .*

A summary of the literature suggests that, although teenage parenting is fraught with greater difficulties than parenting at later ages, it is, nevertheless, not destined to be a failure, as evidenced in the student example just provided. In fact, according to Philliber and Graham (1981), rather than age, the mother's socioeconomic status, particularly whether or not she receives welfare, seems to be more important. The longer the mother was on welfare, the more likely she was to be less emotionally and verbally responsive to her children, the more likely to spank her children more, and to be unable to avoid restriction and punishment. The reasons for this correlation are, at present, unknown. Perhaps those mothers having greater financial difficulties and, therefore, on welfare for long periods of time likewise receive less family support and suffer more severely in a psychological and emotional sense. This

Teenage parenting can be successful; it need not be disastrous although it may be difficult.

suffering may reflect a preoccupation with isolation and helplessness, thereby causing the mother to neglect serious consideration of her parenting responsibilities.

Children of younger mothers, in comparison to children of older mothers, have been shown to have: (1) more physical, emotional, and intellectual handicaps (Menken, 1972; Sugar, 1976); poorer educational attainment (Davie, Butler, & Goldstein, 1972); and poorer verbal and behavioral skills (Wadsworth, Taylor, Osborn, & Butler, 1984). Teenage mothering can be detrimental, it would seem, to child development. These negative effects are likely due to reduced maternal involvement and stimulation of the child, strain from financial difficulties, inadequate knowledge of child development, and personal immaturities.

A teenager's knowledge of infant development is another possible influencer of child outcome. In general, this knowledge is deficient (Epstein, 1979; Roosa & Vaughan, 1984). Adolescent females were particularly deficient in their knowledge of cognitive, social, and language development. Typically, adolescents have not read as extensively as older first-time mothers, nor do they have married friends who can share some of their experience. Marion Howard (1975) relates what she feels is one of the major drawbacks of such ignorance:

> Young parents, in particular, are often [overly] concerned about having a "spoiled" child. A child cannot be spoiled by answering to its legitimate needs. Indeed, more problems will result if the child's cries are misunderstood or ignored. . . . Knowledge of the reasons for a child's behavior can help the parent get through . . . stages with more patience and understanding (p. 206–207).

Delivery of the first child finds tense, bewildered parents feeling inadequate in their roles as providers. What do you do when the infant won't stop crying? How do you know when he or she is hungry, is tired, or needs a diaper change? These questions can be extremely anxiety-provoking for inexperienced teenage parents. Howard (1978) states that recent evidence suggests very young parents are likely to abuse or neglect their children—strains of early child rearing are intense.

Summarizing this section on consequences of early child rearing, we can conclude that the teenage parent faces increased financial and emotional difficulties, compared with other parents. These difficulties are not just a reflection of age, but of maturity, economic resources of the family of origin as well as the parents' own income, knowledge concerning child development, and help with child care. Teenage parenting may be successful or unsuccessful, but the odds are against these young adults.

## Support Systems

*A friend of mine was almost 18 and had a two-year-old son. She was not married and lived with her parents. She worked every day to support herself and the baby, and seemed to enjoy raising her child; she was happy. Having a child has helped her mature and changed her outlook on life. She feels good that it happened to her, for she has grown so much and has started back on the right path.*

*I think she got married two years later. I feel she was successful because her family has supported her emotionally, physically, and financially. She also has a strong religious conviction, which has given her hope.*

This young girl was fortunate because of the support she received. To make the best of a difficult situation, young parents need all the support they can get. Accepting, patient parents are perhaps the major factor in proper adjustment of a teenage parent and her infant. Unwed mothers who continue to live at home are assisted financially and have a greater chance of continuing their education. In addition, the infant has a better chance of receiving adequate discipline, love, and acceptance.

Increased involvement of teenage fathers in their children's well-being also produces positive results. Parke, Power, and Fisher (1980) determined that fathers can influence their infants' development in both direct and indirect ways. Paternal involvement in routine caretaking activities, father–infant interaction, and responsiveness to the child's needs all increase the likelihood that the child will be socially adjusted.

## Summary

The number of teenage parents is increasing. Although these family units are not destined to fail, they nevertheless face additional difficulties that threaten family stability and child development. Some of the difficulties teenage mothers face are social ostracism, undeveloped personal identities, and financial difficulties. Financial difficulties are especially prevalent, as inexperience and truncated educations preclude employment sufficient to provide for a family.

Because of the many difficulties teenage parents face, they often choose to live with parents, who provide both financial and social support. If teenage mothers receive financial and moral support from parents and the child's father, parenting success is more likely. However, in general, children of young mothers have been found to have intellectual, emotional, physical, and behavioral deficits.

*My brother was married at 19; his wife was 15. She had her first child at 17, and nobody expected the marriage to work. But maturity comes quickly when it is forced upon a young couple. To everyone's pleasant surprise, their son brought with him a great increase in their maturity. They are excellent parents, happily married, and will soon celebrate their third anniversary. The marriage worked due to support from the family and a true love between the two partners.*

# S E L F - C H E C K

1. Which population segment is having the smallest increase in pregnancies?
   a. girls under 15 years of age
   b. girls 15 to 19 years of age
   c. girls above 20 years of age
   d. divorced mothers

2. Which of the following factors is a reason mentioned in the text that many teenage mothers decide to keep and raise an illegitimate child?
   a. They developed a certain attachment to the baby during pregnancy
   b. They feel a sense of responsibility.
   c. They feel they deserve the problems of raising a child.
   d. All of the above are good reasons.
   e. All of the above except for c are good reasons.
3. Which of the following is *not* true of teenage mothers?
   a. Many experience social ostracism.
   b. Many are supported by their boyfriends.
   c. Many are still searching for an identity.
   d. Many experience financial difficulties.
4. Of the following patterns of residence found among young mothers, which *two* patterns are most common?
   a. those remaining with their parents
   b. those who, upon discovery of pregnancy, are moving out to marry
   c. those leaving home to establish an independent household
   d. those returning home after being married and subsequently divorced
5. Which of the following is most important in determining the success of teenage parenting?
   a. The teenage mother's socioeconomic status
   b. The teenage mother's knowledge of infant development
   c. Maturity prior to parenthood
   d. The number of previous children
6. Contributing to the financial insecurities teenage mothers face are all the following *except:*
   a. reduced educational attainment
   b. little work experience
   c. low occupational potential
   d. inability to obtain welfare assistance
7. Which of the following is true concerning teenage mothers?
   a. Many remain unmarried.
   b. Many rely on their own families for economic support and living arrangements.
   c. Relatives participate in caring for the new infant.
   d. All of the above are true.
8. Children of younger mothers, in comparison to children of older mothers, have been shown to have:
   a. an equal number of physical, emotional, and intellectual handicaps.
   b. poorer educational attainment.
   c. better verbal skills.

KEY: 1–a; 2–d; 3–b; 4–a,b; 5–a; 6–d; 7–d; 8–b

# CHAPTER 17

# STEPPARENTING

Single parenting is for most a transient state. It has been estimated that 75 percent of divorced or widowed single parents remarry within three to five years (Wald, 1981), creating a situation that itself presents a unique set of expectations, problems, and coping techniques—stepparenting.

Fear and insecurity can cause children to react in ways that frustrate new stepparents. These children and their new parent may have a difficult time adjusting to one another for many reasons. For example, absence of an infancy period—when early love bonds between parent and child can develop—make it harder for the foster parent to tolerate frustrations and irritations that children will always present. In addition, with each passing year, parents and children become more set in their ways. The reconstituted family may find it harder to instigate change.

This chapter will look at the problems reconstituted families face, the natural development of a stepparent, helpful suggestions when assuming the role of stepparent, how to live with differences in the new family, and some solutions to problems that stepparents face.

This section is written to be a practical and insightful guide for stepparents. Obviously, a simple listing of problems would not be helpful; the emphasis is on how to effectively meet the challenge of creating a fully functioning and delightful reconstituted family. The first task is to look at how expectations influence reception of a new parent.

## Negative Expectations

From the beginning of remarriage, the child–stepparent relationship faces inherent difficulties, which can and should be overcome. In fact, more important than the quality of the marital relationship to family happiness is the quality of step-relationships (Crosbie-Burnett, 1984). It behooves stepparents, then, to consider closely the difficulties and negative expectations coming with stepparent–child relationships, and how these problems can be best overcome.

### EXPECTATIONS BASED ON THE PAST

How a person views life is more fundamental than what life really is. A stepparent's humor, orders, requests, and detailing of rules will evoke different reactions in different children because each has unique perceptions and expectations. Conversely, changes within a parent can cause him or her to perceive children's actions differently on each of two days.

A new stepfather told me, "It hardly seems to matter how I try to deal with Danny. He's been so scarred by hearing his own father yell at his mother that he won't let me near him." A stepmother commented sadly, "Even after four years, there is still so much bitterness between Ed and his first wife, so much that is still 'unfinished business,' that my stepson, Alex, can't settle down and accept the fact that I'm part of his life. His attention is still focused on the feeling that I stole his father away, because he can't face the problems his parents had with each other" (LeShan, 1980, p. 58).

A stepparent and stepchild have each accumulated years of habits, ways of speaking, mannerisms, abilities, values, beliefs, and other personality characteristics that can be threatening, irritating, or in other ways unacceptable to each other. Even with the best of intentions, these personality characteristics will only change slowly, if at all. This is especially true of the stepparent who, unlike the child, has acquired personality over decades. As a result, when stepparents and stepchildren do not meet each other's expectations, difficulties may arise. Fortunately, expectations or perceptions can be altered, even in the adult. The most valuable approach for creating positive stepparent–stepchild relations, therefore, is to change negative and inappropriate expectations.

How children perceive the new parent, how the parent perceives the children, and how the biological parent views both are key considerations. More important than whether the new parent is kind, trustworthy, tolerant, and considerate is whether the children *see* him or her that way. If they don't perceive the new parent as having these qualities, he or she will be treated negatively. Likewise, how the parent perceives the new children is also important. Consider the following sequence of events. A stepfather may be seen as a threatening and frightening person when first met. In reality, he might be a genuinely warm, accepting, and kindly man; however, the children's perceptions may cause them to respond with rejection, hostility, or withdrawal, likely causing the stepfather to back off or become mistrusting and unappreciative of the children. As he backs off, he becomes somewhat negative or reserved, causing his wife to perceive him as unloving. Thereupon, sensing her rejection, he perceives her as cold and unaccepting.

Much of the above chain reaction could have been prevented had the children and the husband been prepared in advance. The children could be sat down prior to living with their new father and explained that he is different from their biological dad, and that it may appear as if he does not fit in. The wife could have asked her husband to understand that the children would likely compare him with their previous father, of whom they had unrealistically positive memories. If such things had been discussed in advance, the mother and stepfather might have effected a more positive initial interaction and outcome. False expectations could have been understood and tolerated until they were reformulated appropriately.

## PARENT INADEQUACIES

In remarriage of divorced couples there is almost always a deep sense of self-mistrust on the part of the divorced individual in his or her ability to form and sustain a satisfactory family. As in any aspect of performance, failure makes for intensified fear of future failure (Goldstein, 1974, p. 434).

Even for those couples who do not have a fear of failure, they may feel as if they still lack experience dealing with the spouse's children. Certainly children's problems are more easily tolerated by a parent who has observed the child's past, established loving relationships over the years, and feels obligation and responsibility. A stepparent entering the situation may lack some of the fundamental elements that facilitate patience and undertsanding with particular children. Yet, they need not perceive themselves as unable to deal appropriately with their new stepchildren.

## FAULTY PERCEPTIONS

A faulty image of the stepparent is often created, giving rise to unattainable hopes. According to Dr. Goldenburg:

> TV shows like the "Brady Bunch" and "Eight Is Enough" do stepparents a terrible disservice. . . . They're all so sweet and good that no one knows how hard being a stepparent really is. When they get the real-life version, they become more easily frustrated because their lives are nothing like what they saw on the tube (cited in Kalter, 1978, p. 6).

The tremendous influence of perceptions will form the basis for many recommendations to be presented in this chapter. Differences in perceptions among stepparents and stepchildren may be pronounced. Dealing with and effectively using knowledge about perceptions can change a handicap into an asset.

## Three Stages of Growth for a Stepparent

Stepparents are first met by stepchildren as strangers. They are outsiders and are judged according to the children's perceptions. However, if all goes well, a positive relationship will develop between parent and children. The new parent may first be regarded as a guest, then as a friend, and only later as a parent (see Figure 17.1). However, the goal of "parent" needs clarification. A model of the development of stepparent–child relationships "must allow that the stepparent role might never approximate that of a biological parent, and might be different with different children" (Mills, 1984). Stepparents will never take the place of biological parents. Especially when new stepchildren are older, the stepparent lacks sufficient history with the children to approximate relationships that existed previously with the biological parent.

Development from outsider to parent is not rapid, and will vary with

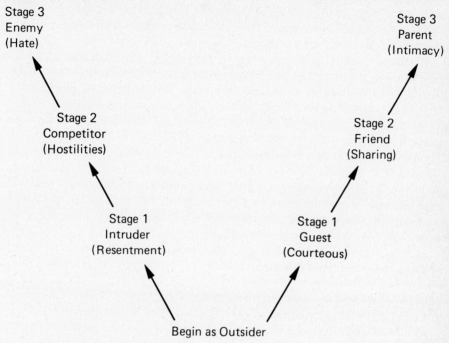

Figure 17.1   Growth of Stepparent into the Psychological World of the Child

Stage 3
Enemy
(Hate)

Stage 3
Parent
(Intimacy)

Stage 2
Competitor
(Hostilities)

Stage 2
Friend
(Sharing)

Stage 1
Intruder
(Resentment)

Stage 1
Guest
(Courteous)

Begin as Outsider

the child's age. It has been suggested, for example, that to equal half of the mutual history a biological parent has with a child will take as long as the child's age at remarriage (Mills, 1984). For example, if a child is five upon remarriage, it will take roughly five years to become a "parent."

In approaching this developmental process, the direction of growth may be negative. The child may view the parent as an intruder, as a competitor, and later as an enemy, instead of as a friend and parent. Figure 17.1 depicts these two possible directions of growth.

## STAGE ONE: GUEST OR INTRUDER

To illustrate this process, consider the hypothetical case of a stepfather, Fred. Introduction to Fred began as the children watched him pick up their mother for a date. Fred greets the children courteously, but as far as the children are concerned, he is still an outsider, a stranger. Psychologically, he is not their guest but is still at the bottom of the V in Figure 17.1.

As weeks elapse, Fred begins to spend evenings in the home when the children are present. They become gradually acquainted and begin to recognize his presence. At this time, depending on Fred's or the children's perceptions, Fred could become either a *guest* or an *intruder*.

If Fred is perceived as warm, the children will be *courteous* toward him.

He will receive courtesies, such as "Would you like a cookie?" or the children may move so he can have the best chair for watching TV. The children will respond to light conversation. If, however, Fred is received negatively, the children will *resent* his presence. They will not be accommodating nor will they respond to conversational gestures.

When married, Fred, as the guest, will find he is living in a social group with rules he never expected. Furthermore, an unexpressed belief may exist that he should adapt to these unwritten rules. Rules about the subtleties of life appear, including such things as how, when, and what is served at dinner. Does he handle any dishes? When is bedtime and what formalities precede going to sleep?

In general, Fred will be expected to follow established rules, but little else will be expected of him because psychologically he is still a guest. Mother might say, "Oh, don't worry, I'll take care of things now. Why don't you just sit down and relax while I put Kimberly to sleep." Fred can be sure he is still a guest when children actually interpret the rules for him: "Put the soap here" and "You're not supposed to touch that dish."

At this point children still see Fred as a newcomer. He is certainly not accepted as a rule maker or disciplinarian. If Fred were to start making rules or punishing children, they would consider him to be out of place. Instead of being perceived as a *guest,* he would then be seen as an *intruder.* The reason for moving in this negative direction is not that Fred is doing anything wrong "for a father" but that the children view him as a guest out of line. Imagine a guest making rules and disciplining!

## STAGE TWO: FRIEND OR COMPETITOR

Later, Fred's status will move ahead to that of either a *friend* or a *competitor.* However, even if Fred moves ahead in the positive direction, he is still not yet considered "a parent," psychologically, by his stepchildren. A friend is a person you like and trust, and with whom you share. Fred could share, but only on a limited basis. Children will listen to him out of trust and respect, and value what he has to say. However, friends still have limitations. Usually, affection is somewhat reserved with friends. Personal property or possessions are definitely regarded as private. Certainly, use of personal property is restricted to what is offered, and a friend is not obligated to share.

While the couple may have decided to begin promoting Fred to a *law-making,* disciplinary role, they would be wise to take this step slowly. Friends exist on an equal level, and Fred, in the children's eyes, should himself be following previously set rules and not upset the system too abruptly.

Before Fred can be psychologically accepted as a parent, children must see him as a noncompeting friend or equal. The wife might help him appreciate restrictions unwillingly placed upon him by the children's perceptions. He can be helped to see that in order to avoid being a competitor, he needs to temporarily interact with the children in their framework—as friends, rather than as a leader or policy maker. Perhaps, when children are in their

Stepparents can eventually be accepted by their stepchildren, and a warm, close relationship can develop.

teens and are resistant to accepting him, friendship may be a sensible, final level of interaction. However, for a fully functioning family with younger children, attaining the status of parent is necessary.

## STAGE THREE: PARENT OR ENEMY

Parenthood, or its likeness, can be said to have been achieved when Fred functions as—and is simultaneously perceived by his children as being—a policy maker, disciplinarian, giver of emotional security, comforter, and psychological caretaker of the children's welfare. Physical and emotional intimacies will develop, children will share fears, doubts, hopes, dreams, and tender feelings, and a special closeness will be felt.

Obviously, such a high level of interpersonal closeness and dependence is not found in relationships with outsiders, guests, and often even friends. Although this process will require time, parent functions can be assumed in small increments. For example, Fred may observe that the children trust him and accept his feelings. He will then find he can express his feelings, and instead of these feelings being just another request to be considered by Mother, they now have the impact of a policy statement. "I don't like waking up to a messy house" becomes a prescription. Yet, Mother's example and response to Fred's expressions may still influence how the children perceive them. They may use their mother's reactions to the father's requests as a standard or frame of reference.

However, looking again at Figure 17.1, we see that the natural progression could lead to the stepparent being considered as an enemy rather than a parent. If Fred begins as an intruder, and then tries to "force" his role as parent through discipline and policy making, he will be seen as an intruder. If this pattern continues, Fred will soon become an enemy to his stepchildren. A happily functioning family is impossible if an enemy exists; warfare is the inevitable result. If this condition persists, professional help is also often warranted.

The two possible paths a stepparent may take have been described, and now we turn to the question of how to facilitate advancement along the most desirable route.

## Facilitating Positive Family Relations

### ALLOW INDIVIDUALITY

Stepparents will usually become parents in their own way. Expecting them to fit a preconceived mold would be unjust, resulting in years of frustration to spouse and children. Relationships between stepparents and their stepchildren will have to be discovered or developed, rather than decided in advance. Definite expectations, however noble or desirable, can be a source of future disappointment because humans rarely meet the ideal. Each person will present his or her own unique style.

It would be well for a mother, for example, to avoid telling her children that someday they will have a father who will save them from whatever problem they are currently facing. Such children listen, hope, and then imagine that their new father will buy them presents, take away fears, protect them from negative happenings, or take them on trips.

It may be better to down play what a father can do and instead help children understand limitations of the person who will become their stepfather. By helping them avoid imagining a preconceived idea, his unique style of fathering is more likely to satisfy all family members.

Schulman, writing professionaly about stepparenting, states:

> [T]here is often an underlying requirement for instant love and devotion on the part of both the child and stepparent-to-be, which turns the healthy motivation into something unrealistic and possibly pathogenic. No other relationship is burdened by such an expectation. Even men who become fathers are permitted to go through an adjustment period (Schulman, 1972, p. 138).

The fact that genuine love ordinarily requires time and growth through interaction and understanding is often overlooked as a stepparent is selected. He or she is supposed to assume automatically a parent role and, in particular, be able to love. It is critical, however, that a stepparent who is capable of loving allow time for this to develop. The same is true for children. Loving a stepparent may require some forgotten memories and a willingness to lay aside jealousies and rivalries with the new parent. Success must be measured in terms of months and years, not days or weeks.

Lowering expectations is often the first step toward a healthy, loving relationship. If high expectations are held initially, disappointment and resentment will most likely result, providing a negative beginning. It is simply unfair to children to promise them an ideal stepparent.

## DEVELOP LOVE, TRUST, AND UNDERSTANDING

In this book we have emphasized a dual approach to family leadership that can be successfully implemented—developing a positive home climate and managing consequences appropriately. This approach applies to families containing stepparents as well. (Discipline was discussed in Chapters 7 through 10; review these chapters if necessary.) It is important that the reconstituted family be familiar with the principle of governing behavior through consequences and reward. Alternatives to punishment—high-power, moderate-power, and low-power techniques to produce or weaken behavior—are as appropriate for the stepparent as they are for biological parents and should be considered.

In addition to the skillful use of rewards, leadership is often more effective when done with love. An emphasis should be placed on internal growth and controls rather than external control. This type of leadership requires faith that within each individual is the capacity for positive growth, and that a parent's function is to nurture and develop the positive elements within children. The parent is analogous to a gardener who provides adequate water, sun, and nutrients during germination, later weeding and nursing the young plant. However, the final outcome is not in the hands of the gardener but resides from the beginning within the seed. Providing a positive home climate with emotions, freedom of choice, love, affection, and a feeling of belonging helps produce this growth. (Review Chapters 5 and 6 if necessary.)

## AVOID THE PASSIVE APPROACH

A word of caution is appropriate when implementing both of the above suggestions for effective family leadership. Administration of the family government should not be turned over completely to the biological parent, who has already developed interpersonal relationships with the children. This approach supposes that the stepparent can later move into his or her role as the necessary love and rapport with the children are acquired.

This solution would start the stepparent off in a weak, passive position which may actually delay reaching a fully functioning family state. In one reconstituted family a passive approach was attempted with disastrous results. The children sensed the stepfather's tentativeness and uncertainty and were soon using their skills to keep him in place. They interpreted rules for him, told him where he was off limits, and ignored his requests. When he made requests it was through the mother, so the children only regarded him as an inconvenience. The mother was also dissatisfied, for she would have liked to share child-rearing responsibilities.

## INSTILL CONFIDENCE IN THE STEPPARENT

While mothers, if they remain home with children, most frequently discipline children, fathers often help determine guidelines and the range of acceptable child behavior. In this function, a stepfather is often resented, as his limits may encroach on the children's wishes and desires, especially as children reach adolescent years. In addition, the father, not having yet been completely accepted, may not be confident in his abilities, becoming hesitant and unsure in this role. Consider the following quote from the Director of the Outpatient Department, Division of Child and Adolescent Psychiatry, State University of New York, in Brooklyn:

> Let us consider the father's dilemma first and see how it is expressed. As the ultimate *enforcer* of discipline (mothers of course administer most discipline) this breakdown of function is expressed in the areas of limit-setting and rule-enforcing. The stepfather is at best reluctant and at worst unable to provide discipline for his adopted children. The father may recognize and express his inability to set appropriate limits but crucial to the resolution of the problem is whether the mother supports him in his role enactment, or whether she acquiesces in her children's denying him the right to discipline them.
>
> Joan and Jean were 14- and 15-year-old daughters by their mother's first marriage, which had terminated in divorce when the girls were 4 and 5, respectively. Although their stepfather had been their sole father for 9 years, he still harbored the feeling that the girls resented him. Well they might have, but not much more than adolescents in general resent the family limit-setter. Yet his concern over their resentment prevented him from following through with the quite appropriate guidelines he had set up. The consequence was that the girls were becoming more and more involved in a deviant subculture. What made it especially hard for him was the fact that his wife, still guilty over the harm she felt she had done her children by her first marriage to an abusive man, could not bring herself to support her husband in his fathering even though she shared his norms (Goldstein, 1974, p. 436).

It is understandable that a mother may be reluctant to support her second husband in some decisions when they result in strong negative reactions from her children. Typically, her role may be one of being an affectionate and nurturant supporter, and as such, she is quite capable of empathizing with a child experiencing distress from limits set by a stepfather. The couple, however, should work out decisions to problems in advance and anticipate children's reactions. In this manner, a stepparent's confidence in self is increased, as is the child's respect for the stepparent.

# DEAL WITH DIFFERENCES IN ADVANCE

The luxury of time to develop common beliefs, habits, and preferences is missing in the reconstituted family. Second marriages are more prone to have larger differences between spouses in age, education, and religious identification (Dean & Gurak, 1978). Racially and culturally intermarried stepfamilies are even more open to difficulties than nonmixed stepfamilies (Baptiste, 1984). When a stepparent, who may be different in terms of age, race, socioeconomic status, religion, or values, enters a family, difficulties are imminent. The marriage will likely lack initial support from internal family relationships. In addition, unless the children are very young, the stepparent may experience difficulty in accepting children different from himself or herself. Yet, if the future stepparent anticipates the problems resulting from differences in age, religion, education, and values, these important issues can be dealt with in advance.

First, it is important that each partner become aware of differences and be able to verbalize and discuss them openly. Removal of judgmental attitudes toward discovered individual differences becomes necessary.

Second, after parents achieve some understanding and knowledge about differences, this awareness could be communicated to children before they notice them. Failure to do so may cause them to remain silent, or to openly criticize the stepparent upon realization of these differences. A boy might say, "You have no right to boss me around because in our religion we don't think like you."

Third, while both spouse's characteristics must be lived with, some are more acceptable or more disturbing than others. Partners must decide which differences can be lived with compatibly and which must be modified. Even if modifiable, change may be a long-term process. For example, religious and educational differences are usually not subject to immediate change. A gradual trend toward similarity may occur over a period of years. Sometimes a marriage partner does not ask for immediate change, but simply hopes that future changes might occur.

Fourth, change ironically occurs more readily in a climate of acceptance rather than a climate of pressures, expectations, or demands. When criticized, people often become defensive and resistant to change. However, when a person feels accepted as he or she is, that person will sometimes honestly examine present development and independently decide that change would be best. Children, too, can come to recognize the wisdom of not exerting pressure for change. For example, counseling will help them realize that over time their new mother may become more like women they have loved and accepted.

In a second marriage, learning to live with differences is more of a key to success than helping the other person change. A phrase spoken in one wedding ceremony reflects this attitude: "Success in marriage depends not upon finding the right person but in *being* the right person."

## HELP THE NEW SPOUSE DISPLAY AFFECTION

Affection includes physical comfort and psychological assurance. While the absence of affection in a home does not indicate failure, its observance does suggest a certain amount of harmony. The amount, type, and openness of affection will vary greatly from one person to another. Individual differences must be accepted and considered. However, while differences do exist, most experts concur that movement toward more frequent affectional displays indicates improvement.

Biological parents will be concerned that their children receive affectional expressions from the new spouse. To facilitate this interchange, they can identify and help their spouse express those affections that come easiest. If, for example, a stepfather is uncomfortable with high levels of physical affection, ways might be suggested in which he can respond without hurting the feelings of a spontaneous child. In addition, the mother may demonstrate affection to her new husband, achieving two goals. First, father will become familiar with ways affection is shared in the family. Second, children will benefit from the experience. It is the opinion of psychologists and family researchers that an open expression of affection between husband and wife has a healthy impact on children.

## RETAIN PERSONAL TIME

In the reconstituted family, time will be short—especially personal time—because developing new relationships demands effort. Doubts, insecurities, and the need for verbal assurances are coupled with working out general household and social activities. To take advantage of and to insure proper usage of precious time, one wife arranged a special 15-minute slot each evening for her husband to be alone. The offer to relax upon coming home from work was a gift he received with kindness. Other innovations or changes in family functioning, like that above, may need to be implemented. Budgeting daily activities may now be required, whereas before it was not.

Time for talking and visiting, including children, may need to be placed high on the list of priorities. During the first part of a new marriage, a couple naturally wants to spend lots of time together. Therefore, in the reconstituted family children will receive less attention from their biological parent, and may feel jealous. To counter this worry, time for children needs to be budgeted.

## RESOLVE OWNERSHIP ISSUES

The immediate transference of what is mine to what is ours may be resisted by some stepparents who attach much value to material possessions. An automobile, for example, though previously belonging only to the stepmother, now takes on "family status." Because children are often naturally rough on such items, the stepmother may find herself being quite possessive. Similarly, a stepfather may be reluctant to let children use his athletic equipment, bicycle, books, magazines, records, television set, or tape recorder.

Family membership entitles the child to use with reasonable care items formerly belonging to the stepparent alone. On the other hand, the stepparent will expect to retain management and rights to personal property. In this case it may be well for the biological parent to immediately bring the question of use into open discussion, relieving strain and allowing questions. Opinions can be aired and policies established. For example, in one family the stepfather arrived with a stereo component set that had in the past received gentle personal care. When elementary-school children now wanted to play their records, he was at first reluctant. After being petitioned by the children, he agreed on the condition that, following proper instructions, one designated child could put records on for the other children.

## SET DOWN FINANCIAL GUIDELINES

Money problems are a leading cause of family difficulties, and are often particularly stressful in a second marriage. A stepfather may be making support payments to a previous wife, and must now assume financial responsibility for someone else's children—his new family. In addition, because of previous marital difficulties, both partners may be guarded about personal finances. These and other circumstances require that the couple set down some guidelines before financial decisions become disrupting. Below are some general principles that have wide applicability.

1. When large amounts of cash, property, or estate are brought into a second marriage, it is better to discuss their disposition prior to marriage. Legal advice or a financial consultant will result in later savings and harmony.
2. To handle salaries, advance budgeting will help avoid later misunderstanding. When setting up a budget, it is almost mandatory that it be written down. Agreements, solutions, and plans can and should be open to continual modification, but it is important that they be made.
3. While mechanics may vary as to whether there should be one or two checking accounts, who is to pay the bills, etc., it is most important that there be understanding of what responsibilities, limits, and expectations are given to each partner. Again, this should be established in advance and subject to change.
4. Because most partners will have had prior experience in budgeting family finances with a spouse, certain preconceived procedural notions are usually the case. Prior experiences with management failures may result in rigidity. Only through frank discussion and sharing of feelings can spouses appreciate each other's concerns.
5. The rights and interests of children remain a legitimate concern even if they do not participate in the decision-making process. Under current law parents are financially responsible for children, and the logic extends morally to stepchildren, whether adopted or not. In the reconstituted family, both partners should, prior to marriage, express their desires and feel an obligation to financially assist chil-

dren. Discrepancies in viewpoint can be resolved prior to marriage better than when the budget is dwindling. At times, money requested for a spouse's children may not seem appropriate. An early and prior recognition of this type of sacrifice will be beneficial.

6. Money represents so many things! Money has been said to buy prestige, power, pleasure, and time, but it cannot buy goodwill or love from a partner. In fact, it has a destructive potential in even the best of relationships. If both partners can acquire an attitude that relationships are valued more than anything purchasable with money, resolving financial conflicts will be much easier.

7. Lastly, there may be a tendency when managing funds to be selfish and dishonest. Putting some of the budget aside for personal use or keeping some outside earnings secret seems harmless, but from such practices grows distrust. Unless understanding of exceptions to the policy exists, the rule of honesty seems mandatory.

In summary, these seven principles, while not specific, can provide a foundation for averting some inevitable financial difficulties in a second marriage. Differences over expenditures will occur, but most budget expenses or practices are not worth serious deterioration of goodwill.

## PRACTICE EQUALITY AND FAIRNESS

Try cutting two equal pieces of pie and serving them to two hungry children. To each child the piece served seems smaller. This phenomenon forms the basis of many disputes, and the inexperienced parent tries to answer the complaint "You're not fair" by being meticulous, making everything fair or perfectly equal. A child's perception that the other person is being treated better is heightened when a stepparent treats his or her natural child just a little better. It is certain to be noticed and certainly resented. A stepparent may at first be unaware that this will happen, but will soon discover the consequences.

One father was looking forward to the time his child would visit him for two weeks. He reasoned that since he had given so many weeks to his stepchildren and none to his natural child, he would go all out during the two-week visit. Prior to the divorce he had been very close to this child, and so when the reunion came, the father and child immediately entered a renewed, intense, and personal relationship. The wife was able to understand what was happening, but the stepchildren were unprepared and unable to comprehend the event, only recognizing that the treatment the natural child was receiving was better than what they had enjoyed.

While the stepfather could logically justify the extra time and energy given his child, he was shortsighted in not being aware of the impact on his stepchildren. What could have been done? First, if the intense relationship was necessary, it could have been arranged to take place away from the other children. Second, both father and children could have been prepared. Even before the first day, a discussion might have emerged to help the father and children see each other's perceptions. Third, the mother could have used the time to compensate and give additional personal attention to her children. Fourth, if an abundance of time was going to be spent in fun activities, inclusion of all the children might have resulted in a more-the-merrier atmosphere. Instead of feeling resentment toward the natural child, the stepchildren might unconsciously feel, "Hey, when he comes, we have fun." However, avoid the situation where a child would say, "Why do we only have fun when he comes?" The natural child might have had an equally good time without the extra attention.

## ESTABLISH RULES OF ORDER

> Adolescents are sensitive to unbalance by parental controls, and use every opportunity to play one parent against the other in an effort to make the natural parent choose between the stepparent and the child. The stepparent is faced with a much more difficult situation, in that accommodation must not only be made to the new mate but to the stepchild as well. Frequently, the success of the remarital venture depends more on the adjustment to the stepchild than to that of the mate (Smith, 1953, p. 236).

In one instance, when two large families were united, the father brought seven children and the mother four. A solution to discipline was needed. After five years, these parents reported a successful approach. They agreed that each parent would always administer negative sanctions to their own children even though the recommendation for punishment originated with the stepparent. They reported that the children never realized this separation of discipline took place. In a similar fashion, Mills (1984) suggests that parents be in charge of setting and enforcing limits for their own biological children. Even if both parent and stepparent are present when the stepparent sees the need to define behavioral limits, the stepparent could turn to his or her spouse and say, "Would you ask your child to . . . " In addition, if parents cannot agree on a given rule or limitation, the final decision should support the children's biological parent.

Psychologists disagree about whether parents should present a united front to children during disputes. Those against maintain it is not honest that parents always appear to agree, and that it presents an unfair advantage to have parents continually agree when confronting a child's demands. Those in favor feel the child will benefit from not being exposed to conflicting views, and that greater stability and order are engendered when parents agree. For the reconstituted family, the need for initial unity between parents may be more important than in the natural family, for two reasons. First, it is often the stepparent who must make a request or present an unpopular decision. A united front will cushion the friction. Second, if a stepchild is having difficulty, he or she may have a tendency to attribute some of these problems to the stepparent, creating a psychological wedge between parents. By being united, parents can insulate themselves from attempts to cause separation.

# Problems of Stepchildren

We have discussed many of the difficulties stepparents face when beginning a new marriage. In summary, negative family influences include unrealistic child expectations, faulty perceptions, and parental feelings of inadequacy. A number of suggestions were presented to help the new stepparent avoid major family disruptions and proceed along the path to becoming an accepted family member. However, stepparents are not the only ones experiencing uncertainties, anxieties, and difficulties. What about stepchildren?

## NAMES

During a workshop on how to help reconstituted families adjust, the lecturer was explaining that young children will often desire to call the new parent "Mother" or "Father." At this point, one man became incensed as he reflected on his son calling a stepfather "Dad." Another young boy told his stepmother that he could not call her "Mother" because it bothered his other mother. It is unfortunate that this burden be carried by a young child, but a biological parent's feelings, although possibly unjustifiable, are real. There is no simple solution to problems of this kind. Persons who are the most psychologically stable must often be the ones who give the most. Hopefully, adult emotional jealousies will not infringe upon a young child's desire to call someone "Mother" or "Father."

## RIVALRY

Sibling rivalry is a common term because of the frequent, almost natural conflicts between siblings in seeking family attention, affection, and other resources. Rivalries are often emotional-psychological, but sometimes involve physical conflicts. A child may feel neglected or dethroned when competing with brothers or sisters. Imagine the increased emotional shock of a child who is faced with a total stranger as a sibling.

Children may perceive favoritism even if both parents are careful to be objective and impartial. Sibling rivalries can then cause biological and stepparents to overreact and come to the assistance of "their" child.

Typically, parents learn to adjust to demands, requests, and expectations according to a child's needs and abilities. Some children are brighter, others more athletic, and some have emotional insecurities. Gender and age differences also require differential treatment. As a result, children will be treated differently, which may be perceived by children as favoritism. To avoid this feeling, stepparents often react by becoming rigidly fair, treating all children alike, and thereby destroying uniqueness.

It would be better to strive for trust and understanding. Children can understand that parents are doing their best, and although they at times make

Although sibling rivalry is often normal, conflict may become intense when a total stranger suddenly becomes a sibling.

unfair decisions, they will, over the long run, be good to all the children. They can realize that decisions are made out of love and consideration for individual children.

## DEPENDENCE, LOVE, COMFORT, LETTING GO

When discussing single parenting in Chapter 15, we suggested that single mothers may turn to their children during distressing moments. Children enjoy this comfort-giving role because it brings them closer to their mothers. However, upon remarrying she begins to turn to the new mate. This change will be noticed by the children, and they may begin to resent both parents. Resentment may be particularly noticeable if sleeping arrangements are changed. The mother may leave a room she occupied with a child, now sleeping in a new room with the door closed.

An experience in one family illustrates how to compensate for initial feelings of comfort loss. One evening when the children were feeling a loss of closeness, the mother decided to spend some time with them in a manner similar to what they were accustomed to prior to her second marriage. In this instance, this mother of three elementary-school girls said, "Let's go out together the way we used to." They then left the house for a walk through the streets and a visit to the ice cream parlor. About an hour or so later they returned, full of positive, close feelings they had previously known. This spirit of unity and closeness did not detract from positive feelings for the father.

Natural rivalry and competitiveness between men for a woman's love can negatively influence a stepfather–son relationship. A stepson often resembles the natural father in facial features, hair color, or body build. Even subtle personality, mood, and behavioral characteristics may resemble the first father. As a result, he may become threatening to the stepfather. Since most of these characteristics are unchangeable, acceptance of them is mandatory. Failure to do so will result in continued friction and sometimes even hostility toward the stepson. This conflict is often at an unconscious level, and the stepfather may state simply that he has a personality clash with the son, not knowing it is because the son reminds him of his wife's earlier mate.

To help alleviate this type of unconscious or conscious friction, a mother can do two things. First, she may openly discuss how resemblances between the son and his biological father may cause problems. The stepfather may be able to adapt after recognizing openly the dynamics of this situation. Ideally, he will recognize that these unique personality and constitutional characteristics are a natural part of the child and do not constitute a threat. Second, the stepfather may be helped to become aware of growing similarities between his stepson and himself. As he sees more similarities, he will experience some pride and identify more closely with him. Similarities may include things such as work habits, recreational interests, religious beliefs, mannerisms, or television program preferences.

## NEW FEELINGS AND OLD FEELINGS

Feelings, emotions, and attachments that children have to their previous father or mother will influence how they react to a new one. Accordingly, it is well to help children maintain positive feelings toward the previous parent, in order for them to more readily accept a new one into their lives. If a father has convinced his children that their mother was a deserter and a bum, then they may believe that the new mother is similar, if not the same. Generally, building a negative image of a previous spouse will work against acceptance of a new one. Little is achieved by creating images of irresponsible adults in young children's minds.

Children will be curious about their previous parent, asking questions and comparing him or her with their stepparent. Occasional visits and memories may not be adequate to satisfy their search for information about their biological parent. If resentful of or bothered by this inquisitiveness, the mother may construct a negative picture, frequently doing so to assure her new spouse that she is no longer emotionally attached to her first husband. Again, it is erroneous to believe that if the first father is portrayed as a demon, then children will, by contrast, love the second father more. It is advisable to report objectively and accurately the original father's basic personality characteristics.

## CLOSENESS BETWEEN MOTHER AND SON

Whiteside and Auerback (1978) of the Children's Psychiatric Hospital, University of Michigan Medical Center, report that mothers will frequently develop a strong dependency on an older child, usually a son. This dependency enhances a mother's feelings of security while she is single, and this relationship is frequently later condoned by the stepfather. He finds this a convenient way to handle some of his wife's demands by letting the stepson share his responsibilities. To reduce this type of dependency, Whiteside and Auerback recommend: (1) strengthening the relationship between mother and stepfather, (2) strengthening the child's relationship with other siblings, and (3) allowing the stepfather to interact more with the child. The child must also understand that as he becomes closely attached to the stepfather, this is in no way disloyal to the natural parent.

## NEW AND OLD WAYS

A stepparent will likely introduce into the family different ways of doing things (e.g., expressions, holiday practices, and other stylistic behaviors). However, children may believe their way to be proper because they rely upon familiarity to define rightness. For example, an adult may overhear half-siblings arguing about whether to call the evening meal supper or dinner. To an adult these descriptions are minor, almost trivial, but they mean more to children. A stepparent eager to establish that what he or she believes will be an improvement, may interpret children's resistance as stubbornness or personal rejection.

To avoid this conflict, an attitude of "Let's try new ideas" will help the child be more accepting. Parents need to model diplomacy in making compromises of new and old ways. Imagine children who at mealtime normally gulp their food, some standing, some watching TV, some of them having decided that they are on a diet. Now, enter a woman who wants a large, three-course dinner every evening at precisely 5:45 PM. She expects a neat table, courtesy, order, and manners. Accommodation to this new situation will be required! The father will have to handle the situation diplomatically. In this scenario the father chooses to support the organized family dinner concept. He can begin by discussing with the children that they should allow time between 5:45 and 6:30 PM for dinner. He might explain to the new mother that some children may look restless during the first few meals. Without being specific, he might prepare her to accept some variance in table manners, table conversation, and rate of consumption.

This mealtime example illustrates how family traditions can at first be a problem. However, developing and accepting new ways of doing things will soon accomplish one function of tradition—stabilizing and solidifying groups. As new traditions are accepted, the family will become a more cohesive unit.

# The Ideal

An ideal is unobtainable, but it is discouraging if one has no hope of even coming close. How close can one come? Duberman (1975), a researcher and writer, was divorced and later remarried to a man who brought four children to live with her three. She became interested in reconstructed families and eventually studied 88 middle-class families in Cleveland, Ohio. All families had remarried with children under 18 at the time of remarriage.

Her findings present a note of optimism. She constructed 24 characteristics of the ideal family and then determined how close the traditional and reconstituted family came to meeting the 24 ideals. The traditional family was similar to the ideal family in 17 of 24 characteristics, while the reconstituted family was similar in 20!

She claims that reconstituted, second-family parents are more self-conscious of their need for improvement. They are more aware of where they are and where they must go—they work harder.

In her study Duberman (1975) found that second-marriage homes reported a higher percentage of husband and wife loving each other in comparison to studies of the traditional family. In fact, she found that 90 percent of the wives and 93 percent of the husbands felt love toward and loved by their spouses. In addition, 52 percent of men and women believed their sexual relationships were excellent (Duberman, 1975, p. 127).

Working toward a loving relationship with a partner is the first step to becoming a successful stepparent. Stepparents need to take time to share mutual events and have open conversations and positive experiences between themselves, which will engender stability and love. Time should be taken prior to remarriage to develop a friendship. Time should be taken from work, housekeeping, and social life to spend with each other.

One book on stepparenting states:

> Parent–child relationships have preceded the new couple relationship. Because of this, many parents feel that it is a betrayal of the parent–child bond to form a primary relationship with their new partner. A primary couple relationship, however, is usually crucial for the continuing existence of the stepfamily, and therefore is very important for the children as well as for the adults. A strong adult bond can protect the children from another family loss, and it also can provide the children with a positive model for their own eventual marriage relationship. The adults often need to arrange time alone to help nourish this important couple relationship (Visher & Visher, 1979, p. 261).

The point is that getting *there* from *here* begins and ends with an enjoyable relationship between spouses. If parents love one another, they are willing and eager to work together. And good spouse and stepparent–child relationships are most important in assuring stepfamily success. Research indicates, for example, that children in close stepfamilies do not differ from children in "intact" families on: attitudes toward marriage; marriage role expectations; and attitudes toward divorce (Coleman & Ganong, 1984).

## Summary

This chapter has attempted to consider the role of stepparent in general, although many examples were given depicting stepfathers or stepmothers in their respective roles. We feel that the content of this chapter is equally applicable to both stepmothers and stepfathers. This assumption is based on the findings of Clingempeel, Brand, and Ievoli (1984) that stepmother–stepchild relationships are not plagued with greater difficulties than stepfather–stepchild relationships.

Reconstituted families face inherent difficulties, especially if stepchildren are older. Negative expectations by children influence their perceptions of the stepparent. Stepparents differ from the original family unit in issues of affectional displays, ownership of material possessions, financial planning, and discipline, not to mention the pervasive racial and cultural differences present in mixed remarriages. Simply stated, the stepparent is not part of the family's previous history and, therefore, must overcome additional obstacles that first-time marriages do not face.

However, stepparenting can be and often is successful. Parents effectively troubleshoot potential family disruptions by: (1) allowing individuality and creating "new" family traditions; (2) dealing with financial, child-rearing, and other differences in advance; (3) dealing with faulty expectations and perceptions; and (4) providing a warm, accepting, and organized home climate. Although a stepparent's trek from outsider, to guest, to friend, and ultimately to parent may take some time, it can be fulfilling. In addition, a review of the literature suggests that "stepchildren evidence no more problems in social behavior, in general, than other children" (Ganong & Coleman, 1984).

# SELF-CHECK

1. A key element in creating a happy reconstituted family is:
   a. the new father's socioeconomic status being equal to that of the mother.
   b. the distinction between external reality and perceived reality (expectations).
   c. the ability to create a positive picture of the new father or mother, even if somewhat embellished.
   d. None of the above is a key element.
2. This chapter depicted three stages of growth for a stepfather. Before becoming an enemy or an accepted parent, all stepfathers tend to start at which of the following stages as depicted in the chart?
   a. friend
   b. intruder
   c. outsider or stranger
   d. guest
3. The following things should be understood when becoming a stepfather *except:*
   a. stepfathers should try to be substitutes for natural fathers.
   b. stepfathers may be perceived as rivals for mother's attention.

    c. stepfathers may need to meet multifamily financial obligations.
    d. stepfathers may be "scapegoated" by children.
 4. Which of the following is *not* a way to avoid the passive approach?
    a. Help the father move into an effective leadership role.
    b. Help the father acquire trust and love for the children.
    c. Leave administration of the family up to the mother until the father is accepted.
    d. Provide order in the home.
 5. Which of the following is true of second marriages?
    a. The luxury of time to develop love and common beliefs, habits, and preferences is missing.
    b. They are prone to have larger differences between spouses than first marriages.
    c. Transference of family possessions may cause conflicts.
    d. All except for b are true.
    e. All of the above are true.
 6. Which of the following is *not* true?
    a. Stepparents should be allowed their own individuality.
    b. The home climate and managing consequences discussed in previous chapters apply to stepfamilies as well.
    c. The new couple should not attempt to work out differences between them prior to remarriage.
    d. The new spouse should be helped to display affection with his or her new stepchildren.
 7. To avoid financial difficulties, the new couple should:
    a. budget in advance.
    b. maintain two checking accounts.
    c. engage in frank discussion and sharing of feelings.
    d. a and c are true.
 8. Stepchildren face the following problems *except:*
    a. knowing what to call the new parent.
    b. sibling rivalry.
    c. strong dependency feelings for the new parent.
    d. learning new ways of doing things.

KEY: 1–b; 2–c; 3–a; 4–c; 5–e; 6–c; 7–d; 8–c

C H A P T E R  18

# FOSTER PARENTING

At this point, the reader probably has a good idea of what we as authors consider important components of a positive home climate. Ideas presented throughout this text are as applicable to parents who have foster children in their homes. In addition, many of the considerations presented in the step-parenting chapter (Chapter 17) are pertinent for foster parents. So, to avoid unnecessary repetition, this chapter is merely an informative description of foster parenting. Specific applications to the foster-home environment (e.g., discipline, warm environment) should be possible after thoroughly digesting previous chapter material.

## Description

Approximately 170,000 married couples are involved in foster parenting throughout the United States. These couples are usually in their forties, and foster fathers are generally a few years older than foster mothers. Although foster parents represent a wide range of educational levels, most foster parents are generally not educated beyond high school. The majority of foster parents are white. Black foster parents are also represented in the literature and account for anywhere from 10 to 44 percent of the foster-parent population. Foster-parent incomes are generally in the low- to middle-class income range. Foster fathers are typically employed in skilled labor, yet unskilled laborers and managerial professionals also become foster parents. Foster mothers are usually homemakers or are employed in unskilled positions. The majority of foster parents are married and have their own children, often adolescents. There are an insufficient number of studies to assess the extent of "single" foster-parenting participation, but they are a minority.

### FOSTER-PARENT ROLES

Meeting certain qualifications is logically necessary before becoming foster parents. Yet, role expectations are ambiguous and inconsistent across the country. Many conflicing ideas of what orientation and training foster-parents receive, what functions they will undertake, what services will be available to them, and what they are to be paid produce frustration among foster-care practitioners, policy makers, fund-raising entities, researchers, communities, and foster parents themselves. Much of the literature contains diverse views and definitions of the foster-parent role.

Most articles define foster parents simply as parents, however. If they are defined as parents and trained as parents, the focus of their role is on parent–child interaction, although they are still obligated to cooperate with social workers in placement of the foster child. Others regard foster parents as colleagues or clients of social workers and foster-care agencies. Foster-parent education training, in this case, focuses primarily on developing roles of teamwork with foster-parent agencies.

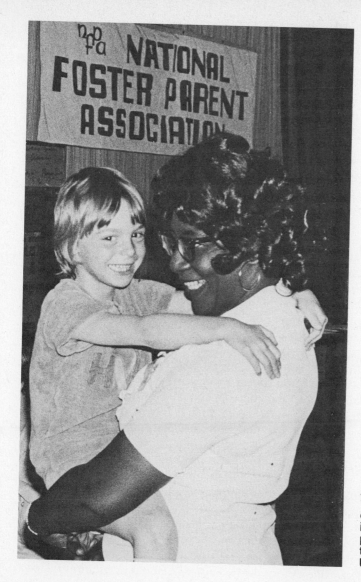

Approximately 170,000 married couples are involved in foster parenting throughout the United States.

In most research, foster fathers are not strongly represented, and case-worker relationships with foster fathers are weak or nonexistent, especially in public agencies. Recruitment, selection activities, and research generally focus on foster mothers, especially in studies of parent–child relationships. It has, therefore, been difficult to do significant research with fathers. However, when foster fathers are located and questioned, they do feel their role as foster father is important, and they seem to enjoy relationships with children they are fostering. Working relationships with foster fathers and social workers are also difficult to establish because of work-schedule incompatibility, making them less available than foster mothers.

Due to inadequate research and study of the foster-father role, important fathering variables cannot be sufficiently summarized. Additionally, information on foster mothers is too often generalized to foster parents, which may reduce the validity of conclusive research findings as they pertain to foster fathers. However, as in the traditional family, the father's role may be a critical factor in the quality of foster parenting as well as the success and length of child placement.

Another problem in defining roles is that many foster children have been found to be manipulative, and will try to make the home environment match that of a previous foster home or the home of their natural parents, creating frustration and feelings of inadequacy on the part of foster parents.

Often plagued with mixed emotions about the child's biological parents, foster parents feel that visits with natural parents are upsetting for the child and therefore a negative experience for the entire foster family. They may also experience jealousy toward these visits after the child has become an emotional part of their own lives. When the child returns from a visit, added strain and stress are often the result.

The above difficulties may be partly responsible for foster-parent role confusion. Yet, a primary purpose of foster care is evident—allowing natural parents to organize themselves financially, emotionally, and otherwise until capable of taking care of their own children. If this role is understood by foster parents, problems revolving around natural-parent visitations are diminished. In this light, a foster parent's role is to create a stable home environment so the child's emotional and educational growth is not indefinitely interrupted. If a child's natural parents do not initiate stable conditions, efforts are taken to terminate parental rights and place the child in an adoptive status.

Current efforts in role definition have provided additional information to foster parents. A listing of foster-parent functions that have been identified include the following: short-term crisis placements; the foster parent as co-worker; academic-year foster care; the foster parent as employee, adoption facilitator, planner, and group leader of foster-parent groups; foster parents as resources to biological parents and as advisors in foster-care replacements. These roles reflect a general broadening of foster-parenting functions, yet at the same time allow for more specific role definition. However, many role definitions are specific to single agency programs existing across the nation.

## Procedures

### RECRUITMENT AND SELECTION

Recruitment of foster parents is usually done by direct presentation to selected groups such as parent-teacher associations or community awareness groups. These presentations are delivered by social workers or current foster

Agencies throughout the United States are dedicated to obtaining and monitoring proper foster-child care.

parents. Newspaper and television have also been used to advertise for applicants. Most agencies, however, prefer referrals from current foster parents.

When responding to an advertisement or referral, most potential foster parents do not end up applying or accepting interviews for placement. If forms and interviews are completed, however, continued screening is necessary to choose stable and responsible couples. Selection is usually based upon the practice, experience, and intuition of the social worker involved. Because there is a great need for foster parents, however, the danger of placing children in unstable homes exists. Requirements for placement are becoming much more flexible than they have been in the past.

## TRAINING

Foster-parent training and education are essential to adequate placement of the foster child. Yet, it is important to note again that most foster parents in the United States have not attained education beyond grade 12. For this reason, programs are widespread throughout the country, varying in sponsorship, content and methods, purposes, levels of participation, and success rates. The majority of training programs and educational seminars emphasize the special roles and relationships involved in foster care. Many focus on foster mother–child interaction, and on behavior management of the foster child. Special-needs programs deal specifically with the emotionally disturbed, mentally retarded, or otherwise handicapped child.

Training programs consist of weekly seminars; topics include child development, foster-care roles, problem solving, and agency–foster-parent cooperation. Many programs offer college credit or completion certificates.

Generally, most foster parents beginning the training program successfully complete it, but low participation is the rule. In addition, most participants are foster mothers. Foster-parent training effectiveness, especially when training is completed after the child is placed, is difficult to assess because of this low rate of participation.

## USING FOSTER PARENTS AS ROLE MODELS

Davies and Bland (1978) reported on a current trend in foster care—using foster parents as role models for natural parents. In this fashion, natural parents upgrade parenting skills while their child is placed elsewhere. A basic assumption of the role-modeling program is that the natural parents have deficits in parenting, and that they are unfamiliar with what is expected of them. In this program, four stages are introduced to help alleviate these deficits. In the first, natural parents teach foster parents about their child's character. In the second, the social worker facilitates the child's transfer to foster parents. In the third stage, the social worker becomes less active, allowing the rapport that has developed between parents and foster parents to grow. In the fourth stage, the social worker helps foster parents and natural parents to separate. Most meetings take place in the foster home, and it is hoped that through this program, biological parents can develop adequate parenting skills by observing foster parents. In addition, foster parents, as evidenced in step 1, are assisted in defining their role.

This procedure begins with a contract, written after a social worker has evaluated the child and family. The purposes of the contract are: (1) to underscore agreement on establishing a permanent plan for the child within a specific time period, usually one year; (2) to clearly define role responsibilities of the natural parents, foster parents, and social worker; (3) to explicate the work to be done in developing child-management techniques; (4) to set limits for both placement and frequency of home visits (usually every weekend); and (5) to require that parents keep weekly appointments (children are also seen weekly). The contract also requires that natural and foster parents meet regularly with the social worker to evaluate progress.

## PAYMENT

Foster-family-care rates are generally low and do not cover the cost of care, nor do they compensate for foster-parent services. Payments often vary according to regional location, and differ according to specific problem; for special problem children board rates are generally higher. In some locations, amount of training determines the salary foster parents receive. There is no change of payment, however, with more training and education after placement of a foster child. Most agencies today believe their rates are high enough to attract and retain foster parents, and there is no actual relationship between recruitment and board rates. Because of the complexity of foster care it is difficult to set a standard rate that is reasonable and prudent for all involved. Most board payments are tailored to the foster child's specific needs, and are differentially affected by standards of living. In 1975, for example, New Mexico allowed $65 a month per child, while Alaska allowed $265 per child.

Foster-care payments reinforce the conception of foster families as substitute biological families, because rates do not adequately cover the costs of care; if they did, foster care would be regarded more as a profession. In fact, monetary compensation has been criticized for that reason. One student in our classes who had been raised in many foster homes since he was three years old objected to payment, feeling that payment attracted persons who took children in for the money and not for love. He felt that removing payment or compensation altogether would be the best screening device for eliminating undesirable foster parents. The counterargument, however, is equally valid—unless foster families are helped with the financial burden there will be a great shortage.

## FOSTER-PARENT ADOPTION

Adoption is a viable alternative for qualified foster parents, especially in instances where the intended outcome of foster placement is not obtained— that natural parents develop sufficient skills to retain custody of their children. In spite of role conceptions emphasizing a working relationship between natural and foster parents, foster parent adoption makes up a large proportion of long-term foster care. Adoption, if included as an option in foster care, could reduce agency caseloads and program costs.

Adoption also has the potential of providing a more permanent, stable environment for older children. Faushel (1978) collected data on New York City foster-care discharges from 1974 to 1977, and found that foster-parent adoptions usually occurred after the child had been in care almost eight years. Nearly 86 percent of the adoptions were subsidized. Nonsubsidized adoptions by foster parents happened much earlier, however—between five and six years after starting foster care. Subsidy, then, appears to make adoption of older children more feasible, helping foster parents who would like to adopt make the decision to do so.

## Outcome

### ATTRITION

Foster care in the United States, according to Cautley and Aldridge (1975), is in trouble not because it is undesirable, but because it is widely misunderstood and poorly utilized. Parents are often poorly informed and inadequately taught. Consider the following example provided by Cautley (1980):

> Well, with Jimmy it is not working out too good. We're thinking about maybe giving up, although we still want to keep his younger brother. . . . One thing, we weren't told exactly what his problems were. Had it been completely clear, maybe it would have been different to start with. We had a trial and error approach that maybe we wouldn't have had to use. I think Jimmy had been fighting us all the way.
>
> I know he's going to feel very badly to leave, but I have to think of my husband and my own family too. Like in the mornings he makes so much noise and wakes everybody. . . . He starts the household out on the wrong foot each day.
>
> We can't feel confident enough that we're doing the right thing for him. If what we are doing is making it harder for Jimmy, like if he's not capable of doing anything better than what he is doing, then maybe we're making it harder on Jimmy by keeping him here expecting him to do more than he's capable of doing (p. 218).

Attrition rates of foster parents are quite high, adding to already present difficulties. High attrition rates lower an agency's resources for substitute care, resulting in overcrowded foster homes and the use of unqualified or unsatisfactory foster parents. Thereupon, large investments of staff time are needed to relocate foster children and to further recruit, select, and train additional couples. In addition, continual relocation is often emotionally disturbing to foster children, producing distrust, fear, and feelings of rejection. Not only does removal cause the social worker, foster-care agency, and foster child to suffer, but foster parents often feel as if they have failed, making them unwilling to accept another child.

One-third of all families studied by Cautley requested that the agency remove the child from their home because, from their point of view, the placement was not working (Cautley, 1980). Most requests took place during the first year; 15 percent took place in less than three months, 21 percent from three to six months, and 23 percent from 6 to 12 months. Cautley determined it was impossible to distinguish or screen out possible quitters before foster-child placement. Reasons cited for termination were inadequate preparation and training on the foster parents' part, inability or unwillingness to cope with the foster child, and poor motivation of the foster family as a whole. Payment was not a factor influencing attrition in this study.

## FOSTER-PARENT SUCCESS

Studies of foster-home success utilize differing criteria for measuring success. However, one common criterion is the number of months foster-home placement continued. Other criteria include worker and researcher ratings of foster-parent understanding, responsiveness, acceptance, and cooperation.

Foster parenting can be an enjoyable, worthwhile endeavor, and may lead to adoption of the foster child.

Rowe (1976) found that better foster parents accepted the child's early-adult behavior, poor academic performance, and social difficulties, and did not require strict religious observance. Social class was found to be unrelated. Qualities for success according to Davies and Bland (1978) were a willingness to work regularly with the social worker, a genuine liking for children, and a capacity for understanding and accepting people. Successful parents were not judgmental of differing values, and were secure in their ability to raise their own children.

Cautley (1980), in suggesting several predictors of successful foster parenting, indicated that social workers should assess or acquire the following:

1. Information about the foster family—the number of siblings each foster parent has, the age position of each foster parent, and the interest the father takes in his own children and wife;
2. The experience of the wife and her ability to care for other children in her home;
3. The ability of the husband and wife to cope with common behavior difficulties of school-age children, and with more serious defiant, withdrawn, and careless behaviors of foster children;
4. The husband's willingness to cooperate with the social worker;
5. The extent to which a prospective foster parent's own children have been taught individuality;
6. The husband's attitude and development of sensitivity toward his own children, and his self-awareness and self-confidence in being a father;
7. The fact that major decision making is successful, whether accomplished jointly or singly by the father;
8. The foster mother's age (between 35 and 40).

In a study by Bush, Gordon, and LeBailly (1977), children were asked to evaluate their foster homes. Criteria for success that frequently emerged were those of love, understanding, and material resources.

Younger foster mothers and fathers, ages 35 to 40, who had had their own children, and who were of a different religion than their foster children, were more successful in keeping the foster child and allowing for his or her natural emotional growth and development until the child returned to the natural family, or until placement in a permanent residence occurred.

Social class, foster-parent experience, and age or sex of the foster parents' own children are apparently not related to foster-care outcome. Rowe (1976) found that economic status of foster parents is unrelated to successful foster care. He also maintains that foster-mother acceptance is positively associated with successful fostering.

## Summary

Approximately 170,000 married couples are involved in foster parenting throughout the United States. These couples are generally in their forties and members of the lower to middle class. Although foster parents can be described demographically, their role is not so easily identified. Their actual responsibilities may vary from state to state. Even within the same state, many foster parents feel they were not adequately informed or trained, and as a result attrition rates are fairly high.

A constellation of factors and variables is involved in successful foster-child care. However, tolerance, patience, acceptance, and responsiveness to the child's needs seem to be the key to harmony in foster parenting. This theme should be familiar by now, as these elements are important facilitators of growth in other family configurations as well. Foster parents exemplifying these characteristics not only benefit the foster child, but can serve as models for the child's natural parents as well, to facilitate the child's return to their own home.

# SELF-CHECK

1. According to statistics, all of the following are true about foster parents *except:*
   a. the majority of foster parents have only young children of their own.
   b. the majority of foster parents are white.
   c. the majority of foster parents are not educated beyond high school.
   d. foster-parent incomes are generally in the lower- to middle-class range.
2. While the foster-parent role is often ambiguous and varied, the majority of foster parents see their roles as similar to those of:
   a. biological parents.
   b. adoptive parents.
   c. hired guardians.
   d. None of the above are true.
3. A basic assumption of the role-modeling program that utilizes foster parents as models for biological parents is that:
   a. biological parents are susceptible to change.

b. biological parents are not familiar with what is expected of them.

c. biological parents have deficits in parenting.

d. b and c are true.

4. Which of the following is true of foster-care payments?

a. Foster-family rates usually cover necessary expenses.

b. Payments are generally the same nationwide.

c. There is no change of payment with more training and education of foster parents after placement.

d. Most agencies feel their rates are not high enough to attract and retain foster parents.

5. All of the following are exhibited by successful foster parents *except:*

a. accepting poorer academic performance and social difficulties from the child.

b. high social class.

c. a genuine liking for children.

d. feeling secure about their own abilities in raising kids.

KEY: 1–a; 2–b; 3–d; 4–c; 5–b

# REFERENCES

## P R E F A C E
## A N D
## C H A P T E R  1

Auerback, A. G. (1968). *Parents learn through discussion: Principles and practices of parent group education.* New York: Wiley.

Baumrind, D. (1971). Current patterns of parental authority. *Developmental Psychology Monographs, 4,* 101.

Belsky, J. (1979). Mother–father–infant interaction: A naturalistic observational study. *Developmental Psychology, 15,* 601–607.

Biehler, R. F. (1981). *Child development: An introduction* (2nd ed.). Boston: Houghton Mifflin.

Bigner, J. J. (1972). Parent education in popular literature: 1950–1970. *Family Coordinator, 21,* 313–319.

Bigner, J. J. (1979). *Parent–child relations: An introduction to parenting.* New York: Macmillan.

Bird, C. (1979). *The two-paycheck marriage.* New York: Rawson Wade.

Brazelton, T. B. (1974). *Toddlers and parents: A declaration of independence.* New York: Delacorte Press.

Bronfenbrenner, U. (1958). Socialization and social class through time and space. In E. E. Maccoby, T. M. Newcomb, & E. C. Hartley (Eds.), *Readings in social psychology* (3rd ed.). New York: Holt, Rinehart and Winston.

Bronfenbrenner, U. (1961). The changing American child. *Journal of Social Issues, 17,* 6–18.

Brown, D. G. (1956). Sex role preference in young children. *Psychological Monographs, 70,* 1–9.

Brown, D. G. (1958). Sex role development in a changing culture. *Psychological Bulletin, 55,* 232–242.

Clarke-Stewart, K. A. (1978). And daddy makes three: The father's impact on mother and young child. *Child Development, 49,* 466–478.

Croake, J., & Glover, K. (1977). A history and evaluation of parent education. *Family Coordinator, 26,* 151–158.

DeFrain, J. (1979). Androgynous parents tell who they are and what they need. *Family Coordinator, 28,* 237–243.

deMause, L. (Ed.). (1974). *The history of childhood.* New York: Psychohistory Press.

Demos, J. (1970). *Little commonwealth: Family life in Plymouth Colony.* New York: Harcourt Brace.

Dennis, W. (1972). *The Hopi child.* New York: Appleton-Century-Crofts.

Dinkmeyer, D., & McKay, G. (1976). *Systematic training for effective parenting.* Circle Pines, MN: American Guidance Services.

Dobson, J. (1970). *Dare to discipline.* Wheaton, IL: Tyndale.

Dodson, F. (1970). *How to parent.* New York: Signet.

Dreikurs, R., & Soltz, V. (1964). *Children: The challenge.* Des Moines, IA: Meredith Press.

Ellis, G. J., Lee, G. R., & Petersen, L. R. (1978). Supervision and conformity: A cross-cultural analysis of parental socialization values. *American Journal of Sociology, 84,* 386–403.

Erlanger, H. S. (1974). Social class and corporal punishment in child-rearing: A reassessment. *American Sociological Review, 39,* 68–85.

Fantini, M. D., & Cardenas, R. (1980). *Parenting in a multicultural society.* New York: Longman.

Gecas, V., & Nye, F. I. (1974). Sex and class differences in parent–child interaction: A test of Kohn's hypothesis. *Journal of Marriage and the Family, 36,* 742–749.

Ginott, H. (1965). *Between parent and child.* New York: Macmillan.

Gordon, H. (1970). *Parent effectiveness training.* New York: Peter H. Wyden.

Harman, D., & Brim, O. G. (1980). *Learning to be parents: Principles, programs, and methods.* Beverly Hills, CA: Sage.

Harmon, C., & Zigler, E. (1980). Parent education in the 1970s: Policy, panacea, or programatism. *Merrill-Palmer Quarterly, 26,* 439–451.

Hess, R. D. (1970). Social class and ethnic influences upon socialization. In P. H. Mussen (Ed.), *Carmichael's manual of child psychology* (Vol. 2). New York: Wiley.

Hoffman, L. W., & Hoffman, M. L. (1973). The value of children to parents. In J. T. Fawcett (Ed.), *Psychological perspectives on population* (pp. 19–76). New York: Basic Books.

Houseknecht, S. K. (1982). Voluntary childlessness: Toward a theoretical integration. *Journal of Family Issues, 3,* 459–471.

Ilg, F. L., & Ames, L. B. (1955). *Child behavior.* New York: Harper & Brothers.

Ilg, F. L., Ames, L. B., & Baker, S. M. (1981). *Child behavior* (rev. ed.). New York: Harper & Row.

Karpowitz, D. H. (1980). A conceptualization of the American family. In M. J. Fines (Ed.), *Handbook on parent education.* New York: Academic Press.

Kephart, W. M. (1981). *The family, society, and the individual.* New York: Houghton Mifflin.

Kohn, M. (1977). *Social competence, symptoms and underachievement in childhood: A longitudinal perspective.* Washington, DC: Winston.

Kotelchuck, M. (1976). The infant's relationship to the father: Experimental evidence. In M. E. Lamb (Ed.), *The role of the father in child development.* New York: Wiley.

Lamb, M. E. (1976). Effects of stress and cohort on mother– and father–infant interaction. *Developmental Psychology, 12,* 435–443.

Lamb, M. E. (1977). The development of mother–infant and father–infant attachments in the second year of life. *Developmental Psychology, 13,* 637–648.

Lamb, M. E. (1978). Qualitative aspects of mother– and father–infant attachments. *Infant Behavior and Development, 1,* 265–275.

Lamb, M. E., & Sagi, A. (1983). *Fatherhood and family policy.* New Jersey: Lawrence Erlbaum Associates.

Lester, B. M., Kotelchuck, M., Spelke, E., Sellers, J. J., & Klein, R. E. (1974). Separation protest in Guatemalan infants: Cross-cultural and cognitive findings. *Developmental Psychology, 10,* 79–85.

Levine, R. A. (1974). Parental goals: A cross-cultural review. *Teachers College Record, 76,* 226–239.

Levine, R. A. (1980). A cross-cultural perspective on parenting. In M. D. Fantini & R. Cardenas (Eds.), *Parenting in a multicultural society.* New York: Longman.

Maccoby, E. E. (1980). *Social development: Psychological growth and the parent–child relationship.* New York: Harcourt Brace.

McClelland, D. C., Constantion, C. A., Regalado, D., & Stone, C. (1978). Making it to maturity. *Psychology Today, 12,* 53.

McLaughlin, M. M. (1974). Survivors and surrogates: Children and parents from the ninth to the thirteenth centuries. In L. deMause (Ed.), *The History of childhood*. New York: The Psychohistory Press.

O'Dell, S. (1974). Training parents in behavior modification: A review. *Psychological Bulletin, 81*, 418–433.

Pickarts, E., & Fargo, J. (1971). *Parent education: Toward parental competence.* New York: Appleton-Century-Crofts.

Plato. (1960). *The collected dialogues* (A. E. Taylor, Trans.). New York: E. P. Dutton.

Pollock, L. A. (1983). *Forgotten children.* Cambridge: Cambridge University Press.

Powell, B. B. (1978). Parenting—A natural instinct? *Health Education, 9,* 8–11.

Radin, N. (1978). *Child-rearing fathers in intact families with preschoolers.* Paper presented at the annual meeting of the American Psychological Association, Toronto.

Radin, N. (1981a). The role of the father in cognitive/academic/intellectual development. In M. E. Lamb (Ed.), *The role of the father in child development* (rev. ed.). New York: Wiley.

Radin, N. (1981b). Childrearing fathers in intact families: An exploration of some antecedents and consequences. *Merrill-Palmer Quarterly, 27,* 489–514.

Radin, N. (1982). Primary caregiving and role-sharing fathers. In M. E. Lamb (Ed.), *Nontraditional families: Parenting and child development.* Hillsdale, NJ: Lawrence Erlbaum Associates.

Ross, G., Kagan, J., Zelzao, P., & Kotelchuck, M. (1975). Separation protest in infants in home and laboratory. *Developmental Psychology, 11,* 256–257.

Rousseau, J. J. (1974). *Émile, or on education.* London: Dent. (Originally published 1762.)

Russell, G., & Radin, N. (1983). Increased paternal participation: The father's perspective. In M. E. Lamb & A. Sagi (Eds.), *Fatherhood and family policy.* New Jersey: Lawrence Erlbaum Associates.

Sagi, A. (1982). Antecedents and consequences of various degrees of paternal involvement in child-rearing: The Israeli project. In M. E. Lamb (Ed.), *Nontraditional families: Parenting and child development.* Hillsdale, NJ: Lawrence Erlbaum Associates.

Santrock, J. W. & Warshak, R. A. (1979). Father custody and social development in boys and girls. *Journal of Social Issues, 35,* 112–125.

Satir, V. (1972). *Peoplemaking.* Palo Alto, CA: Science and Behavior Books.

Sears, R., Maccoby, E., & Levin, H. (1957). *Patterns of childrearing.* Evanston, IL: Row, Peterson.

Soltz, V. (1967). *Study group leader's manual for children: The challenge.* Chicago: Alfred Adler Institute.

Spock, B. (1957). *Baby and child care.* New York: Pocket Books.

Spock, B. (1968). Baby and child care. New York: Hawthorn Books.

Stendler, C. (1950). Sixty years of child training practices. *Journal of Pediatrics, 36,* 122–134.

Stevens, J. H. (1984). Child development knowledge and parenting skills. *Family Relations, 33,* 237–244.

Sunley, R. (1955). Early nineteenth-century American literature on child rearing. In M. Mead & M. Wolfenstein (Eds.), *Childhood in contemporary cultures* (pp. 150–167). Chicago: University of Chicago Press.

Thompson, R. A. (1983). The father's case in child custody disputes: The contributions of psychological research. In M. E. Lamb & A. Sagi (Eds.), *Fatherhood and family policy.* New Jersey: Lawrence Erlbaum Associates.

Tucker, M. J. (1974). The child as beginning and end: Fifteenth and sixteenth century English childhood. In L. deMause (Ed.), *The history of childhood.* New York: Psychohistory Press.

Turnbull, C. M. (1972). *The mountain people.* New York: Simon and Schuster.

Vander Zanden, J. W. (1981). *Human development* (2nd ed.). New York: Alfred A. Knopf.

Veevers, J. E. (1972). Declining childlessness and age at marriage: A test of a hypothesis. *Social Biology, 19,* 285–288.

Waggoner, R. W. (1970). The presidential address: Cultural dissonance and psychiatry. *American Journal of Psychiatry, 12,* 1–8.

White, B. L., Kaban, B. T., Attanucci, J., & Shapiro, B. B. (1978). *Experience and enrichment: Major influences on the development of the young child.* Englewood Cliffs, NJ: Prentice-Hall.

Whiting, J. W. M., & Child, I. L. (1953). *Child training and personality: A cross-cultural study.* New Haven: Yale University Press.

Wood, S. J., Bishop, R. S., & Cohen, D. (1978). *Parenting: Four patterns of childrearing.* New York: Hart.

Wright, J. D., & Wright, S. R. (1976). Social class and parental values for children: A replication and extension of the Kohn thesis. *American Sociological Review, 41,* 527–537.

# CHAPTER 2

Baldwin, A. L. (1949). The effect of home environment on nursery school behavior. *Child Development, 20,* 49–62.

Baldwin, A. L., Kalhorn, J., & Breese, F. (1945). Patterns of parent behavior. *Psychological Monographs, 58* (3, Whole No. 268).

Bandura, A., & Walters, R. H. (1959). *Adolescent aggression.* New York: Ronald Press.

Barron, A. P., & Earls, F. (1984). The relation of temperament and social factors to behavior problems in three-year-old children. *Journal of Child Psychology and Psychiatry, 25,* 23–33.

Baumrind, D. (1967). Child care practices anteceding three patterns of pre-school behavior. *Genetic Psychology Monographs, 75,* 43–88.

Baumrind, D. (1971). Current patterns of parental authority. *Developmental Psychology Monographs, 4* (1, Pt. 2).

Baumrind, D. (1973). The development of instrumental competence through socialization. In A. D. Pick (Ed.), *Minnesota Symposium of Child Psychology* (Vol. 7). Minneapolis: University of Minnesota Press.

Becker, W. C. (1964). Consequences of different kinds of parental discipline. In M. L. Hoffman & L. W. Hoffman (Eds.), *Review of child development* (Vol. 1). New York: Sage Foundation.

Becker, W. C., Peterson, D. R., Hellmer, L. A., Shoemaker, D. J., & Quay, H. C. (1959). Factors in parental behavior and personality as related to problem behavior in children. *Journal of Consulting Psychology, 23,* 107–118.

Becker, W. C., Peterson, D. R., Luria, F., Shoemaker, D. J., & Hellmer, L. A. (1962). Relations of factors dervied from parent-interview ratings to behavior problems of five-year-olds. *Child Development, 33,* 509–535.

Belsky, J., & Spanier, G. B. (1984). *The child in the family.* Reading, MA: Addison-Wesley.

Burt, C. (1929). *The young delinquent.* New York: Appleton.

Endsley, R. C., Hutchens, M. A., Garner, A. P., & Martin, M. J. (1979). Interrelationships among selected maternal behaviors, authoritarianism, and pre-school children's verbal and nonverbal curiosity. *Child Development, 50,* 331–339.

Gruenberg, B. C. (Ed.). (1926). *Guidance of childhood and youth: Readings in child study.* New York: Macmillan.

Healy, W., & Bronner, A. F. (1926). *Delinquents and criminals: Their making and unmaking.* New York: Macmillan.

Kagan, J., & Moss, H. A. (1962). *Birth to maturity: The Fels study of psychological development.* New York: Wiley.

Levin, H. (1958). Permissive childrearing and adult role behavior. In D. E. Dunlany, R. L. DeValois, D. C. Beardsley, & M. R. Winterbottom (Eds.), *Contributions to modern psychology* (pp. 307–312). New York: Oxford University Press.

Lewis, H. (1954). *Deprived children.* London: Oxford University Press.

Maccoby, E. E. (1961). The taking of adult roles in middle adulthood. *Journal of Abnormal and Social Psychology, 63,* 493–503.

Maccoby, E. E. (1980). *Social development: Psychological growth and the parent–child relationship.* New York: Harcourt Brace Jovanovich.

McCall, R. B. (1974). Exploratory manipulation and play in the human infant. *Monographs of the Society for Research in Child Development, 39* (No. 155).

Quinton, D., & Rutter, M. (1984). Parents with children in care: I. Current circumstances and parenting. *Journal of Child Psychology and Psychiatry, 25,* 211–229.

Radin, N. (1971). Maternal warmth, achievement motivation and cognitive functioning in lower-class preschool children. *Child Development, 42,* 1560–1565.

Radin, N. (1973). Observed paternal behaviors as antecedents of intellectual functioning in young boys. *Developmental Psychology, 8,* 369–376.

Roff, M. A. (1949). A factorial study of the Fels parent behavior scales. *Child Development, 20,* 29–45.

Rosenthal, M. J. Finkelstein, M., Ni, E., & Robertson, R. E. (1959). A study of mother–child relationships in the emotional disorders of children. *Genetic and Psychological Monographs, 60,* 65–116.

Schaefer, E. S. (1959). A circumplex model for maternal behavior. *Journal of Abnormal and Social Psychology, 59,* 226–235.

Sears, R. R. (1961). The relationship of early socialization experiences to aggression in middle childhood. *Journal of Abnormal and Social Psychology, 63,* 466–492.

Sears, R. R., Maccoby, E. E., & Levin, H. (1957). *Patterns of childrearing.* Evanston, IL: Row, Peterson.

Symonds, P. M. (1939). *The psychology of parent–child relationships.* New York: Appleton-Century.

Takala, M., Nummenmaa, T., & Kauranne, V. I. (1960). Parental attitudes and childrearing practices: A methodological study. *Acta Academiue Paedogagicae Jyvaskylaesis, 19,* 1–75.

Turner, P. H., & Harris, M. B. (1984). Parental attitudes and preschool children's social competence. *Journal of Genetic Psychology, 144,* 105–113.

Watson, G. (1934). A comparison of the effects of lax versus strict home training. *Journal of Social Psychology, 5,* 102–105.

Watson, G. (1957). Some personality differences in children related to strict or permissive parental discipline. *Journal of Psychology, 44,* 227–249.

Watson, J. B. (1928). *Psychological care of infant and child.* New York: Norton.

# CHAPTER 3

Baldwin, A. L. (1967). *Theories of child development.* New York: Wiley.

Beecroft, R. (1966). *Classical conditioning.* Goleta, CA: Psychonomic Press.

Erikson, E. H. (1950). *Childhood and society.* New York: Norton.

Erikson, E. H. (1963). *Childhood and society* (2nd ed.). New York: Norton.

Fasick, F. A. (1984). Parents, peers, youth culture and autonomy in adolescence. *Adolescence, 19,* 143–157.

Ferster, C. B., & Skinner, B. F. (1957). *Schedules of reinforcement.* New York: Appleton-Century-Crofts.

Franklin, B. Excerpt reprinted in *Journal of Applied Behavioral Analysis, 2,* 247, No. 4, 1969.

*A healthy personality for every child* (1951). A digest of the fact-finding report to the Midcentury White House Conference on Children and Youth. Raleigh, N.C.: Health Publications Institute.

Liebert, R. M., Poulos, R. W., & Marmor, G. S. (1977). *Developmental psychology* (2nd ed.). Englewood Cliffs, NJ: Prentice-Hall.

Lomax, E. M. R., Kagan, J., & Rosenkrantz, B. G. (1978). *Science and patterns of child care.* San Francisco: Freeman.

Maier, H. W. (1969). *Three theories of child development.* New York: Harper & Row.

Mischel, W. (1976). *Introduction to personality* (2nd ed.). New York: Holt, Rinehart and Winston.

Rescorla, R. A. (1967). Pavlovian conditioning and its proper control procedures. *Psychological Review, 74,* 83–88.

Sawrey, J., & Telford, C. (1968). *The psychology of adjustment.* Boston: Allyn and Bacon.

Schwartz, B. (1978). *Psychology of learning and behavior.* New York: Norton.

Skinner, B. F. (1948). "Superstition" in the pigeon. *Journal of Experimental Psychology, 38,* 168–172.

Skinner, B. F. (1953). *Science and human behavior.* New York: Macmillan.

Skinner, B. F. (1972). *Cumulative record* (3rd ed.). New York: Appleton-Century-Crofts.

Spock, B. (1945). *Baby and child care.* New York: Hawthorn Books.

Thorndike, E. L. (1898). Animal intelligence: An experimental study of the associative process in animals. *Psychological Review Monograph Supplement, 2* (4, Whole No. 8).

Waterman, A. S. (1982). Identity development from adolescence to adulthood: An extension of theory and a review of research. *Developmental Psychology, 18,* 341–358.

Watson, J. B. (1958). *Behavior: An introduction to comparative psychology.* New York: Henry Holt. (Originally published 1914.)

White, R. W. (1964). *The abnormal personality.* New York: Ronald.

# CHAPTER 4

Asch, S. C. (1944). Forming impressions of personality. *Journal of Abnormal and Social Psychology, 41,* 258–29.

Berlyne, D. E. (1964). Recent developments in Piaget's work. In R. J. C. Harper, C. C. Anderson, C. M. Christensen, & S. M. Hunka (Eds.), *The cognitive processes: Readings.* Englewood Cliffs, NJ: Prentice-Hall.

Brockner, J., Gardner, M., Bierman, J., Mahan, T., Thomas, B., Weiss, W., Winters, L., & Mitchell, A. (1983). The roles of self-esteem and self-consciousness in the Wortman-Brehm Model of reactance and learned helplessness. *Journal of Personality and Social Psychology, 45,* 199–209.

Coopersmith,S. (1967). *The antecedents of self-esteem.* San Francisco: Freeman.

Daly, M. J., & Burton, R. L. (1983). Self-esteem and irrational beliefs: An exploratory investigation with implications for counseling. *Journal of Counseling Psychology, 30,* 361–366.

Elkind, D. (1981). *The hurried child: Growing up too fast too soon.* Reading, MA: Addison-Wesley.

Felker, D. (1974). *Building positive self-concepts.* Minneapolis: Burgess.

Flavell, J. H. (1963). *The developmental psychology of Jean Piaget.* New York: Van Nostrand.

Freedman, J. L., Carlsmith, J. M., & Sears, P. O. (1970). *Social psychology.* Englewood Cliffs, NJ: Prentice-Hall.

Geist, C. R., & Borecki, S. (1982). Social avoidance and distress as a prediction of perceived locus of control and level of self-esteem. *Journal of Clinical Psychology, 38,* 611–613.

Hardy, K. R. (1975). Personal communication.

Hooper, F. H. (1968). Piagetian research and education. In L. E. Sigel & F. H. Hooper (Eds.), *Logical thinking in children*. New York: Holt, Rinehart and Winston.

Inhelder, B., & Piaget, J. (1958) *The growth of logical thinking from childhood to adolescence*. New York: Basic Books.

Lefevre, E. R., & West. M. L. (1981). Assertiveness correlations with self-esteem, locus of control, interpersonal anxiety, fear of disapproval, and depression. *Psychiatric Journal of the University of Ottawa, 6,* 246–251.

Lewin, K. (1935). *A dynamic theory of personality*. New York: McGraw-Hill.

Liebert, R. M., Poulos, R. W., & Marmor, G. S. (1977). *Developmental psychology* (2nd ed.). Englewood Cliffs, NJ: Prentice-Hall.

Maccoby, E. E. (1980). *Social development: Psychological growth and the parent–child relationship*. New York: Harcourt Brace Jovanovich.

Maier, H. W. (1969). *Three theories of cognitive development*. New York: Harper & Row.

Maier, H. W. (1978). *Three theories of child development*. New York: Harper & Row.

Majares, R. L., & Fox, R. (1984). Children's spontaneous use of real-world information in problem solving. *Journal of Genetic Psychology, 144,* 89–97.

Maslow, A. (1954). *Motivation and personality*. New York: Harper & Brothers.

Maslow, A. (1962). Perceiving, behaving, becoming. In *ASCE Yearbook*. New York: ASCD.

McCall, George J., & Simmons, J. R. (1966). *Identities and interactions*. New York: Free Press.

Phillips, J. L. (1969). *The origins of intellect: Piaget's theory*. San Francisco: Freeman.

Piaget, J., & Inhelder, B. (1956). *The child's conception of space*. London: Routledge & Kegan Paul.

Prosen, M., Clark, D. C., Harrow, W., & Fawcett, J. (1983) Guilt and conscience in major depressive episodes. *American Journal of Psychiatry, 140,* 839–844.

Roe, R. (Ed.). (1971). *Developmental psychology today*. Del Mar, CA: Communication Research Machines.

Rogers, C. (1951). *Client-centered counseling*. Boston: Houghton Mifflin.

Rogers, C. (1961). *On becoming a person*. Boston: Houghton Mifflin.

Rogers, L. R. (1969). *Freedom to learn*. Columbus, OH: Charles E. Merrill.

Rubin, Z. (1968). *Liking and loving: An invitation to social psychology*. New York: Holt, Rinehart and Winston.

Sattler, J. M. (1982). *Assessment of children's intelligence and special abilities* (2nd ed.). Boston: Allyn and Bacon.

Sigel, I. E. (1969). The Piagetian system and the world of education. In D. Elkind & J. H. Flavell (Eds.), *Studies in cognitive development: Essays in honor of Jean Piaget*. New York: Oxford University Press.

Snygg, D., & Combs, A. (1949). *Individual behavior*. New York: Harper & Row.

Sorokin, P. A., & Berger, C. A. (1939). *Time budgets of human behavior*. Cambridge: Harvard University Press. Cited in Snygg & Combs, 1949, 30.

Vander Zanden, J. W. (1981). *Human development* (2nd ed.). New York: Alfred A. Knopf.

Zemore, R., & Bretell, D. (1983) Depression-proneness, low self-esteem, unhappy outlook, and narcissistic vulnerability. *Psychological Reports, 52,* 223–230.

# CHAPTER 5

Ainsworth, M. D. S. (1982). Attachment: Retrospect and prospect. In C. M. Parkes & J. Stevenson-Hinde (Eds.), *The place of attachment in human behavior*. New York: Tavistock.

Ainsworth, M. D. S., Blehar, M. C., Waters, E., & Wall, S. (1978). *Patterns of attachment: A psychological study of the strange situation.* Hillsdale. NJ: Lawrence Erlbaum.

Baumrind, D. (1974). Current patterns of parental authority. *Developmental Psychology,* Monographs, 1–103.

Biller, H. B. (1974). *Paternal deprivation.* Lexington, MA: Heath.

Biller, H. B. (1976). The father and personality development: Paternal deprivation and sex-role development. In M. E. Lamb (Ed.), *The role of the father in child development.* New York: Wiley.

Biller, H. B. (1981). The father and sex-role development. In M. E. Lamb (Ed.), *The role of the father in child development.* New York: Wiley.

Block, J. (1971). *Lives through time.* Berkeley, CA: Bancroft Books.

Bloom, B. S. (1964). *Stability and change in human characteristics.* New York: Wiley.

Bowlby, J. (1980). *Attachment and loss (Vol. 3): Loss: Sadness and depression.* New York: Basic Books.

Bradburn, N. M., & Caplovitz, D. (1965). *Reports on happiness: A pilot study of behavior related to mental health.* Chicago: Aldine.

Bradburn, N. M., & Noll, C. E. (1969). *The structure of psychological well-being.* Chicago: Aldine.

Bridger, W. H. (1965). Individual differences in behavior and autonomic activity in newborn infants. *American Journal of Public Health, 55,* 1899–1901.

Brody, E. B., & Brody, N. (1976). *Intelligence: Nature, determinants, and consequences.* New York: Academic Press.

Broverman, D. M., Klaiber, E. L., & Vogel, W. (1980). Gonadal hormones and cognitive functioning. In J. E. Parsons (Ed.), *The psychobiology of sex differences and sex roles.* Washington: Hemisphere.

Cadoret, R., & Cain, C. (1980). Sex differences in predictors of antisocial behavior in adoptees. *Archives of General Psychiatry, 37,* 1171–1175.

Carey, W. B., & McDevitt, S. C. (1978). Stability and change in individual temperament diagnosis from infancy to childhood. *Journal of the American Academy of Child Psychiatry, 17,* 331–337.

Crowe, R. R. (1974). An adoption study of antisocial personality. *Archives of General Psychiatry, 31,* 785–791.

Cummings, E. M., Zahn-Waxler, C., & Radke-Yarrow, M. (1981). Young children's responses to expressions of anger and affection by others in the family. *Child Development, 52,* 1274–1282.

DeChateau, P., & Wilberg, B. (1977). Long-term effect on mother–infant behavior of extra contact during the first hour post partum. *Acta Paediatrica Scandinavia, 66,* 145–151.

Eysenck, H. J. (1982). *Personality, genetics, and behavior.* New York: Praeger.

Fish, K. D., & Biller, H. B. (1973). Perceived childhood paternal relationships and college females' personal adjustment. *Adolescence, 8,* 415–420.

Freedman, D. G. (1979). *Human sociology.* New York: The Free Press.

George, C., & Main, M. (1979). Social interactions of abuse of children: Approach, avoidance and aggression. *Child Development, 50,* 306–318.

Ginott, H. G. (1969). *Between parent and child.* New York: Avon.

Goodwin, D. W., Schulsinger, F., Hermanson, L. Guze, S. B., & Winokur, G. (1973). Alcohol problems in adoptees raised apart from alcoholic biological parents. *Archives of General Psychiatry, 28,* 238–243.

Gottesman, I. I., & Shields, J. (1974). *Schizophrenia and genetics.* New York: Academic Press.

Hales, D. J., Lozoff, B., Sosa, R., & Kennell, J. H. (1977). Defining the limits of the maternal sensitive period. *Developmental Medicine and Child Neurology, 19,* 454–461.

Herrnstein, R. J. (1973). *IQ in the meritocracy.* Boston: Little, Brown.

Hurlock, E. B. (1972). *Child Development.* New York: McGraw-Hill.

Hurlock, E. B. (1980). *Developmental psychology: A life-span approach.* New York: McGraw-Hill.

James, W. (1890). *The principles of psychology.* New York: Henry Holt and Company.

Jencks, C. (1972). *Inequality: A reassessment of the effect of family and schooling in America.* New York: Basic Books.

Jensen, A. R. (1973). *Educability and group differences.* New York: Harper & Row.

Kamin, L. J. (1974). *The science and politics of IQ.* Potomac, MD: Lawrence Erlbaum.

Kety, S. S., Rosenthal, D., Wender, P. H., & Schulsinger, F. (1971). Mental illness in the biological and adoptive families of adopted schizophrenics. *American Journal of Psychiatry, 128,* 302–306.

Klaus, M. H., Jerauld, R., Kreger, N., McAlpine, W., Steffa, M., & Kennell, J. H. (1972). Maternal attachment: Importance of the first post-partum days. *New England Journal of Medicine, 286,* 460–463.

Kramer, L. I., & Pierpoint, M. E. (1976). Rocking waterbeds and auditory stimuli to enhance growth of preterm infants. *Journal of Pediatrics, 88,* 297–299.

Lieberman, A. F. (1977). Preschoolers' competence with a peer: Relations with attachment and peer experiences. *Child Development, 48,* 1277–1287.

Lindon, E., & Young, P. A. (1981). Genetical theory and personality differences. In R. Lynn (Ed.), *Dimensions of personality.* New York: Pergamon Press.

Maccoby, E. E., & Jacklin, C. N. (1974). Myth, reality and shades of grey: What we know and don't know about sex differences. *Psychology Today, 8,* 109–112.

McClearn, G. E., & DeFries, J. C. (1973). Introduction to behavior genetics. San Francisco, CA: Freeman.

McClelland, C. A., Constantian, R. D., & Stone, C. (1978). Making it to maturity. *Psychology Today, 12,* 42.

McGee, M. G. (1979). *Human spatial abilities: Sources of sex differences.* New York: Praeger.

McKnew, D. H., & Cytryn, L. (1973). Historical background in children with affective disorders. *American Journal of Psychiatry, 130,* 1278–1279.

Parke, R. D., & Sawin, D. B. (1977). Fathering: It's a major role. *Psychology Today, 11,* 109–112.

Parsons, J. E. (1980). Psychosexual neutrality: Is anatomy destiny? In J. E. Parsons (Ed.), *The psychobiology of sex differences and sex roles.* Washington: Hemisphere.

Rice, R. D. (1977). Neurophysiological development in premature infants following stimulation. *Developmental Psychology, 13,* 69–76.

Rosenthal, D. (1970). *Genetic theory and abnormal behavior.* New York: McGraw-Hill.

Rosenthal, D. (1971). *Genetics of psychopathology.* New York: McGraw-Hill.

Schaffer, H. R., & Emerson, P. E. 91964). The development of social attachments in infancy. *Monographs of the Society for Research in Child Development, 29*(3), 1–150.

Schulsinger, F. (1972). Psychopathy: Heredity and environment. *International Journal of Mental Health, 1,* 190–206.

Sears, R., Maccoby, E., & Levin, H. (1957). *Patterns of childrearing.* Evanston, IL: Row, Peterson.

Secord, P., & Backman, C. (1974). *Social psychology.* New York: McGraw-Hill.

Segal, J., & Yahraes, H. (1978). *A child's journey.* New York: McGraw-Hill.

Sherman, J. A. (1978). *Sex-related cognitive differences.* Springfield, IL: Charles C Thomas.

Slater, E., & Cowie, V. (1971). *The genetics of mental disorders.* London: Oxford University Press.

Thomas, A. S., Chess, S., & Birch H. G. (1970). The origin of personality. *Scientific American, 223,* 102–109.

Vander Zanden, J.W. (1980). *Human development.* New York: Knopf.

Waters, E., Wippman, J., & Sroufe, L. A. (1979). Attachment, positive affect, and competence in the peer group: Two studies in construct validation. *Child Development, 50,* 821–829.

Yarrow, M. R., Scott, R., & Waxler, C. Z. (1973). Learning concern for others. *Developmental Psychology, 8,* 240–260.

Zern, D. S., & Stern, G. W. (1983). The impact of obedience on intelligence and self-concept: A longitudinal study involving different situational contexts. *Genetic Psychology Monographs, 108,* 245–265.

Ziegler, M. E. (1979). *The father's influence on his school-age child's academic performance and cognitive development.* Doctoral dissertation. University of Michigan.

# CHAPTER 6

Barnett, L. A., & Kleiber, D. A. (1984). Playfulness and the early play environment. *Journal of Genetic Psychology, 144,* 153–164.

Baumrind, D. (1967). Child care practices anteceding three patterns of preschool behavior. *Genetic Psychology Monographs, 75,* 43–88.

Coleman, J. C. (1974). *Contemporary psychology and effective behavior.* Glenville, IL: Scott Foresman.

Frankl, V. (1962). *Man's search for meaning.* New York: Simon and Schuster.

Gander, M. J., & Gardner, H. W. (1981). *Child and adolescent development.* Boston: Little, Brown.

Leon, G. R. (1974). *Case history of deviant behavior.* Boston: Holbrook Press.

Levy, D. M. (1943). *Maternal overprotection.* New York: Columbia University Press.

Macarou, D. (1970). *Incentives to work.* San Francisco: Jossey Bass.

Maccoby, E. (1980). *Social development: Psychological growth and the parent–child relationship.* New York: Harcourt Brace Jovanovich.

Mandelkev, D. R., & Montgomery, R. (1973). *Housing in America.* Indianapolis: Bobbs-Merrill.

Maslow, A. H. (1943). A dynamic theory of human motivation. *Psychological Review, 50,* 370–396.

McCandless, B. R. (1967). *Children: Behavior and development* (2nd ed.). New York: Holt, Rinehart and Winston.

Oswald, I. (1962). *Sleeping and waking.* New York: Elsevier.

Quinton, D., & Rutter, M. (1984). Parents with children in care—I. Current circumstances and parenting. *Journal of Child Psychology and Psychiatry, 25,* 211–229.

Renshaw, S., Miller, V. L., & Marquis, D. P. (1983). *Children's sleep.* New York: Macmillan.

Scrimshaw, N., & Gordon, J. E. (1968). *Malnutrition, learning, and behavior.* Cambridge, MA: MIT Press.

Shneour, E. (1974). *The malnourished mind.* Garden City, NY: Anchor Press/Doubleday.

Staub, E. (1979). *Positive social behavior and morality* (2nd ed.). New York: Academic Press.

Tolstoy, L. (1882). My confession. Quoted in W. James, *The varieties of religious experience* (pp. 153–155). New York: Longmans Green.

Vander Zanden, J. W. (1981). *Human development* (2nd ed.). New York: Alfred A. Knopf.

Wilner, D. M., Walkley, R. P. Pinkerton, T. C. & Tayback, M. (1962). A longitudinal study of the effects of housing on morbidity and mental health. *The housing environment and family life.* Baltimore, MD: Johns Hopkins Press.

# CHAPTER 7

Christie, D. J., Hiss, M., & Lozanoff, B. (1984). Modification of inattentive classroom behavior. *Behavior Modification, 8,* 391–406.

Hartig, M., & Kanfer, F. H. (1973). The role of verbal self-instructions in children's resistance to temptation. *Journal of Personality and Social Psychology, 25,* 259–267.

Madsen, C. H., Becker, W. C., & Thomas, D. R. (1968). Rules, praise, and ignoring: Elements of elementary classroom control. *Journal of Applied Behavioral Analysis, 1,* 139–150.

Michelson, L., Dilorenzo, T. M., & Calpin, J. P. (1981). Modifying excessive lunchroom noise. *Behavior Modification, 5,* 553–564.

O'Leary, K. D. (1968). The effects of self-instruction on immoral behavior. *Journal of Experimental Child Psychology, 6,* 297–301.

Premack, D. (1965). Reinforcement theory. In D. Levine (Ed.), *Nebraska Symposium on Motivation* (Vol. 13) (pp. 123–128). Lincoln: University of Nebraska Press.

Robinson, P. (1981). *Fundamentals of experimental psychology.* Englewood Cliffs, NJ: Prentice-Hall.

Rosen, H. S., & Rosen, L. A. (1983). Elementary stealing. *Behavior Modification, 7,* 56–63.

Schmidt, G. W., & Ulrich, R. E. (1969). Effects of group contingent events upon classroom noise. *Journal of Applied Behavioral Analysis, 2,* 171–179.

Skinner, B. F. (1951, December). How to teach animals. *Scientific American,* 26–29.

Skinner, B. F. (1953). *Science and human behavior.* New York: Macmillan.

Watson, D. L., & Tharp, R. G. (1972). *Self-directed behavior: Self-modification for personal adjustment.* Belmont, CA: Brooks/Cole.

# CHAPTER 8

Abidin, R. R. (1976). *Parenting skills workbook.* New York: Human Sciences Press.

Allen, K. E., Hart, B. M., Buell, T. S., Harris, F. R., & Wolfe, M. N. (1964). Effects of social reinforcement on isolated behavior of a nursery school child. *Child Development, 35,* 511–518.

Aronfreed, J., & Paskal, V. (1968). *Conduct of consciences.* New York: Academic Press.

Aronfreed, J., & Reber, A. (1965). Internalized behavioral suppression and the timing of social punishment. *Journal of Personality and Social Psychology, 1,* 3–16.

Argyle, M., & Dean, J. (1965). Eye contact, distance, and affiliations. *Sociometry, 28,* 289–304.

Azrin, N. H., & Holz, W. C. (1966). Punishment. In W. K. Houig (Ed.), *Operant behavior: Areas of research and application.* New York: Appleton-Century-Crofts.

Bakken, C. A., & Bromley, B. C. (1972). *Effects of facial expression on eliciting and avoidance response among humans.* Unpublished paper, Department of Psychology, Moorhead State College, Moorhead, MN.

Bandura, A., & Walters, R. (1963). *Social learning and personality development.* New York: Holt, Rinehart and Winston.

Berger, S. M. (1962). Conditioning through vicarious instigation. *Psychological Review, 69,* 450–466.

Blackham, G. J., & Silberman, A. (1971). *Modification of child and adolescent behavior.* Belmont, CA: Wadsworth.

Bugenthal, D. B., Love, L. R., Kaswan, J. J., & April, C. (1971). Verbal–nonverbal conflict in parental messages to normal and disturbed children. *Journal of Abnormal Psychology, 77,* 6–10.

Clore, G. L., & Jeffery, K. M. (1972). Emotional role playing, attitude change, and attraction toward a disabled person. *Journal of Personality and Social Psychology, 23,* 105–111.

Corte, H. E., Wolfe, M. N., & Locke, B. J. (1971). A comparison of procedure for eliminating self-injurious behavior of retarded adolescents. *Journal of Applied Behavior Analysis, 4,* 201–213.

Craig, K. D., & Weinstein, M. S. (1965). Conditioning vicarious affective arousal. *Psychological Reports, 17,* 955–963.

Ellsworth, P. J., Carlsmith, J., & Hensen, A. (1972). The state as a stimulus of flight in human subjects: A series of field experiments. *Journal of Personality and Social Psychology, 21,* 302–311.

Feshback, N. P., & Roe, K. (1968). Empathy in six- and seven-year-olds. *Child Development, 39,* 133–145.

Ginott, H. G. (1965). *Between parent and child.* New York: Macmillan.

Knight, J. (1969). *Conscience and guilt.* New York: Appleton-Century-Crofts.

Kogan, K. I., & Wimberger, H. C. (1971). Behavior transactions between disturbed children and their mothers. *Psychological Reports, 28,* 392–404.

Kolko, D. J. (1983). Multicomponent parental treatment of fire-setting in a six-year-old boy. *Journal of Behavior Therapy and Experimental Psychiatry, 14,* 349–353.

Krumboltz, J. P. & Krumboltz, H. B. (1972). *Changing children's behavior.* Englewood Cliffs, NJ: Prentice-Hall.

Liebert, R. M., Poulos, R. W., & Marmor, G. S. (1977). *Developmental psychology.* Englewood Cliffs, NJ: Prentice-Hall.

McCord, W., McCord, J., & Howard, A. (1961). Familial correlates of aggression in nondelinquent male children. *Journal of Abnormal and Social Psychology, 62,* 79–93.

Murphy, L. B. (1937). *Social behavior and child psychology.* New York: Columbia University Press.

Norton, R. G. (1977). *Parenting.* Englewood Cliffs, NJ: Prentice-Hall.

Parke, R. D. (1969). Effectiveness of punishment as an interaction of intensity, timing, agent nurturance and cognitive structuring. *Child Development, 40,* 213–235.

Parke, R. D. (1970). The role of punishment in the socialization process. In R. A. Hoppe, G. A. Milton, & E. C. Simmel (Eds.), *Early experiences and the process of socialization* (pp. 81–108). New York: Academic Press.

Parke, R. D. (1974). Rules, roles and resistance to deviation: Recent advances in punishment, discipline and self-control. In A. D. Pick (Ed.), *Minnesota Symposium on Child Psychology* (Vol. 8). Minneapolis: University of Minnesota Press.

Sears, R. R., Maccoby, E. E., & Levin, H. (1957). *Patterns of childrearing.* Evanston, IL: Row, Peterson.

Sears, R. R., Whiting, J. W. M., Nowlis, V., & Sears, P. S. (1953). Some childbearing antecedents of aggression and dependency in young children. *Genetic Psychology Monographs, 47,* 135–234.

Solomon, R. L., & Wynn, L. C. (1954). Traumatic avoidance learning: The principles of anxiety conservation and partial irreversibility. *Psychological Review, 61,* 353–385.

Tomes, H. (1964). The adaptation, acquisition and extinction of empathetically medicated emotional responses. *Dissertation Abstracts, 24,* 3442–3443.

Walters, G. C., & Grusec, J. E. (1977). *Punishment.* San Francisco, CA: Freeman.

Walters, P. H., Parke, R. D., & Cane, V. (1965). Timing of punishment and the observance of consequences for others as determinants of response inhibition. *Journal of Experimental Child Psychology, 2,* 10–30.

Weiss, R. E., Roger, J. R., Lombardo, J. P., & Stick, M. H. (1973). Altruistic drive and altruistic reinforcement. *Journal of Personality and Social Psychology, 25,* 390–400.

Whaley, D. L., & Malott, R. W. (1971). *Elementary principles of behavior.* New York: Appleton-Century-Crofts.

Zimmerman, E. H., & Zimmerman, J. (1962). The alteration of behavior in a special classroom situation. *Journal of Experimental Analysis of Behavior, 5,* 59–60.

# CHAPTER 9

Allred, H. G. (1968). *Mission for mothers guiding the child.* Salt Lake City: Bookcraft.

Dreikurs, R. (1948). *The challenge of parenthood.* New York: Duell, Sloan, and Pearce.

Dreikurs, R. (1968). *Psychology in the classroom.* New York: Duell, Sloan, and Pearce.

Dreikurs, R. (1972). *The challenge of child training.* New York: Hawthorn Books.

Dreikurs, R., & Grey, L. (1968). *Logical consequences: A handbook of discipline.* New York: Meredith Press.

Dreikurs, R., & Soltz, V. (1967). *Children the challenge.* New York: Duell, Sloan, and Pearce.

Glasser, W. (1965). *Reality therapy: A new approach to psychiatry.* New York: Harper & Row.

Glasser, W. (1969). *Schools without failure.* New York: Harper & Row.

# CHAPTER 10

Brooks, J. B. (1981). *The process of parenting.* Palo Alto, CA: Mayfield.

Gordon, T. (1970). *Parent effectiveness training.* New York: Peter H. Wyden.

Gordon, T. (1980). *Parent effectiveness training* (2nd ed.). New York: Peter H. Wyden.

Hoffman, M. (1970). Moral development. In P. H. Mussen (Ed.), *Carmichael's manual of child development.* New York: Wiley.

Hoffman, M., & Saltzstein, H. D. (1967). Parent discipline and the child's normal development. *Journal of Personality and Social Psychology, 5,* 45–57.

Lepper, M. R. (1973). Dissonance-self-perception and honesty in children. *Journal of Personality and Social Psychology, 25,* 65–75.

Pepitone, A., McCauley, C., & Hammond,, P. (1967). Change in attractiveness of toys as a function of severity of threat. *Journal of Experimental Social Psychology, 3,* 221–229.

Pines, M. (1979). Good Samaritans at age two? *Psychology Today, 13,* 66–77.

Rheingold, H. L., Hay, D. F., & West, M. J. (1976). Sharing in the second year of life. *Child Development, 47,* 1148–1158.

# CHAPTER 11

Bandura, A. (1967). The role of modeling processes in personality development. In W. W. Hartup & N. L. Smothergill (Eds.), *The child: Reviews of research.* Washington, DC: National Association for the Education of Young Children.

Bandura, A. (1969). *Principles of behavior modification.* New York: Holt, Rinehart and Winston.

Bandura, A. (1971). *Social learning theory.* Morristown, NJ: General Learning Press.

Baruch, G. (1972). Maternal influences upon college women's attitudes toward women and work. *Developmental Psychology, 6,* 32–37.

Cline, V. (1972). *The desensitization of children to television violence.* Bethesda, MD: National Institutes of Health.

Day, R. C., & Ghandour, M. (1984). The effect of television-mediated aggression and real-life aggression on the behavior of Lebanese children. *Journal of Experimental Child Psychology, 38,* 7–18.

Eron, L. D., & Huesmann, L. R. (1980). Adolescent aggression and television. *Annals of the New York Academy of Sciences, 347,* 319–331.

Hall, W. M., & Cairns, R. B. (1984). Aggressive behavior in children: An outcome study of modeling or social reciprocity? *Developmental Psychology, 20,* 739–745.

Hoffman, L., & Nye, F. (1974). *Working mothers.* San Francisco: Jossey Bass.

Huessman, L. R., Lagerspetz, K., & Evon, L. D. (1984). Intervening variables in the TV violence–aggression relation: Evidence from two countries. *Developmental Psychology, 20,* 746–775.

Hyde, J. S. (1984). Children's understanding of sexist language. *Developmental Psychology, 20,* 697–706.

Lewis, M. (1972). State as an infant–environment interaction: An analysis of mother–infant interactions as a function of sex. *Merrill-Palmer Quarterly of Behavior and Development, 18,* 95–121.

Liebert, R. M., Sprafkin, J. N., & Davidson, E. S. (1982). *The early window: Effects of television on children and youth* (2nd ed.). New York: Pergamon Press.

Maccoby, E. E., & Jacklin, C. N. (1974). *The psychology of sex differences.* Stanford, CA: Stanford University Press.

Methvin, E. H. (1975, July). What you can do about TV violence. *Readers Digest,* 185–190.

Meyer, W. J., & Dusek, J. B. (1979). *Child Psychology: A developmental perspective.* Lexington, MA: Heath.

Miller, S. (1975). Effects of maternal employment on sex role perception, interests and self-esteem in kindergarten girls. *Developmental Psychology, 11,* 405–406.

Money, J., & Ehrhardt, A. A. (1975). Rearing of a sex-reassigned normal male infant after traumatic loss of the penis. In J. Petras (Ed.), *Sex: Male/Gender: Masculine.* New York: Alfred Publishing.

Nemerowicz, G. M. (1979). *Children's perceptions of gender and work roles.* New York: Praeger.

Parke, R. D., Berkowitz, L., Leyens, J. P., West, S. G., & Sebastian, R. J. (1977). Some effects of violent and nonviolent movies on the behavior of the juvenile delinquents. In L. Berkowitz (Ed.), *Advances in experimental social psychology* (vol. 10). New York: Academic Press.

Rubin, J. Z., Provenzano, F. J., & Luria, Z. (1974). The eye of the beholder: Parents' views on sex of newborns. *American Journal of Orthopsychiatry, 44,* 512–519.

Sears, R. R., Rau, L., & Alpert, R. (1966). *Identification and child rearing.* London: Tavistock.

Singer, D. G., & Singer, J. L. (1980). Television viewing and aggressive behavior in preschool children: A field study. *Forensic Psychology and Psychiatry, 347,* 289–303.

Singer, J. L., Singer, D. G., & Rapaczynski, W. (1984). Children's imagination as predicted by family patterns and television viewing: A longitudinal study. *Genetic Psychology Monographs, 10,* 43–69.

*Television and growing up: The impact of television violence. Report to the Surgeon General.* (1972). Washington, DC: U.S. Government Printing Office.

Van Hasselt, V. B., Griest, D. L., Kazdin, A. E., Esveldt-Dawson, K., & Unis, A. S. (1984). Poor peer interactions and social isolation: A case report of successful "in vivo" social skills training on a child psychiatric inpatient unit. *Journal of Behavior Therapy and Experimental Psychiatry, 15,* 271–276.

Weitz, S. (1977). *Sex roles: Biological, psychological, and social foundations.* New York: Oxford University Press.

Winn, M. (1980). *The plug-in drug.* New York: Viking Press.

# CHAPTER 12

Ainsworth, M. D. S. (1967). *Infancy in Uganda: Infant care and the growth of attachment.* Baltimore, MD: Johns Hopkins Press.

Ainsworth, M. D. S., & Bell, S. M. (1969). Some contemporary patterns of mother–infant interaction in the feeding situation. In A. Ambrose (Ed.), *Stimulation in early infancy.* New York: Academic Press.

Ainsworth, M. D. S., Bell, S. M., & Stayton, D. J. (1971). Individual differences in strange-situation behavior of one-year-olds. In H. R. Schaffer (Ed.), *The origins of human social relations.* London: Academic Press.

Azrin, N. H., & Foxx, R. M. (1974). *Toilet training in less than a day.* New York: Simon and Schuster.

Bell, S. M., & Ainsworth, M. D. S. (1972). Infant crying and maternal responsiveness. *Child Development, 43,* 1171–1190.

Belsky, J., Lerner, R. M., & Spanier, G. B. (1984). *The child in the family.* Reading, MA: Addison-Wesley.

Berger, K. (1980). *The developing person.* New York: Worth Publishers.

Birns, G., Blank, M., & Bridger, W. H. (1966). The effectiveness of various soothing techniques on human neonates. *Psychosomatic Medicine, 28,* 316–322.

Brazelton, T. B. (1962). A child-oriented approach to toilet-training. *Pediatrics, 29,* 121–127.

Burgess, E. W., & Wallin, P. (1953). *Engagement and marriage.* Philadelphia: Lippincott.

Butler, J. F. (1976). The toilet training success of parents after reading *Toilet Training in Less than a Day. Behavior Therapy, 7,* 185–191.

Davie, R., Butler, N., & Goldstein, H. (1972). *From birth to seven.* London: William Clowes.

Dion, K. (1974). Children's physical attractiveness and sex and determinants of adult punitiveness. *Developmental Psychology, 10,* 772–778.

Dunn, H., McBurner, S., Ingram, S., & Hunter C. (1977). Maternal cigarette smoking during pregnancy and the child's subsequent development: II. Neurological and intellectual maturation to the age of 6½ years. *Canadian Journal of Public Health, 68,* 43–50.

Flynn, M. A. (1975). The portly, corpulent or obese American. In B. Q. Hafen (Ed.), *Overweight and obesity: Causes, fallacies, treatment.* Provo, UT: Brigham Young University Press.

Foman, S. J., Filer, L. J., Thomas, L. N., Rogers, R. R., & Proksch, A. M. (1969). Relationship between formula concentration and rate of growth of normal children. *Journal of Nutrition, 98,* 241–254.

Gath, A. (1978). *Down's syndrome and the family: The early years.* New York: Academic Press.

Goujard, J., Rumeau, C., & Schwartz, D. (1975). Smoking during pregnancy, stillbirth and abruptio placentae. *Biomedica, 23,* 20–22.

Grossman, F. K., Eichler, L. S., & Winickoff, S. A. (1980). *Pregnancy, birth and parenthood.* San Francisco: Jossey-Bass.

Hafen, B. Q. (1981). *Nutrition, food and weight control.* Boston: Allyn and Bacon.

Hafen, B. Q. Thygerson, A. L., & Rhodes, R. L. (1966). *Prescriptions for health.* Provo, UT: Brigham Young University Press.

Harlow, H., & Harlow, M. K. (1969). Effects of various mother–infant relationships on rhesus monkey behaviors. In B. M. Foss (Ed.), *Determinants of infant behavior* (Vol. 4). London: Methuen.

Hobbs, D. F. (1968). Transition to parenthood: A replication and an extension. *Journal of Marriage and the Family, 30,* 413–417.

Hobbs, D. F., & Wimbish, J. (1977). Transition to parenthood by black couples. *Journal of Marriage and the Family, 39,* 677–689.

Isenberg, S. (1982). *Keep your kids thin.* New York: St. Martin's Press.

Kach, J., & McGhee, P. Adjustment to early parenthood: The role of accuracy of pre-parenthood expectations. *Journal of Family Issues, 3,* 375–388.

Kennell, J. H., Jerauld, R., Wolfe, H., Chester, D., Kreger, N., McAlpine, W., Steffa, M., & Klaus, M. H. (1974). Maternal behavior one year after early and extended postpartum contact. *Developmental Medicine and Child Neurology, 16,* 172–179.

Knittle, J. L. (1975). Obesity in childhood: A problem in adipose tissue cellular development. In B. Q. Hafen (Ed.), *Overweight and obesity: Causes, fallacies, treatment.* Provo, UT: Brigham Young University Press.

Korner, A. F., & Thoman, E. B. (1972). The relative efficacy of contact and vestibular-proprioceptive stimulation in soothing neonates. *Child Development, 43,* 443–453.

LaRossa, R., & LaRossa, M. M. (1981). *Transition to parenthood: How infants change families.* Beverly Hills: Sage Publications.

Leifer, A. D., Leiderman, P. H., Barnett, C. R., & Williams, J. A. (1972). Effect of mother–infant separation on maternal attachment behavior. *Child Development, 43,* 1203–1218.

McCall, R. B. (1979). *Infants.* Cambridge, Harvard University Press.

Maccoby, E. E. (1980). *Social development: Psychological growth and the parent–child relationship.* New York: Harcourt Brace Jovanovich.

MacKieth, R., & Wood, C. (1977). *Infant feeding and feeding difficulties.* London: Churchill Livingstone.

Main, M. (1973). *Play exploration and competence as related to child–adult attachment.* Unpublished doctoral dissertation, Johns Hopkins University Press.

Marcus, R. F. (1975). The child as elicitor of parental sanctions for independent and dependent behavior: A simulation of parent–child interaction. *Developmental Psychology, 11,* 443–452.

Matas, L., Arend, R. A., & Sroufe, L. A. (1978). Continuity of adaptation in the second year: The relationship between quality of attachment and later competence. *Child Development, 49,* 547–556.

Matson, J. L. (1975). Some practical considerations for using the Foxx and Azrin rapid method of toilet training. *Psychological Reports, 37,* 350.

Mayer, J. (1975). Fat babies grow into fat people. In B. Q. Hafen (Ed.), *Overweight and obesity: Causes, fallacies, treatment.* Provo, UT: Brigham Young University Press.

Meredith, H. (1975). Relation between tobacco smoking of pregnant women and body size of their progeny: A compilation and synthesis of published studies. *Human Biology, 47,* 451–472.

Meyer, M., Jonas, B., & Tonascia, J. (1976). Perinatal events associated with maternal smoking during pregnancy. *American Journal of Epidemiology, 103,* 464–476.

Montgomery, J. C. (1951). *America's baby book.* New York: Scribners.

Myers-Walls, J. A. (1984). Balancing multiple role responsibilities during the transition to parenthood. *Family Relations, 33,* 267–271.

Olds, S. W., & Eiger, M. S. (1973). *The complete book of breastfeeding.* New York: Bantam Books.

Osofsky, J. D., & Danzger, B. (1974). Relationships between neonatal characteristics and mother–infant interactions. *Developmental Psychology, 10,* 124–130.

Pederson, D. R., Champagne, L., & Pederson, L. (1969, March). *Relative soothing effects of vertical and horizontal rocking.* Paper presented at the meeting of the Society for Research in Child Development, Santa Monica, CA.

Pryor, K. (1973). *Nursing your baby.* New York: Pocket Books.

Roedell, W. C., & Slaby, R. G. (1977). The role of distal and proximal interaction in infant social preference formation. *Developmental Psychology, 13,* 266–273.

Rollins, B. C, & Feldman H. (1970). Marital satisfaction over the family life cycle. *Journal of Marriage and the Family, 32,* 20–28.

Ross, H. S., & Goldman, B. D. (1977). Establishing new social relations in infancy. In T. Alloway, P. Pliner, & L. Krames (Eds.), *Attachment behavior.* New York: Plenum.

Schaefer, C. E. (1979). *Childhood encopresis and enuresis.* New York: Van Nostrand Reinhold.

Sluckin, W., Herbert, M., & Sluckin, A. (1983). *Maternal bonding.* Oxford, Basil Blackwell.

Smart, M. S., & Smart, R. C. (1978). *Infant development and relationships.* New York: Macmillan.

Sollie, D. L., & Miller, B. C. (1980). The transition to parenthood as a critical time for building family strengths. In N. Stinnett, B. Chesser, J. DeFain, & P. Kraul (Eds.), *Family strengths: Positive models of family life.* Lincoln: University of Nebraska Press.

Spock, B. (1968, 1976). *Baby and child care.* New York: Pocket Books.

Sroufe, L. A., & Waters, E. (1977). Attachment as an organized construct. *Child Development, 48,* 1184–1199.

Streissguth, A. P. (1982). Maternal alcoholism and the outcome of pregnancy: A review of the fetal alcohol syndrome. In J. Belsky (Ed.), *In the beginning: Readings on infancy.* New York: Columbia University Press.

Thoman, E. B., Korner, A. F., & Beason-Williams, L. (1977) Modification of responsiveness of maternal vocalization in the neonate. *Child Development, 48,* 563–569.

Thomas, A., & Chess, S. (1977). *Temperament and development.* New York: Brunner/Mazel.

Thomas, A., Chess, S., & Birch, H. G. (1968). *Temperament and behavior disorders in children.* New York: New York University Press.

Thomas, A., Chess, S., & Birch, H. G. (1970). The origin of personality. *Scientific American, 223,* 102–109.

Waters, E., Whippman, J., & Sroufe, L. A. (1979). Attachment, positive affect, and competence in the peer-group: Two studies in construct-validation. *Child Development, 50,* 821–829.

White, B. L. (1975). *The first three years of life.* Englewood Cliffs, NJ: Prentice-Hall.

Winnick, M. (1975). Childhood obesity. In B.Q. Hafen (Ed.), *Overweight and obesity: Causes, fallacies, treatment.* Provo, UT: Brigham Young University Press.

Winter, R. (1980). Bottle-fed baby phase fades as mothers take over. *Science Digest, 88,* 76–81.

Yarrow, M. R., Waxler, C. Z., & Scott, P. M. (1971). Child effects on adult behavior. *Developmental Psychology, 5,* 300–311.

# CHAPTER 13

American Psychiatric Association. (1968). *Diagnostic and statistical manual of mental disorders* (2nd ed.). Washington, DC: American Psychiatric Association.

American Psychiatric Association. (1980). *Diagnostic and statistical manual of mental disorders* (3rd ed.). Washington, DC: American Psychiatric Association.

Barkley, R. A., & Cunningham, C. E. (1978). Do stimulant drugs improve the academic performance of hyperactive children? A review of outcome research. *Clinical Pediatrics, 17,* 85–93.

Bauer, E. E. (1967). *Suggested curriculum for educable mentally retarded children.* Unpublished paper, Indiana University.

Bender, L. (1955). Twenty years of research on schizophrenic children with special reference to those under twenty years of age. In G. Kaplan (Ed.), *Emotional problems of early childhood.* New York: Basic Books.

Bettelheim, B. (1967). *The empty fortress.* New York: Free Press.

Blacher, J. (1984). Sequential stages of parental adjustment to the birth of a child with handicaps: Fact or artifact? *Mental Retardation, 22,* 55–68.

Bristor, M. W. (1984). The birth of a handicapped child: A holistic model for grief. *Family Relations, 33,* 25–32.

Bryan, T. H. (1978). Social relationships and verbal interactions of learning disabled children. *Journal of Learning Disabilities, 11,* 107–115.

Cairns, N. V., Clark, G. M., Smith, S. D., & Lansky, S. B. (1979). Adaptation of siblings to childhood malignancy. *Journal of Pediatrics, 95,* 484–487.

Caldwell, B. M., & Guze, S. B. (1960). A study of the adjustment of parents and siblings of institutionalized and noninstitutionalized retarded children. *American Journal of Mental Deficiency, 64,* 845–861.

Cantwell, D. P. (1975). Natural history and prognosis in the hyperactive child syndrome. In D. P. Cantwell (Ed.), *The hyperactive child.* New York: Spectrum.

Chilman, C. S. (1965). Childrearing and family relationships patterns of the very poor. *Welfare in Review,* 9–19.

Cleveland, D. W., & Miller, N. (1977). Attitudes and life commitments of older siblings of mentally retarded adults: An exploratory study. *Mental Retardation, 15,* 38–41.

Coleman, J. C., Butcher, J. H. & Carson, R. C. (1980). *Abnormal psychology and modern life* (6th ed.). Glenview, IL: Scott Foresman.

Darling, R. B. (1979). *Families against society: A study of reactions to children with birth defects.* Beverly Hills, CA: Sage.

Davison, G. C., & Neale, J. M..(1978). *Abnormal psychology: An experimental clinical approach* (2nd ed.). New York: Wiley.

DeMyer, M. K., Barton, S., Alpern, G. D., Kimberlin, C., Allen, J., Yange, E., & Steele, R. (1974). The measured intelligence of autistic children. *Journal of Autism and Childhood Schizophrenia, 4,* 42–60.

Diamond, S., Baldwin, R., & Diamond, R. (1963). *Inhibition and choice.* New York: Harper & Row.

Dor-Shav, N. K., & Horowitz, Z. (1984). Intelligence and personality variables of parents of autistic children. *Journal of Genetic Psychology, 144,* 39–50.

Feingold, B. F. (1975). *Why your child is hyperactive.* New York: Random House.

Ferster, C. B. (1961). Positive reinforcement and behavioral deficits of autistic children. *Child Development, 32,* 437–456.

Fine, M. J. (1980). *Intervention with hyperactive children: A case study approach.* New York: Spectrum.

Fortier, L. M., & Wanlass, R. L. (1984). Family crisis following the diagnosis of a handicapped child. *Family Relations, 33,* 13–24.

Foxx, R. M., McMorrow, M. J., Storey, K., & Rogers, B. M. (1984). Teaching social/sexual skills to mentally retarded adults. *American Journal of Mental Deficiency, 89,* 9–15.

Gath, A. (1972). The mental health of siblings of congenitally abnormal children. *Journal of Child Psychology and Psychiatry, 13,* 211–218.

Gillberg, C. (1984). Infantile autism and other childhood psychoses in a Swedish urban region: Epidemiological aspects. *Journal of Child Psychology and Psychiatry, 25,* 35–43.

Goffman, E. (1963). *Stigma.* New Jersey: Prentice-Hall.

Goldstein, H., Moss, J. W., & Jordan, L. J. (1965). *The efficacy of special class training of the development of mentally retarded children* (Cooperative Research Project No. 619). Washington, DC: U.S. Office of Education.

Goodman, H., Gottlieb, J., & Harrison, R. H. (1972). Social acceptance of EMRs integrated into a non-graded elementary school. *American Journal of Mental Deficiency, 76,* 412–417.

Grossman, H. J. (1973). *Manual on terminology and classification in mental retardation* (1973 rev.). American Association on Mental Deficiency. Baltimore: Garamond/Pridemark Press.

Harvey, D. H. P., & Greenway, A. P. (1984). The self-concept of physically handicapped children and their nonhandicapped siblings: An experimental investigation. *Journal of Child Psychology and Psychiatry, 25,* 273–284.

Heal, L. W., Colson, L. S., & Gross, J. C. (1984). A true experiment evaluating adult skill training for severely mentally retarded secondary students. *American Journal of Mental Deficiency, 89,* 146–155.

Hingtgen, J. N., & Bryson, C. Q. (1972). Recent developments in the study of early childhood psychoses: Infantile autism, childhood schizophrenia, and related disorders. *Schizophrenia Bulletin,* No. 5, 8–54.

Intagliata, J., & Doyle, N. (1984). Enhancing social support for parents of develop-mentally disabled children: Training in interpersonal problem-solving skills. *Mental Retardation, 22,* 4–11.

Janicki, M. P., Mayeda, T., & Eppel, W. A. (1983). Availability of group homes for persons with mental retardation in the United States. *Mental Retardation, 21,* 45–51.

Kanner, L. (1949). Problems of nosology and psychodynamics of early infantile autism. *American Journal of Orthopsychiatry, 19,* 416–426.

Keogh, B. K. (1971). Hyperactivity and learning disorders: Review and speculation. *Exceptional Children, 38,* 101–109.

Kew, S. (1975). *Handicap and family crisis: A study of the siblings of handicapped chidren.* London: Pitman.

Knobloch, H., & Pasamanick, B. (1974). *Gesell and Amatruda's developmental diag-nosis* (3rd ed.). New York: Harper & Row.

Lavigne, J. V., & Ryan, M. (1979). Psychologic adjustment of siblings of children with chronic illness. *Pediatrics, 63,* 616–627.

Liebert, R. M., Poulos, R. W., & Marmor, G. S. (1977). *Developmental psychology* (2nd ed.). Englewood Cliffs, NJ: Prentice-Hall.

Longo, D. C., & Bond, L. (1984). Families of the handicapped child: Research and prac-tice. *Family Relations, 33,* 57–65.

Lorenz, K. (1935). Der Kumpan in der Umwelt des Vogels. *Journal für Ornithologie, 83,* 137–413.

Lotter, V. (1974). Factors related to outcome in autistic children. *Journal of Autism and Childhood Schizophrenia, 4,* 263–277.

Lovaas, O. I. (1968). Some studies on the treatment of childhood schizophrenia. In J. M. Shlien (Ed.), *Research in psychotherapy: Proceedings of the Third Conference* (pp. 103–121). Washington, DC: American Psychological Asso-ciation.

Love, H. D. (1970). *Parental attitudes toward exceptional children.* Springfield, IL: Charles C Thomas.

Moore, C., & Shiek, D. (1971). Toward a theory of early infantile autism. *Psychological Review, 78,* 451–456.

Ornitz, E. M., & Ritro, E. R. (1976). Medical assessment. In E. R. Ritro (Ed.), *Autism: Diagnosis, current research and management.* New York: Halstead Press.

Ornitz, E. M., & Ritro, E. R. (1977). The syndrome of autism: A critical review. In S. Chess & A. Thomas (Eds.), *Annual progress in psychiatry and child develop-ment.* New York: Brunner/Mazel.

Paulauskas, S. L., & Campbell, S. B. (1979). Social perspective-taking and teacher rat-ings of peer interaction in hyperactive boys. *Journal of Abnormal Child Psy-chology, 7,* 483–493.

Poznanski, E. (1969). Psychiatric difficulties in siblings of handicapped children. *Clin-ical Pediatrics, 8,* 232–234.

President's Task Force on Manpower Conservation. (1964). *One-third of a nation.* Washington, DC: U.S. Government Printing Office.

Reid, M. K., & Borkowski, J. G. (1984). Effects of methylphenidate (Ritalin) on infor-mation processing in hyperactive children. *Journal of Abnormal Child Psychol-ogy, 12,* 169–186.

Rie, E. D., & Rie, H. E. (1977). Recall, retention, and Ritalin. *Journal of Consulting and Clinical Psychology, 44,* 250–260.

Rimland, B. (1964). *Infantile autism.* New York: Appleton-Century-Crofts.

Robins, L. N. (1979). Follow-up studies. In H. C. Quay & J. S. Werry (Eds.), *Psycho-pathological disorders of childhood* (2nd ed.). New York: Wiley.

Robinson, H. B. (1967). *Social-cultural deprivation as a form of child abuse.* Raleigh: North Carolina State Board of Health. Governor's Council on Child Abuse.

Robinson, H. B., & Robinson, N. M. (1976). *The mentally retarded child: A psychological approach* (2nd ed.). New York: McGraw-Hill.

Rosenbaum, M., & Baker, E. (1984). Self-control in hyperactive and nonhyperactive children. *Journal of Abnormal Child Psychology, 12,* 303–318.

Ross, A. O., & Pelham, W. E. (1981). Child psychopathology. *Annual Review of Psychology, 32,* 243–278.

Ross, D., & Ross, S. (1976). *Hyperactivity: Research, theory, and action.* New York: Wiley.

Rutter, M. (1966). Prognosis: Psychotic children in adolescence and early adult life. In *Childhood autism: Clinical, educational, and social aspects.* Elmsford, NY: Pergamon Press.

Rutter, M. (1968). Concepts of autism: A review of research. *Journal of Child Psychology and Psychiatry, 9,* 1–25.

Rutter, M. (1974). The development of infantile autism. *Psychological Medicine, 4,* 147–163.

Rutter, M. (1977). Infantile autism and other child psychoses. In M. Rutter & L. Hersov (Eds.), *Child psychiatry: Modern approaches.* Oxford: Blackwell Scientific.

Sattler, J. M. (1982). *Assessment of children's intelligence and special abilities* (2nd ed.). Boston, MA: Allyn and Bacon.

Schonell, F., & Watts, B. (1957). A first survey on the effects of a subnormal child on the family unit. *American Journal of Mental Deficiency, 61,* 210.

Shaffer, H. R., & Emerson, P. F. (1964). Patterns of response to physical contact in early human development. *Journal of Child Psychology and Psychiatry, 5,* 1–13.

Sloan, W., & Birch, J. W. (1955). A rationale for degree of retardation. *American Journal of Mental Deficiency, 60,* 258–264.

Smith, L. (1976). *Improving your child's behavior chemistry.* Englewood Cliffs, NJ: Prentice-Hall.

Spitzer, R. L., Skodol, A. E., Gibbon, M., & Williams, J. B. W. (1981). *Diagnostic and statistical manual of mental disorders: Case book.* Washington, DC: American Psychiatric Association.

Stevens-Long, J. & Lovaas, I. O. (1974). Research and treatment with autistic children in a program of behavior therapy. In A. Davids (Ed.), *Child personality and psychopathology: Current topics* (Vol. 1). New York: Wiley Interscience.

Stewart, M., Cummings, C., Singer, S., & DeBlois, S. (1981). The overlap between hyperactive and unsocialized aggressive children. *Journal of Child Psychiatry, 22,* 35–45.

Tew, B., & Laurence, K. M. (1973). Mothers, brothers and sisters of patients with spinal bifida. *Developmental Medicine and Child Neurology, 15,* 69–76.

Tizard, J., & Grad, J. (1961). *The mentally handicapped and their families.* New York: Oxford University Press.

Trites, R. L., Tryphonas, H., & Ferguson, B. (1980). Case study #21: Treatment of hyperactivity in a child with allergies to foods. In M. J. Fine (Ed.), *Intervention with hyperactive children: A case study approach.* New York: Spectrum.

Walker, S. (1974). Drugging the American child: We're too cavalier about hyperactivity. *Psychology Today, 8,* 43–48.

Weiss, G., & Hechtman, L. (1979). The hyperactive child syndrome. *Science, 206,* 309–314.

Weiss, G., Kruger, E., Danielson, V., & Elman, M. (1975). Effect of long-term treatment of hyperactive children with methylphenidate. *Canadian Medical Association Journal, 112,* 159–165.

Wender, P. H. (1971). *Minimal brain dysfunction in children.* New York: Wiley-Interscience Press.

Wender, P. H., Reimherr, F. W., & Wood, D. R. (1981). Attention deficit disorder (minimal brain dysfunction) in adults. *Archives of General Psychiatry, 38,* 449–456.

Wentworth, E. H. (1974). *Listen to your hearts: A message to parents of handicapped children.* Boston: Houghton Mifflin.

Werner, E. E. (1971). *The children of Kauai.* Honolulu: University of Hawaii Press.

Werry, J. S. (1979). Organic factors. In H. C. Quay & J. S. Werry (Eds.), *Psychopathological disorders of childhood* (2nd ed.). New York: John Wiley.

Zentall, S. S. (1984). Context effects in the behavioral ratings of hyperactivity. *Journal of Abnormal Child Psychology, 12,* 345–352.

# CHAPTER 14

American Psychiatric Association. (1980). *Diagnostic and statistical manual of mental disorders* (3rd ed.). Washington, DC: APA.

Ax, A. F. (1953). The physiological differentiation between fear and anger in humans. *Psychosomatic Medicine, 15,* 433–442.

Bentler, P. M. (1962). An infant's phobia treated with reciprocal inhibition therapy. *Journal of Child Psychology and Psychiatry, 3,* 185–189.

Bridges, K. M. B. (1932). *The social and emotional development of the pre-school child.* London: Routledge Kegan Paul.

Brooks, J. B. (1981). *The process of parenting.* Palo Alto, CA: Mayfield.

Brown, V. L., Jr. (1981). *Human intimacy: Illusion and reality.* Salt Lake City, UT: Parliament Publishers.

Caine, L. (1975). *Widow.* New York: Bantam Books.

Chess, S. (1979). Explaining death to a child. *Childcraft—The how and why library worldbook* (Vol. 15). Chicago: World Book/Childcraft International.

Clayton, R. R. (1979). *The family, marriage, and social change.* Lexington, MA: Heath.

Cline, V. B. (Ed.). (1974). *Where do you draw the line?* Provo, UT: Brigham Young University Press.

Cummings, E. M., Zahn-Waxler, C., Radke-Yarrow, M. (1984). Developmental changes in children's reactions to anger in the home. *Journal of Child Psychology and Psychiatry, 25,* 63–74.

Ende, R. N., Gaensbauer, T. J., & Harmon, R. J. (1976). *Emotional expression in infancy: A biobehavioral study.* New York: International Universities Press.

Ferrari, M. (1984). Chronic illness: Psychosocial effects on siblings: I. Chronically ill boys. *Journal of Child Psychology and Psychiatry, 25,* 459–476.

Hartup, W. W., & Smothergill, M. L. (Eds). (1967). The young child: Review of research. In *Social psychology* (pp. 214–248). Washington, DC: National Association for Young Children.

Hetherington, E. M., Cox, M., & Cox, R. (1979). Stress and coping in divorce: A focus on women. In J. E. Gullahorn (Ed.), *Psychology and women: In transition.* Washington, DC: V. H. Winston.

Hodges, W. F., Tierney, C. W., & Buchsbaum, H. K. (1984). The cumulative effects of stress on preschool children of divorced and intact families. *Journal of Marriage and the Family, 46,* 611–617.

Hoffman, M. L. (1976). Empathy, role-taking, guilt, and development of altruistic motives. In T. Lickona (Ed.), *Moral development and behavior.* New York: Holt, Rinehart and Winston.

Ilg, F. L., & Ames, L. B. (1955). *Child behavior.* New York: Harper & Row.

Jersild, A. T., & Holmes, F. B. (1935). Children's fears. *Child Development Monograph, 20.*

Kagan, J., & Moss, H. A. (1962). *Birth to maturity.* New York: Wiley.

Maccoby, E. E. (1980). *Social development: Psychological growth and the parent-child relationship.* New York: Harcourt Brace Jovanovich.

Mahler, M. S. (1950). Helping children to accept death. *Child Study, 27,* 98–99, 119–120.

Malatesta, C. Z. (1982). The expression and regulation of emotions: A lifespan perspective. In F. Tiffany & A. Fogel (Eds.), *Emotion and early interaction*. Hillsdale, NJ: Lawrence Erlbaum.

Mischel, W., & Grusec, J. (1967). Waiting for larger rewards and punishments: Effects of time and probability on choice. *Journal of Personality and Social Psychology, 5,* 24–31.

Mischel, W., & Metzner, R. (1962). Preference for delayed reward as a function of age, intelligence, and length of delay internal. *Journal of Abnormal and Social Psychology, 64,* 425–431.

Mischel, W., & Staub, E. (1965). Effects of expectancy on working and waiting for larger reward. *Journal of Personality and Social Psychology, 2,* 625–633.

Mischel, W., & Underwood, B. (1974). Instrumental idealism and delay of gratification. *Child Development, 45,* 1083–1088.

Mischel, W., Coates, B., & Raskoff, A. (1968) Effects of success and failure on self-gratification. *Journal of Personality and Social Psychology, 10,* 381–390.

Mischel, W., Zeiss, R., & Zeiss, A. (1974). Internal–external control and persistence: Validation and implications of the Stanford Preschool Internal–External Scale. *Journal of Personality and Social Psychology, 29,* 265–278.

Norton, G. R. (1977). *Parenting.* Englewood Cliffs, NJ: Prentice-Hall.

Rosenberg, M. (1965). *Society and the adolescent self-image.* Princeton, NJ: Princeton University Press.

Rutter, M. (1970). Sex differences in children's responses to family stress. In E. J. Anthony & C. Kouperwik (Eds.), *The child in his family.* New York: Wiley.

Schachter, S., & Singer, J. (1962). Cognitive, social and physiological determinants of emotional state. *Psychological Review, 69,* 379–399.

Staley, A. A., & O'Donnell, J. P. (1984). A developmental analysis of mothers' reports of normal children's fears. *Journal of Genetic Psychology, 144,* 165–178.

Taylor, D. A., & Harris, P. L. (1984). Knowledge of strategies for the expression of emotion among normal and maladjusted boys: A research note. *Journal of Child Psychology and Psychiatry, 24,* 141–145.

Van Leishout, C. F. M. (1975). Young children's reactions to barriers placed by their mothers. *Child Development, 46,* 879–886.

Wallerstein, J. S., & Kelly, J. B. (1977). Divorce counseling: A community service for families in the midst of divorce. *American Journal of Orthopsychiatry, 47,* 4–22.

# CHAPTER 15

Benjamin, S. (1978). *The one-parent family.* Toronto: University of Toronto Press.

Bigner, J. J. (1979). *Parent–child relations: An introduction to parenting.* New York: Macmillan.

Blanchard, R. W., & Biller, H. B. (1971). Father availability and academic performance among third-grade boys. *Developmental Psychology, 4,* 301–305.

Brooks, J. B. (1981). *The process of parenting.* Palo Alto, CA: Mayfield.

Burgess, J. (1970). The single-parent family: A social and sociological problem. *Family Coordinator, 19,* 137–144.

Carter, H., & Glick, P. (1970). *Marriage and divorce: A social and economic study.* Cambridge, MA: Harvard University Press.

Dodson, F. (1977). *How to discipline with love.* New York: Rawson Associates.

Esphenshade, T. J. (1979). The economic consequences of divorce. *Journal of Marriage and the Family, 41,* 615–625.

Fergusson, D. M., Horwood, L. J., & Shannon, F. T. (1984). A proportional hazards model of family breakdown. *Journal of Marriage and the Family, 46,* 539–549.

Finkelstein, H., & Rosenthal, K. (1978, May). Single-parent fathers: A new study. *Children Today,* pp. 14–15.

Gasser, R., & Taylor, C. (1976). Role adjustment of single-parent fathers with dependent children. *Family Coordinator, 25,* 397–401.

Gaylin, J. (1977). The single father is doing well. *Psychology Today, 10,* 36.

Glenn, N. D., & Supancic, M. (1984). The social and demographic correlates of divorce and separation in the United States: An update and reconsideration. *Journal of Marriage and the Family, 46,* 563–575.

Groller, I. (1981). A fresh start for single parents. *Parents, 56,* pp. 66–69.

Guyatt, D. (1971). *The one-parent family in Canada.* Ottawa: Vanier Institute of the Family.

Hetherington, E. M. (1972). Effects of father-absence on personality development in adolescent daughters. *Developmental Psychology, 7,* 313–326.

Hoffman, M. L. (1971). Father absence and conscience development. *Developmental Psychology, 4,* 400–406.

Hope, K., & Young, N. (Eds.). (1976). *Momma: The sourcebook for single mothers.* New York: New American Library.

Kempe, R. S., & Kempe, C. H. (1978). *Child abuse.* Cambridge, MA: Harvard University Press.

Kogelschatz, J., Adams, P., & Tucker, D. (1972). Family styles of fatherless households. *Journal of American Academy of Child Psychiatry, 11,* 365–383.

Kriesberg, L. (1970). *Mothers in poverty: A study of fatherless families.* Chicago: Aldine.

Lamb, M. E. (1977). The effects of divorce on children's personality development. *Journal of Divorce, 1,* 163–174.

LeMasters, E. E. (1977). *Parents in modern America: A sociological analysis* (3rd ed.). Homewood IL: Dorsey Press.

Lindeman, B. (1976). Widower, heal thyself. In R. H. Moos (Ed.), *Human adaptation: Coping with life crises.* Lexington, MA: D. C. Heath.

Marsden, D. (1973). *Mothers alone: Poverty and the fatherless family* (rev. ed.). London: Penguin Press.

Mendes, H. (1976). Single fathers. *Family Coordinator, 25,* 439–444.

Nye, I. (1959). Child adjustment in broken and in unhappy, unbroken homes. *Marriage and Family Living, 19,* 356–361.

Orthner, D., Brown, T., & Ferguson, D. (1976). Single-parent fatherhood: An emerging family style. *Family Coordinator, 26,* 420–437.

Ostrovsky, E. S. (1959). *Father to the child: Case studies of the experiences of a male teacher.* New York: Putnam.

Ricci, I. (1980). *Mom's house/dad's house.* New York: Macmillan.

Rice, F. P. (1979). *The adolescent: Development, relationships, and culture.* Boston, MA: Allyn and Bacon.

Schlesinger, B. (1975). *The one-parent family: Perspectives and annotated bibliography* (3rd ed.). Toronto: University of Toronto Press.

Smith, M. (1980). The social consequences of single parenthood: A longitudinal perspective. *Family Relations, 29,* 75–81.

Smith, R. M., & Smith, C. W. (1981). Child rearing and single-parent fathers. *Family Relations, 30, 411–417.*

Sorosky, A. (1977). The psychological effects of divorce on adolescents. *Adolescence, 12,* 123–135.

Stuart, I. R. (1981). *Children of separation and divorce.* New York: Van Nostrand Reinhold.

U.S. Bureau of the Census. (1974). Households and family characteristics. *Current Population Reports, 276,* 20. Washington, DC: U.S. Government Printing Office.

U.S. Bureau of the Census. (1976). *Statistical abstract of the United States: 1976* (97th ed.). Washington, DC: U.S. Bureau of the Census.

U.S. Bureau of the Census. (1980). *Census of the population: General social and economic characteristics.* Washington, DC: U.S. Bureau of the Census.

Vander Zanden, J. W. (1981). *Human development* (2nd ed.). New York: Knopf.

Weiss, R. (1973). The contributions of an organization of single parents to the well-being of its members. *Family Coordinator, 22,* 321–326.

Weiss, R. S. (1984). The impact of marital dissolution on income and consumption in single-parent households. *Journal of Marriage and the Family, 46,* 115–127.

# CHAPTER 16

Abernathy, V., & Abernathy, F. (1974). Risk for unwanted pregnancy among mentally ill adolescent girls. *American Journal of Orthopsychiatry, 44,* 442–450.

Alan Guttmacher Institute (1981). *Teenage pregnancy: The problem that hasn't gone away.* New York: Alan Guttmacher Institute.

Blood, R. O. (1969). *Marriage* (2nd ed.). New York: Free Press.

Brunswick, A. F. (1971). Adolescent health, sex and fertility. *American Journal of Public Health, 61,* 711–729.

Davie, R., Butler, N. R., & Goldstein, H. (1972). *From birth to seven.* London: Longmans.

Epstein, A. S. (1979, March). *Pregnant teenagers' knowledge of infant development.* Paper presented at the biennial meeting of the Society for Research in Child Development, San Francisco, CA.

Furstenberg, F. F. (1976). *Unplanned parenthood.* New York: Free Press.

Furstenberg, F. F. (1980). Burdens and benefits: The impact of early child rearing on the family. *Journal of Social Issues, 36,* 64–87.

Goldfarb, J. L., Mumford, D. M., Shurn, D. A., Smith, P. B., Flowers, C., & Shum, C. (1977). An attempt to detect "pregnancy susceptibility" in indigent adolescent girls. *Journal of Youth and Adolescence, 6,* 127–144.

Gottschalk, L. A., Titchener, J. L., Piker, H. N., & Stewart, S. S. (1964). Psychosocial factors associated with pregnancy in adolescent girls: A preliminary report. *Journal of Nervous and Mental Diseases, 138,* 524–534.

Howard, M. (1975). *Only human.* New York: Seasbury Press.

Howard, M. (1978, February/March). How can classroom teacher help? *Today's Education,* p. 64.

Kaplan, H. B., Smith, P. B., & Pokorny, A. D. (1974). Psychosocial antecedents of unwed motherhood among indigent adolescents. *Journal of Youth and Adolescence, 3,* 181–207.

Lewis, H. R., & Lewis, M. E. (1980). *The parent's guide to teenage sex and pregnancy.* New York: St. Martin's Press.

Lowe, G. D., & Witt, D. D. (1984). Early marriage as a career contingency: The prediction of education attainment. *Journal of Marriage and the Family, 46,* 689–698.

Menken, J. (1972). The health and social consequences of teenage child rearing. *Family Planning and Perspective, 4,* 45–53.

Parke, R. D., Power, T. G., & Fisher, T. (1980). The adolescent father's impact on the mother and child. *Journal of Social Issues, 36,* 88–106.

Philliber, S. G. & Graham, E. H. (1981, February). The impact of age of mother on mother–child interaction patterns. *Journal of Marriage and the Family,* 109–115.

Population trends 1980. (1981). Editorial in *Population Trends, 25,* 1–10.

Presser, H. B. (1980). Sally's corner: Coping with unmarried motherhood. *Journal of Social Issues, 36,* 107–129.

Ralph, N., Lochman, J., & Thomas, T. (1984). Psychosocial characteristics of pregnant and nulliparous adolescents. *Adolescence, 19,* 283–294.

Rice, F. P. (1984). *The adolescent: Development, relationships, and culture.* Newtown, MA: Allyn and Bacon.

Rossa, M. W., & Vaughan, L. (1984). A comparison of teenage and older mothers with preschool-age children. *Family Relations, 33,* 259–265.

Steinhoff, P. G. (1978). Premarital pregnancy and the first birth. In W. Miller & L. Newman (Eds.), *The first child and family formation.* Chapel Hill, NC: Carolina Population Center.

Sugar, M. (1976). At-risk factors for the adolescent mother and her infant. *Journal of Youth and Adolescence, 5,* 251–270.

United States Bureau of the Census (1984). *Statistical abstract of the United States: 1985* (105th ed.). Washington, D.C.: U.S. Bureau of the Census.

Wadsworth, J., Taylor, B., Osborn, A., & Butler, N. (1984). Teenage mothering: Child development at five years. *Journal of Child Psychology and Psychiatry, 25,* 305–313.

Zongker, C. E. (1977). The self-concept of pregnant adolescent girls. *Adolescence, 12,* 477–488.

# CHAPTER 17

Baptiste, D. A. (1984). Marital and family therapy with racially/culturally intermarried stepfamilies: Issues and guidelines. *Family Relations, 33,* 73–380.

Clingempeel, W. G., Brand, E., & Ievoli, R. (1984). Stepparent–stepchild relationships in stepmother and stepfather families: A multimethod study. *Family Relations, 33,* 465–473.

Coleman, M., & Ganong, L. H. (1984). Effect of family structure on family attitudes and expectations. *Family Relations. 33,* 425–432.

Crosbie-Burnett, M. (1984). The centrality of the step relationship: A challenge to family theory and practice. *Family Relations, 33,* 459–463.

Dean, G., & Gurak, D. (1978). Marital homogamy the second time around. *Journal of Marriage and the Family, 40,* 559–570.

Duberman, L. (1975). *Reconstituted family: A study of remarried couples and their children.* Chicago, IL: Nelson Hall.

Ganong, L. H., & Coleman, M. (1984) The effects of remarriage on children: A review of the empirical literature. *Family Relations, 33,* 389–406.

Goldstein, H. (1974). Reconstituted families: The second marriage and its children. *Psychiatric Quarterly, 48,* 431–440.

Kalter, S. (1978, November 19). Stepparents are people, too. *Family Weekly/Logan Herald Journal,* p. 6.

LeShan, E. (1980). Stepmothers aren't wicked anymore! *Parents, 55,* pp. 57–61.

Mills, D. M. (1984). A model for stepfamily development. *Family Relations, 33,* 365–372.

Schulman, G. (1972). Myths that intrude on the adaptation of the step-family. *Social Casework, 53,* 131–139.

Smith, W. C. (1953). *The stepchild.* Chicago: University of Chicago Press.

Visher, E. B., & Visher, J. S. (1979). *Stepfamilies: A guide to working with stepparents and stepchildren.* New York: Brunner-Mazel.

Wald, E. (1981). *The remarried family: Challenge and promise.* New York: Family Service Association of America.

Whiteside, M., & Auerback, L. (1978). Can the daughter of my father's new wife be my sister? Families of remarriage in family therapy. *Journal of Divorce, 1,* 271–283.

# CHAPTER 18

Bush, M., Gordon, A. C., & LeBailly, R. (1977). Evaluating child welfare services: A contribution from the clients. *Social Services Review, 51,* 491–501.

Cautley, P. W. (1980). *New foster parents: The first experience.* New York: Human Sciences Press.

Cautley, P. W., & Aldridge, M. J. (1975). Predicting success for new foster parents. *Social Work, 20,* 48–53.

Davies, L. J., & Bland, D. C. (1978). The use of foster parents as role models for parents. *Child Welfare, 57,* 380–386.

Faushel, D. (1978). Children discharged from foster care in New York City: Where to—when—at what age? *Child Welfare, 57,* 467–483.

Rowe, D. (1976). Attitudes, social class, and the quality of foster care. *Social Services Review, 50,* 506–514.

# NAME INDEX

Ferster, C. B., 76, 350
Feshback, N. R., 210
Filer, L. J., 300
Fine, M. J., 337
Finkelstein, H., 391
Finkelstein, M., 47
Fish, K. D., 137
Fisher, T., 413
Flavell, J. H., 92
Flowers, C., 403
Flynn, M. A., 300
Fomon, S. J., 300
Fortier, L. M., 326
Fox, R., 96
Foxx, R. M., 314–318, 341
Frankl, V., 165
Franklin, B., 79
Freedman, D. G., 129
Freedman, J. L., 100
Freud, S., 17, 33, 53, 57–63, 69, 72, 320, 371
Furstenberg, F. F., 408, 410

Gaensbauer, T. J., 357
Gander, M. J., 158
Gardner, H. W., 158
Gardner, M., 105
Garner, A. P., 46
Gasser, R., 387
Gath, A., 295, 329
Gaylin, J., 387, 391
Gecas, V., 27
Geist, C. R., 105
George, C., 133
Ghandour, M., 282
Gibbon, M., 346
Ginott, H., 28, 204
Glasser, W., 237–241
Glenn, N. D., 386
Glick, P., 389
Glover, K., 29
Goffman, E., 330
Goldfarb, J. L., 403
Goldman, B. D., 321
Goldstein, H., 296, 341, 411, 418, 424
Goodman, H., 342
Goodwin, D. W., 127
Gordon, A. C., 446
Gordon, H., 28
Gordon, T., 245, 248–256
Gottesman, I. I., 127
Gottlieb, J., 342
Gottschalk, L. A., 403
Goujard, J., 296
Grad, J., 330
Graham, E. H., 410
Greenway, A. P., 329
Grey, L., 235
Griest, D. L., 271
Groller, I., 397
Gross, J. C., 341
Grossman, F. K., 284, 295
Grossman, H. J., 338

Gruenberg, B. C., 33
Grusec, J., 199, 359
Gurak, D., 425
Guyatt, D., 398
Guze, S. B., 127, 330

Hafen, B. Q., 299, 300
Hales, D. J., 132
Hall, W. M., 282
Hammond, P., 245
Hardy, K. R., 101
Harlow, H., 320
Harlow, M. K., 320
Harman, D., 28
Harmon, C., 28
Harmon, R. J., 357
Harris, F. R., 222
Harris, M. B., 48
Harris, P. L., 358
Harrison, R. H., 342
Harrow, W., 105
Hart, B. M., 222
Hartig, 192, 193
Hartup, W. W., 365
Harvey, D. H. P., 329
Hay, D. F., 257
Heal, L. S., 341
Healy, W., 47
Hechtman, L., 335
Hellmer, L. A., 36
Hensen, A., 211
Herbert, M., 321
Hermanson, L., 127
Herrnstein, R. J., 128
Hess, R. D., 27
Hetherington, E. M., 374, 393
Hingten, J. N., 349, 352
Hiss, M., 185
Hobbs, D. F., 294, 295
Hodges, W. F., 375
Hoffman, L., 280
Hoffman, L. W., 4, 5, 9
Hoffman, M., 259
Hoffman, M. L., 4, 5, 9, 363, 393
Holmes, F. B., 366, 371
Holz, W. C., 202
Hooper, F. H., 95
Hope, R., 397
Horowitz, Z., 350
Houseknecht, S. K., 5
Howard, A., 207
Howard, M., 412
Huesmann, L. R., 282
Hunter, C., 296
Hurlock, E. B., 121
Hutchens, M. A., 46

Ilg, F. L., 17, 373
Ingram, S., 296
Inhelder, B., 89, 93, 94
Intagliata, J., 342
Isenberg, S., 300

Stuart, I. R., 394
Sugar, M., 411
Sullivan, H. S., 105
Supancic, M., 386
Symonds, P. M., 46
Syngg, D., 104

Takala, M., 36
Tayback, M., 170
Taylor, B., 411
Taylor, C., 387
Taylor, D. A., 358
Telford, C., 65, 66, 70
Tew, B., 329
Tharp, R. G., 182
Thoman, E. B., 310
Thomas, A., 308
Thomas, A. S., 126
Thomas, B., 105
Thomas, D. R., 190
Thomas, L. N., 300
Thomas, T., 403
Thompson, R. A., 19
Thorndike, E. L., 73, 75
Thygerson, A. L., 299
Tierney, C. W., 375
Titchener, J. L., 403
Tizard, J., 330
Tolstoy, L., 162–163
Tomes, H., 211
Tonascia, J., 296
Trites, R. L., 334
Tryphonas, H., 334
Tucker, D., 387
Tucker, M. J., 12
Turnbull, C. M., 26
Turner, P. H., 48

Ulrich, R. E., 190
Underwood, B., 359
Unis, A. S., 271

Van Hasselt, V. B., 271
Van Leishout, C. F. M., 358
Vander Zanden, J. W., 28, 88, 132, 158, 386
Vaughan, L., 406, 411
Veevers, J. E., 5
Visher, E. B., 434
Vogel, W., 128

Wadsworth, J., 411
Waggoner, R. W., 28
Wald, E., 416
Walker, S., 334
Walkley, R. P., 169
Wall, S., 133
Wallerstein, J. S., 374, 375
Wallin, P., 294
Walters, G. C., 199
Walters, P. H., 202

Walters, R., 204
Walters, R. H., 47
Wanlass, R. L., 326
Warshak, R. A., 20
Waterman, A. S., 71
Waters, E., 133, 319, 320
Watson, D. L., 182
Watson, G., 47, 49
Watson, J. B., 17, 33, 34, 53, 73–75
Watts, B., 330
Waxler, C. Z., 133, 309
Weinstein, M. S., 211
Weiss, G., 335, 336
Weiss, R. E., 211
Weiss, R. S., 389
Weiss, W., 105
Weiss, W., 396
Weitz, S., 277
Wender, P. H., 127, 333, 334
Wentworth, E. H., 326, 328, 329
Werner, E. E., 333
Werry, J. S., 332
West, M. J., 257
West, S. G., 282
Whaley, D. L., 216
Whippman, J., 320
White, B., 306
White, B. L., 17, 296
White, R. W., 59
Whiteside, M., 433
Whiting, J. W. M., 25, 26, 207
Wilberg, B., 132
Williams, J. A., 321
Williams, J. B. W., 346
Wilner, D. M., 169
Wimberger, H. C., 207
Wimbish, J., 295
Winickoff, S. A., 294, 295
Winn, M., 283
Winnick, M., 300
Winokur, G., 127
Winter, R., 300
Winters, L., 105
Wippman, J., 133
Witt, D. D., 406
Wolfe, H., 321
Wolfe, M. N., 220, 222
Wood, C., 304
Wood, D. R., 333
Wood, S. J., 20
Wright, J. D., 28
Wright, S. R., 28
Wynn, L. C., 209

Yahraes, H., 127
Yange, E., 344
Yarrow, M. R., 133, 309
Young, N., 397
Young, P. A., 128

# SUBJECT INDEX

# Copyright Acknowledgments

Wadsworth Publications and author: pp. 318–319, from C. E. Schaefer, *Childhood Encopresis and Enuresis*, 1979.

John Wiley & Sons: pp. 349–350, from G. C. Davison and J. M. Neale, *Abnormal Psychology: An Experimental Approach*, 2nd ed. © 1978. Reprinted by permission of John Wiley & Sons, Inc.

Yale University Press: pp. 25–26, from John W. M. Whiting and Irvin L. Child, Child Training and Personality, published by Yale University Press, 1953.

# Photo Credits

p. ii, Erika Stone.

*Part Opening I:* The Image Works Archives/The Image Works, Inc.

*Chapter 1:* p. 6, © Bohdan Hrynewych/Stock, Boston; p. 7, © Erika Stone; p. 9, © George W. Gardner/Stock, Boston; p. 15, © Mary Evans Picture Library/Photo Researchers, Inc.; p. 20, Jean-Claude Lejeune/Stock, Boston.

*Chapter 2:* p. 34, Owen Franken/Stock, Boston; p. 39, Katrina Thomas/Photo Researchers, Inc.; p. 41, © Alice Kandell/Photo Researchers, Inc.

*Part Opening II:* Mark Antman/The Image Works, Inc.

*Chapter 3:* p. 60, © Bruce Roberts/Photo Researchers, Inc.; p. 65, © Michal/Woodfin Camp & Associates; p. 70, © Jan Lukas/Photo Researchers, Inc.; p. 72, Michael Kagan/Monkmeyer Press Photo; p. 75, Mimi Forsyth/Monkmeyer Press Photo.

*Chapter 4:* p. 86, Stock, Boston; p. 90, Mimi Forsyth/Monkmeyer Press Photo; p. 93, © Elizabeth Hamlin/Stock, Boston; p. 99, Suzanne Szasz/Photo Researchers, Inc.; p. 103, David Powers/Stock, Boston; p. 107, Peter Vandermark/Stock, Boston.

*Part Opening III:* © Erika Stone.

*Chapter 5:* Peter Vandermark/Stock, Boston; p. 122, David S. Strickler/Monkmeyer Press Photo; p. 125, © Elizabeth Crews/Stock, Boston; p. 130, David S. Strickler/Monkmeyer Press Photo; p. 136, © Maureen Fennelli/Photo Researchers, Inc.; p. 140, © Alice Kandell/ Photo Researchers, Inc.

*Chapter 6:* p. 152, © Erika Stone; p. 157, Mimi Forsyth/Monkmeyer Press Photo; p. 160, © Erika Stone; p. 169, Peter Menzel/Stock, Boston.

*Part Opening IV:* © Chester Higgins, Jr./Photo Researchers, Inc.

*Chapter 7:* p. 189 © Christopher Brown/Stock, Boston; page 190, © Elizabeth Crews; p. 194, David Strickler/Monkmeyer Press Photo.

*Chapter 8:* p. 203, © Alan Carey/The Image Works; p. 205, © Hazel Hankin; p. 208, Peter Vandermark/Stock, Boston; p. 210, Mimi Forsyth/Monkmeyer Press Photo; p. 217, Lionel J.M. Delevingne/Stock, Boston.

*Chapter 9:* p. 228, Michael Hayman/Stock, Boston; p. 229, © Bob Kalman/The Image Works; p. 239, Stock, Boston; p. 239, © Jim Anderson/Woodfin Camp & Associates.

*Chapter 10:* p. 246, Peter Vandermark/Stock, Boston; p. 248, © 1983 Christa Armstrong; p. 249, Mimi Forsyth/Monkmeyer Press Photo; p. 257, © David M. Grossman/Photo Researchers, Inc.

*Chapter 11:* p. 265, © Alice Kandell/Photo Researchers, Inc.; p. 269, © Michel Euler/EPU/ Lehtikuva/Woodfin Camp & Associates; p. 273, © Frostie, 1978/Woodfin Camp & Associates; p. 276, James Holland/Stock, Boston; p. 282, © Alice Kandell/Photo Researchers, Inc.; p. 285, © Elizabeth Crews.

*Part Opening V:* © Elizabeth Crews.

*Chapter 12:* p. 298, © Erika Stone, 1979; p. 303, James R. Holland/Stock, Boston; p. 306, © Beryl Goldberg; p. 310, © Erika Stone, 1984; p. 314, © Elizabeth Crews; p. 316, Michael Weisbrot/Stock, Boston.